WALKING THE EXODUS

WALKING
THE
EXODUS

My Journey in the
Footsteps of Moses

MARGARET MALKA RAWICZ

URIM PUBLICATIONS
Jerusalem • New York

Walking the Exodus:
My Journey in the Footsteps of Moses
by Margaret Malka Rawitcz

Typeset by Ariel Walden

Printed in Israel

First Edition

ISBN 978-965-524-248-5

Urim Publications
P.O. Box 52287
Jerusalem 9152102 Israel
www.UrimPublications.com

Library of Congress Cataloging-in-Publication Data
Names: Rawicz, Margaret Malka, author.
Title: Walking the Exodus : my journey in the footsteps of Moses / Margaret
  Malka Rawicz.
Description: First edition. | Brooklyn, NY : Urim Publications, [2018] | Includes
  bibliographical references.
Identifiers: LCCN 2017058301 | ISBN 9789655242485 (hardcover : alk. paper)
Subjects: LCSH: Bible. Exodus—Antiquities. | Rawicz, Margaret Malka—Travel.
Classification: LCC BS1245.55 .R39 2018 | DDC 222/.12—dc23 LC record
  available at https://lccn.loc.GOV/2017058301

Contents

Contents

Acknowledgements

This book is based on many months of research and travel. I am grateful to my late husband, Richard Rawicz, and my family for their encouragement throughout this journey. Their support and love allowed me to persevere.

Thanks to G-d Almighty -- Hashem -- the Author of knowledge and wisdom, for all His guidance and protection.

I am grateful to the editors who assisted at various stages: Rita Lewis, Mary Hazelton, Ian Fleming, Sue Randal, Shanoo Chupty, and Paula Levin.

Thank you to Rabbi Levy Wineberg of Chabad, Hamaor Synagogue, Johannesburg, for his encouragement.

A special word of gratitude to my friends Carmen Emanuel and Sybil Perlstein for their suggestions, and to Irene Taviv who read the draft book and made valuable comments.

Thank you to the many people who suggested that I write this book and who have taken an interest in it.

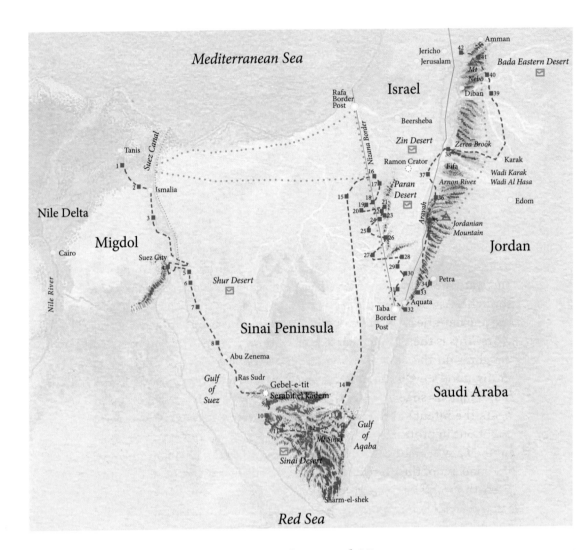

Camp Number and Name

(adapted from *The Living Torah*)

1	Rameses	11	Rephadim	21	Haradah	32	Ezion Gaber
2	Sukkot	12	Mount Sinai	22	Makheloth	33	Kadesh
3	Etham Desert	13	Kivroth Hataavah	23	Tahath	34	Mount Hor
4	Pi-Hahiroth, /	14	Hazerot	24	Tarah	35	Zalmonah
	Migdol	15	Kadesh Barnea /	25	Mithkah	36	Punon
5	Marrah		Ritma	26	Hashmonah	37	Oboth
6	Elim	16	Rimmon perez	27	Moseroth	38	Iyay Ha'avarim
7	Red Sea	17	Libnah	28	Benei Jaakan	39	Dibongad
8	Wilderness of Sin	18	Rissah	29	Hor hagidgad	40	Almon Divlathaymah
9	Dophka	19	Kehethah	30	Jotvathah	41	Abarim
10	Alush	20	Shapher	31	Ebronah	42	B'Arvos

Chapter 1

Beginning in Egypt

The waters of the Nile River seem larger than life and sparkle in the sunlight. As I look at its timeless banks in wonder, my mind leaps to the journey ahead and at once flashes back three-and-a-half thousand years. This is the spot, they say, where Moses was rescued by Pharaoh's daughter on the banks of the Nile. I stare down into the depths and in my mind's eye I can see the princess in her white robes, with her handmaidens shadowing close behind. Then, from the bulrushes, she hears the infant's cry. Startled, she wades into the water. Her escorts shout out in protest, for there are crocodiles here; but no, she will pick up the baby . . . and change the future of the world.

I snap out of the vision and can barely believe it is only a few days and a few thousand kilometers, that separate me from the home and loving family I have left behind. I smile, thinking of their reactions when I decided to forsake safety and sanctity for this "undoable" epic. Arched eyebrows and the kind of silence one expects after an untimely death had greeted my announcement. My sister's jaw practically unhinged itself and I thought my mother would collapse when I said, "I'm going to do it. I'm taking the plunge." My father's eyes did that thing when he is dumbfounded: he squeezes them closed very tight, as if by doing so he may persuade G-d to take his plea to restore me to sanity more seriously. Or better still, prevent me from leaving, by giving a sure sign of His disapproval. But even if the menorah had fallen off the mantelpiece, nothing would deter me. I was like the princess, called from deep inside.

Soon enough, word was out. My friends began calling in sympathy, as if I had a potentially fatal illness. Some tried a different stance, offering what sounded like condolences. Others were more blatant: "You'll get yourself killed." Perhaps I *am* mad, I thought, as I imagined their questions after I had seemingly disappeared off the face of the earth. "Why haven't you heard from her, after so long?" "When will she be back?" "Do you at least know where she is?" And the vague answers: "Somewhere in the desert. Alive. We hope." The answers would all be the same, resigned . . . "We have no idea."

My decision to venture into the deserts of the Middle East on my own and to retrace the footsteps of the biblical Exodus, which forged a nation and changed the course of humanity forever, had taken many months of research and years of dreaming. I wanted to lift the miracles and stories from the ancient biblical texts and feel them come back to life again.

I also wanted to escape my own personal incarceration, the futility I'd been drowning in, just as the enslaved Israelites had escaped the Pharaoh. Searching for freedom and finding it is one thing; knowing what to do with it is quite another. I too had no idea whether liberation or enlightenment, imprisonment or death lay in wait. But as I set out to walk the story of the Israelites' Exodus from Egypt, I began to sense how sweet the taste of freedom can be.

I had been building up to the moment of no return for months, and I knew the fears and concerns of my family were rational enough. I was, after all, a Jewish woman in her mid-fifties and would be traveling through extremely volatile parts of the Middle East, through territories where criminals and terrorists are hailed as liberators, where water is infinitely more precious than gold or oil, and where satellites are redundant specks of light dimly circling the earth. It would be no ordinary adventure. And I would be doing it alone, for the most part, without anyone I know, only a local person to take me where I want to go. No wonder my mother finally said: "May G-d bless you and protect you, my child."

The Book of Exodus has always fascinated me. I had often wondered about the trials and miracles that the Israelites experienced. A child believes these things, even knows them to be true; but the sense of awe and wonder tends to fade as life's duties and obligations take hold. Over time, I had come to understand the Israelites' journey through the wilderness as a metaphor for my own life and others'. It could have destroyed them, but it transformed them from being an oppressed people to an uplifted nation. Such a collective transformation enthralled me, and I craved such an experience on a personal level.

I was particularly intrigued to see where the miracle of the splitting of the Red Sea had occurred. I wanted to stand on the narrow beach with impassable mountains behind, where the people had no route for escape when the Egyptian army pursued them. As it turned out, that was indeed one of many places that would bring about a realization, almost an epiphany that was to change my life forever.

In traveling the same route from Egypt, through the Sinai, to Israel and up into Jordan, I wanted to immerse myself in the ancient Israelites' world during their forty years of wandering. I felt compelled to uncover, as much as humanly possible, what some archaeologists regard as myth and religious people call reality; what can be traced through archaeological and historical fact, and what will remain a mystery forever.

At last, in November 2003 on a Monday morning, I left Johannesburg for Cairo. For two days I joined a tour group and we explored the city, home to sixteen million people and known for its bad air, congested traffic and excessive noise. More recently it has been famous because of the Arab Spring revolution. I was one of thousands of tourists milling around, with heavily armed policemen stationed everywhere. Looking back, perhaps their presence indicated a concern to protect tourists, and maybe the first hint of the Arab Spring – which later threatened to set the entire Middle East ablaze. But at the time, I was simply mesmerized by the thronging madness and color of it all. In Cairo city itself, I was stunned by the sight of magnificent modern office blocks, hotels, restaurants, shopping malls and monuments.

Little did I know that it was the early days of a revolution to come. President Mubarak, with his autocratic and extremely corrupt control, would face massive street protests as thousands of people joined to overthrow him during the Arab Spring of 2011. This would be followed by the Egyptain military assuming control. Even less could I imagine that in the subsequent elections, in 2012, the head of the Muslim Brotherhood, Mohamed Morsi, would become president. As Morsi began to impose strict Islamic law, there followed a resurgence of violence, more political upheaval, the military imposing a full-scale crackdown, with Egypt becoming a most dangerous place. Then the overthrow of Morsi came after just one year of his presidential term in a coup led by his Minister of Defense, Abdel Fatah Al-Sisi. Now many Egyptians cannot even afford to buy bread.

But as I stood there in 2003, Egypt was normal. Big tourist buses choked the streets and coughed out people from every corner of the world. They had come to marvel at the inexplicable, at sheer human genius, or perhaps to contemplate supposed alien interventions and sunken civilizations. We all wanted to travel back in time in some way or another. However, I believe my purpose might have been unique among the brochure-wielding masses.

Taking a break from the back-to-back tour itinerary, I took a walk beside the Nile. I felt a sense of connection to the distant past. This area around the river had marked the cradle of civilization, and it was here that empires had been born that were splendid and wrathful, with incredibly advanced architecture. We know, of course, who did the hard labor: slaves. And I would be tracking the route which those slaves eventually traveled through the endless expanses of desert and sky.

A lady from the tour group joined me on a bench overlooking the water. Her name was Carol. "Why have you come here?" she asked.

"I'm going to follow the Exodus route of Moses and the Israelites," I replied. "From here to Israel."

"How interesting! Which tour group are you going with?"

"No, I'm traveling alone," I smiled. "I want to walk the route . . . well, parts of it at least. I'm going to figure it all out myself. I will just have a local person to take me where I want to go."

Carol stared at me in disbelief and gave a wry smile, probably thinking she'd indulge this odd South African for a bit and then go back to mix with more normal people on the bus.

Trying to lend a bit of credibility to myself, I said, "I'm an environmental consultant, and I want to explore the land, ecology and any archaeological remains along the biblical Exodus route. I travel a lot whenever I do environmental work. So I feel confident that I can cope with the challenge of the deserts. I'm going to travel by foot and on camels, as well as by jeep and car along the way."

"But . . ." Carol seemed to think things over, and then she snapped out of her cynicism. She said, "It sounds fascinating. I learned about the Exodus when I was younger. But what made you want to take such an unusual journey?"

I had gathered that she was not Jewish. I explained, "Jews recall the Exodus every year during Passover. It's one of the main Jewish holy days. Passover inspired several revolutions in many countries around the world, whenever downtrodden people fought to gain their freedom. Actually, the three big religions – Judaism, Christianity and Islam – all recognize the importance of Passover. In Hebrew, the idea of "leaving

Egypt" also means moving beyond one's personal limitations.

"It took me six months of planning and doing research," I went on. "I read the five books of the Bible of Moses. I found a list of all the encampments of the Exodus route in the Book of Numbers, in Chapter 33. Scholars of the Bible and archaeologists have argued about the exact route for centuries. So, I've researched many different points of view."

"I wondered whether the Exodus actually happened, and what the route may have been," said Carol.

"One thing is for sure," I said. "A whole nation of millions of people, including women, children, elderly people, and all their livestock could not have climbed huge mountains. My trip will last many weeks, I suspect about six, but I can't say exactly because I will have to see how it goes along the way. I will keep a log book to record how many days it will take, but I won't travel on Saturday as it's the Jewish Sabbath."

I told her that, from what I had learned, there was one route along the shores of the Mediterranean, a second through the northern Sinai Peninsula, a third through the southern parts of the Sinai Peninsula, and a fourth around the southern tip of the Sinai Peninsula. Some archeologists say it never occurred.

I had decided to follow the route shown in a sketch from a copy of the five books of Moses called *The Living Torah* by Rabbi Aryeh Kaplan,[1] which is shown in Annexure 1. This route was depicted in sketch format in 1868 by Adolf Neubauer, a Talmudic scholar and geographer. He analyzed the entire set of Jewish biblical books and then published *La Geographie du Talmud*. Neubauer's route fit best with the travel times described in the Bible.[2]

I realised that archeological findings along this route would include various eras such as Middle Bronze Age: 2000–1750 BCE; Joseph in Egypt; Late Bronze Age: 1550 – Exodus to start of biblical judges; Iron I 1200–1000 biblical kings, prophets and temple destroyed; Iron II 1000–550 states of Judah and Israel; 722/721 – northern state of Israel obliterated; 700 Jerusalem conquered and exile in Babylon and thereafter.

"I'll explore the other possible routes in the future," I told Carol. "But for now, all I want is to see how the biblical and archaeological information can be linked."

I told her that I had read widely on the geography, history and archaeology of the forty-two Exodus encampments that are described in the Book of Numbers, Chapter 33. I went on to explain how I had pored

Ancient text kept in the geniza room in the Old City Synagogue in Cairo. |
M Rawicz Trip Photo

over maps of the countries through which the Israelites walked: ten
maps in all, one of which dated as far back as the thirteenth century.
But there was no map showing the whole route that gave essential
information about the land, such as sand tracks, roads, settlements,
topography and historical sites. I had struggled to correlate Arabic, English, and Hebrew hard-copy cartography with additional maps which
I found on the internet. Some of them showed topographical features,
but others were just satellite images.[3–17]

"It sounds terribly complicated!" Carol exclaimed. "What will you do
about sleeping, eating, and toilet facilities?"

"I will see what life brings. I have to trust the local people, whoever
I meet."

My journey into the depths of time continued later that day when
our tour group went to view the 1130-year-old Ibn Ezra Synagogue.
There I met Eliezer, one of Cairo's last remaining Jews, in the Old City.
He was sitting at the door of the synagogue issuing tickets. I looked at
the gloriously refurbished white marble columns of the synagogue. The
lectern and pulpit had elaborate gold trimmings. The walls and Holy
Ark, where the Torah Scrolls are kept in the front of the synagogue,
were made of magnificent and intricately carved wooden panels. The

Moses' well. According to tradition, this is the location where Pharaoh's daughter rescued Moses from the Nile. This spot used to be in the Nile itself, but the riverbanks have since shifted. | M Rawicz Trip Photo

entire building was a richly embellished work of art. Hidden in its interior were thousands of ancient biblical texts, kept in a room called a *geniza*. In the gardens is a well, allegedly where Moses was rescued by Pharaoh's daughter on the banks of the Nile. The river banks have changed since that ancient time.

I asked Eliezer about the local Jewish community.

He whispered, "When the State of Israel was established, many Jews left and by 1956, almost half of the community had gone to Israel. There were still over 78,000 Jews, but after the Six-Day War in 1967 nearly all Jewish men were either thrown out of the country or jailed and tortured. Most Jews who fled went to Israel. There are less than 100 Jews

Ibn Ezra Synagogue in the Old City. | Ask-Aladdin, Egypt Travel Experts https:// www.ask-aladdin.com/Egypt-Sites/Coptic-Monuments/benezra.html

left now. We live in fear, as many citizens treat them badly. The official policy is religious freedom but it is not so in daily life."

I shared with him the nature of my quest. He asked whether my religious beliefs had motivated me to travel. I replied, "I want to understand the biblical experience of "going out of Egypt" from many viewpoints. The prayers that religious Jews say daily refer to the Exodus many times."

"Yes, yes," he muttered. "I remember my father telling me the story when we celebrated Passover."

I became emotional at having met Eliezer, a fellow Jew from across the sands of time and geography, astonished at the knowledge that we shared this common bond. Our fathers had retold this story year after year. As had their fathers. I began to describe this cherished tale and related the biblical story of Moses and the Israelite enslavement. Eliezer's eyes glistened with delight at the memory of this almost forgotten story. The old man became almost childlike as he was transported into the tale.

The historical scene flashed into vivid reality in my mind. I imagined the thundering roar of hundreds of horses as the huge Egyptian army swept down, whipping the desert sands up into the trembling sky. Following the enraged call of their god-king, the chariots had raced out of the vast stables – which covered almost a square kilometer at Pi-Rameses and Tel el Daba – and stormed down the exact route I would soon be traveling.

I imagined the army's divisions fanning out to block the entire area from the Gebel Atâqa Mountains in the west to the beach, baying for the Israelites' obliteration. Escape would have been impossible.

Charging down a dune face came Pharaoh's golden chariot, followed by the soldiers with their armor and thick leather straps worn across the chest. The leather tunics with metal scales sewn onto them made a thudding cacophony as the army drew closer. I saw the powerful composite shooting bows; the long, metal-tipped arrows; the piercing axes, spears and swords glistening in the sun . . . weapons raised high and ready for the kill.

I saw the Pharaoh, adorned in jewelry of turquoise, gold and precious stones, his sandals painted in gold and maroon, and his golden headdress resplendent above the seething mass of the army. The Pharoah wanted to reclaim his Hebrew slaves.

No doubt Eliezer was also picturing the scene; he was in no rush for me to complete the story.

I imagined an enormous twister curling down from roiling clouds and great stabbing sheets of lightning ripping across the desert. This was the "pillar of cloud and light" that had spiraled down between the fleeing slaves and their captors. I tasted the fear that haunted the Israelites; and I pictured Nachshon ben Aminadav – the first person to heed the command, wading heroically into the sea . . . perhaps the first and most ancient "giant leap for mankind." It was only then, at the last moment, with the water at his neck, that the miracle happened and the sea opened, creating a pathway for the rest of the Israelites to escape from an otherwise certain death. As the waters drew back and parted, the people were surrounded on either side by high banks of water, liquid cliffs like skyscrapers.

I heard the frenzied whinnying of the Pharaoh's cavalry, and saw the terror on the Egyptians' faces as they became bogged down in the mud behind the Israelites. Then the walls of water came crashing down on them. The mighty ruler's delusion of omnipotence was flattened.

I empathized with the incredible feeling of liberation as I imagined the Israelites reaching the other side of the sea. I was awakened to my own potential personal and spiritual growth. I was going to transform my prayers and faith into action, so that I too might be blessed with a miracle. Through the help of G-d, perhaps I could experience an emotional shift that would remain with me forever. I intended to be standing at the site I had just seen in my mind's eye within a few short days.

The old man coughed and I continued to give my summary of the Exodus.

"The Israelites' journey took them through the desert and to Mount Sinai, where they received the Ten Commandments and the Torah from G-d. Many of the people who had left Egypt were punished and died in the desert because of their disobedient and ungrateful ways. They stopped at many campsites during their forty years on the way to Canaan."

Eliezer was suddenly on the verge of tears. "Yes, yes," he muttered. "I remember my father telling me the story when we celebrated Passover."

Our next stop was in the Giza areas of Cairo. We visited a life-size ancient pharaonic village from the era between 1650 and 1450 BCE. We saw Egyptian village activities come to life, with people dressed in ancient tunics and head-dresses. Some were making clothes, bakers kneaded dough for bread, weavers manipulated the reeds they used to weave baskets, and other people were crafting implements. Men were

At Cairo's Giza ancient pharaonic village we saw a replica of Pharaoh's statue.

fishing, ploughing and winnowing, or building using ancient technology. I understood more of what daily life was like in biblical times.

Next we visited the eclectic Cairo Antiquities Museum. Carol and I explored on our own as she was a history teacher and had her own interests. In this museum I learned a lot about ancient Egypt's numerous pharaohs, and I was keen to see what remained from the era of the Exodus. Several renowned archaeologists and Jewish scholars believe that the Israelites lived in Egypt between 1650 and 1450 BCE, during the Thirteenth Dynasty of the pharaohs. I had heard about displays of life-size ancient pharaonic boats. This was the period I was intent on exploring.

We went into the Mummy Room where the embalmed pharaohs, including those from the time of Moses – such as Rameses II – lay in state. I was particularly drawn to one of the mummies: Pharaoh Merneptah, under whom the Israelites are believed to have labored. His remains were lying in a glass display cabinet. His dark brown face was well preserved and his arms were crossed over his chest. I could see his teeth and fingernails. It was mind-boggling to stand and look at his body at such close range, to think of his mouth shouting the command for the total onslaught.

I gazed around at the golden chariots and all the weaponry and regalia on display. There was also a resplendent, magnificent gold bed in the shape of a leopard housed in the museum. I moved on to view an elaborately decorated throne. Perhaps it was from this seat that Merneptah had barked the order to annihilate the people of Moses.

Ancient papyrus scrolls depicted personal stories, including descriptions of slave life. Colossal statues of pharaohs lined the passages, and their enormous sarcophagi stood in rows. Royal chariots from the largest pharaonic stables at the cities of Pithom and Rameses – which the Israelites had built – stood immobile, never again to race across the Sahara. I saw ceramic pottery glazed with tin, and cylinder seals, from the cities where slaves had labored to make bricks. These special items would never again be touched by the hands of the ancient rulers.

To my astonishment, the display included a life-size golden calf which had been crafted by the Egyptian priests and represented the cow-god Hathor. Mummified crocodiles, baboons, falcons, cobras, frogs, hippopotami, jackals and cats revealed the extent of Egyptian reverence for animals.

A huge stone tablet, known as a *stele*, from the time of Pharaoh

A "golden calf" idol, which was an Egyptian cow-god called Hathor, in the Cairo museum. | Wikipedia-Hathor. | http://en.academic.ru/dic.nsf/enwiki/59235

Merneptah made reference to the expulsion of the Hyksos people. Some scholars think that the Hyksos and Israelites may have been one and the same people.

The more I explored the museum, the more my journey ahead came to life. What I saw in the Cairo Museum was to prove invaluable in my retracing of the Exodus route. The museum visit left me with a profound sense of the culture, lifestyle and values of the history of Egypt, and placed the Israelites' journey into a far more meaningful context. The artifacts I saw, populated my later visions in rich detail. From the ancient city of Tanis I saw finely-carved masks made of solid gold which had been worn by the pharaohs. I also saw a solid silver coffin bearing a falcon's head; spectacular gold jewelry inlaid with green and royal blue stones; magnificently crafted scarab beetles – created from purple and red precious stones; a turquoise and gold bracelet with the large embedded black-and-white eye seen so often in Egyptian artwork; gold and silver bowls and cups; and sandals made of gold. It was breathtaking to see so many precious treasures, now on show for all to view. I saw many ancient papyrus scrolls depicting personal stories, art and conquests over their slaves. My visual well full, it was time for me to rejoin the tour group. The people were busy looking at fascinating pictures of the Egyptian gods.

"I have heard that the Egyptian god was Ra, the sun god, but there are so many different ones here," I said, turning to our tour guide.

He replied, "Their religion was complicated. They believed that the supreme god had many representations or sub-gods. They believed that original chaos was the god Nun. The god Atom created all the other gods, including the sun god Ra. Nut had a brother Geb, and their son was Osiris. Of the sub-gods, Nepthys symbolizes death, and Seth evil. Geb's daughter Isis was the protective goddess. Isis married her bother Osiris, and gave birth to their son called Horus. So, you can see how incestuous relationships were an integral part of the beliefs. No wonder the pharaohs themselves were incestuous." The guide smiled briefly. "This was one of the fundamental values that the Israelites learned to reject when they received their Bible."[18]

I learned that Hathor was considered the mother of pharaohs as well as being the goddess of protection, love and joy. Hathor was depicted as a calf.[19] When the Israelites created the golden calf at Mount Sinai, they may have used Hathor as their model.[20] The worship of a bovine goddess, Hathor, mother of the sun, may have led to the Golden Calf and given the Israelites hope.[21]

And then we visited the pyramids. As I crawled into the deep, dark inner chamber of the Great Pyramid or Pyramid of Cheops, where Pharaoh Khufu has lain for thousands of years, an eerie and even frightening chill swept through me. I thought of men carving the convoluted tunnels, of grave robbers and obsessed archaeologists. But although I was fascinated and overwhelmed by the pyramids and the Sphinx, my real interest lay elsewhere.

I saw the statue of Pharaoh Akhenaten who abandoned traditional Egyptian polytheistic religion and introduced a form of quasi monotheism. The practice was not widely accepted by Egyptian society.

Sailing down the Nile past ancient Egyptian palaces and temples. | M Rawicz Trip Photo

Cruising down the Nile in a small felucca. | M Rawicz Trip Photo

After our whirlwind exploration of Cairo, some of our tour group went cruising down the Nile in small felucca boats. We sailed past Egyptian palaces and temples. The gigantic temple of Abu Simbel, built by Pharaoh Rameses II, bore witness to yet more astonishing feats – both ancient and modern (that is, built in the twentieth century). The ancient temple was built at the time of Moses.

Modern engineers had gone to extraordinary measures to preserve

Pyramids and Sphinx. | M Rawicz Trip Photo

the statues when the Aswan Dam was built. They had carved the ancient monolithic statues of Rameses II into blocks, and transported them to higher ground where they could be reconstructed. Pharaohs Rameses' statues were so huge that my head only just drew level with their ankles.

We moved on to the Valley of the Kings. As we walked into the bowels of the mountain to see the sarcophagi and burial chambers of the pharaohs, my heart began to race with excitement. At last, there it was: the burial chamber of Pharaoh Merneptah, who is believed to have ruled at the time of the Exodus. His life story was painted on the walls in great detail with vibrant colors that have survived the millennia. Was Merneptah, son of Rameses II, the pharaoh who had been killed by G-d at the splitting of the Red Sea?

We made our way back to the bus and drove to the main synagogue, Chaar Hachamaim (Shaar Hashamayim), which is a large grey building with two huge towers and an enormous circular window. It also has windows shaped in the style of the ancient Egyptian buildings. This synagogue was built in 1899 in a style similar to ancient Egyptian temples as a reminder that Moses was the prince of Egypt. There was a big military tank with Egyptian solders standing outside guarding it. Inside there was a large library which housed books from before the 17th century.

I learned more about Jewish history in Egypt from the guide.

During the Greek Ptolemaic period, rulers took control from the pharaoh in 323 BCE and 120,000 Jewish captives were brought to Egypt from Jerusalem. After that, many other free Jews were attracted by Egypt's fertile soil and immigrated of their own accord to settle around Alexandria. During the Roman period from 30 BCE onward, an important Jewish community lived on the eastern side of the Nile River south of Cairo. Jews continued to live in Egypt relatively peacefully through the Islamic Empire of more than two thousand years. There was even a time when the 60,000 Jews flourished and ran Talmudic schools. In the 17th to the 19th centuries Jewish communities continued during the French and British rule, and were sometimes oppressed. The number of Jews, however, has dwindled since 1948.

I felt sad at seeing the lonely emptiness of such a beautiful synagogue that was reminiscent of a more glorious past.

Later that evening, at our hotel, Carol and I reminisced about our trip. One of the lounges was called a *hookah* and we lay on scatter cushions on the floor. People sat smoking from "hubbly bubblies" or shisha water pipes, and vapor with exotically fruity flavors wafted through the air.

This would be my last night with the tour group. Carol wanted to know more about my journey, so I told her about my intention to follow the Exodus route in greater detail.

"I'm interested in many aspects of the Israelites' experience," I said. "At each of the forty-two Exodus camps they had to learn certain spiritual lessons. Their forty years in the desert changed them from being demoralized slaves to confident conquerors. They managed this by doing what some religious people call "work of the heart," like becoming compassionate, sensitive, disciplined and strong. They also realized that they had to be persevering, humble and unified. They also had training in becoming faithful, trusting, and so much more. These are traits we all aspire towards. I know about the spiritual lessons they learned because I've studied some of the insights given by the Jewish Kabbalah teachers."

I told Carol that after the Israelites left Egypt, it took them forty-nine days to get to Mount Sinai and receive the Ten Commandments. On the

Second night of Passover each year, Jews still begin to count forty-nine days until they celebrate the Feast of Weeks, which commemorates the receiving of the Ten Commandments. People use this period to work on their personal characteristics in the same way they understand that the Israelites had to.

I hoped that this journey would yield some emotional and spiritual transformation for me as well. I had read various texts about the meanings of the various camps. I had found the works of Rabbi Simon Jacobson called *42 Journeys* from the Meaningful Life Center and the lesson of Rabbi Hillel ben David called *The Journeys of the Sons of Israel* particularly interesting. I took copies of their writings with me so that I could learn what psychological and spiritual lessons might be valid for each campsite. Carol asked, "But Margaret, why now?"

"In the last few years I have been through a difficult and stressful time, raising three teenagers, coping with trying relationships, the death of my father and a demanding job. Recently, I have been one of the team leaders on a project to develop a "new national strategy for holistic pollution control for South Africa." It has taken its toll on me. I feel I could also benefit from some emotional and spiritual rejuvenation. My outlook on life could do with some improvements! So, I'm hoping to go through a transformation similar to that of the Israelites."

I continued, "The Israelites needed to learn certain traits to prepare them to receive the Ten Commandments. They needed to be raised from a lowly state to one of uplifted spiritual sensitivity. The desert offered them this opportunity. I want to find a sense of what they experienced in that environment, and see if I can move beyond my own limitations, my own inner Egypt."

Carol asked, "But how on earth are you going to survive in the desert?"

"I've hired a private Egyptian driver to take me through Egypt to a place after the Red Sea crossing. I also managed to track down a Bedouin from the Sinai. I contacted him and he agreed to take me along the route that I've planned to travel. We're going to meet at a bus stop on the border of the desert. Somehow, I think it will be all right, but that's when the dangerous part will begin. I will have to trust the people I meet. I will show them respect and hope for the best. I guess I'll have to take my chances and trust in G-d."

It was late and we parted company for the night . . . or perhaps forever. The physically and spiritually challenging part of my adventure was about to start.

Chapter 2

Exodus Journey Begins: Camps 1–6

The following day I left Cairo. I was traveling in a hired car with a driver called Hashim, and a guide called Yaman who knew a fair deal about Egyptian history and could speak English. We spent our first day together heading northward to the far reaches of the Nile River Delta where it fans out into the Mediterranean Sea. The land of Goshen is mentioned in the Bible as the place where the descendants of the patriarch Jacob (and his eleven sons and their families) took refuge during the seven years of drought and famine. It was from Goshen that Moses led the Israelites in their flight from Egypt.

After an hour of driving through partly built-up areas, the landscape turned to bare desert. As nature would have it, we soon needed to relieve ourselves, and I wondered how we would deal with this small challenge. The protocol turned out to be rather simple: men on one side of the car, ladies on the other; find a suitable rock to provide a screen – and then get on with it. I did as I was told and went to the ladies' side.

When I was ready to return to the car, thinking I would have to get used to this lifestyle as it would be mine for many days to come, I shrieked – and froze. There, a foot in front of me, lying coiled up on the ground, was a large black snake. It was a Palestine Mole Viper, extremely venomous and the most dangerous snake in the region. These snakes are known to have poor eyesight, so I stood still, barely daring to breathe and immobilized like a statue, as if I was hypnotized by the snake.

In my mind's eye, other snakes reared up before me. I pictured Moses and Aaron smashing the staff down before the Pharaoh in his cobra headdress, and turning solid wood into a writhing serpent – an unheeded warning to let the Israelites go free.

Later, on reflection, I wondered whether the viper that could so easily have ended my journey was an omen of good or ill. Back in the here and now, the snake simply slithered away, but its image had curled into my brain and I would be more careful from now on.

Hashim knew a short-cut and turned off the main road, onto a dusty track running alongside a *wadi*. The word "wadi" means a river channel, usually a dry river bed. He tried to navigate a tight bend in the path, and almost lost control of the vehicle, but then the car bounced back onto the track.

Yaman muttered, "Whoops, nearly lost her there."

The way forward became increasingly sandy, threatening with every slow second to sink the car's wheels and trap us down. But Hashim had done battle with the desert before, and we slowly and painfully made some progress. The mood in the car was becoming tense and frustrated as we negotiated the treacherous track for what seemed an eternity. Yaman was angry about Hashim's bad decision. I decided that it was not worth worrying about the driving, and instead drifted off in thought.

Suddenly, I saw what looked like a strange yellow funnel ahead. Hashim swerved the car and the tires skidded dangerously. Then he revved the engine to breaking point and the vehicle roared off the side of the road, ramping up a meter-high sand embankment. Still at full throttle and virtually airborne, we careened into the open desert. Then the car came to an abrupt halt.

"Duck down!" Yaman yelled.

I crouched, terrified, as the sandstorm hit us. It had come as if from nowhere, and began to blast the car with such intensity that I thought the sand would surely strip the paintwork. I'd heard stories of storms like this ripping car doors from their hinges. We waited it out breathlessly. Eventually, as quickly as it had arrived, the fury passed. Everything went quiet, and we slowly righted ourselves, glancing at each other nervously. My heart was pounding and I felt stunned by the encounter.

We carried on in silence for the next twenty minutes. This was the world I had entered, unpredictable and dangerous, where the might of the elements could snuff us out in an instant.

Eventually we returned to the main road. After a few more hours there was a sudden change in the landscape as we approached the delta.

Lush farmlands of the Nile Delta spread out for hundreds of kilometers – no wonder Joseph's brothers came to live here. | M Rawicz Trip Photo

This northernmost area of Egypt was strikingly different from the desert that dominated the rest of the country. The lifeless, yellow sand gave way to lush green fields, and farmlands spread out for hundreds of kilometers.

The Nile Delta measures 160 kilometers from north to south, and 185 kilometers from west to east: a total area of approximately 29,000 square kilometers. The region contains sixty percent of Egypt's farmland as well as extensive swamps and shallow lakes. The biblical land of Goshen, in the eastern part of the Nile Delta, extends across 2,500 square kilometers and forms a substantial part of the eastern delta.[1]

Tributaries of the Nile flow gently through this area which has the richest and most fertile soil I have ever seen. The soil is dark brown to black and is filled with nutrients from the Nile's silt. It was clear why this area is the "breadbasket of the Middle East."

We passed farmers with their donkeys pulling carts loaded with supernatural-looking, outsized fruits and vegetables. Apples as large as normal green melons, artichokes the size of big pineapples, butternuts

Tributaries of the Nile flow gently through the "breadbasket of the Middle East." |
M Rawicz Trip Photo

Outsized butternuts from the rich Nile farms. | *M Rawicz Trip Photo*

Lush farms make the Nile Delta a major contributor to the wealth of Egypt. |
M Rawicz Trip Photo

with the girth of watermelons, and cabbages like overblown footballs all boasted of the earth's bounty. Everywhere I looked I saw fields of cotton, maize, bananas, vegetables, vineyards, citrus and sugarcane – and not just normal crops, but super-crops. Date palms, that symbol of Egypt, stretched into the sky along the roads . . . and on into the distance. The contrast between this profusion of life and the deathly desert was breathtaking.

We passed thousands of water birds flocking above us. This area is famous for its birdlife and is crisscrossed by one of the world's greatest bird migration routes, lending credibility to the miracle at Kibrothhat-taavah (the "graves of craving") to the east of this area. Kibrothhattaa-vah was the thirteenth Israelite encampment, where millions of quails had fallen from the sky and given food to the fleeing people. However, the birds' meat turned out to be a mixed blessing.

At that camp, the Israelites had learned to surrender themselves to their Higher Power after they became consumed and obsessed. They then began the process of rehabilitation, learning to overcome the seductive power of lust, desire and addiction. They learned to steer away from cravings that cause a person to become buried in personal desire, figuratively digging one's own grave. This was a vital lesson for them and it was hugely important for me too. I had been a workaholic, an addiction that had threatened to ruin my life.

At one of the Nile River tributaries, we stopped to watch some fishermen mending their nets. They told my guides there was an abundance of fish, including striped mullet and sole. As we watched, one of the men threw out his nets, just as the earliest Egyptians had; others ate what they'd just caught and cooked on the spot. The scene was beautiful and tranquil, with the wide river flowing slowly, shimmering under the eternal blue sky.

We drove on and the sights around me reflected images I had seen in the Cairo Museum: heavy-browed bulls, such as those hammered out in gold or carved in stone; slender cats with upright tails and big conical ears that had once been depicted on papyrus, and now ran through the alleyways we passed; mummified animals springing to life in front of my eyes. People still drove donkey carts and water buffaloes still ploughed the fields, although the occasional tractor jolted me back into the 21st century. Sheep and goats walked in flocks, tended by shepherds. A row of camels, heavily laden with goods, sauntered past. It was easy to visu-

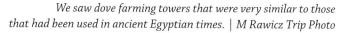

We saw dove farming towers that were very similar to those that had been used in ancient Egyptian times. | *M Rawicz Trip Photo*

Buffaloes are still used to plough the fields in the location of Biblical Goshen. |
M Rawicz Trip Photo

alize how the Israelites and ancient Egyptians had lived.

No wonder Jacob's sons had come here during the drought, I thought. It was to these rich lands that they had brought their sheep, goats and cattle to graze, and where they had labored and flourished under the reign of the "good" Pharaoh. The story is recorded in Exodus 1:8–2:10.

We stopped several times to view the river's banks. Crocodiles no longer live in the delta, because the Aswan Dam, built in the 1960s, prevents them from moving northward; but of course, anywhere you go in Africa, crocodiles live in the minds of people. Men wearing white robes and skullcaps labored in the fields, and boys walked along the road carrying farm implements. The area was paradisiacal, sublime, and probably not that different from the way it had been thousands of years ago.

At midday, we arrived at a village and bought fruit and vegetables from a genial stallholder in the bazaar, where melons, grapes, beans, coffee and spices were sold in abundance. We ate our lunch and then took a quick look around. Some homes were poorly constructed mud

We saw simple irrigation structures to channel water from the Nile into fields, just as had been done in ancient Egyptian times. | M Rawicz Trip Photo

houses, and the village was swarming with barefoot children who ran among the rubbish strewn in the streets. Canals filled with refuse and even sewage coursed sluggishly between these elementary homes.

"You know, tourists come to Egypt and do not see our poor," Yaman said. "It is a big problem. The communities here are getting bigger very fast. Every year, we have a million-and-a-half more people being born. So many Egyptians are too much for our economy to support. Islam forbids birth control. Egypt has a shortage of homes and community services."

"People have food. Nothing else," Yaman said dolefully.

With that, a few villagers came out of their houses to gawk at us and a group of children began to follow us. One young boy was jumping from one foot to the other with a toy weapon raised high. "Hamas! Hamas! Hamas!" he yelled. Another boy rushed at us, armed with a bamboo gun. He was wearing a band across his forehead with Arabic writing scrawled on it. When the younger children saw him, they began to pick up goat turds and throw them at us.

A village in the Nile Delta which was there in biblical times, located in the area where the Muslim brotherhood is now powerful. | M Rawicz Trip Photo

"Poor children," Yaman said, turning to me. "They're brainwashed by politically motivated people and they go mad at the sight of Westerners."

I would be meeting more angry people in the weeks to come, many of whom had been brainwashed by politically motivated masters; people who were desperate because of poverty. But I was deeply disturbed to see such hatred in the minds of mere children. I was stunned that parents could teach their children such hatred, but I tried to act as if nothing had happened.

As we walked back to the car, an older man walked past us and spat on the ground. I had seen other people spit and knew it was acceptable behavior in the rural areas, but this had been deliberately aimed at my feet. His action made me feel resolute to dissuade people from expressing racial hatred in the future. We walked on in silence.

Yaman said, "Many of these people cannot read. They know little about the world. They just accept what they are told about Americans and other Westerners. *Insha Allah*, things will improve."

At the time I did not realize that I was in the heart of one of the largest concentrations of Sunni Islamists, the center of the Muslim Brotherhood. From this area would emerge in 2012 a major political force and massive political movement in Egypt, headed by Mohamed

Morsi. This area would be the center for the support of espionage and sabotage and future terrorist activities.

I could understand that tourists are fascinated by the ruins of temples and scenes of offerings made to green or blue gods, but many Egyptians are annoyed by this attitude. Tourists indeed seldom do get to see the squalid conditions in which most Egyptians live. I felt enthralled to have this glimpse into the real lives of the locals. It gave me far deeper insight into the plight of the general population.

GOSHEN AND TANIS

In the middle of the afternoon on the third day of my journey, we arrived at the northern border of the land called Goshen in the Bible, in the region known also as Avaris. According to early Egyptian records, Avaris had been home to the Israelites, Asiatics and Hyksos people.[2]

We reached a village called San el-Hagar, and saw behind it what looked like a hill but was actually a *tel*, a mound formed by the accumulated remains of age-old settlements. This huge tel spread out for 2.5 kilometers ahead, and spanned 1.5 kilometers from left to right – a total of almost four square kilometers full of a city's relics. Yaman told me that the tel consisted of the remains of a massive biblical city called Tanis, and it was the largest tel from that era. It was a remarkable sight.

I was particularly interested in this area because of its proximity to the Israelites' land. In the Bible, Tanis is referred to as the City of Zoan or the Field of Zoan, and this is verified by two Egyptologists who are also archaeologists, Kitchen[3] and Redford. One tradition locates the confrontation between Moses and Pharaoh as having happened here.[4] At that time, Tanis was the Egyptian capital city. Oddly, relatively few tourists visit Tanis.

Here, spread out in front of me, were the remains of an important city, which archaeologists have uncovered and continue to explore. Security guards from the Egyptian Antiquities Department granted us access to the tel, which was fenced off. On our way in, we met a middle-aged portly man with blond hair, who was examining the hieroglyphs on a huge stone. We greeted him and I asked if he knew much about the site. He introduced himself as Mustafa, an archaeologist. When Yaman asked him to show us around, Mustafa was so delighted that he gave Yaman a great bear hug.

Tanis was a capital city of ancient Egypt and is a major excavation site. The buildings that were erected by the Israelites at Pitom and Rameses were eventually moved here due to flooding at their original site. | M Rawicz Trip Photo

Mustafa spoke English enthusiastically, with a heavy Egyptian accent. We began to follow him on an impromptu tour.

"I've read that the capital of the pharaohs was originally at Heliopolis,[5] near what is now Cairo." Mustafa looked at me with interest. "But they moved their capital to this area of the delta," I continued. "The Bible says that the big new capital cities were known as Pithom and Rameses. They were storage cities, built by the Israelite slaves for the pharaohs."[6,7,8]

"Yes," said Mustafa. "The city is known as Pi-Rameses and is about twenty kilometers south of here. Pi-Rameses was a magnificent city, but it was abandoned in about 1070 BCE and the city of Tanis was built to replace it. When the pharaohs needed stones to build their new temples, they ordered that the stones should be transported from Pi-Rameses to Tanis. And so they ravaged the buildings of Pi-Rameses."[9]

"Why did they come to Tanis?" I asked.

"Well, from what we know, Tanis was built for several reasons," Mustafa explained. "Mostly, it served as a strategic trade and cultural exchange center, but also as a new capital to get away from the political and religious control of the priests of Memphis and Heliopolis. Traders trekking from east to west also stopped here with their spices and other enticing goods."

I commented, "From what I've read, the area where the Israelites lived in Goshen must have been close to here."

He replied excitedly, "Yes, Tanis was originally a city just north of the area of Goshen."

We continued walking through the historical site, talking as we went.

"Tanis went through various stages of building – and various pharaohs," Mustafa explained. "Originally it was the site of Zoan, built in about 1700 BCE. It is referred to in the Bible. Later, it became the capital of the legendary Hyksos, the Shepherd Kings, who ruled Egypt for more than 500 years. After that it became the frontier town of Goshen."[10]

Just ahead, some massive statues loomed as we approached. Mustafa glanced up at them as if they were old friends. "Today," he said, "all traces of Zoan lie buried deeply beneath the many layers of Tanis. It's a city built upon a city."

"And the pharaohs?"

"The pharaohs in the north favored Tanis for themselves and their fabulous treasures."

Mustafa gestured towards the gigantic columns. "These were part of the palace and public buildings. The hieroglyphics you see were an anthem which told of the power and splendor of the previous pharaohs." The size of the columns was intimidating. Mustafa dramatically punched his arm into the air to show how the pharaohs had ruled with an iron fist over the lives of their subjects, their slaves and conquered people.

I found myself becoming quite angry, and felt uneasy standing there – in the shadow of the pharaohs' arrogance. We walked a little further, and then Mustafa pointed to a hill.

"Look," he said. "There are the remains of a great Egyptian temple. Its entrance has a huge gate. Behind it there's a vast area full of monuments that were part of the temple."

We headed towards this central temple site, examining the remains of items along the way, and passing 25-meter-high statues of pharaohs. Some were still standing but others had fallen and were lying on their backs. Each statue represented a specific pharaoh and they all had exotic names, such as Pusinis I, Amenembit and Shishnik; they had all

Archeological remains from Tanis much of which was taken from the city of Rameses. | M Rawicz Trip Photo

been part of the 21st Dynasty. Many statues showed the typical pharaonic headdress and square plaited beard that had been worn only by pharaohs. I stood beside a statue so that Mustafa could take my photograph, and my head was level with the top of its knees.

Further on, in the central temple area, I counted at least twenty-three obelisks. All of them were engraved with hieroglyphics, and most stood at least 4.5 meters high and were made of red granite. Mustafa told me that some of the obelisks had stood at the House of Rameses under Pharaoh Rameses II. I recognized that era as the time when the Israelites had been in Egypt. The remains of some obelisks that had fallen down were lying in broken pieces, with their parts lined up and waiting for archaeologists to restore them.

We continued walking deeper into the heart of the site, passing more densely engraved relief blocks. I could imagine the slaves, stonemasons and the Israelites laboring with such enormous stones. After I had viewed the temple itself, Mustafa took me to see the tomb area, which housed the remains of at least seven different pharaohs who had reigned from 1040 to 850 BCE.

A huge pharaonic statue at Tanis. | M Rawicz Trip Photo

Mustafa showed me the site where, in the late 1930s and 1940s, the archaeologist Montet[11] had discovered an entire complex of royal tombs of the kings, with structures half-buried in the ground. Stepping down into the excavation, I moved across to the opening and cautiously peered through it, then crept on my hands and knees into a shadowy,

An obelisk with hieroglyphics at Tanis. | *M Rawicz Trip Photo*

dank tomb. As I gazed into the gloom, a sense of foreboding overcame me and I retreated into the daylight.

I began to feel as if I was being sucked into a vortex, as I slowly walked over to one of the square pits from which a sarcophagus had been removed. I stared into the pit's black hole. The ominous feeling was quite powerful now and gave a tugging sensation at my heart. And then my foot slipped! Just as I was about to tumble in to join the long-dead, Mustafa grabbed my arm and yanked me back.

The sense of teetering on the edge of a tomb belonging to such a powerful, cruel ruler had been eerie. I made a mental note to listen to my intuition better in the future. After almost stepping on the viper, this was the second close shave I'd had, and I suspected it might not be the last.

From what Mustafa had told me, I realized that although the Israelites would have witnessed the start of the building of Tanis, large parts of the city would have been constructed only after they had left Egypt. I would have liked to explore more, but it was late in the day. The sun was low so we drove to the nearby village of San-el-Hagar, where we stayed overnight at a bed-and-breakfast in a private home. In the morning we would explore Pi-Rameses.

I opened a notebook that I had brought with me, and wrote the first entry of my traveler's journal. "Tanis is a major city with temples, palaces, and wells, spectacular gold jewellery, with some features still intact."

BURIED CITY – RAMESES

CAMP 1

"And they departed from Rameses in the first month, on the fifteenth day of the first month; on the morrow after the Passover the children of Israel went out with a high hand in the sight of all the Egyptians."[1]

On a spiritual level, Rameses symbolizes the first event of a person's life journey: our birth. It spells out the purpose of the entire voyage, which is to free ourselves of the constraints of the womb and its physical boundaries. At birth we come armed with the strength and tools to overcome all our future challenges, but we will need to be trained and educated to realize our potential. Birth is thus a joyous occasion, coupled with anticipation about how we will do on our long journey ahead. This is alluded to in the word "*Rameses*," which also means the "best of the land."[2]

The following day, Friday, the fourth day of my journey, after breakfast (which included a delightful array of colorful salads) we carried on for twenty-one kilometers with Mustafa to Pi-Rameses. The book of Numbers 33:3 describes how the Children of Israel journeyed from Rameses. The word "*Rameses*" also means "to trample down"[3] and in my quest to find this camp I wanted to search for something that had been trampled. It seemed an unusual criterion, but I was keeping an open mind.

After going the twenty-one kilometers in a southerly direction, we reached a large farming area that marks the site of the ancient cities of Pithom and Rameses. Today, the nearest village is Qantir. My map of the delta showed that Qantir was ninety-six kilometers northeast of Cairo. As we approached Qantir, my driver turned the car off the main road and we proceeded to travel along a back lane to reach the area of Pi-Rameses.

Yaman continued telling me about his life, until eventually Hashim pulled the car to a halt at our destination. A short stocky man wearing a striped shirt met us, as had been arranged. His face was friendly and intelligent and he had a grey moustache and greying black hair. He introduced himself to me as Achmud, saying, "I am the representative of the authorities, and I am here to show you around. You have been granted special permission to visit this site." He was a specialist archaeologist with great knowledge of the area, and his job was to guide us and explain the excavations and findings of the archaeological surveys. His English was good, and his manner was energetic.

I had studied maps of the city's layout and buildings that had been discovered by archaeologists such as Manfred Bietak,[4] so I already knew a little about Pi-Rameses and its rulers. Pharaoh Seti I (who ruled from 1291 to 1279 BCE) was the father of Pharaoh Rameses II (1279 to 1212 BCE). Seti had owned a summer residence at the site of the future Pi-Rameses when it was still a small town. Rameses II, who is widely thought to have been the pharaoh who ruled in Moses' time, moved his main palace to this site and built the town into a vibrant city.

The son of Rameses II was Pharaoh Merneptah. He ruled from 1212 to 1202 BCE, and is thought by other archaeologists to have been the pharaoh at the time of the Exodus.[5]

Rameses II was one of the most powerful and successful of all the pharaohs. He built great architectural developments to deify himself, one of which was the new capital of Pi-Rameses. Thus Pi-Rameses was transformed into a royal residence and the seat of the government; the city was also important for military and strategic reasons. Rameses hoped that by shifting the capital from Thebes to this delta region, the influence of the priesthood would be curtailed. He evidently also wanted to protect Egypt's borders, especially the eastern one, which had been vulnerable to invasions by neighboring countries. Similarly to Tanis, the new city of Pi-Rameses served as a commercial connection between Egypt and Asia.[6] The town itself was extremely wealthy.

However, the glory of Pi-Rameses was eclipsed when the pharaohs of the Twenty-First Dynasty (1070 to 945 BCE) moved the capital yet again. This time, as Mustafa had explained, they chose Tanis. The river on which Pi-Rameses was located had dried up at the start of the Twentieth Dynasty, and this problem appears to have been one of the main reasons for the shift to Tanis. The pharaohs moved virtually all the monuments, item by item, to the new capital.

When we arrived at the site of Pi-Rameses, Mustafa pointed out the undulating terrain around the city, and gave us some information about its history.

A satellite image of the huge ancient city known as Pi-Rameses, now called Tel El Daba, in Avaris in the Nile Delta. We call it Pithom and Ramses in Goshen, in the Pesach Hagganda. | Google Earth, Orion-Me, DigitalGlobe

"The city was built on a Nile tributary, which split into several branches at this site," he explained. "Between the branches, islands of higher ground remained which were safe from the annual flooding. The archaeologist Ian Wilson believes that Pi-Rameses was built across these islands to protect it from such floods."[7]

He then showed us the incredible layout of this ancient city which the Israelites had built. It was vast: an astounding 30 square kilometers.

"Another archaeologist, Manfred Bietak,[8] excavated the site," Mustafa said. "He worked as part of a German expedition in which the Austrian Archaeological Institute was also involved. They used a magnetometer, which can detect what lies beneath the ground. The team surveyed the site meter by meter, a bit like when you use a metal detector to find a landmine. They worked their way across the site, making records of the findings, long before they started to excavate. The team covered seventy-five square kilometers, and found that the ruins of Pi-Rameses stretched over thirty square kilometers. Later, their actual diggings uncovered some astounding artifacts."

Achmud led the way as we walked across the grey clay ground. Mustafa pointed out several areas containing archaeological indicators of

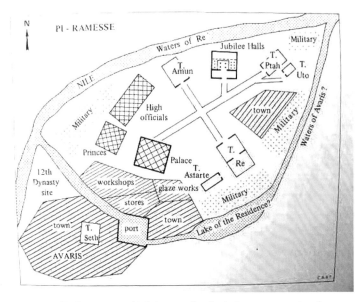

A map of Pi-Rameses, which is an archeologist's reconstruction from
magnetic testing. It shows palaces, temples, halls, military quarters,
factory area, port, residential area, and more. | Map of Rameses (Ramses)
from which the Exodus began, Egyptian: Pi-Ramesses or Per-Ramesses. |
Walter Reinhold Warttig Mattfeld y de la Torre | 16 Sept 2005 |
http://www.bibleorigins.net/RamesesMapAvaris.html

the city's layout and buildings. I had read about some of them. Today, the city remains largely buried.

Large shafts descended into the ground at an angle and then opened up into underground chambers. We went in to explore them.

The city layout consisted of a large central crossroad. At the top of the southern road were the palaces of the Pharaoh, princes and homes of high officials. On the top of the northern, eastern and western roads were temples. Next to one of the temples was a large jubilee hall. These main buildings were flanked by military barracks, I presume for the protection of these important places. Further away to the south were workshops, stores, glaze works, stables and behind them a section of the town for less important people. This whole area was surrounded by water canals, I presume also for protection. The canals led into a tributary of the Nile River. Behind these canals was another residential area in which could be found a Twelfth-Dynasty temple to the god Seth with a sacred lake and a Twelfth-Dynasty palace.

As we drove over the vast area, Mustafa pointed out areas that had accommodated these various facilities. We examined some of the tunnels that led to the city remains. We saw the area where Seti's palace and its private lake had been uncovered.

Tunnels led to the huge stables, with factories next door where the royal chariots and arms would have been made. The stables alone covered almost seventeen square kilometers and had held more than 460 horses. There were six rows of halls connected to a vast courtyard. This is the largest ancient stable discovered in Egypt. In fact, the second level of stables discovered here would have been built by Rameses II. From here the Pharaoh must have pursued the Israelites to the Red Sea.

Mustafa explained, "Next door to these stables were workshops for making glass, faience, cylinder seals, beads, scarabs, inlays, pots and statuettes. There were halls where cloth was dyed and leather was made. They even found equipment which would have been used to make fertilizer for the vineyards."

In the south-westerly direction was the Twelfth-Dynasty temple, a large rectangular structure with a few atriums and chambers for worship. It too had been identified, complete with columns and walls, by the archaeologist Bietak.[9] This temple was located near an existing village called Ezbet Rushdi.

A kilometer beyond this was the excavation tunnel of the Twelfth-Dynasty palace. The palace had a large hall, administrative quarters, and spacious lodgings. It had been excavated by the archaeologist Edouard Naville in the 1880s.[10]

Another kilometer on, we arrived at the tunnel to the temple of the god Seth, where the floor of a sacred lake was still visible.

Finally, outside the city perimeter, Bietak had found a cemetery with hundreds of gravestones and mausoleums built of stone. Many of the rooms contained pottery and offerings made to the gods on behalf of the deceased.

By now I was looking around in a stupor of amazement. The biblical cities of Pithom and Rameses that the Israelites had slaved to construct had become larger than life in my mind. From now on, whenever these cities were mentioned at Passover, I would find myself mentally travelling back to these massive archaeological diggings.

I couldn't help but gasp in amazement, but deeper feelings surfaced as well. This was where Pharaoh had made the Israelites' lives particularly bitter. The children of Israel had increased in numbers, and Pharaoh was worried that they might join his enemies. So he had enslaved them, and made them build these treasure cities of Pithom and Rameses.[11]

I imagined the Israelites laboring under that cruel ruler, hewing mammoth stones in the blazing sun and hauling them across long distances and up great heights. Here they had also slaved to make extremely large quotas of bricks each day. And just to top things off, they had been forced to build everything on the sinking marshy ground of the Nile's tributary islands. Walls might collapse or sink even as the people were trying to build them.[12]

The true meaning of "Rameses" suddenly became clearer to me. The Hebrew meaning – "trample down" – must have referred to the conditions under which the Israelites had labored. Scholars have recorded that the ground at the sites of the storage cities of Pithom and Rameses was marshy. The suffering of my ancestors seemed to cry out from the earth as they begged G-d to save them.

They were like babies, totally dependent, with only hope that they would be helped or rescued. The people had been utterly dispirited by the futility of their task. Their self-image was shattered and they had no way of visualizing any other reality for themselves. They could only hope that they would be rescued. They felt abandoned and unable to exercise free choice against their Egyptian taskmasters.[13]

I felt close to tears. This place of horror and wonder was the first encampment of the Hebrew people's first step towards liberation. They must have been terrified, trampled down as they had been in both body and spirit just as the Hebrew meaning of 'rameses.'

⬒ Emerging from Oppression

The Hebrew meaning of the word Rameses, "to trample down," could refer to the utter subjugation of the spirits and bodies of the Israelites when they were struck down to the ground. On leaving the Rameses camp, the Israelites would have had their first taste of liberation.

This is where the Israelites learned their first lesson in emerging from oppression. A person may find themselves in a situation in which they are highly controlled and even oppressed. The person is unhappy and feels extremely limited in personal choice and freedom. He fears the consequences of departing from the restrictive rules of the environment and repressors. The days go by and no future or way out seems possible. One's own behaviors, habits or even addictions can be bondage. If one is not living consciously, then one might not even be aware that life could be different.

However, it is possible that one can go through a mind shift that enables one to break free mentally. One can begin to see a way to becoming more independent, make plans and eventually break free of the bondage. This requires one to have a concept of living free that can be pursued. One can also break free from a personal bondage when one's consciousness is awakened; then one can think and act for a better future. This can lead to a faith and hope that the future can be brighter – faith that G-d can help turn the situation toward a better one.

This mental breaking free is the teaching of this camp of Rameses which was the start of the Israelites' liberation, as referred to in the explanations of Jacobson, a prominent Chassidic scholar.[14,15]

As I reflected on this, I became more aware of my own feelings of uncertainty. I carried a great deal of life's stresses and accompanying depression in my heart over the past few years, but I, too, could emerge from the sense of oppression. I could live with greater hope and love of G-d. I felt like a new-born, at the beginning of my personal transformation. My own Exodus offered me the opportunity to change my life and mature, so that I could start to make more balanced choices about my work, relationships and my need to rest. The prospect was exciting.

I imagined crowds of Israelite families amassing here to move to the next village. Their goods and animals were bundled along with them as a steadily growing group gathered behind Moses. The celebration of Passover and its liberating meaning suddenly took on a new light.

MYSTERIOUS TEL AND MIRACULOUS CLOUDS – SUKKOT

CAMP 2

"The children of Israel journeyed from Rameses and encamped in Sukkoth."[1,2]

I was tired, my eyes heavy with the need to sleep, as we continued on the next stage of our journey. To entertain themselves, Hashim and

Yaman turned on the car radio and the Egyptian music blared out its typical rhythm. My companions proceeded to shout above the music as they conversed in their own language. I hid my head under some clothes and dozed off. By the time I awoke, we had travelled further southeast towards the Israelites' second main camp, at Sukkot.

Sukkot means "temporary shelters." This fact set me the challenge of finding an ancient place of shelter, which seemed unlikely in the modern bustling environment. How could a temporary shelter have survived thousands of years? On the other hand, "temporary shelter" could refer to the "clouds of glory" that had sheltered and protected the people as they journeyed.[3] That might indeed be impossible to find, I thought. It was here that the Israelites had to choose from the various routes eastwards to Canaan and Asia that I had explained to Carol.

The most northern route was along the shores of the Mediterranean, called the Way of the Philistines, because the route skirted the area of the fierce Philistines, now known as Gaza C.[4] The Israelites would have taken just three days to reach Israel by the first of these routes,[5] but G-d did not want them to abandon their cause and turn around and return to Egypt,[6] as they would have risked running into the militant Philistines.[7] They would have encountered the corpses of the people of the tribe of Ephraim who had died along that route after having left Egypt before the appointed time. As it says in the *Jewish Encyclopedia*, "The tribe of Ephraim miscalculated the time of the deliverance of the Children of Israel from Egypt, and left the country thirty years before the appointed time. They were met by a hostile host of Philistines."[8] Such a sight would surely have demoralized the Israelites and undermined their faith in G-d. However, they obeyed G-d's command to avoid this route.

The route which runs through the northern Sinai Peninsula, in biblical times was called Darb-es-Shur or "Way to Shur." Today, the route runs along a dry riverbed called Wadi Tumilat, passes the town of Abu Suwayr or Suweir to the town of Ismailia, then turns eastwards to Muweileh via Halatza, and on to the Negev Desert in southern Israel. The third possible route ran through a valley from west to east, between the mountain ranges of the central Sinai; this was called the "Way to Hagg" or "Suez to Taba" route. This route goes down the peninsula's western coastline and then through its central mountain passes, via what is today St Catherine's monastery, and continues towards Israel. This slower journey would give the Israelites time to develop greater

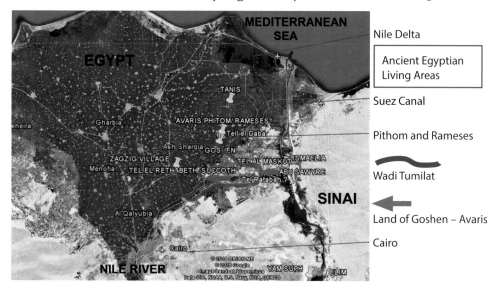

The Nile Delta showing the location of the Land of Goshen, where the Israelites lived. It is next to Pithom and Rameses and alongside Wadi Tumilat, a strategic route to the "eastern door" of Egypt, leading to Canaan. | Google Earth image amended by M Rawicz

faith in G-d.[9] The fourth route is around the southern coast to the tip of the Sinai Peninsula on the road to Sharm-el-Sheikh. It skirts around enormously high mountain ranges and is too long to match the Bible's versions of the journey.

According to Neubauer, the Israelites took the "Way to Hagg" route. I wanted to follow this route that the Israelites had taken through central Sinai, so we proceeded southwards from Rameses and Tel el Daba. As we moved further away from the nutrient-rich Nile tributaries, the land began to look less fertile. The rural road took us to the village of Ikyad. Here we passed more mud-brick homes with roofs made of palm leaves. We stopped for refreshments and I bought an apple that was double the size of both my hands together.

Further on, we passed another small village called As-Salihyah-Al-Jadidah. The soil looked extremely sandy and the vegetation was sparse, but modern irrigation methods had allowed the people to cultivate what was once pure desert.

Eventually we passed a modern town called Al Qassasin, near Wadi Tumilat. The wadi runs towards the border of Egypt with the Sinai Peninsula, culminating at a large lake called Timsah. Small towns lie on both sides of the valley, which has long been a strategic route to the "eastern door" of Egypt. In biblical times, the valley linked the eastern and western sides of Egypt, and also linked Egypt to Canaan, Babylon, Persia and other parts of Asia.

This is still regarded as a key route from Egypt and an important area of development, with the large town of Ismailia on the Suez Canal bearing witness to this development. On the day we visited the area, the main road running parallel to the wadi was crowded with cars and large trucks. The traffic rushed by noisily. People were busy with commerce and import and export activities, just as their forebears had been in ancient times.

Water has periodically flowed through the wadi, giving rise to settlements on either side at various times. In some places wells had been sunk to provide water during the dry periods. Today, the settlements of the ancient past remain visible in the numerous tels along the wadi. These included Tel-el-Retabeh and Tel-el-Muskhuta,[10] which we intended to visit. The tels are believed to be near the site of the ancient Sukkot encampment. We turned off the main road onto a dusty track running alongside the wadi. The track became increasingly muddy, with a growing risk of the wheels becoming stuck in the ground, but Hashim persevered. I was reminded of our seemingly endless trip on a sandy track a few days earlier, and the mood in the car now resembled that day's too. To take my mind off the mundane reality of the trip, I thought about the journey Moses had undertaken with the multitudes, coming to rest at Sukkot.

It was logical that they would have walked along this route because their livestock would have had ample grazing from the desert scrub. The wadi was surrounded by small bushes, herbs, and grasses, which included the ground-hugging bright green Cynodon and long grassy Panicum with its prolific grey tufts. There were beautiful trees, which would have provided food for camels, including varieties of Acacia such as Acacia Nilotica (Scented-Pod Acacia). The wild figs on the banks of the wadi would have yielded fruit for the people and chewy treats for the children; and the willows – Salix Alba – might have been used for medicinal purposes, to treat ailments like arthritis, abdominal cramps, colds, cuts and wounds. I could visualize the Israelites passing rapidly along this way in their flight.

I decided to keep a list of the plants and animals that we encountered on the journey, so I wrote down the names of the plants I had just seen.

The Bible recounts that the Israelites arrived at Sukkot in the evening of the first day of the Exodus. This was the 15th day of the month of Nissan, which scholars have calculated fell on a Thursday in the biblical time of the Exodus according to the Jewish calendar. Nissan corresponds roughly with April. At the Sukkot encampment, the people were able to rest after their hasty departure from the previous site.

We also know from biblical texts that Sukkot refers to the protection of G-d. "The cloud of G-d was over the tabernacle. . . . in the sight of all the Israelites during all their travels."[11] "G-d went before them by day in a pillar of a cloud, to lead them along the way; and by night in a pillar of fire, to give them light."[12] The sages comment that the Israelites were escorted under the protection of the cloud of G-d's glory.

This Divine protection is remembered during the Jewish festival of Sukkot, when people make symbolic temporary dwellings using palm leaves for the roof. They eat their meals in the *sukkah* for a week, to commemorate G-d's protection. I was interested to note that some farmers along the wadi still lived in huts with palm leaf roofs, as in other rural areas.

I now understood what was meant by "the edge of the wilderness." The boundary of the cultivated land was a sharp line that cut through the landscape, with the far side being completely barren desert. There was a stark contrast between the fertile land of the irrigated fields and the more distant yellow expanse of desert. Clearly, one needed the protection of a loving G-d to survive in this desert.

Thirty-one kilometers from the point at which we entered Wadi Tumilat, we arrived at Tel-el-Retabeh, which is thought to be the location of the Sukkot encampment.[13] I saw a large mound which I estimated to be roughly one square kilometer, surrounded by neat square fields of cultivated vegetables and fruit trees planted in rows.

I wondered if the locals ever thought about that huge mound and reflected on its historical meaning, or whether they just accepted it as part of the landscape. Our driver stopped the car and we climbed out. A tall grey-haired man, probably in his sixties, approached us; he wore a white turban and a long blue desert robe. He was the representative of the authorities whom we had arranged to assist us in this area. He introduced himself as Hamed, with a strong handshake and a broad smile.

"I'm the local representative of the specialist archaeologist for this site," Hamed told us. "I am delighted to show you around."

We followed him across the open ground to the mound of the tel.

I had read that this tel was the remains of a settlement built during the reign of the Ramesside pharaohs, including Rameses II, who reigned in Moses' time. Ramesside pottery debris has been found in this mound.[14] Tel-el-Retabeh was at its glorious peak during the era when the Israelites lived in Egypt, and it boasted its own Egyptian temple. Vast stables have been excavated by the archaeologist Hans Goedicke here, and[15] Goedicke also found a great fortress of Pharaoh Merneptah. Merneptah might have been the pharaoh who pursued the Israelites to the Red Sea, as I had seen in the Cairo museum. The fortress was an important defense point for protecting Egypt's borders.[16]

An ancient Egyptian papyrus letter called *Anastasi 6*, dating from the thirteenth century BCE, states that "Bedouin with cattle were being allowed to pass Merneptah's fortress to obtain water at the pools of Pr-Tum." The archaeologist Hoffmeier[17] regarded this place as the site known as Tjeku, which housed Egyptian military forces, including horses and possibly chariots. These armies protected Egypt's border.

Hoffmeier also suggested that the site might have housed the very chariots used to pursue the Israelites as they proceeded toward the Sinai desert when Pharaoh realized that he was losing his slaves. Further evidence that Tjeku was probably a militarized zone is found in Egyptian military documents associated with officers assigned to defend that area. An Egyptian text that was found refers to "the troop commander of Tjeku."[18]

I had read that Josephus Flavius,[19] the famous historian, had commented on an ancient letter that a prince of Gezer had sent with soldiers to the Pharaoh, requesting urgent assistance to prevent the slaves from running away. A chief archer was sent to Tjeku but the help arrived too late: the slaves had been seen crossing the north wall of the fortress town of Merneptah. These slaves may have been the Israelites.[20]

I imagined the Pharaoh's officers riding in their golden chariots, drawn by strong Arabian horses, thundering out from the stables in front of the spot where I now stood. I recalled the verse in the book of Exodus (14:5–7): "The heart of Pharaoh and his servants was turned against the people, and they said, why have we done this, to let Israel go from serving us?" Pharaoh ordered his 600 chariots and the captains to be prepared for the chase. According to the Torah, "G-d had hardened the heart of Pharaoh and he pursued after the children of Israel."

As I examined the site under Hamed's guidance, I told him that I had read that archaeologists had found a long line of fortresses along the entire eastern border of Egypt. These had prevented people from passing in and out without permission; evidently, the system was similar to modern passport control. The fortresses were built parallel to the present Suez Canal, from the Mediterranean Sea to the top of the Gulf of the Red Sea.[21] Those in the north guarded the Way of the Philistines, which G-d had instructed the Israelites not to follow. The fort at Tel-el-Retabah, the ancient Sukkot encampment, was midway in the line of fortresses running from north to south. Hamed told me that he knew all this, and vividly described what he had seen at the remains of a fortress he had visited.

As I was about to embark on the next portion of the journey through the Etham Desert, I reflected on the teachings of the Sukkot encampment.

✢ Shelter, self-confidence and self-esteem

On a personal level, the Sukkot encampment can represent the shelter that parents provide for their children in nurturing, secure homes. The child's needs are anticipated and catered for, and their safety, education and well-being are supervised. With this sense of security, a child perceives the world as a safe place and develops a healthy, socially acceptable attitude. This can assist the child's ability to navigate the world adequately in the future.

G-d catered for the Israelites in the desert in a similar fashion by providing protection with the "cloud" that accompanied them. In our daily lives, the sense of security that G-d provides for us can give us a better sense of well-being and an ability to cope. It can also bolster our confidence, and this is what Sukkot represents in our lives, according to Jacobson's suggestion.[22]

At the very early stage of their exodus the Israelites were still like dependent babies and needed this kind of protection.[23]

For me personally, knowing that I was travelling towards the Sukkot camp encouraged me to believe that G-d would protect me. I hoped to succeed in spiritual growth and better understanding of the Torah on my journey, and knew that to do so I would have to rely on G-d's protection. This attitude became a feature of my mindset from that day forward. It guided my physical journey and I have maintained that same outlook in life.

Hillel Ben David, in his book *Journeys of the Sons of Israel* explains that the Children of Israel were growing up emotionally, mentally and spiritually as if from infancy into old age as they moved from Egypt through the forty-two camps until they reached the Promised Land. Of all the commentaries about the Exodus that I had come across, I resonated particularly with this metaphor, with the idea of evolving and maturing as I progressed on my journey tracing the footsteps of Moses, Miriam, Aaron and the Children of Israel. I worked extensively with Hillel's ideas because they echoed the process I was hoping to achieve for myself, in my relations with others and with G-d in a more authentic manner, beginning with baby steps, and growing more sure-footed as I travelled deeper into the Sinai and into my soul.

After a short break we continued eastwards along Wadi Tumilat for another fourteen kilometers, where we passed a tel called Tel-el-Maskhuta. Here we saw a portion of a large canal with military outposts along its length, which the pharaohs had built to prevent people escaping from Egypt.

Long before the Suez Canal had been built, the ancients had recognized the advantage of having a route that provided access between the Mediterranean and Red Seas. A Twelfth-Dynasty king named Sesostris began work on a canal to connect the Great Bitter Lakes, south of Wadi Tumilat, with the Red Sea. Archaeologists believe that such a canal was completed in ancient times.[24]

On the way, we visited several stelae in Wadi Tumilat which had been erected by Pharaoh Rameses II. They indicated the position of the canal in the Nineteenth Dynasty, which lasted from 1293 to 1185 BCE. The French Egyptologist and archaeologist Pierre Montet had discovered the stelae.[25]

As in ancient times, there was still a huge Egyptian military presence in the area. Many large outposts are still located in this area to prevent interference with the Suez Canal. I noticed a police vehicle following us, and asked my guide what the reason might be.

Yaman said, "They've been driving behind us all the way through the delta. Have you only seen them now?"

I was astonished to learn that the Egyptian police were trailing us to make sure that we did not deviate from the route we had declared to the authorities. Yaman said they also wanted to ensure my personal safety

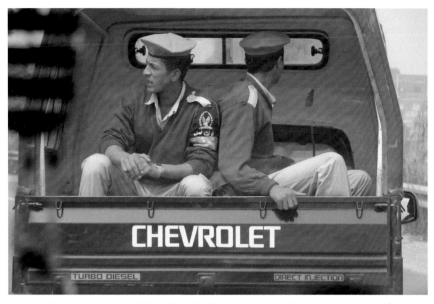

Egyptian police trailed us through Northern Egypt, for our own security. |
M Rawicz Trip Photo

as a tourist. The tourist trade is highly valued in Egypt, and travellers who venture off the beaten track are often protected. Yaman also told me that although police officers study for five or six years at the Cairo Police Academy, none of them can speak English.

As we approached the mouth of Wadi Tumilat, I saw that it had been made into a concrete canal a short distance before flowing into Lake Timsah. There were rows and rows of small homes surrounded by gardens of fruit and vegetables; the impression was of small farmers living in a suburb engaged with small-scale intensive food production.

We drove on to visit the town of Ismailia on the border of Lake Timsah, strategically situated. Hashim drove us to the busy port, where we saw large ships en route to the Suez Canal. Cargo ships sail in both directions as they enter and leave the long Suez passage. Like metal giants, roughly 15,000 ships a year make their way along these waters, representing more than a third of global maritime traffic. A huge amount of oil is transported via the Suez en route to Europe and North America.

Visiting the area brought home to me the fact that Suez is one of the most strategically important places on earth, and nations will go to any length – even war – to protect it. It is a potential "hotspot" because the entire world uses this channel. Trade makes the world go round, but it also causes wars.

Lovely holiday resorts and hotels grace the lake border of modern Ismailia, with picturesque fishing boats lined up along the shores. The town is an administrative doorway to Egypt and has an attractive, busy commercial center. In addition to being the agricultural hub for the movement of fresh produce from the delta, it is also a transit hub for people and cargo navigating from north to south (Europe to Africa) and from east to west. This was also the case in ancient Egyptian times, rendering it a strategic area.

We made a quick but fascinating visit to the town's archaeological and maritime museums, where we saw relics of its past.

From this point onwards, the most logical alternative for the Israelites' route would have been for them to turn southwards into the Etham Desert and move parallel to the watercourse that connects Lake Timsah to the "Large Bitter Lake" and "Small Bitter Lake," on the way to the Red Sea. They would then have continued southwards until they reached the Gulf of the Red Sea. We would follow in their footsteps, but not today: it was already evening.

What a pleasure it was to check into a large modern hotel, with a lovely comfortable room and private bathroom – a luxury! I looked forward to dinner, as we had eaten very little during the day. That evening, from the hotel's window I watched the sun set in brilliant red over Lake Timsah, and the lights of the town come on as the sky darkened.

After eating, I recorded the day's sights in my log book: "Two more Egyptian cities, Tel-el-Retabeh with its vast fortress and the largest stables of antiquity, and Tel-el-Muskhuta; both had Egyptian temples. This made it six Egyptian cities seen to date, along a trade route and within the ambit of civilization. Each had a significant water supply from a Nile tributary and the pharaonic channel." My log book was going to record what archaeological and ancient historical finds there were. I wanted to see if there were any patterns in the evidence that I might see along the way. I also wanted to keep a record of the flora and fauna to understand the ecology of the route. The next day was Saturday, the sixth day of my journey. I planned to spend the day resting and enjoying my stay at the lakeside hotel, as it would be the Sabbath day. As I drifted off to sleep, my heart was singing with joy at having seen the Bible come alive.

Dusk over Lake Timsah, which the Israelites passed on their Exodus, and which is alongside the Suez Canal. | *M Rawicz Trip Photo*

TASTE OF DESERT AND ARAB REVOLUTION – ETHAM DESERT

CAMP 3

"They took their journey from Sukkot, and encamped in Etham on the edge of the wilderness."[1] G-d had promised to take them by the Red Sea and they would go from Sukkot via Etham out of Egypt.[2]

Etham has various meanings. It means "from them," "their ploughshare" and "contemplation."[3] I wondered how one might find a ploughshare in the desert, and how this could be connected to contemplation. It seemed a mystery, and I looked forward to finding the answer. Maybe there was a special place for contemplation in the desert.

Early on Sunday morning there was an urgent knock at my door. Yaman stood there, freshly showered. I rushed to finish my packing and met him and Hashim in the lobby, where we sat down for a quick cup of tea.

"The radio said we can expect a day of wind and dust," Yaman told me.

Evidently, this is typical weather for the area. As Yaman sipped his tea, he told me that he had enjoyed visiting his friends the previous day and was now ready for more adventure. We planned our day and mulled over the Exodus route options.

South of Wadi Tumilat is the extensive Etham Desert, which stretches all the way down the eastern coast of Egypt to the Red Sea Gulf. In ancient times, the canal built by the pharaohs was a crucial barrier to prevent people from entering and leaving the eastern border of Egypt without permission. The Israelites trekked parallel to the ancient canal before crossing the Red Sea. It was logical for them to have moved southwards, because this is a short route leading directly to one of the most suitable places to cross into the Sinai Desert – from which they would reach the Promised Land. Our journey essentially took the same route, but went parallel to the Suez Canal through Etham Desert.

We travelled for half an hour, during which we covered twenty-one kilometers. We were driving on one of the ancient roads in the desert that leads to the Red Sea. We moved through large expanses of yellow sands with occasional small sand dunes. This was my first experience of being surrounded by real desert landscape. Initially I could see only sand, sand, and more sand, as far as the distant horizon. The heat became intensive and stifling. Some dunes were covered with stumpy grey desert bushes. These plants stabilize the drift sands because their roots spread underground and bind the loose grains together.

Occasionally, we saw a larger and tougher bush species called Casduarina, which has needle-like leaves and brown cones; we also saw some trees called Dalbergia, which have thin dark-green leaves. This part of the desert receives an average of just sixty-two mm of rain annually, so wildlife is scarce.

Suddenly, we were treated to the delightful sight of flocks of local birds. One of the species we saw was the Lammergeyer, a large red-and-grey-breasted vulture with a black back. This bird is becoming rare worldwide but it still breeds in small numbers in this area. When we slowed down we also saw the Sinai Banded Snake, with its rings of white and light-brown, and the thick Hoogstraal's Cat Snake, which has a black-and-white spotted back and grey spotted underbelly. We stayed in the car while viewing the snakes.

Our route through the bleak expanse of flat sand ran parallel to the Suez Canal, which was between one-and-a half and three kilometers away from the road at any point. In some places we saw a glimmer of water on the horizon, and where our route was closer to the canal we saw irrigated lands. A narrow "green zone" existed beside the canal, made possible by modern irrigation; it was filled with palm trees, cultivated fields and other vegetation. In biblical times, however, this whole area would have been bare sandy desert, with no more than a few sheep grazing under the intense sun.

Kilometer after dusty kilometer of slowly changing landscapes blurred past. I had a sense of physical movement, but it was not matched by any variety in the visual landscape. The car windows framed the world like the edges of a television screen. The scenes I saw were like unending shots of the same thing.

Because of the heat, we had to keep the windows closed. I felt like a passenger in a hermetically sealed compartment that precluded contact with the real world; it was unlike any trip I had experienced before. Even on safari in South Africa, there is some feeling of contact with the earth because of rivers to be crossed, branches to be avoided, and rocks to be skirted. Here, we just drove. And drove. And drove.

The ancient route that we followed took us to the northern point of the Large Bitter Lake, where suddenly the view changed dramatically. In front of us stretched an enormous expanse of salt water, some ten kilometers wide and twenty kilometers long. All around the shimmering lake, farms that used fresh-water irrigation stretched back about a kilometer from the water's edge.

We began to pass many impoverished villages and a few small towns. At a village called Fayid we took a break, and I was struck by the impressive sight of red brick schools, which stood out above the miserable dwellings. The schools had been built by the government in a drive to improve education. The homes, however, were poorly constructed mud houses. Dirty barefoot children ran around in the streets.

We also passed farmers working in small sugarcane plots and palm plantations, alongside narrow railways that would carry the harvest to the processing factories. Women were bent over in the fields as they picked tomatoes and crated them. Their brightly colored clothing gave some cheer to the landscape. My thoughts drifted back to the ancient Israelites. We had seen places where people could plough, which left me wondering whether even in ancient times the route might have been cultivated rather than complete desert all the way.

We strolled over to buy some cool drinks and were mobbed by children at our heels. They were running and began shouting something and picked up stones to throw at me. Hashim shouted at the boys and they backed off. I was stunned to be exposed to this once again.

"Just take no notice of them," Hashim told me as we hurried back to the car. "Not everyone is like this. It's just some of the people are narrow-minded with a prejudiced background. In the bigger towns where people have been to school more and have seen more of life, they understand better. These people feel very unhappy about us being here. They feel we are coming to their place and we should not do that. There are not enough homes and community services. Our sanitation, electricity, piped water and hospitals are not enough. Only schooling is making some progress. So the people are angry and upset."

We drove and I gazed out of the window, trying to assimilate the underlying conditions of the locals in parts of Egypt not normally seen by tourists. Silently, I hoped that one day the people would be in a better situation. I noted that I was fortunate enough to number among a more privileged population.

We continued travelling southwards and came to a point where the lake narrows. Here the water became shallow and brackish, full of salt and other chemicals washed down from the desert sands. This section is known as the "Small Bitter Lake." We skirted the lake on a road that is now called Hugada-el-Ishmaelia.

The Etham encampment of the Israelites had been somewhere in this region.[4] Hashim stopped the car, and Yaman and I climbed out. I wanted to get a feel of the land. I sat down on the sand to reflect on this part of the Exodus journey and the meaning of the word "etham."

⧉ Developing from dependency to independence

The Hebrew grammar for the word "you" in the plural is contained in the word, Etham. The plural implies that the people had begun to think of themselves as a community or a more cohesive group.

Just as young children are more self-centered and not keen on sharing until they mature or are socialized to do so, the Israelites were at an early stage of their maturity.

At this stage the Israelites had an emergence of some newfound strength deep within themselves but still somewhat hidden. They were beginning to have some thoughts that their future may be better than it had been. They were growing slightly in self-respect and self-determination and away from their previous repressed mentality. They could be compared to children that were testing their early days of freedom but still needing protection and agreement, as I read in the text of Jacobson.[5]

I was still recovering from my recent episode of depression and the effects of a stressful life in South Africa. This was a great self-limiting factor in my sense of wellbeing. I was beginning to explore my own independence in this potentially dangerous, desert environment. I was gradually becoming acquainted with the "new" world around me. I sensed that, with G-d's protection, everything was going to be all right. This insight gave me confidence, and I felt easier about the exploration that still lay ahead of me. I had a sense that some kind of personal mission, still unknown to me, would emerge from my trip.   ◤

GREAT IDOL AND RED SEA SPLITTING –   CAMP 4
PI-HAHIROTH AND MIGDOL

"They journeyed from Etham and camped in Pi-Hahiroth, which faces Baal Zephon; and they camped in front of Migdol."[1]

Migdol means "tower."[2] I needed to find something that looked like a tower and which had survived for more than three-and-a-half millennia. How could any tower remain standing for that long? Would it be as indestructible and obvious as a pyramid?

The desert to our west was flat. Further on it became an undulating plain, shallow and wide, sloping towards the Bitter Lake. On this side of the lake, many shallow wadis drained towards other lakes that lay at the foothills of a distant ridge. Beyond that ridge, the ground was flat and elevated. The scene presented a marvelous variety of color, with several shades of yellow and deep shadows.

In the distance to the southwest, an unusual small mountain caught my eye. I realized this must be the mountain as mentioned in the Bible,[3] and believed by some archaeologists to be the Migdol landmark.[4] It stood out as a hard grey rocky outcrop in contrast to the yellow sand. The mountain looked like a fortified natural tower, and I could see how it would have been considered intimidating in biblical times. The ancient military could have used it for reconnaissance and to launch ambushes on enemy forces, as they would have needed a tower-like structure[5] or a prominent landmark like Migdol.[6] The hill was situated thirty kilometers west of the place we stood, along a sand track known today as Genaiva. To this day, a large military presence has been maintained in the area, with a security outpost in the desert and a large military barracks.

South of the Small Bitter Lake, we had another thirty kilometers to travel before we reached the northern shore of the Red Sea. This was where the waters had parted to let the Israelites across. On the way, we passed numerous military installations, reminders that the Sinai Peninsula border maintains strict control so that people cannot leave Egypt unlawfully. The Israelites would have moved parallel to the fortified canal built by the pharaohs until they crossed the Red Sea.

After an extremely bumpy ride that left my body feeling a little bruised, we reached the Cairo–Suez road. This road crosses the vast barren desert sands that stretch from the Red Sea Gulf in the east to the distant city of Cairo in the west, situated on the Nile River. In pharaonic times this route was a link to the ancient city of Heliopolis, now part of the northern suburbs of Cairo. Heliopolis was the center of Egyptian government before the capital was moved to the northern Nile Delta near Goshen under the leadership of Pharaoh Rameses. The history of the Egyptians and Israelites was becoming clearer and more real to me every day.

We journeyed through the desert and crossed many small dry river tributaries, running from the higher ground into the shallow valleys leading to the Red Sea coast. At some point a Blanford's Fox ran across our path; this is a beautiful small bushy-tailed fox. An hour later, in an area practically devoid of vegetation, we spotted a silvery grey wolf, a creature seldom seen by humans. We were not lucky enough to see another rare species, the secretive and endangered leopard that inhabits the mountainous area.

"I know some people in this town," Yaman said, as we approached a large village.

Hashim steered the car onto a sand road and soon we were surrounded by small brick houses. We arrived at a simple, square house built of grey brick, and Yaman climbed out of the car and went to knock on the door. He was invited in, and called me to follow him.

We were led into a small, cool lounge with bright blue cushions lining the edges of the room. The patterns on the cushions caught my eye. Yaman and I sat on the floor and Yaman chatted with a middle-aged man, while a slim young woman wearing a light veil over her face brought us tea. The food consisted of homemade bread that had been baked into a flat, round shape and was served with jam. A large round plate with delicious fruit and freshly sliced vegetables was passed around. The hospitality was warm, and I felt immensely comforted after the harsh ride through the arid desert. Three young children with large brown eyes watched us innocently and with great interest, standing in the doorway to the kitchen.

As Yaman conversed, he translated for me. The conversation gave me insight into the lives of this family. The husband had spent his entire youth with his feet in the water of sugarcane plantations, and had contracted bilharzia as a result. This had led to degeneration of his liver. He asked Hashim to tell me that tourists and foreigners do not realize how difficult life is for many Egyptians, and seem to care only about visiting the ancient marvels from the era of the pharaohs.

"Insha Allah, things will improve," our host concluded. "Tourists are fascinated by the ruins of temples and scenes of offerings made to green or blue gods. But many Egyptians are annoyed by this, because the tourists never get to see the squalid conditions in which our people live."

I felt privileged to have this glimpse into the lives of the locals; it gave me far deeper insight into the plight of the general population. I now understood why the police had followed us in the delta and why Hashim had said they were there to protect me. Our host said something that made Hashim laugh, and smile at me. After further congenial conversation we took our leave and left.

Eventually the Red Sea came into view. The landscape in front of us was absolutely flat and featureless, except for the Gebel Atâqa Mountains on the horizon, running parallel to the western coast of the Red Sea. Gradually the mountains loomed larger. They looked like an impassable red stone barrier and appeared extremely close to the edge of the sea. Then I saw a large beach between the mountains and the sea, and Hashim told me the beach was called Pi-Hahiroth. The mountain range was hugely significant to the Exodus, with *Pi-Hahiroth* meaning "mouth of freedom," "redemption" or "freedom valley."[7] I wondered what exactly we would find at the next stop. In the far distance I saw another mountain. This one had unusually steep stone cliffs that looked like pillars. According to my study of the archaeological findings, these two huge natural mountainous pillars were referred to in the Bible as Baal Zephon, an idol which was the center of a great plaza.[8]

I asked Hashim to stop the car so that I could get out and have a good look at the scenery. Right beside my feet was a small brightly colored Ornate Spiny-tailed Lizard running on the rocks. The Bible mentions several animals from this region, including the desert fox and a type of guinea pig called the hyrax, and I would have liked to see the Nubian Ibex and other gazelle known to live here. I glanced across the radiant waters of the Gulf of Suez, the home of a rich array of marine life, including dolphins, and a wide range of birds.

At this stage of our journey to the Red Sea, we had travelled eighty kilometers from our starting point at the Goshen area at Camp Rameses. We resumed exploring and veered eastwards as the Israelites would have done, travelling along the northern tip of the Red Sea towards the Sinai Desert. The traffic became heavier and the countryside more ugly, with fewer sugarcane fields. We soon reached Suez City and travelled through it. We were approaching the canal water's edge and I began to notice some natural vegetation, including the well-known and historic Papyrus. I also saw lovely Lotus plants growing atop the water. The Lotus plant has saucer-shaped leaves and large pink flowers, and is famous in Egyptian history. Occasionally we passed bright green Typha bulrushes with their long brown heads; these plants grow in marshes. In other places, groves of date palms predominated.

Travelling on, we arrived at the point where Wadi Tumilat enters the Red Sea Gulf. This was where the Israelites might have crossed onto the Sinai Peninsula. But why would they have taken this route? They could have entered Sinai simply by crossing the small water inlet between Egypt and Sinai. It is possible to travel from the top of the Red Sea Gulf into the Sinai Desert because the northern shores of the Gulf comprise navigable land. However, the archaeologist Hoffmeier believed that in the distant past, the salty water of the Red Sea was mixed with fresh water from the canal all the way up to Lake Timsah. This would have created an estuary-like environment with reeds or marsh grasses, referred to as Yam Suph – meaning "Reed Sea."[9] At low tide, this area could probably be crossed on foot. It seemed logical that the Israelites would have followed such a route. They could have left Egyptian territory and entered the peninsula, looking for a place where they could safely worship G-d. Even the pharaohs might have used this route to visit their temple to worship the cow-god Hathor in the Sinai Peninsula.

But G-d had another plan for the Israelites. The biblical text narrates: "And they encamped before Migdol."[10] G-d spoke to Moses, saying: "Speak to the children of Israel, and let them turn back and encamp in front of Pi-Hahiroth, between Migdol and the sea; in front of Baal Zephon, you shall encamp opposite it, by the sea."[11]

I was curious to know what would be found at the place where the Israelites had achieved their first taste of freedom. What would I find when we arrived at the place where the Red Sea had parted?

The biblical text continues, "And Pharaoh will say about the children of Israel, they are trapped in the land. The desert has closed in upon them. And I will harden Pharaoh's heart, and he will pursue them, and I will be glorified through Pharaoh and through his entire force, and the Egyptians will know that I am the Lord and they did so."[12] After receiving instruction from G-d, the Israelites backtracked along the eastern shore of the Red Sea and then across its northern shore, until they arrived at the Pi-Hahiroth valley on the western shore. The Israelites had made a U-turn at this part of their journey.[13.] Was this also a plan by G-d to frighten the Israelites and force them to turn to Him for help?[14]

To follow in their footsteps, I too would have to retrace my journey back past Suez City to the point where we had been before entering the city. We would have to return to the western shore of the Red Sea.

"We have to turn around and backtrack," I told Hashim.

He looked at me in bewilderment. I began to persuade and explain, and he finally acceded to my request. He looked exasperated and shook his head, muttering to himself. It took all my concentration to ignore him and stay focused on what we were about to do.

CROSSING RED SEA

We retraced our route, just as the Israelites had been commanded by G-d to do. We turned around at the northern end of the Red Sea and headed back to Suez City, towards that beach of great significance. After passing through the central area of Suez City we turned southwards and skirted the western shore of the Red Sea on the modern Hurgada Ismailia Road, which leads to a small seaside settlement called Adabiya. We then proceeded for about nineteen kilometers and arrived at the foot of the Gebel Atâqa Mountains, beyond which lay the large beach believed to be the Pi-Hahiroth referred to in the Bible.[15] The beach was only a kilometer wide at the foot of the mountains. I climbed out of

The route that was retraced by Moses when G-d commanded the Israelites to turn back and go to Pi-Hahiroth, passing before Baal Zephon. | Google Earth image edited by M Rawicz

the car to experience this sacred place. Facing Pi-Hahiroth valley, the nearby mountaintop bore the large natural pillars we had seen on our previous trip. In this site a huge idol known as "Lord of the North" or Baal Zephon had been erected. The idol is thought to have been made of copper and took the form of a gigantic snarling dog.[16]

The temple of Baal Zephon stood in the center of a great plaza, a place of exceptional beauty. It was the pride of the Egyptians. In biblical days, G-d destroyed all the idols of Egypt except this one, which was the Egyptians' god of wealth. Pharaoh may have believed Baal Zephon would have power over the Israelites, that this idol's concealed evil would help Pharaoh to trap his slaves.[17] The Egyptians concluded that if they remained faithful to this particular god they would regain their wealth and their power over the Israelites.[18] G-d, however, instructed the Israelites to camp directly in front of this idol in Pi-Hahiroth valley. The Egyptian army was destined to suffer its final downfall right under the feet of the last idol.

The place where I stood was hemmed in between the Gebel Atâqa Mountains and the sea. Had anyone been chasing us, we would have had no escape route. To the east was the sea; to the south, the mountains sloped steeply into the sea; to the west were mountains, and the Egyptian army would have blocked the northern route.[19] Pi-Hahiroth, the mouth of freedom, could only be the beach in front of us, the sandy space between the base of the mountain and the shoreline. I was overcome with emotion to realize that I was standing at the very site the Israelites had known. I could hardly believe that I was really here. We were standing at the Yam Suph to which G-d had told them to go.

It was fantastic to be at the Red Sea and to see in reality where the Israelites, physically entrapped by topography, could also be entrapped by their own doubts.

The Bible tells of how Pharaoh pursued the escaping Israelites with his horses, chariots and army.[20] He overtook the people at Pi-Hahiroth. The Israelites were afraid and complained that Moses had brought them into the wilderness merely to die. Moses replied that they would experience salvation from G-d. He stretched out his rod over the sea.

I stood on the beach and imagined the roaring rumble of hundreds of stallions as the massive Egyptian defense force raced down under the infuriated command of Pharaoh. The horses with chariots are galloping at full speed from the stables that I had seen at Pi-Rameses and Tel el Daba. Soldiers block any escape between the seashore and the Gebel Atâqa Mountains. The infuriated soldiers yell, ready to attack and recapture their slave multitude.

Moses obeys G-d's command and Nachshon ben Aminadav walks up to his neck in the calm water. One of the greatest biblical miracles bursts into reality. Water defies its character as G-d shows how He controls nature. The submissive water stands upright and offers its seabed as the passage for escape. G-d combines salvation and destruction in one fell swoop. Pharaoh's authority and delusion of being a god-king are instantly eliminated and G-d claims honor for Himself. The fearful Israelites are liberated and the brazen Egyptians terrified. Death changes sides from the Israelites to the Egyptians as they sink under the returning water. The Israelites understand for all generations that their allegiance can never be to man. They are now appreciative servants of G-d only. They appreciate their Creator's kindness. The slaves walk free and burst into song. "I will sing to G-d, for he is highly exalted: the horse and its rider he threw in the sea."[21]

Part of the topography behind the Red Sea crossing beach, which shows how the Israelites were trapped between the mountains, the sea, and the Egyptian army. | M Rawicz Trip Photo

I walked to the edge of the sea and stood barefoot in the cold water, as Nachshon of the tribe of Judah had done. I waded further into the water until it reached my knees, and in my mind's eye, I saw the miracle begin. I became part of the group of people who forged ahead to the far bank. The sun was beginning to set. I breathed in deeply, and for a moment my body and mind were utterly peaceful. I could feel the beating of my heart. I stood there transfixed until my body decided to exhale with a great sigh, returning me to the present moment. What a privilege it was to stand at this place! I became part of the incredible feeling of liberation of the Israelites. I have never forgotten that moment.

On the horizon across the water, I saw a yellow beach, the western coast of Sinai. I knew it was just seven kilometers away but it looked much further. I glanced at the coastline of the Red Sea Gulf west of Suez City, about six-and-a-half kilometers away across the water, where the Israelites had left the sea. Everything I had learned about the Red Sea crossing suddenly fell into place. When the Israelites left the water, they had actually ended up back on the Egyptian side. One might have thought they would leave Egyptian soil, cross the pathway through the sea, and arrive in Sinai. But contrary to common belief, it appears that

I stood at the Red Sea crossing point and imagined the incredible splitting of the Sea, when G-d allowed the Israelites to escape from Pharaoh's army. | *M Rawicz Trip Photo*

this did not happen. The Talmud *Arachim*,[22] which is part of the Jewish canonical texts, states that the waters parted in such a way that the Israelites made a U-turn and arrived back on Egyptian territory. They were simply further north than they had been. Standing at this site, I finally understood that this interpretation must be correct. The entire event had been designed by G-d primarily to crush Pharaoh's military strength and claim glory for Himself.

I sat down on the beach to gather my composure. My mind was a jangle of images from the past and the present. I tried to focus on the spiritual meaning of this particular piece of biblical history. What was it that the Israelites learned here, and what can we still learn from the narrative of the Red Sea parting?

The Bible recounts that when the Israelites saw the Egyptians closing in from behind, each person reacted in one of four ways: those who wanted to throw themselves into the sea in helpless and hopeless despair; those who advocated surrender; those who wanted to be pragmatic and wage war; and those who believed it was all beyond them and just wanted to pray. However, all of them needed to learn to take responsibility and to act with faith and courage by plunging into the wa-

Looking from the Sinai desert, at camp Elim, back across the Red Sea towards Egypt. The mountains that trapped the Israelites on the beach of Egypt are visible in the far distance. They are on the other side of the Red Sea Gulf. In the foreground is the beach of the Sinai coast to which the Israelites escaped and where they rested at camp Elim. | M Rawicz Trip Photo

ter. This display of faith would bring about the miracle of the splitting of the Red Sea.[23] For G-d had said, "Why do you cry out to Me? Speak to the children of Israel and let them journey forth."[24] G-d expected the people to be willing to endanger their lives in obedience to Him.[25]

The people who wanted to throw themselves into the sea in helpless and hopeless despair had to learn faith. Those who advocated surrender, were too submissive and needed to learn to look forwards, not backwards. Those who wanted to be pragmatic and wage war, had to learn that G-d fights on our behalf, and those who believed it was all beyond them and just wanted to pray, had to learn to take action as well.

⮐ Action triggers miracles

Sometimes when a situation is difficult it is not sufficient to pray for help. Even though we may have faith in G-d, we need to take charge of our situation. It is not enough for us to just ask for help. We need to be prepared to use our own talents and resources to create the opportunity for change to occur. Even though G-d performs miracles in the course of the normal functioning of the world, these are hidden miracles and thus require us to play our part as well. These miracles could include finding the right job or partner. We may need to make decisions and act on them. Acting with daring and inner resolve does not mean a lack of trust in G-d; rather we show our tenacity to make things change. Miracles can happen when G-d shows His intimate involvement in our lives and His control over nature, as Jacobson explains.[26]

Hillel continues his metaphor of a child: "By now the Israelites would have grown and could be compared to youth who are thinking about their future. They would have begun to realize that they may each have their own unique task in life and need to grow spiritually. Their sense of self-worth was awakened. They might have a better destiny and collective identity."[27]

This meaning also includes the experience that teenagers go through when they begin to explore a wider environment and new areas of interest. They begin to do things that were outside the norm of the family and to find out what their true personal direction in life is. This moves them out of their comfort zone and into a wider world of other adults. They then have the opportunity to begin what will become their own personal contribution to the world. There may be temptations to follow trends that are not in line with the worship of G-d. Many such temptations exist in the world and include the unhealthy aspects of striving for wealth, power, status, image and other areas of self-gratification. If teenagers choose worthy and proper courses of action, they can make a difference. The difference that we can make is adding to or improving the world as part of service to G-d, and thus making the world a better place, as understood by Jacobson.[28] ⮐

I was extremely excited and felt a sense of impending change. My emotions were shifting and I was becoming freer of my "false god" of placing too much emphasis on my work, and the depression that it had resulted in. I was acquiring the capacity for more "sober reflection." I felt somehow my life would be different and better in the future if I placed more emphasis on relationships and doing good deeds.

The reality of the miracle seemed within my experience and I was overwhelmed by the miracle and G-d's help.

My own connection to G-d was strengthened by my visit to the Red Sea in a way that has remained with me ever since. The feeling of awe, amazement and relief that the Israelites would have felt flooded through me. Miriam's "Song at the Sea," *Shiru LaHashem*, came to mind and I began to sing it. "I will sing to G-d, for he has triumphed gloriously: the horse and his rider has he thrown into the sea . . . ."[29] I felt in touch with the spirit of Miriam, the sister of Moses. She had picked up a tambourine and led the women in dance and song.

One of the maps I had seen of the seabed of the Red Sea was drawn by a Jewish scholar who had studied the Red Sea crossing. The map showed extensive stone shoals that became exposed at low tide, five kilometers south of the port of Suez.[30] In ancient times these shoals had formed the Camel Ford,[31] a passage that was used by merchants to cross the sea; thus, the Camel Ford was a natural passage by which people could cross from Etham Desert to the Sinai Peninsula. The Franco-Spanish nun Egeria (also known as Etheria), who pilgrimaged to the Holy Land in the fourth century, noted that the crossing was located near a fortress built by Rameses III. In the 1960s the remains of this fortress were found near the Red Sea, and the modern-day town of Qom Qulzoum marks the site. The fortress was used to control people's entry into Egypt[32] and some archaeologists believe this was where Pharaoh's army became mudbound. Perhaps G-d had brought about the miracle at a place where the natural features would facilitate the supernatural event.

I noticed a striking contrast between the terror of the Exodus experience and the natural beauty of the area. The looming red Gebel Atâqa Mountains behind the beach boasted some marvellous rock formations and the red sand that washed down from the mountain into the sea might also have given the Red Sea Gulf its name. This miraculous, magical and beautiful place was a highlight of my trip and left a lasting impression on me.

SUEZ CITY

We spent the night at a hotel in the city of Suez. The next morning, I decided to spend a full day in Suez to gain a better appreciation of the area where the historic event had taken place. The beginning of the eighth day of my journey started with a drive around the city, which lies at the southern end of the Suez Canal and guards and serves it. The first thing I wanted to do was find a bookshop. We did so, and I purchased a book on Suez City and its surrounds to use as our guidebook for the day. Then Hashim helped me find a library, and I used the various books at my disposal to do a little research. The history of the area was informative. I began to gain a greater appreciation of the historical events that had taken place on these shores.

I wanted to know what had happened at this famous biblical place of the splitting of the Red Sea. Before the miracle of the Red Sea, the shoreline of the sea was so arid that humans could not live here. Around 2500 BCE, the Egyptian rulers sought a commercial route to Punt, a distant land possibly on the Horn of Africa. The land at the top of the Red Sea's role as a port began. In the nineteenth century BCE, King Sesostris III ordered the digging of a canal linking the Red Sea and the Mediterranean via the Nile, and the Suez village began to grow.[33] It soon became a trading hub and the starting point for exploration and commercial missions, and a formal trading station of the pharaohs for gold, ivory, ebony, aromatic resins, spices, cattle, animal skins, wild animals, and slaves.

Over the years, several canals were built linking the Nile River to this shore of the Red Sea, but none lasted. However, the pharaohs continued to have a military presence on this beach. From 1500 BCE to the thirteenth century, great empires used these shores. Around 1500 BCE, Pharaoh Hatshepsut used this port for long voyages and as a military outpost.[34] By the seventh century BCE a settlement grew and later a town called Kolzum. From the sixth century BCE to the thirteenth century, soldiers and sailors of great empires arrived, including Persians under Darius, Greeks under Alexander the Great and the Ptolemaic Dynasty to take advantage of its strategic position.[35] During the first century CE, with the discovery of a direct route from the Red Sea to India, a bigger commercial center developed to cater to the passing merchant ships dealing in spice. Later Rome gained control over Egypt, and the Red Sea waters carried an even greater volume of traffic.[36] Some of the ships transported goods from Indian ports that had originated in China, but this route was destroyed by the Aksumite Empire and was then subjected to Byzantine Rule; eventually it was attacked by the Crusaders.[37] Sadly, however, Kolzum and Suez were defeated and by the thirteenth century they lay in ruins.[38]

My concept of the Red Sea was changing with every page that I read. This was no longer a mythical place to me, but a tremendously historical one.

The status of the Red Sea had improved during the Middle Ages when it again became an important part of the spice trade route. The Turks eventually developed this as a Turkish naval station and the city became an even bigger trading station and naval center.[39] Even the great French General Bonaparte came in 1798 when he invaded Egypt and moved to take control of the Red Sea. A plan was made to revitalize the canal that had been envisaged so long ago during the pharaonic era, and Ferdinand de Lesseps, a French engineer, developed a grand plan to construct and operate the Suez Canal. In 1869, the massive waterway of the modern Suez Canal was opened. Huge ships and tankers from all over the world ploughed through its waters, with an immediate and dramatic effect on world trade.[40] After the Second World War, the Americans and Soviets extended their influence and the volume of oil tanker traffic using the Suez Canal intensified. In the late 1960s and early 1970s, the city of Suez was virtually destroyed during battles between the Egyptians and Israelis. The Israelis, descendants of the ancient Israelites who had crossed the Red Sea, now occupied the Sinai Peninsula. Following the Arab-Israeli war in October 1973, reconstruction and widening of the canal began, and continued until Egypt reopened the Suez Canal. A peace treaty with Israel was signed and peace and security returned to the shores of this once holy place.[41]

My understanding of the history of this area had changed radically. Ever since childhood, I had thought of the Red Sea in a stereotypical manner that had been informed mostly by pictures showing Moses with an upraised staff, and the multitudes passing between giant walls of water. Now I could appreciate the living dynamics of the place in a more mature fashion. The romantic image had been tarnished, but the place seemed far more alive and real to me now. Clearly, the shores of the Red Sea had played an increasingly prominent role in international relations through history.

We drove to the coast, intending to examine the port area. There we saw the three harbors, Adabya, Ain Sokhna and Port Tawfiq, and their extensive service facilities. Numerous shipping berths serve the ships that dock at this internationally strategic port. From these shores, the route by which the Israelites would have crossed the Red Sea was clearly visible. It was breathtaking to view the Suez Canal from close up. The sight of so many gigantic ships, tankers and even cruise liners queuing to enter the canal or to cross its waters was spectacular. Approximately fifty ships pass through the canal daily. The canal itself is only about 350 meters wide, so the ships and tankers pass by the land at extremely close range. I saw a variety of enormous vessels, including a crude oil supertanker and a ship carrying petroleum products, followed by a dry bulk carrier, a chemical carrier, and a liquid gas ship. The sheer size of these vehicles and their powerful slow movement through the water left my heart thumping. I had never witnessed anything quite like this, let alone from so close by! A massive container vessel and a colossal vehicle carrier soon followed. Security restrictions, concerned with preventing terrorist acts, meant that I was not able to take any photographs – but the image of those passing ships was forever imprinted on my mind.

Little did I know at the time of my visit in 2003, that the Arab Spring and the rise of ISIS would take place. I was aware that Al-Qaeda and jihadi groups had been assisting Gaza. In the future they would take advantage of the upheaval after the ousting of President Mubarak in 2011. Then late in 2014, following the overthrow of Muslim brotherhood President Mohamed Morsi, ISIS would arise, start to operate in the Sinai, and declare war on the Egyptian government. Thousands of ISIS fighters, assisted by Hamas, would kill hundreds of Egyptian soldiers. But I was traveling along happily, unsuspecting that in the near future most governments would advise against unnecessary travel to this area. I wonder, would I go again?

We moved on to view some of the petrochemical plants and oil refineries that process raw material into finished products. These products are then transported to Cairo through extremely long pipelines. We saw enormous round oil terminals, crude oil storage tanks, and warehouses. The entire area was a fairly polluted industrial zone. Accompanying these mega-structures was an equally huge infrastructure. Massive railway lines and highways connect Suez City with Cairo, Port Said and Ismailia. Citizens and workers have access to multiple transport options such as private taxis, buses and trains. A huge airport facilitates

Egypt's military has wanted to control this place since biblical times. |
M Rawicz Trip Photo

international flight. The Suez Canal contributes significantly to the
Egyptian economy. It would have been the envy of various pharaohs
who had tried to stimulate trade by building canals.

We came across another cluster of military installations, barracks
and army equipment. I wanted to take a photograph.

"No photos, no photos!" Hashim yelled. "You are not allowed to take
photos in a military area. They'll arrest us. Put the camera away, now,
quick, or they will think you are a spy!"

I pushed the camera into my bag, reflecting on the survival of an
element of dictatorship since ancient times.

Suez City, which has a population of about half a million people, was
crammed with cars. It was also abuzz with pedestrians, some of whom
were smartly dressed in Western-style business clothing while others
wore Arab robes. Traders wearing turbans attended to their customers. The city was as busy as any other modern city. I caught the eye
of a woman in the crowd who was selling large bunches of wild dates.
The expression in her dark-brown eyes was clear and intelligent and I

clambered out of the car to buy some of her wares. It was intriguing to observe such advanced facilities in this place where the Israelites had once wandered through open desert. The modern overlay did not in any way detract from the biblical significance of the area.

We drove on to the suburbs, where we saw numerous modern developments. I was becoming accustomed to the sight of densely-built square brick homes and apartment blocks with typical Middle Eastern architecture. We passed a mosque and Hashim spoke to a man there, who told us that Suez City is a stopover for pilgrims on their way to and from Mecca. Part of Suez City's religious history includes the Mahmal, a ceremonial palanquin carried on a camel which was the centerpiece of the pilgrimage caravan. The people carried the cover of the Kaaba, Muslim's most sacred feature, to Mecca each year during that period, from Cairo, where it was made.

We drove on to explore the coastline. At the seafront, we discovered that Suez is a great place for wonderful fresh fish and seafood. We passed attractive oceanfront holiday resorts, luxurious hotels, and villas and private homes offering accommodations. We also drove through a vibrant tourist area with plenty of restaurants, bars and shops. Many people visit Suez to enjoy its traditions and culture, or to relax on its beautiful sparkling beaches. We saw divers, dolphin watchers, and sportspeople taking advantage of the many amenities, open sports areas and other recreation facilities. I had a little fun and got my feet wet in the seawater, which looked very inviting. At an outdoor café, I took the opportunity to interact with other travellers. A middle-aged couple said that they had visited historical sites such as the ancient Masjid Hamza mosque and a teenager told us that he had just come back from hiking in the Ataga Hills, where he had enjoyed the wonderful landscapes.

On the way back to the city center, Hashim took me to see the large site of the new Suez National Museum. This caught my interest, so we went to the tourist information office to find out more. I learned that the museum would be built in a pyramid shape and have halls to show 2500 archaeological pieces that tell the story of the city of Suez, from prehistoric times to the modern era. It would include also the maritime history and boats and a mining hall showing Egypt's industrial achievements from pre-dynastic times to the Islamic period, and all types of mining – gold, silver, copper, lead, iron, and precious stones. There would be a special Suez Canal Hall. The museum was expected to attract more than a million visitors each year and to become one of Egypt's biggest tourist attractions.

Sunset was approaching and we would be staying in Suez City again overnight. By the time we arrived at a restaurant for tea and cool drinks, it was already dark. A large group of youths were gathered, talking noisily, but suddenly the volume rose and they started to sing rowdily.

"Feyn! Feyn! Seyf Allah! Seyf an Nahr! Tahal! Philistin ihtag adala! Ma Zulfakar, Adini beled for el Aqsa! Tahal, Khalid ibn el Walid tahal tani! Hamas! Hamas!" (Where are you? Where are you? Sword of God! Sword of fire! Come! The Palestinians need justice! With Zulfakar! Give El-Aqsa a country! Come! Khalid ibn el-Walid return. Hamas! Hamas!")

What had begun as a relaxing evening outing had become more like a political rally. Words were shouted contemptuously, with repeated angry mention of "Israel" and "America." I overheard two men at the next table conversing in English. "It's good that these youngsters want to drive the Jews and their American friends out of Israel, until the last one is gone."

I felt appalled to realize that the pharaohs' murderous intentions towards the Israelites was still manifested in their modern-day descendants. The group of youths started laughing.

"Twin towers! Twin towers!" someone yelled. They were expressing their hatred of America because of its alliance with Israel on the problems besetting the Middle East and the Palestinian people.

I wanted to preserve my pleasant memories of the day. I asked Hashim to take me to the hotel. On the way, he tried to explain what I already knew.

"These young people think they are victims of American domination. They have no hope for a better life. They know that their government likes the tourists. Egyptian tax money is spent on the police. We have more than two million policemen! Many of them help to protect Westerners, but the villages stay poor and cannot even give the people services they really really need." Hashim explained.

That night, before I fell asleep, I reflected on everything that I had seen that day – from the shores of the Red Sea and the huge ships on the Suez Canal to the angry young men in the restaurant. I thought about the villages I had seen the day before. I could understand the people's resentment. The rural commoners clearly gained nothing from the vast income from tourism, and the gap between the two worlds was extreme. Once again, sleep did not come for a long time.

The following morning I awoke with renewed excitement and anticipation. The next part of my trip would take me into the Sinai Peninsula and the Shur desert. We found a ferry that transported cars as well as people across the Suez Canal, and when we reached the other side we set about finding the biblical encampment of Marrah.[42]

BITTER WATER – MARRAH

CAMP 5

"They walked for three days in the desert of Etham and camped in Marrah."[1]

Marrah in Hebrew means "bitter."[2] My task was to find bitter water at one of the many possible scattered locations. The Bible describes how the Israelites moved from the Red Sea to the Desert of Shur. "For three days they travelled in the desert without finding water. When they came to Marrah, they could not drink its water because it was bitter. So the people grumbled against Moses, saying, 'What are we to drink?' Then Moses cried out to G-d, and G-d showed him a piece of wood. He threw it into the water, and the water became sweet."[3]

We drove until we reached Bir-el-Murr, a village in the region of Qaret-el-Murr close to Wadi-el-Murr. Professor Har-El believes this to be the site of Marrah because of its brackish water.[4] When we arrived, I explored the area on foot and found the shallow stretch of brackish water. The only plants growing around it were species that can survive in salt water, such as Glaucous Glasswort, a spindly bush with stems that look as if they have numerous white bubbles on them. Scattered in patches were a few other species such as the tough long grass called Salt-Marsh-Hay, Tamarix trees with their profusion of tiny pink flowers, the grey succulent groundcover Frankenia, and small woody Yan Jie Mu bushes.[5]

"Bitterness" seemed to describe not only the water but the entire area. I enjoyed the sight of the plants, but not the taste of the water. It made sense that the Israelites would have been unhappy about not finding drinkable water here. They would have used up any water they had carried with them, which would have posed a big problem at this stage. Some scholars think that the wood G-d commanded Moses to throw into the water to sweeten it might have been Oleander, which itself is bitter yet somehow does sweeten water. Although Oleander grows in Egypt, I could not find any at this site.[6]

▸] Facing resource challenges – avoiding being bitter

There are times in our lives when we are confronted by a new situation for which we are completely unprepared. We do not have the physical stamina or equipment and may also be emotionally unprepared to deal with the situation. We could feel shocked, become immobilized by fear and become extremely unhappy or bitter. We might react with grumbling, fretting, losing our self-control and could even fall apart. If we remain like this we embitter ourselves more and could exacerbate the situation over time. The alternative is to make an effort to adapt and ask for help. We could become creative and innovative in seeking a solution. Such experiences make us draw on our ability and inventiveness which ultimately gives us satisfaction, inner sweetness and healing. Jacobson explains this similarly and also points out that "G-d used the Israelites' situation to teach them survival techniques and methods" and "the bitterness of the water of Marrah was similar to the inner state of the Israelites."[6]

Hillel explains that the "Israelites were at a stage equivalent to being young adults who are starting out in life."[7] He also teaches that, "finding no water is also a metaphor for not learning from G-d, and this lack of spiritual motivation caused them to become exhausted."[8]

As I contemplated their condition, in the shade of a Tamarix tree, it also evoked in me a sense of trepidation about proceeding further into the desert. Would I also suffer from a lack of resources, hardship? I too had to overcome this apprehension and be positive.

◀

Hillel explains that at Marrah they were also instructed to keep the Sabbath and to honor their parents.[9] Further commandments would be given only at Mount Sinai. Other lessons had been passed on from previous generations, some of which would eventually be included in the Ten Commandments. From Adam the people had learned not to blaspheme, from the sons of Noah they had learned not to worship idols, or to murder, commit adultery or steal. The Noahide laws also forbade the cutting of flesh from a living animal. Essentially, the laws put in place a system of justice.[10]

G-d also gave them commandments through which they were able to elevate their actions, improve their relationship with Him and attain joy.[11]

We were all famished. Hashim left to look for firewood and I filled a large tin with water to boil for tea. This was my first experience of preparing my own meal in the desert. We made a salad from food we had bought in Suez City, opened a tin of fish, and enjoyed our picnic under a date palm tree. After eating, we proceeded further southwards into the Shur desert to find the next encampment, Elim. It was a baking hot day but we followed the seashore and a lovely cool sea breeze was blowing in.

One of the remaining wells at the camp of Elim, as described in the Bible. | M Rawicz Trip Photo

There are only around forty palm trees at the camp of Elim today, fewer than the number recorded in the Bible. | M Rawicz Trip Photo

RECUPERATION OASIS – ELIM

"They journeyed from Marrah and arrived at Elim."[1] "And they came to Elim, where there were twelve wells of water, and seventy palm trees; and they encamped there by the waters."[2]

According to Hillel[3] *elim* means both "palm tree place" and "strength." I assumed we would find palm trees at the camp we were headed towards, known by today's Sinai residents as Ayn Musa or "the Springs of Moses." As we moved along the eastern shore of the Red Sea, I enjoyed the soft light and yellow sands, and the rich bird life near the water. Sadly we also came upon three dead storks on the desert sands, which might have lost their way during annual migration. We encountered a police roadblock within the first five kilometers of our journey and I had a renewed appreciation of their presence.

We arrived at the oasis of Elim, and stopped to rest as the Israelites had done. The oasis is evidently much the same as it was 3500 years ago and still – to my delight – had roughly forty palm trees and several of the twelve wells described in the Bible. On my initial walk around the site, I could not find any wells. I recalled the writings of various archaeologists. Dr. GD Mumford had written that "Ayn Musa possesses twelve springs."[4] Today, this number has dwindled because, sadly, some were closed during the Israeli occupation of Sinai in the late 1960s. I managed to find only two of the wells as the others had been filled with sand.

Elim is a significant natural feature in an otherwise barren, sandy area. It has become an international tourist attraction because of its connection with the Exodus. Bedouin women sit under the palm trees with wooden benches to display their beadwork and other souvenirs for tourists to buy. I conversed with a young Bedouin woman who sold me a lovely necklace and bangle made from pink seeds and seashells. I wondered whether the ancient Israelite women might also have crafted such jewelry.

I walked a little further and a breeze rustled through the palm leaves above, whispering the events of biblical times. My walk brought me out to a broad, sandy beach. There I stood, recollecting how it must have felt to the Israelites to stand here. Across the blue and beautifully calm water were the Gebel Atâqa Mountains from which we had just fled. They were a soft gray-purple hue.

Later that day, I sat at the edge of a well and peered into its depth. I recalled having read that when the Israelites rested at Elim, they had had a few days in which to contemplate their past. The wells in this area had been dug by their ancestor Jacob, who had partly planned for the people's escape from Egypt. G-d had revealed to Abraham, Jacob's grandfather, that the generations to come would pass through this area, and that provision would be needed for their wellbeing.

⏏ Strength emerges from loss and pain

There are times in a person's life when they have gone through a bitter experience and sit back to reflect on it. Their reality may have changed and perhaps the person they love is no longer there or they have lost their job or moved to a new, strange place. At such times it becomes necessary to gather one's thoughts, consolidate what has transpired and consider how to move forward. This can be a time of deep introspection.

As Jacobson points out, when one introspects on bitter experience they may think of G-d. The name of the camp Elimah has the name of G-d in its letters. When we are able to tap into inner love, like that from G-d, we are awakened to a greater dimension of capacity even during painful experiences.[5]

Elim provides us with the opportunity to think of our future, to engage in self-transformation, and to see our potential future reality from a new perspective. We each need periodically to re-connect with ourselves, with others and G-d and have a new vision for how we want to be in our lives.[6]

Elim made us realize that G-d did not, and will not, forsake us and continues to create our futures in a way that we cannot envisage, as part of the ongoing process of creation.[7]

After this contemplative break, I walked to the southernmost end of the oasis, enjoying the beauty of the palm trees. I noticed a flock of Sinai Rose Finches in the branches of the palms, and the sound of the birds and the gentle breeze filled me with contentment. I also glimpsed a pretty little Garden Dormouse (sometimes called "the bandit" because of the black mask over its eyes) scampering away.

Chapter 3

Journeying to Mount Sinai – Camps 7–12

CAMP 7

"They left Elim and camped near the Red Sea."[1]

Although the Israelites camped near the Red Sea, the actual camp's name means "Reed Sea." This camp was situated on the opposite side of the Red Sea Gulf or the Sea of Suph[2] which the people had miraculously crossed. The word "*suph*" is related to the Hebrew *sof*, meaning "end."

The journey to the next camp, as I understood it, followed the Sinai coastline of the Red Sea Gulf. What might I find that alluded to the meaning of "Red Sea"? The Red Sea Gulf borders Egypt, which raised a rather obvious possibility. Would I discover something interesting related to the sea's name or the miracle that happened there? This seemed a new challenge. I studied the possible route taken by the Israelites further into the Shur desert. To my surprise, I saw a beautiful wadi leading out of Elim from the far southern end through the sand and on into the distance. This must have been the route they followed.

I asked Hashim to drive on for a kilometer while I walked beside the road through the wadi. It was an intriguing experience to walk alone in the quietness – almost total silence. Underfoot there was groundcover in places, small and larger pebbles, and very fine yellow sand, making for an easy walk. The further I walked the more enraptured I became by the wadi's ecology. On my left were the mountains of the Sin Desert. Along the path, bushes, scrub and palm trees offered some shade from the hot sun. Inspired by the pleasant tranquility of this wadi, I took many photos.

Eventually I met Hashim and offloaded my luggage. We had agreed that he would bring me to this point and I would then continue by bus, because he did not usually venture further. So I took leave of Hashim and Yaman, parting with a cheery "*Salem Aleichem*." He left me standing at a bus station in the middle of the desert, waiting alone and wondering what would happen next as I ventured further into the desert.

Some young Arab men arrived and stood waiting too, but they were quite unfriendly and looked at me as if I was some strange creature. I was growing hotter and hotter in that shadeless place, and was becoming uneasy. To my relief, eventually a bus loomed over the horizon. I clambered aboard with all my luggage.

I could see the wadi that I had been exploring running parallel to the road for a few more kilometers. Here and there along its path a natural area of water appeared, where palms grew more prolifically and underground water was available from shallow wells. To the left, looking out of the bus, were the low sand hills of the Shur Desert. We followed the wadi for many kilometers southward, parallel to the west coast of Sinai. I imagined the camels, donkeys, sheep, goats, and throngs of Israelites walking along this clearly defined route. I felt thrilled to experience the setting with such clarity.

We carried on for another ten kilometers and then began to catch sight of some of the developments that have sprung up in this prosperous region of modern Egypt. We passed a large manganese mine that employs thousands of local residents. A little further on, we saw some large upmarket apartment blocks, the kind that wealthy families use as private holiday homes. We also passed some extremely expensive and elite hotels, which are patronized by people wanting to escape the noise and bustle of the cities. They flock to these hotels to enjoy the peaceful environment of Sinai's western coastline and beaches. Along certain parts of the coastline, construction sites were visible, with buildings not yet complete, and I also saw ostentatious verandas and patios, tiles and colonnades, stucco lions, and showy porticos.

Gradually, I began to feel sad. This countryside had changed so much since Moses' time. I found it quite hard to reconcile the sight of such ultramodern buildings in a place that had been bare desert in biblical times. I had somehow imagined that it would still look exactly the same.

And then the buildings and developments were behind us. As the bus carried on, I gazed out of the window and saw only sand and more sand. My sadness began to yield to curiosity. What lay ahead? Eventually we

Elite hotels abound on Sinai's western coastline along the route that the Israelites once walked. | *M Rawicz Trip Photo*

arrived at another bus station. I gathered that I was to disembark here, as there was a hotel nearby – called *Al-Batros Amira*. A man was supposed to meet me and take me to wait in the lobby of a hotel. But no one arrived. I waited alone while considering my options. What was I to do? Maybe there was nothing to fear, so why let my mind play havoc with my emotions?

After about half an hour a small car appeared, and I saw that it was carrying Arab women. I flagged the car down and asked the women about the area. They told me where I was supposed to be and offered to give me a lift. "It's not far," they said. I climbed into the car and started praying. To my relief, the women drove me directly to the hotel.

With true gratitude I said, "*Shokran, Salem Aleycum.*" Sometimes the smallest good deed can mean so much to the recipient. I went inside to wait in reception for my driver who would take me further. The hotel was charming; it was a small resort used by tourists and holidaymakers. I hired a room for the night, wondering what the next day of adventure would bring.

MEETING A BEDOUIN

Early in the morning of the ninth day of my journey, I woke with anticipation. I packed my bags and walked outside, where a handsome and charming Bedouin man greeted me. He wore a long white kaftan and a red headdress or *kaffiya*, held in place with an *agal* – a black ring around the head. It was a typical Arab outfit, seen everywhere in the Middle East. He introduced himself as Rabia, and asked if I was the person who was following in the footsteps of Moses through the Sinai. I was a little taken aback by his effusiveness, but replied that I was the right person.

"I will be driving you through the desert in my jeep with my assistant Hamed," he said, pointing to a tiny old blue-and-yellow miniature jeep in which another man sat.

I was alone in this huge expanse of desert with no other options. I drew a courageous breath and decided to take a leap of trust. I followed Rabia, and he swung my heavy suitcase up onto the roof rack of the jeep and strapped it down tightly with ropes. Then he opened the door and I nervously climbed in. The passenger seat was rather old and shabby. Rabia shut the door with a mighty rattle, and walked around to the driver's seat. The floor of the car was covered with a woven multicolored mat. I imagined that Joseph's coat might have looked a bit like this. Hamed, a Bedouin man in his late twenties was sitting at the back. He would accompany Rabia all the way as an assistant with minor chores. It felt better for me not to be alone with a strange man.

As Rabia started up the engine, my heart sank. "This is it," I thought. The only thing to do was go forward; there could be no turning back now.

Everything shook as Rabia struggled to get the jeep's engine going. My heart was pounding and my head felt light. I said a prayer for my safety and tried to convince myself that G-d would look after me. I thought back to the Israelites standing at the edge of the Red Sea. They could only go forward and have faith; there was no other option. I had put myself in the same position.

Finally the engine began to idle more smoothly. Rabia turned to me and asked, "So where do you want to go?"

I pulled out the map that I had so meticulously prepared and nervously said, "Here." I pointed to the spot where I thought the Israelites would have camped next. Rabia launched the jeep faster with a jolt in a southward direction. I sat in uneasy silence for some fifteen minutes as

*Rabia, the Bedouin guide who took me through the Sinai, with his jeep. |
M Rawicz Trip Photo*

we rattled down the road. Occasionally big trucks carrying manganese passed us. After a while, when I felt a bit more composed, I decided to take out my prayer book and recite some psalms.

Rabia eventually asked, "I want to ask you, what you are doing?" He spoke very good English as he had worked with tourists, but with an Arabic accent.

"Oh, I'm praying," I replied. "I like to do this."

He nodded silently and drove on. We travelled for some fifty kilometers, passing beaches such as Masala Beach and Temarco Rose Beach. Each beach boasted a holiday resort, though some were extremely up-market whereas others were quite homely. Eventually, far ahead of us, I saw a small coastal village called Ras Sudr. The distance between Elim and the site where the Israelites "camped near the Red Sea" is about fifty kilometers. In the vicinity of Ras Sudr is an estuary at the end of a small wadi. I wondered whether the Israelites had stopped here, as it was about halfway to the Sin Desert, their next stop. They might have stopped before Ras Sudr, but the exact location of this camp in today's landscape is unclear. The estuary, however, had an abundance of reeds. This would correlate with the camp's name, Reed Sea. From this observation I felt more confident that it might be the correct location.

The camp near the Red Sea was an opportunity for them to delight in the rejuvenating power of water.

⊟ Seeing miracles

The Hebrew word "sof" means "end." After the Israelites had seen the splitting of the Red Sea and witnessed amazing miracles, they experienced intensified consciousness of G-d's presence. They had seen nature manipulated beyond the laws of physics as we know them and then return to a normal perspective again. They had seen the world as the domain of heaven or celestial beings.[3] However, they needed to continue to appreciate G-d's daily miracles as discussed by Jacobson. These could include saving them from potentially dangerous events in everyday life.

At this camp they had the opportunity to appreciate the presence of G-d in normal, daily life.

I, too, was still basking in the extraordinary experience of seeing this location of the miracle of the Red Sea with an intensified consciousness of G-d's control over nature.   ◧

BUYING FOOD FOR THE DESERT –
WILDERNESS OF SIN

CAMP 8

"They journeyed from the Red Sea and camped in the desert of Sin."[1] "And they took their journey from Elim and all the congregation of the children of Israel came to the wilderness of Sin."[2] The wilderness of Sin lies between Elim and Sinai, and the Israelites reached it on the 15th day of the second month after their departure from Egypt.

Sin means "clay."[3] What might this mean for my journey and ability to move forward? Would we get stuck in a wadi of clay?

To get to Sin we had to journey for another fifty kilometers along a road called El Tour – Ras Sudr, the main route along the west coast of the Sinai Peninsula. The surface of the road was in good condition but the scenery was similar to what I had seen before, with the Red Sea and yellow sands on one side and no distinguishable features on the other, apart from the distant mountains marking the western border

Lovely holiday resorts like Moon Beach are found along the Red Sea coast. |
M Rawicz Trip Photo

of Shur Desert. The road eventually veered towards the sea and I could make out some beaches. We passed one called Moon Beach with huts of wood and thatch to shelter tourists in the holiday season. The area was beautifully developed as a holiday resort, and is known to be a popular destination.

At last we reached Ras Sudr, which we had seen from a distance. We stopped for a few minutes to enjoy the view of a magnificent bay. Then Rabia said, Ï will show you something interesting." We headed for a special place called Pharaoh's Bath or Hammam Pharaoh, forty-six kilometers further, where we stopped to explore, and Rabia told me about the area's history. From a large mountain beside the sea, a spring flows with sulphurous water as hot as 27 °C. It flows from the mountains into a 100-meter long lake right beside the seashore. A small cave has been carved out of the mountainside to form a natural sauna, which is thought to have therapeutic value for many diseases (including rheumatism, kidney disease, lung inflammation and skin diseases). These steaming, boiling, sulphurous waters have been used for healing for hundreds of centuries and were evidently used by the pharaohs.

"Bedouin tradition teaches that Moses came here," Rabia said.

I wondered whether the Israelites had benefited from this unique feature on their journey, but probably not as the pharaohs used it. While we were still at the spring, a busload of Muslim tourists arrived. It must have been their prayer time because we watched fifty-odd men prostrate themselves on the ground, facing east. I have always derived pleasure from seeing people in prayer. The men looked up, glanced around, and departed as fast as they had appeared.

I began to wonder how we would sustain ourselves; the surroundings looked bleak. At first I kept my concerns to myself in an effort to be diplomatic, but my stomach was clenching itself into a knot. I had put my faith in this strange Bedouin man and here I was, taking an extraordinary journey unaccompanied in his car.

Eventually I said, "How are we going to have enough food?"

Rabia shot an irritated glace at me and muttered under his breath, grunting,

"Don't you trust me?"

I too was feeling a bit irritated. The heat was intense and my clothes were stuck to my skin from perspiration. I wanted water. I had silly visions of being driven all the way through the desert without food or water, and for a moment I wondered whether I had made a mistake in trying to take this journey. I stared out of the window at the hard yellow mountains with the sun reflecting off them and the expanses of rough sand. The sea breeze had turned into a strong wind. The silence between Rabia and me dragged on, while worries raced through my mind. I forced my thoughts into a more positive direction. This journey was never meant to be easy. It was a test of character and an opportunity for growth. The Bible contained plenty of stories about personal strength.

"I've put myself in your care and I know that you won't let me down," I told Rabia. "But please, just tell me how we'll get food and water on this trip."

He threw back his head and laughed loudly.

"I have lived in this desert since I was born. I know all the places to get food, and even how to get food from the desert itself in an emergency." He pointed to the horizon and said, "Over there, in about ten kilometers, is a place with shops, a desert restaurant, and anything you need."

I sighed and relaxed into my seat.

"On our way, we'll find Bedouin camps," Rabia continued. "The people enjoy giving tea to travellers. They make bread and give us food. You can help as well. When we go further into the desert, we'll make our own food – just wait and see. In the back of my car, I have bottles of water for you. I can drink the local water from desert wells, but it would give you an upset stomach. You will see many interesting things on this journey. Trust me."

"Oh!" I said, and then sat quietly, staring ahead.

Eventually we arrived at the town. He clambered out of the jeep. Rabia turned to me and said,

"You want food? This is Abu Zenema. Come."

We were standing in front of a small shop that evidently sold everything. Rabia bought rice, a huge bag of flour, many more bottles of water, salad greens, dates, fruit, and some dried fish. All of it was promptly loaded into the back of the jeep. The town also had a bus stop, a small chemist, a sweet shop, a café with a sit-down eating facility, a little supermarket, and a small port.

"This is the last stop where we'll be able to buy anything other than the basics, for a while," Rabia said. "What we get here must carry us through the Sinai Desert for a few days."

I decided to buy a large packet of sweets and a bunch of pencils, in case we saw Bedouin children on the way. As we were leaving, a great booming *muezzin's* voice began calling the faithful to prayer.

"Allah hu akbar," the chant rang out.

The road veered inland from the Red Sea coast and then, after another slight bend, we were driving parallel to the coast. Large yellow mountains made it impossible to journey along the coast itself. The sandstone mountains in this area range from 90 to 200 meters high, and our route gradually climbed upwards. Ten kilometers south of Abu Zenema, we left the Shur Desert and entered the Sin Desert, and the mountain landscape changed. We were silent and my thoughts centered on the geography and archaeology of the surrounding desert. Most scholars associate the wilderness of Sin with the coastal area known as El-Merkha, which is south of Ras Abu Zenema. However, one researcher, Walter Myatt, believes that the wilderness of Sin refers to the flat area called El-Sanawi and Hosan-Abu-Zenna, situated around a wadi called Gharandal.

As I proceeded I experienced a mixture of fear, courage, vulnerability

A small shop where we bought provisions before we went into the Sinai Desert. |
M Rawicz Trip Photo

or naivety, and faith. At this stage, the Israelites had also had a struggle and had needed to continue on despite the difficulty and overcome
their crisis of faith.[4]

Rabia pointed out a large flat plain ahead of us. "Look, there is Hosan-Abu-Zenna. It's close to the sea. We Bedouin know that as the place
where the Israelites camped in the Sin Desert." I looked around but I
could not see any clay as the word "sin" suggests.

Yes," I nodded. "I was wondering, if this is the Sin Desert, then this is
where the Israelites ran out of food. They showed a lack of faith in G-d,
just like I did."

Rabia's expression was a mixture of amusement and concern.

"The Israelites started complaining," I continued. "'If only we had
died in Egypt! At least there we had pots of meat and all the bread we
could eat! But you brought us out into this desert to kill us. We're going to starve to death!'" (Exodus 16:3). I could sense their desperation
and standing in that vacant wasteland I felt myself transported to the
scene. . . .

The unrelenting sun shows no mercy from its scorching zenith and
a strained stillness settles across the red sands. A pale old man on the

verge of fainting sits silently, staring vacantly into nowhere, the fight gone out of him completely now, the final resignation upon him. There is no more food in this sweltering barrenness, every last crumb has been consumed or sucked up by the giant white sun.

Huddled groups of adults glare at empty plates, their eyes flashing in defiance. Furrowed brows stare suspiciously up at Moses, the one who has brought them here, the one who must pay. Dishevelled women with strained long faces hold bawling infants, sunken-eyed, raw-boned with hunger, although most of them have gone quiet already, too weak even to cry. One woman is prostrate, her arms raised in supplication for surely only a miracle can save them now, surely this is the end of all their journeys. Perhaps she is begging not for grace, but for release, not for food but for the welcoming in heaven.

Suddenly a squabble breaks out. A teenage girl has found a morsel clutched in her little brother's hand and she has ripped open his fingers to grab it. He yells and she screams and lashes out, but there is no strength to fight and the instinct to survive, even at the expense of one's own blood bond, is quelled. The smell of pending death hangs heavy in the air. It has skewered the last will to fight for life.

With no warning, there is a sudden surge of movement from the outskirts of the camp. Stamping their bedraggled way forward, a huge crowd of men are chanting, "We need food now, we need food now." These are the strongest survivors and they shove their way through their wraithe-like brethren and move ominously toward Moses. Emaciated arms brandishing sticks are raised in feeble unison, fists clenched in defiance, voices caked in thirst.

Realizing mutiny is upon him, Moses, strengthened not by food but by faith and faith alone, booms, "Wait until tomorrow!" In that instant the rabble is silenced, but revolution thrives on hungry stomachs and will be sated. Moses knows an intervention must come now or it will be too late. But he is in no doubt it will come.

◱ Crisis in faith for livelihood

Here the Israelites "became frightened."[5]

The Israelite encampment in the Sin Desert held a lesson about the difficulty in keeping faith while striving to receive a source of revenue.

People who have no food in a city can resort to begging or

scavenging, but in a desert this is not an option. One cannot turn to other humans for help, but only to the Divine. If faith fails in the desert, one is completely lost.

The gift of manna, however, also teaches us that income is a gift from the Divine. We must make our own best effort, but we need to take cognizance that even our best effort may not succeed. Sometimes only a small effort may be more successful. This is a clear indication that G-d has a big role to play in determining what provisions we will receive, as Jacobson claims.[6]

Yes, we need faith. I needed faith to carry on with this journey too. I was strengthened in my approach from this teaching.   ◀

TEARS, GOLDEN CALF, FRIENDS, DÉJÀ VU AND A MARRIAGE PROPOSAL – DOPHKA `CAMP 9`

"They left the Desert of Sin and camped at Dophka."[1]

Dophka means "attack" or "knock" according to Rabbi Hillel.[2] It seemed there wouldn't be much to look for at this camp, but the idea of being attacked was intimidating and I was still a little uncertain of my Bedouin guide Rabia. He turned to me and said, "Now where you want to go?" I took out my map and pointed to a place on the far side of a mountain range. "This place is called Dophka in the Jewish teachings. Please take me there." He frowned, looked closely at the map, and then gave a deep, long laugh. The jeep sprang into motion and he continued to chuckle.

"Why are you laughing?" I asked eventually.

"This Dophka is my family home. We own the land. It's a famous place."

I was curious to know more, and this was the start of my first more personal conversation with Rabia.

He said, "My uncle is the Sheik of the Alagat tribe of Bedouin that live in the southwestern part of the Sinai Peninsula. My father died, and now his younger brother rules our tribe."

"Are you being serious?" I asked my tough-looking guide. He seemed intelligent and people savvy, with a desire to please. He simply chuckled in response.

"Please tell me about the Bedouin tribes," I asked.

Rabia went on to explain that there are more than sixty thousand Bedouin living in the Sinai. They have lived here for a long time. Now the whole desert is divided into tribal lands. Over the centuries, each tribe moved through its territories in search of grazing for its livestock. Some of them settled around oases during the spring and summer months when the rains come but in very dry years or in autumn, many move to the settled areas where they rely on water supplied by the government. Many Bedouin people have become modernized and at this thought, Rabia seemed to lose interest and went silent for a few seconds.

"But we return to the desert as soon as we can. Our lifestyle goes back more than a thousand years." Then a look of passion flared into his eyes.

"How many tribes are there?"

He explained that there are more than fourteen in the Sinai. In the north, along the beautiful, cool coast of the Mediterranean Sea, live the Aheiwat, Qatawiya and Suwarka tribes. In northern Sinai, in the flat, hard, arid regions the tough Ayaida, Tarabin, Laheiwat and Haweitat squeeze out a living. In the lofty southern mountainous parts the Awarma Qararsha, Awlad Said tribes somehow manage to live. The Gebeliyeh tribe cherishes their beloved Mount Sinai and St Catherine's monastery and the Muzeina tribe lives near the fertile southern tip of the peninsula. In the militant east, close to the Israeli border at the Gulf of Aqaba, is the Laheiwat tribe. Along the Israeli border is the Tiyaha tribe. I realized that I would be passing through many of the Bedouin tribal territories.[3]

"What about your tribe's land?"

"My family owns land around our home village, Serabit el-Kadem. There, on top of a high mountain, is an ancient temple dedicated to the Egyptian cow-god Hathor."

"The pharaohs went there often to pray," said Rabia. I thought of the biblical passages in which Moses had asked Pharaoh to let his people go, so that they could worship G-d in the Sinai desert. The request would have made sense to the Pharaoh because he and his people also went into the Sinai to worship their gods. It seemed obvious that people would search for divinity in the desert. It is so pure, free of matter and material things that I certainly felt closer to Him there, free of societal bonds and boundaries.

Rabia continued, "If you stay at my home for a few days, I will take you to see this great temple. Just trust me, alright?" I listened with an open mind, not yet certain of my plans. With the detailed map of Sinai open on my lap, I traced the route that we were following. In the distant background, the huge Gebel-el-Tih Mountains loomed. This enormous range crosses the Sinai Peninsula from east to west and divides northern and southern Sinai. We trailed towards these through a series of dry riverbeds and then made a few sharp turns to enter the foothills of the mountainous area. After a few more dry riverbeds, we came to a pass called Debbet-el-Qerai near the Gebel um-Rinna Mountain. I was learning to identify the mountains and valleys of the Sinai on the map by looking closely at the landscape. We arrived at a remote spot that housed the tomb of a Bedouin tribal leader, Sheikh Giray.

"I want to pay my respect to the deceased," Rabia said, drawing the car to a halt. While he was busy, I studied my map. Things were starting to fall into place in my mind. Just as one reads a map of a city according to the streets and buildings, so could one read a desert map. The riverbeds were like streets, and the mountains were like buildings. I suddenly felt a lot more at ease being in the desert. Rabia returned and we drove on. He turned the car into a side road and drove through Wadi Nasib, past a well called Bir Nasib. Then he stopped the car and climbed out, motioning me to follow. I plodded after him through the sand for about ten meters until we reached a huge rock. He pointed to some writing on the rock which also had camels carved into it.

"This is an ancient desert instruction to wanderers," he said. "It told them what direction to take."

I stared in amazement at the rock with the inscription which had been so exposed to the vagaries of men and the elements for millennia. These inscriptions date back to Rameses II. For three and a half millennia visitors to the oasis had seen this writing and I wondered if the Israelites had come here too.

Further on, Rabia stopped again and said, "I want to show you this mining site." There, to my astonishment, lay enormous quantities of dark slag. "There are about one hundred thousand tons of this black stuff here." Rabia said. "It comes from the most important mining site at the time of the pharaohs. Copper was extracted and smelted here."

After this foray, we continued by car and eventually left the mountainous region and moved through an area with red-brown, flat sandy land. Rabia pointed to the Gebel el-Tih Mountains. "We Bedouin believe that Musa walked on these mountains." I was surprised to hear

The great Gebel el-Tih Mountain range that divides northern and southern Sinai and on which the Bedouins believe that Moses spent time. | M Rawicz Trip Photo

this knowledge had been passed down through generations of Bedouin people. I was finally starting to trust my guide. By now we were crossing extremely soft sand and the jeep was sliding around all over the place, threatening to become embedded. I hung onto the rattling door holding my breath while my insides started to feel like the contents of a mixing bowl. I hoped we would be safe as we followed some vehicle tracks between sparse yellow and grey-green bushes. Then the car stopped. We were stuck. Rabia calmly got out, checked the vehicle, and deftly wedged some stones under the wheels. He climbed back in, started the car and jerked it sharply, and away we drove. My trust in him grew all the more. I was starting to feel quite carefree.

Finally, we arrived at a Bedouin village of seven small dwellings. Rabia stopped the car, jumped out and Hamed started lifting my bags off the top of the jeep. He gestured towards the village and shouted,

"This is your Dophka camp!"

We were greeted by five young children who came running towards us, shouting "*Salaam, salaam!*" (Hello, hello). A middle-aged woman

The Barakat encampment at the Dopkah Exodus camp location. | *M Rawicz Trip Photo*

dressed in black, her face covered by a black veil, followed them. I was escorted into a three-room home. It was small, about the size of a three-car garage, but was well constructed, built of concrete blocks painted white. Half of the house was a living area that had palm leaves for the roof and a desert sand floor. Two small square windows set into the wall had no glass, but I noticed wooden shutters which might keep the sand out on a windy day. The second half of the home was taken up by a small kitchen area and two bedrooms, one for the man and his wife, the other for their five children. This area had a cement floor and a tin roof.

Colorful woven mats lay on the sand floor. I was offered a seat in the lounge with the luxury of cushions on the floor. Four men and two women were already seated on cushions. They were introduced to me as Rabia's brothers Shihab and Sulaiman, his nephews Faraj and Tolba, his wife Sa'diyah and his mother-in-law Fteha. I greeted them and sat looking and smiling at them, wondering how we would communicate.

"Our family does not move about all the time, so we have this home and not a traditional one made of goats' hair," Rabia explained. "We still keep our homes open to nature and to people, all year round. We are an open people."

The philosophy of Bedouin hospitality includes three stages. Accordingly, I was first greeted, in the stage of *salaam*, then offered drink and food in *ta'aam* and then spoken to in *kelaam*. I felt the people's attitude of acceptance, their openness of heart and lack of prejudice. Tea was served, followed by flat bread – *shrak*. The tea was poured from a metal teapot that had been standing on a fire in a small square metal box in the middle of the room.

Tolba started talking to me in reasonable English. He translated the conversation that ensued from Arabic to English and slowly information was exchanged. I told them that I had been journeying for ten days and mentioned some of the places I had seen. The conversation turned to the family history and Tolba showed me an article that had been written in a newspaper about the late Sheik and various other family members. The more he read, the more emotional I became, until I started crying. Fteha was watching me intensely. Her dark eyes were just visible above her veil. Suddenly, I felt an intense bond with her as emotion overcame me. By now I was crying uncontrollably. Fteha reached out and held my hand and unfamiliar emotions were released within me like a dam wall breaking. Everyone else was just sitting and watching me quietly. Eventually, my emotion subsided and I wiped the tears from my face.

Tolba asked, "Why do you cry so much?"

"I feel as if I belong here!" I blurted out. "This feels like coming home. Maybe I lived here before."

The lounge of Rabia's home and some of his family members. | M Rawicz Trip Photo

I slept on the floor in the family room of Rabia's Bedouin home with a thick camel-wool blanket to protect me. | M Rawicz Trip Photo

My heart was pounding and I did not understand the words I had just spoken, though they were somehow true. My head was starting to spin. *Dophka . . . I've been here before.* The sense of déjà vu was overwhelming. Or maybe it was just a release of pent-up emotions because I felt safe in this family setting.

A noisy discussion ensued among Rabia's family members and I gleaned a little more of their family history. By now I was exhausted. Eventually, Fteha motioned for me to follow her to the next room. This was the family room and dining room where guests would sleep. It had light blue painted walls, a sand floor, a window without glass and the palm roof. I unrolled a camping mattress, sleeping bag and a cushion and Fteha laid out a thick camel-wool blanket on the floor.

Smiling, she indicated I should lie down and sleep, and then gently covered me and blew me a kiss. I had learned to sleep almost anywhere and quickly fell into a deep sleep.

When I woke in the morning, the first thing I saw was a young camel looking in through the window. Two lambs were standing at the doorway bleating for milk. Fteha came over to me and gestured if I wanted to eat. She spoke only Arabic but we were able to communicate fairly well using sign language and facial expressions. She had prepared some cucumber and tomato salad and was about to bake bread over an open flame. I sat next to her, fascinated by the way people survive in a desert. Their customs could surely teach me about the daily activities of the ancient Israelites.

I motioned to Fteha that I would like to help her with the baking. First, she mixed flour and water and showed me what size to make the dough balls. Then she rolled them out in an expertly made pizza shape but double the size and half as thin. Deftly she placed them on a grid over the fireplace. I helped make a few doughballs, and in a few minutes a delicious breakfast was ready. We all sat around the metal box filled with hot coals on which the teapot stood. Washing my hands and saying the prayer before eating bread took on a new meaning and the meal satisfied more than my hunger. I felt at home, that I belonged. After breakfast, with rejuvenated energy and encouragement from Fteha, I explored the Dophka camp. Today it is called the Barakat encampment, after Rabia's family name. Some camels sauntered around outside and several goats, sheep and chickens occupied the yard. I spent a blissful

Fteha, Rabia's mother-in-law, sat at the fireplace and taught me to make their typical flat bread called Shrak. | *M Rawicz Trip Photo*

day wandering around and acquainting myself with everything. Time passed quickly.

As the sunset approached, I went to the well beside the house, wanting to bathe. A stone platform provided a firm place on which to stand and two stone pillars were joined by a piece of wood at the top which held the bucket for drawing up the water. Tolba watched while I lowered the bucket on a long rope which unrolled for a long time until it reached the water. With all my strength I tried to haul it up, but Tolba had to take over. Eventually the bucket emerged and I splashed some water over my hands and face. The water was invigorating. I poured some into a dish and carried it inside so that I could wash in private. Water from the well was extremely precious to the family and was treated with great care to ensure that it did not become dirty. I could appreciate the gratitude of the Israelites on receiving water in the desert.

With the light softening, I took a walk up the hill behind the houses and had a magnificent view of the surrounding hills and vast stretches of desert. Two shy young girls with scarves over their heads followed me, giggling and waving. As I sat watching the sun set in a ball of brilliant red, the evening wind brushed my face. The stars gradually appeared and soon the night was ablaze with them. Such a sight is possible only when the skies are pure and far more real when the heart is untroubled.

That night, I joined the Bedouin family sleeping outside the house on the cool sand, covered with splendid camel-hair blankets. Men slept on one side of the house and women on the other and the children snuggled next to the women. The friendly atmosphere was delightful and soothing. This tiny desert community had embraced me and it felt wonderful.

In the morning I rose early to start the journey that Rabia had spoken about, to the pharaonic temple at Serabit el-Kadim, one of the most significant archaeological features of the Sinai Desert. We would explore by camel, something I had never done before. At first I was scared of the animals but felt more at ease once I had watched the Bedouin preparing them for the trip. A young man named Shareef placed a soft cloth on the camel's back, then the camel seat – a piece of smooth and beautifully shaped wood which slipped neatly into the hollow of the camel's back between its hump and the pelvis. At the front of the seat was an upright handle which could be grasped when mounting and riding. On top of the seat, another soft blanket was placed for the rider's comfort. A second wooden upright pole at the back of the saddle served

Fteha's daughter helping to prepare simple food for the family meal. |
M Rawicz Trip Photo

as a hook for baggage. The design of the saddle enabled the rider to stay firmly seated while the camel stood up or knelt down. On another camel, Shareef placed a large water container, a bag of flour, a pot for tea, some plates and utensils, a tent, thick woven mats, a foam mattress and some warm camel-hair blankets.

PHARAOH'S WILDERNESS TEMPLE

Then I faced the daunting experience of climbing onto a camel for the first time. It sat down with its front and back legs tucked under its body and I was instructed to swing my foot high to reach the seat and then hoist myself up. I could not reach. Shareef led the camel to a large rock and told it to sit down again. I climbed onto the rock and was now able to put my foot over the animal's back and swing myself into the saddle. When I was seated, the camel started to stand up. First it rose onto its hind legs, throwing me forwards, face down, almost parallel to the ground. I hung on for dear life and let out a scream. Then the camel righted itself onto its front legs, throwing me backwards again, so that I was almost lying on my back and I screamed again. However, in a moment I experienced the terrific sensation of being some three meters above the desert floor. Shareef helped me to maneuver my feet into the strong leather stirrups and I was set to go.

"I will see you later when you come down," Rabia said.

Tolba, Faraj and Shareef mounted their camels and we rode together for about five kilometers through the desert. I watched the shadow cast by my camel as it moved at a steady pace across the sand and captivated, I began talking to him. Camels make various sounds that indicate how they feel and they roar when displeased. If a male blows a big pink bubble out of his mouth, it means he wants a mate. They liked to snack on one particular type of bush and seemed unable to pass those plants without taking a bite. They needed encouragement to walk down a slope and I learned to give my camel reassurance and encouragement by saying, "Urgh, urgh, urgh!" I found myself wondering how it would be to own one.

We eventually arrived at the base of the mountain called Gebel Serabit el-Kadim. Here we started a three-hour climb on foot along a very steep winding slope to the summit, another 200 meters. A stone pathway twisted between the rocks. As we climbed, I chatted to Shareef, who could speak some English.

"In Arabic, Serabit el-Kadim means 'columns of the slaves,'" he told me. "Look, this is how you should walk on the mountain path. If you find a stone on the path, you must move it to the side. This is a very old tradition of the desert people. In this way we help to keep the path clear and safe for the next person."

I was reminded of the Jewish law that requires one to remove obsta-

The pharaohs' Hathor temple, one of the largest archeological finds in the Sinai. |
M Rawicz Trip Photo

cles from the path of a blind person, taken literally or metaphorically.

It was very hot, and as we walked I started to strip off the layers of my clothing. Having left early in the morning with warm clothes, eventually all I was wearing was a loose kaftan with a cool scarf to protect my head and shoulders from the sun. The main struggle was simply to keep moving.

"The Hathor temple that we will see soon was a very important site for Egyptians, here in the Sinai," Shareef continued.

Just then we passed a large hollow chamber carved into the mountains.

"Look, there's a huge carving of a pharaoh at its entrance," Shareef pointed out. "Inside, there's some Egyptian writing about Pharaoh Thuthmose IV."

Tolba added, "This was the entrance to a mine that was set up in about 3000 BCE by the pharaohs. They had engineers who were very good in mining turquoise in the Sinai desert. For two thousand years they mined a lot of turquoise here and sent it to ships near Abu Zenema on the Red Sea. I'll show you something great in a moment."

We arrived at a spot where the rocks beside the path had been engraved.

"These were carved by the ancient miners," Tolba said. "Look at the donkeys carrying goods and the ships. They were carrying the turquoise from the mines to the sea and then it went by ship to the cities to be made into jewelry for the pharaohs."

"I visited Abu Zenema," I said. "That was where the Israelites stopped beside the Red Sea. I also visited the Cairo museum and saw many objects made of turquoise, or enameled with powdered turquoise."

According to archaeologist Jeffrey Zorn, the word *Dophka* is associated with the Egyptian word *mfkt*, meaning turquoise.[4]

We spent time exploring the area. Some scholars believe this might have been the area where the people called the "mixed multitude," who were not of Israelite origin, had joined the Exodus.[5]

"Some books say that at times, Canaanites worked in these mines, which supplied turquoise. Archeological remains of this turquoise were found at Tanis and others ancient cities," I told my guides. "They might have seen the Israelites passing during the Exodus, helped them to find their way, showed them where to find water, and then joined the Exodus crowd."[6]

This was borne out by the book *Ancient Mesopotamian Materials and Industries: The Archaeological Evidence* by Peter Roger Stuart Moorey.[7] Eventually we reached the summit and the huge remains of Serabit el-Kadim temple which covers 200 square meters. The temple had been built during the Twelfth Dynasty of the pharaohs on a Semitic cultural site. Prayer rooms were cut into the rock and a long line of halls, several bas-reliefs and stelae, some as tall as two meters with inscriptions on all sides, all showed how deeply Hathor was revered. According to my guides, the inscriptions recounted spells or religious sayings and stories of mining.[8]

Shareef said, "You know, the first people who came here thought this was a cemetery."[9]

The story of the Israelites and the golden calf was on my mind. The calf was supposedly a deity of hope and joy, emotions that were in short supply when Moses stayed on Mount Sinai for forty days. Some archaeologists think the Israelites based the golden calf on the myths of the Egyptian goddess Hathor, based on artifacts that had been found.[10] The Egyptians believed that Hathor, the cow godess, "the Golden One," gave birth to the sungod every morning as a golden calf and then swallowed it every night, and it represented hope.[11]

I told Shareef what I had learned at the Cairo museum:

The extensive remains of Serabit el-Kadim Hathor Temple that was built during the Twelfth Dynasty of the pharaohs. The pharaohs came here to worship. They understood Moses' request to go into the desert to worship his G-d. | M Rawicz Trip Photo

"According to Egyptian legend, the sun god Re made Nut pregnant. She was the goddess of the west or sky goddess. Each morning, Nut gave birth to the sun, which was a bull calf known as the Bull of Heaven. This sun then started to shine every day. They thought that the bull was swallowed by its mother Nut every night and was reborn from her the next morning. Nut, the queen mother of the sky, was called 'the cow which bore the bull.'"[12]

"How strange," commented Shareef.

I continued, "They called their sun bull the 'youthful sun of the horizon' and drew him as a winged sun-disk. It explains why we see Hathor sometimes shown as a cow wearing the sun-disc between her horns. One of her names was 'the golden one,' probably because she reflected the sun's golden glow."

Shareef explained that archaeologists uncovered Egyptian inscriptions near the Hathor shrine which tell about the sacrifice of bullocks to Hathor. Bones of a bullock had also been found there. He pointed out carvings of hornless calf heads in some of the offerings that were cut into the stelae.

I later learned that pot shards and scarab seals had been found here, similar to those found in an area once inhabited by western Asian Hyksos people in the Nile Delta.[13]

I wandered over to a rock overlooking the desert. The Gebel-el-Tit mountain range stretched out for hundreds of kilometers above a desert carved out by the massive forces of wind, earth and extreme temperatures and one mountain looked like enormous mushrooms. The dynamic geological forces of the Great Rift Valley were evident here in the Sinai. The mountains were composed of sandstone with an upper layer of schist, rich in turquoise. Huge rifts were visible in the mountainsides where tectonic forces had shifted the earth. Feeling utterly uninhibited, I sang the prayer that proclaims the unity of G-d, *Shema Israel*. This is the central prayer of the Jewish people, and I sang it loudly.

It was time to eat. Tolba made typical Bedouin *shrak* bread. He also served goat's cheese and yoghurt, tuna from a tin, and onion, tomatoes, eggplant, cucumber and greens. We washed it down with hot herbal tea made from desert berries and had halva for dessert.

Soon after, Rabia's oldest brother Selim, the current Sheik, met up with us. He had evidently been roaming the mountain. He was a tall man with dark skin, a strong intelligent face, piercing brown eyes and a small black moustache and was dressed in traditional Arab robes with a jacket over them. He sat down next to me and to my surprise and delight began to speak in Hebrew. We conversed for about an hour about Bedouin life, the issues that a sheik has to deal with, Middle Eastern politics and my religious beliefs. He was such a charming man that I took a liking to him. It was a strange but warming experience for me – a religious Jewish woman camping out in the mountains with Muslim Bedouins in an atmosphere of comradeship.

The biblical teaching from Camp 6 called Elim came to mind. We should nurture a vision of what we want in our lives and trust G-d to act within natural laws to unfurl His plan. From that moment on, I knew that I was capable of a far greater effort to love and tolerate all people, no matter their background, and that from now on I would insist that no person would speak in a racist manner in my presence, as in the past I had tolerated this poor behavior. I pondered this as I ended the night in six layers of clothing with a balaclava and two thick scarves over my head and sat on the mattress on the floor of a little cave in which I had chosen to sleep. Then I tucked myself into my sleeping bag and threw two thick camel-hair blankets over myself in preparation for a freezing night on the mountain.

When we travelled in the desert our typical meal was Shrak *bread made on twig ashes in the sand. After baking for 13 minutes the end product was similar to matzos.* | *M Rawicz Trip Photo*

Here, away from the controlled environment of city life, I was learning to accept whatever the desert offered in the way of food, water, temperature or shelter. I was shedding irrational fears and a new awakening was being nurtured within me. The image of the desert as something to fear was yielding to one of great value. I was learning to accept life on its own terms without trying to change things. My appreciation of the Israelites' experiences was deepening every day.

The next morning, we started the extremely steep descent by a different pathway. This proved to be a difficult and dangerous task that at times entailed stepping down a sheer rock face. Tolba and Shareef guided my steps to ensure that my feet found the crevices and I did not fall. I wished we had a rope ladder, but my guides insisted that if I

When I was on the high mountains, I slept on the floor of a little cave covered in six layers of clothing and several head scarves to stay warm in the freezing desert nights. | *M Rawicz Trip Photo*

followed their lead I would be fine. As we proceeded, the path became even more dangerous until I was dangling against a sheer cliff face, with one Bedouin man holding my hand from above and another clasping my ankle from below. One slip would have meant my demise. My mind was racing, telling me that death could be close, but I forced myself to remain focused and listened to my guides. I prayed, and prayed, and thankfully made it down safely. After the cliff, we walked in single file, it seemed for hours and hours. I was exhausted but had to push on. The others were communicating by shouting across the distances as we walked, entertaining each other.

When we eventually reached the lowest slopes, I looked back and saw four huge flat mountains close to each other. The pathway that we had descended looked like a snake stretching from the flat top all the way down the steep rocky mountainside for about two kilometers. I felt rather proud of myself for having survived that formidable descent. The lower slopes of the mountain were covered with soft yellow sand and by this time I was so tired that I just sat down and slid down the remainder of the slope on my backside. It was a fun ending to a long adventure.

At last, we were back on flat ground. Close by, standing under an Acacia tree, was a traditional black Bedouin tent woven from goat-hair, called a *beit shaar* or "house of hair." This type of tent has been used for generations by the Bedouin who carry them as they migrate from place to place. Women have traditionally been responsible for the tents: their weaving, striking, packing, and re-erecting. The Bedouin have started to build modest fixed homes of the type I had already seen with Rabia's family only since they had started earning wages by working in the open economy. Rabia was there to greet us. It felt authentic to be sitting in a *beit shaar* helping the men make bread on the sand.

Our camels had been led around the mountain while we were climbing it and I felt greatly relieved to be riding my "ship of the desert" again, after our meal. I began to hum and Sulaiman, Faraj and Tolba caught the mood and started singing some of their ancient songs loudly in unison. I joined in where I could. We all rejoiced at the top of our voices, celebrating the freedom of being in the desert, unencumbered by the stuffy formality of modern city life. It was exhilarating. I had connected with a lifestyle that was countless years old. This simple and pure life made me feel closer to the Creator. My spirituality was opening up in a way I had not anticipated. The strange and haunting sound of Bedouin songs reverberated through the vastness, and I felt a deep affection for my guides. I added my version by singing Hebrew songs. The only background noise was that of the wind blowing across the sand.

Rabia said that he wanted to go past his sister's home. Nadira was a dark-skinned woman who wore a bright multicolored dress with a floral pattern and a red scarf over her head. Her face was oval and her amber eyes were deep-set as she returned my greeting with a quick smile. She served the traditional tea and I noticed that she had been embroidering. After tea, she got up and left the room. When she returned, she squatted before me and spread out a cloth, unrolling it to display typical Bedouin beadwork jewelry.

"Please buy some," she said and I perceived sadness in her gentle and sweet voice.

"Thank you, but I already have some," I replied.

She looked greatly disappointed. Five young children joined us and Rabia explained that Nadira lived alone with them because her husband had been arrested for trying to smuggle drugs through the Sinai.

Bedouins making bread and waiting to greet us, in a typical tent woven from goat-hair. |
M Rawicz Trip Photo

"He was trying to make a little money," Rabia commented. "But now he's in jail and she has to raise the kids alone."

Nadira's expression changed and I sensed her shame and anxiety. She rushed off and returned almost immediately carrying a magnificent black embroidered and beaded skirt.

"Thirty US dollars," she said, looking at me wistfully.

It had seven vertical panels, each looking like an intricately embellished peacock's tail. Across each section, complex patterns of beads in silver, gold, blue, turquoise and green, ran the length of the fabric down to the eye of the peacock at the base of the skirt. The skirt surely had at least a thousand beads. I nodded my acceptance and handed Nadira $40. She looked at me with surprise and gratitude.

"She's trying to make money any way she can," Rabia said.

His sister showed the same quiet determination I had noticed in the other Bedouin. I loved the skirt so much that I later wore it to extremely posh weddings where, dare I say it, the dress threatened to upstage the bride's. I resolved to compensate Nadira more and find a way to help

*The magnificent black embroidered and beaded skirt that the Bedouin lady sold to me. |
M Rawicz Trip Photo*

her. On the way back to Rabia's home, I thought about the possibility of buying a camel that could be part-owned by Fteha and Nadira.
Fteha could look after it and use it to transport goods or people with
the understanding that they would share the proceeds with Nadira.
This would be the equivalent of buying the women a car. Months after
my journey, eventually I had enough cash to transfer to an account in
Egypt and the money was delivered to Rabia. He arranged for a camel
to be bought from the camel market at Cairo. A young male animal was
selected and transported to Rabia's home. To the women's absolute
elation, they were presented with the surprise gift. I was told the camel
had a beige face and tufts of black hair on the top of its head and the
family named it "Margaret's *arbed*" - Margaret's "black one."

In turn, Rabia's family decided to give me a surprise as well. On a subsequent visit to the Sinai, I was invited to watch them weaving goat hair.
I found the process fascinating and they offered to teach me the art,
using their home-made wooden loom. Absorbed in the activity, I didn't
notice Rabia's relatives disappear and suddenly I was presented with a

brilliantly colorful and beautiful rug that they had woven for me. I cherish that rug to this day and it takes pride of place on my dining room table as a throw over on special occasions such as our Passover meal.

It was afternoon by the time our small caravan arrived back at the Barakat encampment. I was then invited to a wonderful experience in the form of a traditional Bedouin treatment. Fteha is renowned in the area as a healer and clairvoyant. Tolba told me that approximately forty species of plants growing in the Sinai Peninsula are used by Bedouin healers as medicines for a wide range of illnesses – everything from diabetes to upset stomachs – and Fteha knew most of these plants and could concoct compounds from more than one plant. Patients came from near and far to consult with her.

Fteha was also skilled in energy healing, and offered to give me an ancient Bedouin cleansing treatment. This sounded fascinating and I agreed. She first placed tiny pieces of metal into a ladle and melted them over a fire. She waved the ladle around my head and body and under my skirt, allowing the smoke to encircle me, and then moved the ladle over the seven energy centers of the body called *chakras*, known also in Red Indian and Chinese healing. Finally, she threw the molten metal into a bowl of cold water, which made it solidify in fragments which she examined to provide a clairvoyant reading. I was astounded by the shape that emerged. It looked exactly like a tiny, well-formed doll. Fteha proceeded to tell me, through Tolba the family interpreter, what she saw. The details were extremely relevant to my life and I was amazed at how she accessed such deep truths about my family and personal history.

Fteha then told me to rest, and she did the same. Her daughter Sa'diyah indicated to me that Fteha needed to rest because during the process, issues affecting her patients are transferred to her as part of the healing, so she needed to recuperate just as they did. When I awoke, I felt extremely content and somehow different. Evidently the cleansing process had had a deep and genuinely beneficial effect on me. It was Friday afternoon which is the Muslim Sabbath. Fteha dressed herself in a beautiful multicolored veil with little gold coins around the edges, and sat next to me reading from the Koran before saying the afternoon prayers. We enjoyed sitting together holding hands, laughing and smiling, and cherishing each other's company.

Fteha left for a while and then returned to tell me that Rabia's brother, Sulaima, liked me and was lonely and would consider marrying me. Sulaima was a tour guide and prior to that had worked at a Jewish hospital for years, when the Israelis occupied the Sinai. He had sent Fteha as a messenger to ask me whether I would consider marrying him.

"He feels you have a good heart," Fteha explained with the help of Tolba.

The proposal came as a shock. Although I felt it was a great compliment, I had to explain that marriage would not be possible because I was already married and I lived in a very different country and culture. They completely understood and we laughed together but I also thought about how our cultures often supersede our collective identity.

I told Fteha that because it was Friday afternoon, I needed to prepare for the Jewish Sabbath and wanted to bake some *kitka* bread. She helped me to make the dough which I plaited into three large kitka breads and placed into the ashes to bake. I made enough bread to last two days because baking on the Sabbath is prohibited. Fteha helped me find a suitable place to set up my Sabbath candles in her private room, and helped me cook rice and vegetables in a pot I had brought from home so that I could enjoy a hot Sabbath meal. I had also brought some dried kosher meat from home, as a Sabbath treat, and grape juice with which to make the traditional blessing.

The whole family ate together, listening respectfully when I recited the evening blessing over the meal. I sensed a wonderful feeling of comradeship. I explained that I was on a journey to follow in the footsteps of Moses and they excitedly acknowledged that I was on a "Hajj of Moses." They seemed to understand my intention completely for indeed this was a pilgrimage, with a difference.

I was falling in love with the Dophka camp and its inhabitants. We exchanged, in simple terms, the views of our respective religions. We agreed that there were many similarities but that all people are obliged to draw closer to G-d by whatever route they know, and that mutual respect is essential. Fteha did her Muslim prayers which I decided to learn:

Allahu Akbar. Asyhadu An La Ilaha Ill Lal. Lah Ash Hadu An Na Muhammad Ar Rasoolul Lah. Ash Hadu An Na Ali An Wali Ullah. Hayya Al Las Salah. Hayya Al Lal Falah. Hayya Ala Khairil Amal. Allahu Akbar. La Ilaha Ill Lal Lah	God is Great. I bear witness that there is no God but Allah. I bear witness that Mohammad is the Messenger of Allah. I bear witness that Ali is the Friend of Allah. Hasten towards prayer. Hasten towards prosperity. Hasten towards the best of action. Allah is Great. There is no God except Allah.

In the evening, I lit my Sabbath candles in the Bedouin home. | M Rawicz Trip Photo

The next day was the thirteenth day of my trip. After rising, I spent part of the morning reciting the Sabbath morning prayers which seemed especially inspirational. I also read the weekly Bible portion and again the text was more real. My private service lasted the whole morning. Then I walked to a small hill at the edge of the encampment and sat down to enjoy the view. The shadow of a rock sheltered me from the sun. Ahead of me was a vast expanse of light yellow sand which in the distance took on the appearance of a network of rivers running between the dark low mountains as far as the eye could see. I sat there meditating and picturing in my mind's eye how the Israelites would have walked along the sand, led by a pillar of smoke. It was uplifting to visualize this in the very place it had occurred. My gratitude to G-d took wings in glorious flight through the clear desert air.

✪ Fear of deprivation – emotional control

Jacobson discusses that Dophka in the Bible represented the place where the Israelites' hearts beat in fear for lack of bread.[14]

When people experience severe anxiety about how they are going to survive, it is easy to panic and lose control. That is when their heart rate increases with distress. It is a time when they can become very emotional, cry and express being terrified of the future.

Here the Israelites had to learn to avoid giving in to their distress and to access their deepest emotional resources and beliefs that help would come in time. This is an integral part of faith and trust in G-d as discussed by Jacobson.[15]

In our daily quest for survival we may also feel insecure. "Knocking" is another meaning of the word Dophka and can allude to the prospect of asking G-d for help and enhancing our own capabilities to meet our challenges.[16]

I made kitka / challah bread for Sabbath, which I then baked on hot ashes on the desert sand on Friday afternoon. | M Rawicz Trip Photo

At Dophka the Israelites were at a stage of life in their Exodus similar to young people starting out in life.[17] This was possibly why anxiety was an issue. They had begun to run out of bread and became afraid. They needed to turn to heaven for help. Here they learned to try doors of opportunity and discover inner, deeper resources, control their emotions and refrain from fear.

I resolved to integrate this lesson in my heart by appreciating what I ate daily. The meaning of the lesson was all the more powerful after having been treated with such great hospitality in the Bedouin family home.

I went back to the house and enjoyed a Sabbath lunch with Fteha. Then I ventured alone into the desert again, but soon took shelter from the sun under an Acacia tree before finding a rock with a hollow shape where I could sit in the shade on the soft sand. In these surroundings, hosted by Bedouin people, my perception of the Bible was shifting radically away from a worldview informed by European scholars and I felt myself becoming increasingly aligned with a new awareness of the Divine.

People who live in the desert typically nap at midday to avoid the heat, as do sheep and goats. The camels can withstand the sun but even they rest in the midday heat. It occurred to me that the Israelites must have risen early in the mornings to move forwards while it was still relatively cool, taking shelter from the sun at noon. Watching the lives of the Bedouin had given me a far greater appreciation of how the Israelites would have lived. All of it seemed so real to me!

I, too, took some time after resting to pray and deepen my connection to G-d, and to contemplate the lessons I was learning. I sensed a Divine embrace that left me feeling utterly tranquil and loved. I drifted into a contented sleep, the traditional Sabbath afternoon sleep. At dusk, I returned to Rabia's family and spent another night in their home.

Early Sunday, I awoke to the sound of sheep bleating and goats waiting impatiently to be taken into the desert to graze. I helped the women milk the goats and sheep so that cream cheese and yogurt could be made. We then ate breakfast with the children – fresh goat's milk and cream cheese, freshly baked bread, yogurt, date jam, eggs (from the chickens in the yard) and tea. The baby lambs and kid goats came begging for scraps and the giggling children played with them as if they were pets.

Fteha gave me lessons on how to shephard the sheep and goats in the desert. |
M Rawicz Trip Photo

After the meal, Fteha beckoned me to follow as she led the sheep and goats into the desert to graze. Our ability to communicate in sign language amazed me and her psychic powers seemed to include partly reading my mind. I too have some telepathic ability, possibly because I am a twin and my interactions with my twin sister over the years have led to a natural form of unspoken communication. Tolba accompanied us on his camel. As a shepherdess, Fteha ensured that the sheep and goats stayed together and that no animals wandered off alone. She taught me the clicking and rolling sounds used to encourage the herds while walking uphill and to slow them down on the descent.

My spirit basked in the silence and beauty of the desert. I understood the value of the biblical shepherds who became great leaders, particularly Moses and King David. Fteha also taught me to pick berries from the desert plants to make tea. We collected dry branches which she carried in a sack with a hood that she wore over her head with the branches hanging against her back. Her long brown dress with its blue and white bodice fluttered in the breeze. A black veil, called an *asaba*, covered her face from just below the eyes.

We walked for two and a half hours to reach the grazing area. Eventually we arrived at a small oasis with palm trees and a spring which welcomed us with its cold water gushing from a rock in the side of a cliff. Bedouin legend says that Moses spent time alone here. We splashed our hot faces and bodies with water and Tolba's camel enjoyed a long drink. Fteha gave me a much-needed hug and we settled down in the shade of a palm tree. She began to prepare a fire for tea, using the branches she had been carrying and forming a hollow in the sand. Then she twisted the branches into a circular shape to fit into the hollow, and Tolba lit the fire. Fteha leaned over it, shielding it from the breeze, and blew gently onto the spark until the twigs began to burn. She boiled water in a small metal jug with the berries we had picked and soon we had a soothing tea.

To prepare lunch, she took out a packet of flour which we kneaded into dough. We waited for the fire to die down to glowing embers, and then placed the dough into the ashes to bake. This reminded me of the Passover bread, *Matzah*. In just fifteen minutes, the other typical flat Bedouin bread called *tab-banna* was ready. Fteha pulled the bread from the embers and beat it gently to get rid of the ashes that still clung to it, and then it was ready to eat, with just a few flecks of grey on its edge. The flavor was delicious.

I felt comfortable with Fteha. Unexpectedly, I became extremely emotional and let my inner hurt show, from many unpleasant experiences that I had undergone in the past. Being here felt like being in a wonderful loving home. I identified with the family and felt as if I had been here before and now I was coming home.

With Tolba acting as interpreter, Fteha told me more about her culture.

"We Bedouin use things from the desert in our daily lives," she said. "Goatskins are a good surface for preparing food and hyrax skins make good curdling bags. We make camel saddles from various kinds of wood – almond, castor, and quince. Desert plants give us powerful medicines. Boiled lavender is good for eye infections, wild mint can ease an earache, and wormwood broth is good for headaches."

In the late afternoon, Fteha called the sheep and goats. By now they were just specks on the horizon, but somehow they understood her call and obediently returned. I walked ahead for a short while, wanting a

Fteha and Tolba prepare a fire for wild desert berry tea on our trip to look after the sheep in the desert for the day. | *M Rawicz Trip Photo*

little solitude, but I soon became lost. The path had crossed through a valley but evidently I had taken a wrong turn and I did not know where to go. I stood still, waiting to be rescued, and eventually Fteha showed up and smiled wistfully at me and took me back to the correct track. I was like one of her sheep that had strayed off the path.

When we got home, I reluctantly began to prepare for my departure the next day. In the evening, the seven other women who lived in the village came to say goodbye. Sa'diyah, Fteha, Nadira, their companions and I sat around the room against the walls, and it was a colorful sight. Fteha's daughter was dressed in a shiny long pink dress and a black *asaba* with a gold stripe. Fteha had given me one of her dresses as a present and I was wearing this; it was made of shiny black material with a beautiful pattern of blue and red squares and oblongs. On my return home, it became one of my most prized garments and I wear it with joy. On my subsequent visit to the Bedouin, I gave each woman a beautiful decorated black dress of the kind worn by sophisticated Arab women, a real treat for them.

Fteha had also given me a navy-blue face scarf embroidered with flowers of yellow, green and red. I wore it to cover my face when I was among Bedouin women. My own religious tradition requires me to cover my hair in public and I usually wear caps or scarves for this, so wearing a veil over my face did not seem strange. I viewed it as just another step in enhancing feminine modesty. I felt comfortable in the presence of these beautiful, gentle Bedouin ladies with their alluring eyes. Fteha also gave me one of her rings and I wore it for years after my trip because I felt so close to her. In return, I gave her a large tube of hand cream as one's skin becomes dry and flaky in the desert. This was a luxury for her.

As we sat around the room, we started to sing and clap and later danced together. I felt grateful for the women's hospitality and companionship and the bond that had developed between us would last for years. I resolved to encourage everyone to understand that if each of us desists from negative talk about others, they might do the same for us. In our own small way, we can all help to nurture tolerance and mutual respect. This kind of empathy is especially necessary to offset the negative sentiments caused by extremist Muslim movements that support terrorism in today's world and the tension in the Middle East between Israelis and Muslims. I also realized that if this was how the Israelites had socialized in the desert, I was all for it.

We left the next day and my heart ached a little. I promised Fteha that I would be back one day. I had a big lump in my throat. So far my experiences were proving to be one of warm human connection and spiritual growth.

MANNA VALLEY – ALUSH   CAMP 10

"They left Dophka and camped at Alush."[1]

Alush means "powerful city" or "wild place."[2] These terms seemed contradictory, so I wondered what I would find at the site. What kind of wildness would I encounter? I hoped it would not be wild dangerous animals.

Rabia drove us into the desert, stopping at a hill far away from anything.

"If you want to use your cell phone to call your family in South Africa," he said, "this is where you can get a signal. You have to stand right here, look . . . and hold your phone at this height." He demonstrated.

Apparently this was one of the few spots that received a signal via satellites. There was absolutely nothing to mark the hill, and without

In the evening, the seven other women who lived in the village came to say goodbye at a farewell party. I dressed in the blue scarf and clothes that Fteha had given me (sitting in the middle). | M Rawicz Trip Photo

someone like Rabia to show me around I would not have thought it possible to make any calls from the desert. With delight, I called home immediately.

"I'm well," I said. "And I'm so happy here! I love being with the Bedouin. In fact, I might even consider coming to live among them."

My family sounded surprised, but the allure of the desert and its special lifestyle had really crept into my heart.

Rabia, Tolba and I then travelled southwards again. We passed through a plain of soft red sand with mountains as a backdrop, and then turned into a steep ravine called Wadi Sein, which was 120 meters wide with foreboding dark-grey granite mountains on each side. Some of the mountains formed sheer cliffs on which almost no vegetation could survive. These cliffs towered over us and dwarfed our vehicle; some of the peaks were as high as 350 meters. In this contorted and winding valley we crept along slowly for about twenty kilometers. The valley was shrouded in shadow, and the ground was stony and hard on the vehicle. The terrain left me feeling constrained in space, with a strange kind of uneasiness. The track led into Wadi Sidri.

I enjoyed Fteha's company as we relaxed. She wore her beautiful beaded veil on Friday afternoon, her Sabbath. | *M Rawicz Trip Photo*

Rabia said, "I want to show you something."

He made a detour of approximately 500 meters along Wadi Maghara, which means "Valley of Mines." There we came to another turquoise mine dug into the side of the mountain, which we explored.

As we walked, Tolba pointed to an engraving.

"Look, this one is of King Sekhemkhet and it shows him fighting Egypt's enemies."

We passed ancient tunnels, miners' huts, and stelae.[3] Twelve bas reliefs have been found in this wadi, but most have been damaged over the centuries. Tolba led me on another small diversion to show me something amazing. Near the mine entrance, carved into the rock of the mountainside, we saw some more inscriptions.

Tolba said, "I know a lot about this place, because many archaeologists have come here."

"Oh, I've read about this site," I replied. "These inscriptions were carved by ancient Asiatic miners from a southern Canaanite people, not by the Egyptians."[4] Some of the inscriptions honored El, the Canaanites' god.[5] One inscription related the death of a miner, and reads "O Father El, grant to my companion Heber rest beside him."[6] Other scripts were hieroglyphic signs showing the names of Semitic miners and keeping account of their labors. Writings on stone tablets have also been found on the ground in this area. Some of these tablets were thought to be burial stones for miners that had died.[7]

Tolba pointed to one inscription and said, "This is very ancient Hebrew writing."

"I've read about this too!" I exclaimed. "It's one of the earliest alphabets, from about three thousand years ago."

The script in question was the Proto-Sinaitic Script, often called Old Hebrew, which was used to record the Pan-Canaanite language. It is believed that this developed into modern Hebrew script.[8] "Some scholars believe that the Ten Commandments were written in Proto-Sinaitic Script," I added.[9]

"Yes," Tolba replied, "we've also heard that."

He proceeded to tell me that the inscriptions at Wadi Mughara and previously at Wadi Nasib are very important. Archaeologists have visited these sites and deciphered some of the writings, but thirty-five inscriptions still have not been translated. One of these is a stele with an Egyptian god, Ptah, on it. There are three stelae dedicated to Hathor.

"We know all this because our land at Serabit el-Kadim has many stelae, and archaeologists who learn about Egyptian history come to see them," Tolba said.

I was intrigued to see these real-life examples of the ancient script I had read about.

At this stage of their journey, the Israelites had been in an ongoing state of anxiety about food. I could understand how one would feel unhappy wandering through this terrain. Eventually we reached the lower end of the valley, which opened out onto a wide floodplain measuring six square kilometers – an area large enough to hold many tents. This had probably been what was known as the Alush valley, at the confluence of Wadis Seir and Mukkatab. Today, a small village comprising a few Bedouin homesteads marks the site. Rabia stopped the car so that I could view the area more closely. Small yellow bushes were scattered across the land, with a couple of Acacia trees, and I saw some Tamarisks at the sides of the plain.

He said, "We Bedouins believe that this is where manna fell for the first time."

I said, "The Bible says that[10] 'in the morning the dew lay round about the peoples' campsite. It looked like small round things, as small as the hoar frost on the ground. When the children of Israel saw it, they said each to the other, 'It is manna (what is it?),' for they did not know what it was.[11] It was like coriander seed, white; and the taste of it was like wafers made with honey.'"

Rabia responded, "Yes, we have this in our tradition too and we have eaten what you call "manna" for hundreds of years. In June, if we have enough rain, we can collect a white sticky stuff, which drops from the thorns of the Tamarisk trees. It covers the ground under the trees. We collect it as soon as the sun comes up, because when the sun rises the stuff melts away. We eat it and it tastes like honey. If we boil it and strain it through a cloth it can stay for a long time. Then we can eat it with our bread like a jam. Some people say it comes from the tree itself. Other people say it comes when a tiny insect that lives on the trees makes a hole in the tree stems. Anyway we like to eat it."

I was completely intrigued. After my trip I did research on manna. I found out that a Dr. Bodenheimer had observed and photographed some insects, including Trabutina mannipara and Najococcus serpentinus minor, in the act of actually excreting a substance which Arabs regard as manna-like. The insects feed on the tree and the substance drops to the ground. This consists of beads of manna, transparent, hard syrup that crystallizes into a milky white substance.[11.1]

This biological explanation was very interesting, but the fact that manna was given in quantities suitable for the many thousands of Israelites at the time of their Exodus is certainly a miracle.

I continued talking to Rabia, "Moses then told them that it is the bread which G-d had given them and that they must take only what they needed for the day except for the sixth day on which they must gather twice as much food, to keep for the holy Sabbath day of rest.[12] Here the Israelites were tested to see whether they would observe the commandment and remember that G-d had saved them from Egypt."

According to Bible commentaries, known in the Jewish tradition as Midrash, G-d fulfilled His promise to "cause food to rain down from the sky" at the Alush encampment. The people's complaints about food were addressed. That evening, a large flock of quails flew in to the camp, and the people slaughtered many of the birds for their sustenance. I stood at the site contemplating these historical events. The Israelites first received the gift of manna at Alush, but it continued for the next forty years while they wandered in the desert.[13] The reality was a bare desert but in my mind's eye the image was one of plenty.

I saw people waking to the most astonishing sight. The usual cloudless dawn sky heralding another merciless and hungry day has changed from blue to a shiny white haze. It is raining! But this is no ordinary rain, for the drops are fine and flaky and they rest upon the earth like frost. What strange portent is this? Another curse? Another blessing? Perhaps a heavy dew has fallen overnight. It takes but a few seconds to realize that it is manna falling from the sky and coating the ground in white and effulgent swathes. Manna! G-d has answered the hungry plea! Where once was endless sand and sparse desert grass, now lies pearl white manna sparkling like jewels in the morning light.

A jubilant cry rises up in unison as women and men, old and young, run through the bounty, followed by their shadows leaping in the rising sun. Stunned and dazed, people walk through the miracle harvest, some staring in curiosity, others in disbelief. Children shout in ecstasy and men crawl on all fours to gather the unheralded nourishment, their grumblings and calls for mutiny from the day before forgotten. Young and middle-aged mothers plunge their baskets deep and when these are brimming over, every possible container is used and filled to overflowing. Some women are panic-stricken and gather as much as they can in the folds of their robes, for this gift from G-d might disappear as quickly as it fell from heaven – there is no telling when it comes to G-d's bounty or his wrathful lessons because for some, it appears, there is no end to doubting.

In between the densely-packed tents, salivating children lick manna directly from the ground, their hands sticky and faces soft with wonder. The sounds of laughing and weeping, cries of joy and whisperings of reverence, fill the air, but soon only the hum of delight at the manna's varied tastes can be heard. The manna's delicious smell of honey, rich and sweet, has sent the people into a state of rapture.

Moses stands watching his delirious flock and after a time, for he knows the crippling power of excess, with his staff waving heavenward, he commands: "Do not take more than you need for one day!" Many are puzzled at this call for restraint but most are kneeling and bowing their heads to the ground in thankful supplication. Others raise their arms in praise and cast their eyes gratefully heavenwards.

Soon the scent of sweet cakes baking will silence every last soul.

I snapped out of my imagination and continued to explain to Rabia and Tolba that the lesson from Alush for the Israelites, and indeed for people for all times, is the recognition that sustenance comes entirely from G-d no matter what the circumstances.

"We live with this daily," he responded. "Allah provides for those who have faith in Him."

⊡ Learning to trust

I continued, "The challenge and lesson to be learned, both for them and for us, is to always remember that G-d gives us our food."

While in the desert the Israelites would receive food by miraculous means, however, when they were in the Promised Land they would have to use natural means of agriculture only. They had to learn to recognize G-d's role in providing food in all circumstances.[14]

It is easy for a person to believe that one's daily effort results in one's livelihood. G-d, however, wanted to teach the Israelites that their efforts only created the opportunity for sustenance, but it was ultimately in His control. This lesson was administered with the people receiving manna for only one day at a time. Any left over became inedible on the following day. Only the portion collected on Friday for the Sabbath remained fresh. The insight that they gained from this is that for the Sabbath G-d will provide independently of the person's efforts. This was proof that they should keep the Sabbath and not worry that its income would be forfeited.[15]

G-d was teaching the people to trust Him. Both poverty and wealth test us at many levels. Some examples are at a level of faith, endurance, contentment, honesty, generosity and integrity. Indeed, the manna had two opposite factors. It had every taste a person could desire, symbolic of abundance, richness and fullness.[16]

Jacobson explains also that another lesson from Alush, which means "power," is that "it symbolizes the stage in life when we rise to power – either at work or in another position of influence. Power is a double-edged sword, which can be used either toward achieving greatness or corruption." We have to meet the challenges morally.[17]

◄

To honor the receiving of manna, I asked my guides if we could have a meal at Alush. Rabia stopped the car so that we could have a mid-morning meal. He spread a multicolored mat on the stony ground beneath an Acacia tree, and brought out the paper bag we had packed with provisions.

"Here are the serviettes," he said, producing a roll of toilet paper.

I laughed. The remains of the flat bread which had been made the day before by Fteha were also unpacked and placed on a plate. Tolba unpacked a plastic washing bowl in which to prepare the salads: sliced green peppers, tomato and finely-diced cucumber. We also sliced some hard-boiled eggs, and had cream cheese and yogurt that Fteha had made from goats' milk. A packet of crisps and also halva that had been bought at Abu Zenema were opened as a special treat. The halva I imagined could symbolize the sweet white fluffy manna that tasted like wafers and honey.

Rabia carried a large container of drinking water out of the car and Tolba prepared some tea.

Before eating, I washed my hands with a little drinking water and said the customary blessing over bread. I felt privileged to say this grace before meals, and to eat with relish, experiencing renewed gratitude for my food. We enjoyed our delicious meal and used pieces of the flat bread – held in our fingers – to scoop food out of the communal bowls. Enjoying this sumptuous meal in the middle of a sea of sand certainly reinforced the teachings from Alush, as I recognized the truth that our sustenance comes from G-d. Yet we so easily take our daily food for granted. I resolved to be grateful for what I had to eat each day.

⊷

At this stage the Israelites had moved through the phase experienced by young adults.[18] They had begun to realize that if they worked on having a more positive attitude and took responsibility for their attitudes and actions, they could go through a self-transformation. They started to change pain and bitterness to a dimension of love. They realized that they could envision a future and learn to take proper action. They also improved in having faith. They realized that even if at first the situation appeared hopeless, they could muster inner, deep resources and create opportunities or even aim for greatness.

I also had to move through the phase which one could compare to that of young adults. I too realized that if I could be more positive, in so doing my despondency and feelings of stress could dissipate. I was going through a mini transformation, and could envision a better future of more balanced effort towards work and other activities in life. Even though it is a strain to earn a livelihood, bring up a family and deal with difficult relationships, I could act differently. I could work towards more balance in my life. I would have more faith that life would give me only as much as I could handle. I would need to find the proper means of achieving progress on each front.   ◄

As we prepared to leave, I saw that we had been picnicking close to a rocky mountain, which might have been home to a mountain lion or perhaps even a cheetah. I did not see any such animals but knew they had probably lived in this area in the past. I did not comment on this to my guides.

AMALEKITES WAR – REPHADIM   CAMP 11

The Israelites still had to go through the stage of adults[1] who are finding their way and struggling with the difficulties or challenges of life. They started out with doubt and apathy, cynicism and indifference. There was strife, useless competing with each other and even obsession with their desires or cravings. Many had acted in a rebellious way that led to harmful consequences for themselves and was undermining their destiny.

After the Israelites left Alush, they went on to camp at Rephadim.[2] The word *rephadim* means "weakness," "railing," or "baluster."[3] What would I find at this place, either in the environment or within myself? How would such a weakness manifest? The biblical text narrates that "[at] Rephadim, there was no water there for the people to drink."[4]

After our meal, Rabia, Tolba and I proceeded along Wadi Mukkatab, the "Valley of Inscriptions." Rocks in the wadi bore inscriptions re-sembling graffiti, dating back to the times of the Nabataeans. The in-scriptions we saw included a boat, human figures walking or mounted on camels or horses, animals such as camels, horses, gazelles, ibexes and bats. The engravings had a simple but strong sense of line, almost like gifted children's drawings. Numerous such inscriptions have been discovered. The Nabataeans were ancient traders of Aramaic or Arab descent, who transported goods from eastern and western areas during the years 37 CE to 100 CE. Their trade routes passed from Egypt through Petra, central Arabia, as far as the Euphrates in Babylonia. They maintained a line of fortresses and loosely-controlled trading posts which included oasis settlements. Eventually the Romans conquered the Nabataeans, and parts of their territory became integrated into the Roman Empire; other areas in Arabia were later abandoned.[5]

From Wadi Mukkatab we went to the next wadi, Wadi Ferrain, and then to the oasis of Ferrain. This oasis is widely accepted by archaeologists and biblical scholars as the camp of Rephadim. This route took us along a narrow valley running through the mountainous area that spreads over most of the southern Sinai Peninsula. This region cannot be crossed easily, and can only be traversed by following a convolution of narrow steep valleys. The route we took had the widest path, ranging from 0.25 to 1 kilometer wide. In ancient times, this route linked Egypt with countries east of the Sinai, including today's Saudi Arabia, Iraq, and Israel. The route constitutes a logical and direct path from west to east and was probably used by the Israelites in their Exodus.

As an environmentalist, I was fascinated by the landscape. The mountains in this region are mostly composed of hard granite and basalt, produced by volcanic activity in the distant past. The areas we had passed through until now had been composed of yellow sandstone and limestone, which is relatively soft, both of which are formed by layers of sedimentation deposited beneath the oceans millennia ago. The change in geology meant that we were no longer surrounded by soft yellow sand with yellow hills in the background, but steep jagged cliffs of grey and red.

The desert scrub that we had seen until now had included Camel Thorn trees, Tamarisks and various Goosefoot species (such as Hammada and Anabasis), and Bean Capers (such as Zygophyllum). However, nothing grew easily here and the mountain peaks were virtually bare. Extreme aridity and searing daytime temperatures, huge variation between nighttime and daytime temperatures, and the effects of desert winds make for an inhospitable habitat on the mountain slopes. Only small shrub species such as Primula boveana grow here. Of the entire Sinai, this area shows the greatest poverty of species.

As we journeyed on, the mountains became steeper and the cliffs

The road which runs between high southern Sinai mountain ranges in Wadi Ferrain.
It leads to the oasis of Ferrain, identified as the Israelite camp of Rephadim. |
M Rawicz Trip Photo

closer to the road, until we were moving through a narrow ravine. For about four kilometers the route was extremely narrow and winding and we made slow progress because the road made numerous sharp zigzags. Deep shadow alternated with bright sunlight. Then the valley began to widen and eventually we were travelling through the slightly wider flood plain of an ancient river that had cut though the rocks to form this valley. The ground was hard and stony. However, at last we saw some sign of human habitation. Homesteads with small vegetable gardens dotted the wide plain, evidence of the fertile soil commonly found in such valleys. Some of these settlements looked as old as the hills. The further we went, the larger the settlements became. At first we had seen perhaps three or four homes in each place, but now each cluster included seven or eight houses. I felt that we were approaching somewhere special, a place of significance. The mountains were beautiful.

Rabia steered around a sharp curve on the way to an oasis. He pointed to a rock at the side of the road, and said, "This is the rock that we Bedouin call Hesi-el-Khattatin, meaning 'Spring Hidden by the

Scribes.' Our tradition teaches that G-d told Moses to strike this rock to give water to the people."

The Bible recounts the story of the Israelites' complaints about a lack of water at Rephadim.[6] They said that Moses had brought them out of Egypt only to kill them and their children and animals through thirst. Moses asked the people not to test G-d, but he also cried out to G-d, saying, "What shall I do unto this people? They are almost ready to stone me." G-d told Moses to go to the river and to strike the rock there with his staff, "and there shall come water out of it, that the people may drink." Moses did so, and called the place *Massah and Meribah*, after the people's questioning of G-d. *Massah* means "tempting" or "proving" and *meribah* means "chiding" or "striving." These names would forever be a symbol reminding us of the wayward attitude of the Israelites.[7]

Rabia stopped the car so that I could explore the rock in delight. It is a huge square rock under the north side of Wadi Ferrain. The Bedouin have a tradition that when they pass it they throw stones at it, to commemorate its sanctity. Great piles of stones have accumulated over the thousands of years.

This incident had been the first of its kind in producing water from a rock. A second, similar instance happened much later in the Exodus, when G-d told Moses to speak to the rock but instead Moses struck it; for this, G-d forbade him to enter the Promised Land.

After this exciting stop, we continued on our way and reached the outskirts of the Ferrain oasis with its ancient village and tel. This site had been settled by the Nabataeans around the year 37 CE. The village included the remains of the foundations of approximately ten houses, which evidently had low doorways to provide some protection against the extreme heat and cold. We also saw the remains of storerooms and graves. Painted ceramic debris from the early Bronze and Iron Ages have been found at Ferrain, and we saw some of the pottery shards. There were also Roman-Byzantine, early Arab, Hellenistic period, and Persian shards. There were even shards from the kingdom of Judah belonging to Iron Age II, and from the period of the kings of Judah during the time of the First Temple.[8]

We continued by car until we reached the center of the flourishing village at the oasis. This site had been the biblical camp of Rephadim, where the Israelites were attacked by the Amalekites. The Bible narrates that the Amalekites attacked the Israelites from the rear, pouncing on the weakest and most exhausted members of the clan. Paradoxically,

As we approached the oasis of Ferrain there were hundreds of trees along the road and people from the local village were walking on the road. | M Rawicz Trip Photo

G-d had led the Israelites to set up their camp at Rephadim despite the danger.[9]

The archaeologist David Rohl believes that during this era, thousands of Amalekites were migrating through the Sinai, heading in the opposite direction to the Israelites. The Amalek tribe hailed from the southern Negev and northern Arabia; they were travelling to the Nile Valley as refugees from famine and in the hope of gaining Egyptian riches. They had heard that the land of pharaohs had been crippled by disastrous plagues and that Egypt was now undefended because its army had drowned in the Red Sea. This was recorded in the writings of the Egyptian priest Manetho, and was quoted by Josephus the famous Jewish historian of the First Century, CE.[10]

After the initial attack, Moses said to Joshua, "Choose men and go out and fight with Amalek. Tomorrow I will stand on the top of the hill with the staff of G-d in my hand." Once again, Moses' staff became the sign of G-d's authority. The following day, Moses, Aaron and Hur climbed to the top of the hill. "And Joshua mowed down Amalek and his people with the edge of the sword."[11] According to tradition, Joshua defeated the Amalekites in Wadi Ferrain. Moses and Aaron supported Joshua's group with prayers while they viewed the fighting from the mountain.

From where I stood, I could visualize the battle . . .

At first they come as marauders preying on the weak and exhausted who straggle behind the multitude – the women and children and the old and infirm at the back of the column. And then the sun goes dark for an instant as glistening arrows shower down and the screaming begins. The people are unprepared for war, let alone this cowardly attack, this sniping against the defenseless ones. It is clear the Amalekites have but one purpose – total extermination.

And then they charge full force, led by the thundering of camels at full gallop. The rugged horde of Amalekites, those descendants of Esau, is upon the Israelites now, baying for blood. Their terrifying yells rip across the plain of Rephadim and echo off the mountains under the dark sky. People scatter, trying to find shelter behind bushes, rocks and mounds but there is scant protection here and soon the bodies begin to pile up. Animals run amok and howl in panic for they too are falling to the rain of arrows. With spears pointing heavenward, the Amalekites launch their bloody assault. As if resigned to their fate, many of the Israelites stand praying or fall on their faces begging for mercy from G-d because resistance seems futile – they have never fought a battle without G-d's help before; they did not come here seeking war.

Then Moses, standing above the battleground with Aaron and Hur by his side, holds his hands high and the almost defenseless Israelite men begin to retaliate, to fight for their lives. Echoing against the surrounding mountains, the clash of the battle and the wailing of the dying is amplified, but with their leader's arms stretching up towards the heavens, the Israelites begin to gain courage and courage fuels strength. The tribal leaders form into fighting groups. Fires are breaking out everywhere as the Amalekites hurl burning wood in their unspeakable cruelty, but the Israelites have rallied now under the outspread arms of their leader. He stands high on the hill and they know G-d is speaking through him. They have not been deserted.

As the long hours pass, Moses becomes weary and his heavy arms begin to droop down. With this, the tide turns again and the Amalekites regain advantage, ever closer to the final obliteration. It is then that Aaron and Hur find a rock for Moses to rest on while these two attendants, one on each side, hold the great leader's arms upright and they remain so until the going down of the sun, until the Israelites have finally vanquished the Amalekite army.

Then G-d's booming command rings out. "I will utterly blot out the memory of Amalek from under heaven[12] . . . I will have war with Amalek from generation to generation."[13]

Remembering these words as I stood rooted at the scene of the battle, sent shivers down my spine. My people are still at war with forces that would obliterate us.

The attack at Rephadim left the Israelites stunned and apprehensive. This was the first time they had been attacked since leaving Egypt. The biblical narrative states that "G-d said to Moses, write this for a memorial in a document, and rehearse it in the ears of Joshua, that I will utterly blot out the remembering of Amalek from under the heavens . . . And Moses built an altar and called the name of it El-nissi [G-d is my banner] and he said, 'Truly with a hand to the throne of G-d I swear, G-d will have war with Amalek from generation to generation.'"[14]

As I looked around the site, Rabia pointed to a mountain and said:

"There's Gabal-al-Tahona. That is the mountain where Musa held up his hands so that the Israelites would win the battle. There's a shrine to Moses at the top of it."

The mountain was high, but looked possible to climb. Rabia told me that from the summit I would be able to look down over the entire wadi, so I decided to give it a try and we began the ascent using an ancient path. The climb was arduous. We passed a church built in the fourth century to commemorate the battle, and when we finally arrived at the top I was rewarded by the sight of the memorial shrine to Moses. Pilgrims regularly visit this site. Close by stood an ancient cross and the ruins of a small church, also built in the fourth century.

From this vantage point I could see the two mountains of Gabal-al-Banat and Gabal Sirbal, between which Wadi Ferrain lies. I could also see the Greek Orthodox Monastery of Moses, a community within the oasis that has existed since the second century. Their principle of caring for other people led its religious inhabitants to serve the local population for no return, a practice that has been maintained for centuries. I also saw the ruins of several ancient churches, some dating back to the early Christian era. These were established as a religious center for monks and pilgrims in Ferrain. Many of these spiritual people were travelling to Mount Sinai and St. Catherine's Monastery, further east.

⤷   Feeling vulnerable – handling apathy

I felt a bit like a pilgrim myself. I sat down to contemplate the shrine.

Rephadim means weakness. The type of weakness referred to can occur when, as adults, we have to deal with the demands of our lives. We may not always know exactly what we are meant to be doing and can become overwhelmed. This weakness could mean losing sight of our goals, losing direction, becoming vulnerable through a lack of spiritual commitment – which allows the inner enemy to wage war against us. The enemy is our own indifference and irrationality, and the battle is lost when we become indifferent or cynical towards life.[15]

At Rephadim the Israelites went through a serious dilemma in their belief, acceptance and confidence in G-d. They were not convinced that G-d was looking after them. There was a disconnect between what they thought they ought to believe and what they were experiencing. They were seriously questioning whether G-d was supporting and looking after them. The strength and support that comes from being certain that G-d is with one can be weakened as it must have been for the Israelites. A person is then more spiritually vulnerable and exposed to indifference in following G-d's leadership, as Jacobson maintains.[16]

It is recorded in the Bible that Moses therefore named this camp "the place of challenge and strife" and that the Amalekite army arrived and attacked Israel in Rephadim."[17] Amalek represents an unfounded, senseless indifference in that one does not contest the truth but just ignores it.[18]

An "Amalek" state of mind is thus, the waning of spiritual responsibility and being susceptible to the formidable influences of uncertainty and unresponsiveness. This is a negative core state of mind that we are, therefore, urged to guard against during our lives.

The effect of the battle with Amalek was that the Israelites were in doubt and weakened, which caused strife amongst them. They had to learn that it can be useless to compete with others and to create strife. They learned to call forth reserves of confidence in G-d's support and access some inner harmony.

I resolved not to become vulnerable to doubt and apathy, but to maintain my spiritual commitment and to strengthen my awareness of G-d's presence in my life. This kind of awareness, I resolved, needed to be nurtured every day. I too gained some inner harmony through my contact with the openhearted Bedouin. My rough edge of competitiveness was beginning to wear down. ◼

After we descended Gabal-al-Tahona, we returned to the car and Rabia drove us towards the heart of the Ferrain oasis. We passed a small cemetery on the way. Hundreds of palm trees stretched from the side of the road to the foot of the mountains, with the trees ranging in height from five to fifteen meters. I was surprised to find that the road running through the center of the oasis village was tarred.

"It's because so many people use this road," Rabia explained.

We arrived at another Bedouin restaurant and vegetable garden, something like a tea-garden to entertain visitors in the desert. I recalled that Abraham had also hosted guests during his desert sojourn. At the entrance we were met by a short barefooted Bedouin man dressed in a long royal-blue desert robe that reached to his ankles. He wore a white *kaffiya* on his head, wrapped in the Muslim style. His skin was a ruddy brown and his bushy hair was black, as were his moustache and beard, and his friendly dark eyes glittered with energy. His name was Mohamed and he invited us to view the garden while he organized our meal. In the garden, we found a three-sided hut made entirely of palm branches, which reminded me of the *sukkah* huts that Jews build every year for the Festival of Tabernacles. The palm leaves had dried out and become brown. The walls were built of upright palm branches and the roof consisted of palm leaves thrown over a wooden lattice. The hut looked cool and inviting, and blended in perfectly with the surroundings.

At the back of the hut, in deep shade, were pottery vessels filled with water. The containers were oval, with a narrow top and bottom and a wider middle; the top was open and the containers were stored upright in a metal tripod. They were covered in dark cloth or skins to keep the contents cool. I was graciously given some of the cool delicious contents.

A Bedouin restaurant and vegetable garden, similar to a tea-garden, was a refreshing sight in the desert. | *M Rawicz Trip Photo*

Rabia and Tolba walked ahead as we entered an enclosure containing a few goats. A woman wearing a dark brown robe and black scarf, with a white upper garment, smiled at us. Around her were a dozen white and black goats, eating and bleating and milling around. The path led through a garden gate into a beautiful herb garden. The soil here was a yellow-grey color and the small patch of land had been divided into squares, with different vegetables and herbs growing in each section. The squares were bordered by berms of sand to control the flow of water. Most of the herbs were small, but I noticed some larger bushes of red or green.

Mohamed arrived to proudly show me around his herb garden.

"This is *Gaisoom,* Lavender Cotton, used to help if a person has headaches, colds and low blood sugar. This plant is *Sheeh,* Wormwood and *Buaytharaan,* Judean Wormwood, good for stomach problems, to treat stomach worms and parasites. Here you see *Rubayaan,* Wild Chamomile, good to help a person to relax. We use this one here, *Nihaida,* to heal the kidneys."

A palm leaf hut exactly like the sukkah that Jews build for the holiday of Sukkot, with pottery vessels that contain cool water. | *M Rawicz Trip Photo*

"The plants are beautiful," I said. "I can see that you really care for them."

"Please, follow me to the vegetable area."

We walked on until Mohamed stopped to point out his favorites.

"Here you can see our young watermelons, tomatoes, and chili peppers. We also grow garlic, olives and nuts, and of course some fruit."

Rabia went to socialize with his friends, and I asked Mohamed about his family, who were clearly industrious and dedicated. As we left the garden, three Bedouin greeted us with nods of delight. A woman was carrying a basket to a man who was squatting to weed the vegetable patch.

"She's come to fetch vegetables to make the meal," Mohamed told me.

The woman was dressed in a light-blue robe with a black floral pattern, and a black scarf. I was wearing a green-and-black kaftan with a dark green scarf over my head. I was pleased at how easy it was to blend in with the locals.

Rephadim oasis with its beautiful herb garden and date palms, where we bought some greens for our trip. Rephadim is where the ancient Israelites were attacked by the Amalekites. | M Rawicz Trip Photo

"We also grow corn, barley, wheat and tamarind," Mohamed said. "But really our main crop is dates."

He showed me around the border of his garden. The fence was made of palm leaves with an occasional palm stump supporting them. At the very back of the plot were the people's living quarters, square stone huts that blended in with the yellow sand. A large tree opposite the huts acted as a handy place to hang things: blankets and brown striped bags for carrying provisions.

"It's so lush and green in your garden," I said. "It's a lovely sight after having seen the desert for a few days."

Mohamed led me to an extremely deep well. "The sides are made of clay," he said. "We still use a bucket to get the water out, but as soon as I have more money I will buy a pump from Cairo."

The late afternoon meal was ready. I was invited to sit with Mohamed and his companions, but a slight distance away because Bedouin men and women do not sit together while eating. Mohamed's warm hospitality was typical of the Bedouin I had met. We chatted, and the conversation turned to my "Hajj Musa."

"How long have your been travelling?" he asked.

"Today is day fifteen," I said.

Mohamed and his companions asked questions about what I had seen and experienced. While we spoke, I thoroughly enjoyed the meal, which included dates, salad (from the garden), Bedouin tea, freshly made bread, and potato crisps bought as a treat for visitors. As I sat and ate, the Jewish Passover feast came to mind. I was eating herbs, both bitter and sweet, and bread that was similar to the unleavened Passover *Matzah*. We were sitting on the ground and I was reclining; one of the four questions traditionally asked at the *Seder* (the Passover meal) discusses reclining. I dipped the herbs into salted water, recalling yet another aspect of the *Seder*. However, to be doing all this at a real oasis on the Exodus route was an amazing experience. I explained this to my Bedouin acquaintances, who listened with great curiosity.

Mohamed asked, "So, how has this trip been for you so far?"

"Since I left the Nile Delta," I replied, "I've been observing how people live. It's given me a new insight into the desert and the meaning of each camp the Israelites stopped at. Also, I'm starting to feel very independent. I guess my ancestors felt the same sort of freedom. You know, my friends and family wondered if I was mad – to make a trip like this alone. But it's helped me find my inner strength. I'm gaining more serenity with each new day, and I don't feel weak or vulnerable out here in the desert like I thought I would. And the kindnesses of people like you have made me feel that there are strangers who can be trusted . . . and so can the desert itself!"

He chuckled and said, "Yes people from the city are afraid of this desert. But you must tell them about it when you return home."

"Observing how your people live has made me appreciate everything G-d gives us," I added. "It's G-d who gives us shelter and food and rejuvenates us, even when we are far from the usual comforts. My experience of the desert has given me an idea of what the Israelites went through, and has made me realize how foolish it is to worship idols such as unnecessary material things."

"Yes, that's how we see life too," said Mohamed.

"My understanding of the Bible stories has grown so much," I said. "And I've learned something about inner healing, too. I've seen that people from all walks of life can become stronger as a result of pain and

The meal that I ate, which reminded me of the Passover feast when we eat bitter and sweet herbs and Matzah. | M Rawicz Trip Photo

sorrow. It's made me more determined to become a better person. Even in the short time that I've been here, something inside me has started to heal."

Mohamed seemed pleased at what I had told him. He called the rest of his family to come and meet me, including the women who tended the garden. Rabia spoke to them in Arabic, and I was starting to recognize a few phrases. Arabic and Hebrew share some similarity in certain words and expressions.

Mohamed pointed in the direction of the mountain I had climbed.

He said, "That mountain is very important because of the miracle G-d performed when Moses was there. We Bedouin walk to the top on special days in honor of that miracle. Moses is a big part of our tradition, and we feel at home with the stories about him because we still live where he walked."

One of the other men told me, "At this oasis, we're a mixed group of Bedouin people from a few Sinai tribes. Here we have people from the tribes of Uzbeliya, Muszeina, Sawalha, Huwaitat, Oualed, Saied and Alleget, as well as some Egyptians who came to live with us. In other parts of the Sinai, each tribe sticks to its own land."

I chatted with the wonderful Bedouin who ran the restaurant and tea-garden. |
M Rawicz Trip Photo

By the end of our visit, I had bonded in a special way with these people. I spent a short time with the wives: Namar, Baseema and Ghazal. I
noticed that the women's skin was rough and dry, so I rubbed some of
my hand cream onto each of their hands, which was a treat for them –
and another reminder for me not to take the small comforts of life for
granted. I also noticed that a woman called Jabirah had a bad cut on her
toe, which was slightly infected. I dug out my medical kit to clean and
disinfect the wound and bind it with a dressing.

I had found no physical evidence of railings or balusters at this camp,
but the emotional, practical and spiritual meanings associated with
Rephadim, such as not becoming vulnerable to attack from the forces
of doubt and apathy, had made an impression on me. As we left the
village, I noted the following in my log book: "Rephadim, the first relic
of an ancient Nabataean settlement, still has relatively well-preserved
remains and an underground water supply. The Israelites had left the
Egyptian temples, cities, and all else behind but were still on a main
desert 'highway' crossing the Sinai, which had been used by many peo-

Rabia (left) introduced me to the Bedouins from the oasis and I bonded with them in a special way. | M Rawicz Trip Photo

ple including Egypt's enemies, such as the Amalekites. This was one of four main west–easts Sinai routes used very commonly, including by the powerful Nabataean traders."

We travelled onwards to the next camp in silence, as I contemplated what I had seen.

MOONLIGHT TREK UP MOUNT SINAI   CAMP 12

"They journeyed from Rephadim and they encamped in the Wilderness of Sinai."[1]

I was shocked to learn that *Sinai* comes from the Hebrew word *sin-ah*, meaning "hatred."[2] I had always simply thought of the Sinai Desert as the place where Mount Sinai stood, where the Ten Commandments had been given. I was greatly puzzled as to what I might find at this camp.

The location of Mount Sinai is of tremendous interest and has been researched for centuries by archaeologists and travellers, and various scholars have proposed different locations without consensus being

A magnificent view with typical Acacia trees on the route between the Dopkah camp and the Sinai encampment location. | M Rawicz Trip Photo

reached. Some people believe the exact site will never be known and prefer a mythological interpretation of the biblical narrative. The proposals of specific locations depend on the assumed Exodus route. Did the Israelites take the course I had been following, or did they move through northern Sinai above the Gebel-el-Tit mountainous divide?

Archaeologists and secular scholars have also not reached consensus on the likely timing of the Exodus. Many think it never occurred. Most scholars agree that it took place during the Late Bronze or First Iron Age, but some cite a lack of physical evidence that the journey occurred at all. Scholars also differ in their opinions on how many kilometers were covered in a given day. Several people have proposed as little as ten kilometers, while others say as many as thirty or forty kilometers per day. These estimates are generally based on observations of the movements of Bedouin people grazing their herds. The speed made by the Israelites would not have, under normal circumstances, exceeded the pace at which herds can be driven in a day without exhaustion and death.[3]

Of the fifteen researchers who have studied the location of Mount Sinai, three have proposed Gebel Musa, eight have suggested sites close to Gebel Musa, three believe it was in Jordan, another three think it was in northern Sinai, and one believes it was in Saudi Arabia. I was following the route detailed in a book recognized as a Jewish biblical text,[4] which indicated that Gebel Musa might be the correct mountain. I therefore chose to go to the famous St. Catherine's monastery which is located at the base of Gebel Musa.

I started to talk to Rabia about this as we camped on the sand.

"This is a big subject, let's make some tea and sit and talk about it," he suggested. So we camped on the sand and conversed.

I told him what I had learned when I was researching this Exodus route. There are a few route options. The Northern Sinai possible route crosses through completely barren flat land, but has two mountains as likely choices for Mount Sinai. The nineteenth-century archaeologist Jarvis[5] said that it was Gebel Hallal, and another scholar said it was at Gebel Sin Bishr. Not many other scholars agree with the route nor the mountains.

I had read the opinions of many archaeologists. The archaeologist Burckhardt,[6] from the eighteenth century, suggested the southern route which has Gebel Serbal and nearby Gebel Musa. Sir William Flinders Petrie[7] in the early nineteenth century also thought that Gebel Serbal was Mount Sinai. Mattfeld y de la Torre[8] of the twentieth century said that Gebel Saniya near Rabia's home at Serabitel-Kadim was the right one. His view was based on his archaeological findings from the Late Bronze Age. He identified those stone carvings on two tablets similar to the ones bearing the Ten Commandments. Aharoni,[9] an early nineteenth-century archaeologist, said that Mount Paran or Mount Horeb was the right mountain. This is found somewhere in the southern part of Sinai. They are both close to Gebel Musa. It is interesting that a very early pilgrim nun from the sixth century, Egeria,[10] wrote in her travel diary that Mount Sinai was Gebel Aribeh. This mountain is east-northeast of Gebel Musa. Her opinion was backed by Palmer, a twentieth-century scholar, because this mountain had a larger plain at its base on which the Israelites could camp.[11] Gebel Musa itself was preferred by Robinson, the admired eighteenth-century archaeologist.[12] His views were supported by Kenneth A. Kitchen,[13] the famous twentieth-century archaeologist. They both agreed that Gebel Musa had a huge plain beneath it on which the Israelites could have camped.

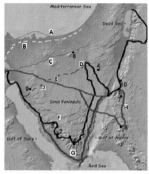

Options for Mount Sinai
1. Gebel Musa
2. Gebel Serbal
3. Gebel Sinya
A Mediterranean Sea Islands   4. Har Karkom
B Philistines   5. Jebel-Al-Lawz
C Way of Shur   6. Gebel Hallal
D Kadesh Barnea Section   7. Mount Zibbatuf
E Way of Hajj   8. Mount Paran or Mount Horeb
F Traditional route – St. Catherine's   9. Gebel Sin Bishr
G Sharm-El-Sheik   10. Gebel Al Medhbah
H Saudia Arabia   11. Gebel Aribeh

Alternative Exodus routes and options for Mount Sinai posited by various scholars. (The brown route is the one taken in this book.) | http://www.biblicalzionist.com/RedSea.htm adapted by M Rawicz

An Israeli archaeologist Anati claimed that Mount Sinai is Har Karkom in the southern Israeli Negev desert. He found rocks bearing carved images of a snake like the one Moses's rod became, a rock with carvings of the Ten Commandment tablets, and much more. I will be seeing that when I progress further on this journey into Israel.[14]

Actually, there are more opinions that Mount Sinai is in Jordan but they are not well supported. In the eighteenth century, researchers Beke[15] and Lucas[16] designated a mountain near the Gulf of Aqaba. Another archaeologist, Nielsen,[17] from the nineteenth century, believes it to be Mount Zibb'atuf in lower Jordan (just south of Petra). A mountain called Gebel al Medhbah has also been a candidate. I will also be seeing these when I progress further on this journey into Jordan.

There has been a lot of information spread by two archaeologists, Cornuke and Halbrook.[18] They say Mount Sinai is Jebel-al-Lawz in northwestern Saudi Arabia (north of Mecca). They found a rock carving of a golden calf, twelve altars for the twelve tribes, and more. I have heard a lot of criticism about this, as the location is too far for the Israelites to have gone in seven weeks. I would love to see the site but unfortunately it is strictly off limits. Anyway, I am not allowed to get a visa into Saudi Arabia, as I am not a Muslim and am not doing official business there either. This will be the only option that I won't be visiting.

Rabia said to me, "Bedouins believe that the Exodus was on a southern route, the one we are on now, in this valley. The mountains that people have said may be Mount Sinai are Gebel Musa, Gebel Sirbal,

Gebal Siniya and Gebel Aribeh. I will take you to see each of them as they are not far apart and close to the way we are going.

These are all on this southern route but we Bedouins say that Mount Sinai is Gebel Musa, the mountain to which I want to go now. I don't know the details like you but we see thousands of people over the years and they say that Gebel Musa is the right one. You can talk to my friend Gebeli whose tribe has lived there for centuries. I don't know about the other mountains, only about some in the Sinai.

We Bedouin have grown up knowing this to be an important place. We know its history. Earlier it was called Mount Horeb and then it was called Gebel Musa, which means 'mountain of Moses.' At the bottom of the mountain is the flat area called Plains of Melga and Raha. Close by is the town of Saint Catherine. The wadi in this area is called Wadi Shoeib, meaning 'the valley of Horeb.' It's also known as Wadi Jethro, after Moses's father-in-law. When we get there, you'll see a small hill with a little prayer room built on it, called the Chapel of the Golden Calf."

We continued driving away from Rephadim through a long valley with yellow sands towards Gebel Musa. We saw whirlwinds and dust clouds, and camels roaming freely in the desert to graze while their owners were busy elsewhere. The road was tarred because of the heavy tourist traffic travelling to the possible location of Mount Sinai and St. Catherine's monastery. On the way, we stopped to greet some friends of Rabia's. The family lived in a small yellow hut with an open patio, where several men and women were sitting when we arrived. As is the custom, a woman immediately offered us tea and the host invited us to sit on cushions around a fire, above which was perched the kettle. He poured a little tea into each glass and then tossed it out, warming the glasses before filling them carefully with piping-hot tea. With a flourish, he nodded and said a blessing over the tea and we then sipped it. The liquid was extremely sweet. Because I was a guest, in this instance I was allowed to sit with the men. The friendliness and warmth of the people was by now a familiar experience. After my first cup of tea, I slipped out to join the women in another room. I chatted to a woman called Alhena, who could understand a bit of English. After half an hour or so, we set off again. By now I was filled with excitement at what I might find at the alleged site of Mount Sinai.

Dusk was approaching, and the desert grew hazy. We continued in silence and arrived at the campsite in the dark. The night was already cold and I needed a hot meal, so Rabia went to a small shop and bought some frozen fish, pumpkin, potatoes, onions and carrots. I made a fish barbeque and a thick vegetable stew over a gas stove provided for campers. All the other campers had gathered in a long hall around a central table and sang songs while they ate. They clapped their hands and were clearly enjoying themselves; most of them were young people with lots of energy. The evening was lively. It was my first encounter with tourists in the Sinai.

Eventually, we retired for the night, having arranged to meet at 2 o'clock to start the journey up Mount Sinai. It is tradition to set out for Mount Sinai three hours before dawn so as to enjoy the spectacular view of first light from the summit. I overslept, and at 3 o'clock Rabia thumped on my door and called out, "It's time to go!"

CLIMBING MOUNT SINAI

I dressed hurriedly in warm clothes. I had been advised to take a torch and wear hiking boots and warm garments, because the temperature at the summit falls sharply and often a freezing wind blows. I pulled on a thermal vest and long thermal underpants, a thick pair of warm slacks and a long-sleeved top, a winter tracksuit and a long heavy kaftan. After adding a sturdy pair of gloves, a balaclava, warm socks and boots, I was ready.

Rabia led me outside the camp, where three camels were waiting. Two Bedouin men would accompany me. Gebeli was about 23 years old and was wearing a red-and-white *keffiyeh* with the traditional black *agal* (rope circlet) and a white loose robe. The second guide was his friend Butrus.

We rode by camel for about half an hour before arriving at the foot of the mountain. Gebeli had worked with tourists and spoke English very well. On the way we chatted.

Gebeli told me, "I am from the Gebeliya tribe, which means mountaineers, because we live in these high mountains of St. Catherine's. Our ancestors were brought from Eastern Europe, and we think they were descendants of either Bosnian or Wallachian serfs. Or we might be descended from a group of slaves that were brought here by a ruler called Justinian about fifteen hundred years ago, to build and serve St. Catherine's monastery. Our ancestors converted to Islam and also became nomads. We still serve the monastery and make a living by taking visitors up this mountain."[19]

Dusk at the base of Gebel Musa, that many people believe is Mount Sinai. |
M Rawicz Trip Photo

"I've read a bit about St. Catherine's monastery," I ventured, "For many hundreds of years religious people have lived at the foot of Gebel Musa mountain. Early Christian pilgrims apparently visited the area and stayed to form communities of monks who built the monastery in the sixth century. In 330 CE, Helena of Constantine built a small church and the community grew over the centuries. In the Byzantine era they built the monastery, which still stands today. The monks welcomed Muslims and even built a mosque in the monastery. Bedouins respected this special religious community.[20] This monastery is a great example of tolerance between Christians and Muslims."

Gebeli added, "At some stage we local Bedouins were given gardens where we could grow food. Many of us make a living from this, but others do tourism work here and at coastal towns in the Sinai. We help tourists who come here. We have camels, and we get good money for letting people ride on them. We've been able to survive here for centuries because of this."

The first part of the ascent of Gebel Musa can be made by one of two routes. We were ascending by camel on the Route of the Pasha. Some people walk the entire way up, but I decided that was an option best left to younger people – not a city woman in her mid-fifties. It was pitch dark and totally silent, and thousands of stars were visible. At first I had to concentrate on sitting correctly on the camel as we climbed the slope, but once I was accustomed to the rhythmic movement, my mind turned to the reason I was going up this mountain.

We learn in the Bible that G-d told Moses that He would speak to the Israelites from out of a dense cloud. Through Moses, G-d told the people to sanctify themselves and wash their clothes. On the third day after these instructions, Moses led the people out of the camp to meet with G-d,[21] whose presence was marked by thunder and lightning and a cloud on the mountain.[22] G-d spoke with a voice so loud that the people were in awe. Moses then climbed the mountain and G-d instructed him what to "tell the children of Israel."[23] Moses remained on the summit for forty days[24] while the Divine presence dwelled at Mount Sinai.[25] This was the momentous event at which G-d gave Moses the Ten Commandments to convey to the Israelites, describing the spiritual laws they were to follow.[26]

I was inspired to think that I might actually be ascending the same mountain myself. I sat quietly on the camel and peered into the darkness or stared up at the stars as we made our way slowly towards the halfway mark. This became another highlight of my trip, and unexpectedly I found myself receiving a profound new insight into my life. I was born a twin, but sadly my sister died tragically when we were twenty years old. The insight that now came to me was that I had been born with a twin because my soul had needed her help during childhood and the early years of adulthood. Once she had completed her task of guiding me through these challenging years, her own soul was called back.

I had been living with a suppressed sadness – unconsciously – for more than thirty years, feeling bereft because of the loss of my twin. During the slow journey up Gebel Musa I gained the insight that she had been here only to assist me for a while but had another destiny. I resolved to truly accept her departure, and to overcome my sadness. It was the beginning of a phase of rehabilitation that made me happier. I have since regarded the insight as a precious gift from G-d. The night wore on in silence.

In the dim light I saw an amphitheatre that is believed to have been the stopping point for the seventy wise men who accompanied Moses part of the way, but then had to halt because they were not allowed to enter the presence of G-d.[27] Two chapels have been built in this amphitheatre, one dedicated to Moses and the other to the prophet Elijah. Additional minor chapels were also vaguely visible.

After travelling for about an hour and a half, we reached the intersection with the second route and the starting point of the final ascent. The summit was just 700 steps away and from here on I would have to walk. The pathway up the rest of the mountain was steep and steps had been hewn into the stone to assist climbers. I was one of many people making the ascent on this particular morning. Each person carried a paraffin torch, forming a beautiful row of lights winding up the slope in the dark.

Gebeli and I chatted again. I found him easy-going and modest, with an ability to relate to others in a charming, cheerful way. As if he was my guardian, he accompanied and helped me throughout the hike. Other Bedouin men from his tribe were skillfully guiding other people. Gebeli would listen to my breathing and watch my body language to judge when to slow down, stop, or rest, and to make sure that I was not taking too much strain.

The slope became steeper near the summit and our pace dropped as my breathing became heavy. I had to draw on all my inner resources to keep going. Now and then I glanced at the sheer cliffs beside the path, and their size seemed to reinforce the immensity of the task. By now it was about four-thirty in the morning. My companion was tireless and kept me distracted through conversation.

"We love our camels," he said. "Mine is my best possession." A few minutes later he told me, "My tribe lives in the desert and we're attached to our land, but we guide visitors who come from all over the world."

Perhaps this explained his open-minded approach to life. Eventually, to my great relief, we reached the summit. It was about five o'clock and was still dark, but I could see that many had arrived ahead of us. Gebeli took me to a small flat area where members of his tribe had set up a stone hut to sell drinks, snacks and loan piles of camel-hair blankets. My guide opened a blanket and spread it out on a rock so that I could lie down and snooze, and then he covered me with a second blanket. As I had been warned, it was freezing at this altitude and the chill bit to the bone despite many layers of warm clothing.

During the next hour, hundreds of people arrived at the summit until a vast number had gathered. People were waiting, sitting or standing around.

I was confronted with the buzz of connection in many languages. To add to the excitement were beating drummers and the hum of song, prayers of praise, and horn blasts wafting on the air.

African men donning colorful striped red, purple and orange kaftans were expressing their joy in euphonious harmony. The delighted women wore bulky bright multicolored floral African headdresses and swayed while waving their arms in flowing synchronization. A group from Nigeria were soulfully blowing a ram's horn. Short Japanese men in dark grey kimonos were waving white and red flags in celebration and gleefully chanting. The soulful moans of animal horns added to the cacophony. A group of Koreans sat silently in meditative contemplation. Two Brazilian girls were braving the chill with heart-felt warmth. The silent eternal mountains witnessed the expectant crowds.

I chatted with a Russian lady called Mayitshka, who gave me some vodka that warmed me up a little. There were South Americans, Israelis, Americans and Australians, but I appeared to be the only South African. Virtually every European country was represented, including Russia and Britain.

Slowly streaks of light appeared. We stared at the gentle brilliant early dawn colors. All noise died down to an awed silence. It was as if new life was being born.

Gebel Musa is a major pilgrimage destination for people from all over the world, who climb the mountain to watch the sun rise over the Sinai Mountains. The place is a symbol of hope and worship of G-d, where people of the Abrahamic religions contemplate the Messiah's arrival.

I was profoundly moved to think that this might have been the place where G-d's presence descended and G-d spoke to Moses. I imagined Moses staying on this mountain for forty days and nights. But I was bothered that the encampment in the Sinai Desert below meant "place of hatred." Who had done the hating, and what had they hated? I had once read that after the Israelites received the Ten Commandments, people from the other nations became jealous of their relationship with the Divine and began to hate them. My sadness at such hatred was softened by knowing that many of the main world religions subsequently accepted the five Books of Moses as part of their traditions and have their own special relationship with the Divine.

I looked around as the dawn broke, to see if there was any other

Streaks of light appeared at sunrise over Gebel Musa as people stood in awed silence. | M Rawicz Trip Photo

evidence of Moses having been here. All I could see was the magnificent beauty of Mount Sinai; thankfully, the hatred seemed to have diminished in the sands of time. The bonds between Christians, Jews, Muslims and other people at this place attested to the greater unity among all humankind.

As the sun rose, it cast streaks of color over the mountaintops and the dark sky took on hues of red, pink, lavender and gold. The light struck the red granite peaks all around us and set the mountains ablaze with color – a truly awesome sight. We could see as far as Eilat in Israel. People spontaneously burst into song and started playing the musical instruments they had brought with them, giving rise to a great celebratory cacophony. The unity between these many diverse strangers from all over the world was amazing. A feeling of hopeful expectation and joy arose as we celebrated the revelation of the Ten Commandments and the Bible, and acknowledged our Creator with renewed desire to serve Him. It was a completely unexpected experience. I wondered whether the entire world might become like this in time. Would people put aside their differences and focus on their common humanity, and let love prevail? I was inspired to recite the Shema prayer of Unity. I learned

Strangers from all over the world celebrated, in unity, the revelation of the Ten Commandments and the Bible, as light struck the red granite peaks all around us. | *M Rawicz Trip Photo*

a greater degree of community cohesiveness with other people of the world. I was being awakened as the Israelites had been at Sinai to a new awareness, a heightened state of consciousness, a keener ability to sense G-d's presence.

Heightened consciousness, harmony and inspired unity

This camp was where the Israelites experienced totally new, profound revelations and their consciousness of G-d's existence and manifestation was intensified.

There are times in our lives when exceptional circumstances occur that can heighten our consciousness of G-d's presence. It could be a birth, a recovery from a terrible illness, an escape with our lives and many more. There are also times when this consciousness is awakened in more gentle ways such as when we see a magnificent, natural sight.

At such special times a person might sense G-d's reality in an extraordinary way. In the still of the night, while ascending Mount

Sinai, the penetrating insight entered my mind that perhaps one of the purposes of my twin sister's short life had been to guide my own when I most needed her. And that when she left, though it felt to me like a tragedy for so many years, like her work was unfinished, she left because she had a different destiny than mine, and I than hers. In the beauty of that setting, in the quiet of my soul's sadness, G-d offered me some consolation, which I will always treasure.

I realized that of everything I had anticipated about this journey, I could never have imagined I would feel any sort of comfort from the loss I had carried for over three decades. The journey was never about that – or so I had thought. But I understood that G-d wants us to prepare the path, to do the work and He will provide the results Himself. For me, that meant using every skill and resource I had at my disposal, mapping out every stretch of territory, reading every historical opinion, and going about the task as an academic and a passionate environmentalist. I had been methodical in my approaching the trip with painstaking attention to detail about each camp's archaeology, geography, flora and fauna. And here, possibly my most transformative moment had come out of the blue, not from my own efforts at all. It was humbling and awe inspiring.

Hillel explains that the fact that the "Torah referred to the entire Israelite nation in the singular was to allude to the tremendous unity inspired by the awesome event of receiving the Torah. The reason that this is referred to in the Torah at this stage is because such unity is not merely a measure of social harmony, it is also the measure of objectivity, an imperative for receiving the Torah . . . the way G-d wants it to be received."[32]

When people are in a heightened state of awareness they can be drawn together in celebration rather than driven apart by dissension. Jacobson[28] explains that the Israelites experienced a great cohesive and connected unity when they were more aware of G-dliness.

The original encampment at Sinai showed how important it was to be "as one man, with one heart."[29] The Israelites' cohesiveness made them worthy of receiving the Bible, and they in turn followed the principle to love their neighbor as they did themselves to bring more peace into the world. Although people are individuals who possess unique physical and mental characteristics, these differences need not separate and divide but should rather encourage each to complement another. This unity between people brings us to a higher level of perfection.30 In essence, we share a common denominator, as explained by Rabbi Shneur Zalman of Liadi in the Tanya: 31 souls are "all of a kind, and all having one Father, therefore are called real brothers, by virtue of the source of their souls in the One G-d." I was witnessing some of this harmony here on Gebel Musa.

I recalled a book I had read, *A Time to Actualise*, which stated that one day there will be new insights, and greater understanding of things that are presently obscure about G-d, to the extent that a human is capable. It would be a time of much greater peace and harmony, with neither famine nor war and a time of love, without envy and hatred.[33]

The Bible narrates that the Israelites camped at the base of Mount Sinai for one year and one month.[34] This would have given them time to settle down and start to refocus their energies. As I stood there looking in all directions – north, south, east and west – I pondered the possibility that this might have been where the Israelites were told how to build the Holy Tabernacle that they then carried wherever they went.

I was transported into the scene of the building site of the Holy Tabernacle. The Israelites were working energetically, creatively and conscientiously.

I could visualize strong men beating silver into poles for the outer walls of the Tabernacle. There was a deafening sound as they beat and shaped the silver with many hammers. Other men in dark brown tunics were pounding copper for the huge washbasin and sacrificial altar and pouring liquid gold into bars for the holy vessels. The fire was roasting them. There was a cacophony of deafening noises so the men could hardly talk to each other.

Groups of men were hauling completed silver poles, to test them, to stand upright with many ropes. One man stood precariously on a wooden ladder manipulating his ropes to bring the poles into vertical alignment. The men were sweating profusely as they focused intensely on the difficult work.

Supply workers were heavily laden as they dragged new wood and other materials into the area.

Young men were labouring to chop the prized acacia wood. These were passed to carpenters who scraped, sawed, filed and shaped it. Shavings were blowing around into their faces. The best wood would be used for the Holy Ark.

At the edge of the working area, tough looking men were busy working with leather. One thickset man was skinning carcasses. His neighbour was salting and preparing skins for tanning. A terrible odor from the tanning work wafted my way as the wind changed direction. The prepared leather was taken to three men who were carefully smoothing and scraping it and cutting it into shape to form the cover for the Mishkan, which was made of ram and tachash skin. Their leader's deeply furrowed eyes were sharply focused as he conscientiously marked the shapes.

A separate area was designated for women. Several women in yellow and green kaftans were standing around steaming pots with bubbling red dye which would be used to dye the ram skin, to emphasize the significance of blood. The steam of the dyes filled the air through the smoky haze of the burning fires.

A queue of excited women with flowing headdresses had formed. Each one had something precious to give away. Some handed over their precious copper mirrors, others their jewels. This was to form the holy vessels. Smiling children skipped around with coins hoping to also make a contribution.

Teenage boys were busy with the animals. A group was shearing bleating sheep and passing the wool to their companions. Impatient and frustrated boys sat with this unenviable task of disentangling the wool. This was passed onto the next group who were combing the wool and loading it onto donkeys. The poor beasts were moaning under the weight of white fluff as they carried it to the women to be dyed.

Children were running around trying to participate in all the new-found crafts unfolding so industriously in the barren desert.

The older women were receiving the dyed product and spinning and then weaving it into beautiful cloth, as they chatted.

On the opposite side of the area, in a very clean section, middle-aged women were preparing flour which they would much later knead and bake into loaves for the inner courtyard of the Tabernacle when it was completely ready. Enthusiastically they hummed delightful tunes.

Other women dressed in white were working with rare and precious spices. They had the rare spices for the Tabernacle such as onycha, gal-

banum, myrrh, cassia, spikenard, saffron, costus, aromatic bark, cinnamon, and carshina lye. They were getting them ready for the priest who
would use them for incense. The smell wafting from this corner was
delightful.

Betzalel and his top-class artists were carefully measuring out the
dimension for the golden cherubs, for the cover of the ark, in reverent
silence.

Moses and Aaron sat in a commanding position to give instruction
and ensure that all was going according to plan.

This might have been the place where they were taught how to worship G-d, to show their faith and belief; here that they learned the moral
code that underpins the three Abrahamic religions (Judaism, Christianity and Islam) and indeed Western civilization. It might have been
here that Moses helped the freed slaves to became well-organized and
disciplined tribal groups. The Israelites were being taught the power of
unity, respect for diversity among others, and belief in the Oneness of
G-d. They had a lot of work to do to follow G-d's instructions.

People were beginning to descend the mountain, but I was not
ready to leave. It was eight o'clock. I went exploring, wanting to see
the cave discussed in Exodus 33:21–22 in which Moses is said to have
hidden when G-d passed by, revealing "not His face but Himself from
behind."[35] This indentation in the rock has the shape of a human body;
one can slip into the space but there is no room for movement. The
little cave fascinated me.

I also learned about the one-roomed chapel built in the fourth or
fifth century and rebuilt in 1934. Inside it has frescoes depicting the
life of Moses. To the west of the chapel was a small mosque built in
the twelfth century. Beneath the mosque is the cave where Moses
supposedly spent forty days and where G-d appeared to the prophet
Elijah.

I ventured further afield and came to the edge of a cliff. From there,
to my amazement, I could see the plain below the mountain where the
Israelites are thought to have encamped. In my mind's eye, I could see
the people gathered behind the barrier that had been erected to keep
them away from the mountain. Perhaps this was the view that Moses
had had when G-d said, "Go and look, your people have made an idol
of a golden calf."[36] I recalled the Proto-Sinaitic script I had seen, and
the writing of the Ten Commandments on stone tablets. I imagined
Moses descending this mountain and shattering the tablets at the bot-

The view from the summit of Gebel Musa onto the open plain below, where the Israelites could have been camping while Moses was receiving the Torah. | *M Rawicz Trip Photo*

tom, and how he pleaded for the lives of the Israelites when G-d wanted to destroy them. Moses then climbed the mountain a second time to receive new tablets. I envisaged the people living on the plain below me for an entire year while they learned to live by the new laws.

By ten o'clock I was tired. I went to one of the stone huts, where the Bedouin guides who lived on top of the mountain kindly let me lie down on one of their sleeping benches. A young man called Misbah gave me a camel-hair blanket and I had a good rest. When I arose, I spent some time talking to the Gebeliya youths.

"We bring the provisions for the pilgrims up the mountain every day, by donkey," one man told me.

"Where are you from?" another ventured.

"South Africa," I replied. "I work in the environmental field."

Hearing this, Misbah began to tell me about the environment of the Sinai. He was extremely knowledgeable and well-spoken, and seemed to take a genuine interest in speaking with people from all backgrounds who visit the mountain.

The stone huts on the top of Gebel Musa. Bedouin guides who live on top of the mountain give provisions to the hundreds of daily visitors. | M Rawicz Trip Photo

"St. Catherine's monastery is a UNESCO World Heritage Site," he informed me. "And the Egyptian Ministry of Culture is busy deciding whether to make this whole area around Gebel Musa a heritage site."

"I didn't know that," I said, "but I'm not surprised."

"They say this area has played a special role in human history . . . and it is still a place where spiritual values can be exchanged. People can learn to understand each other's religious traditions. And many religious monuments have been built here over the years, as you've seen. You know, more than a third of all people belong to one of the three religions that honor this site – Judaism, Christianity, and Islam. Gebel Musa and St. Catherine's monastery are proof that people from different faiths throughout the centuries can live together peacefully. The authorities were also interested in the Gebeliya tribe because of our connection with the monks. And, of course, the natural qualities in this area are outstanding – thousands of tourists come here to enjoy our natural beauty. A lot of people want to see the sunrise, like you did. And we have some rare or endangered plants and animals in this area,

People gathered on the summit of Gebel Musa in the early morning. |
M Rawicz Trip Photo

that aren't found anywhere else in the world. When the World Heritage Committee visited us, I spoke to them personally."

"That must have been an interesting experience," I said.

"Yes, for them and for us. They liked the landscape and range of different plants here so much that they wanted to make an even bigger area into a World Heritage Site."

"What's your biggest environmental challenge?"

"Well, there's so much waste coming out of the café" – he pointed to the place that served drinks and snacks to tourists – "that the donkeys struggle to take it all down to the bottom of the mountain."

I was impressed by his articulateness as well as his insight.

I promised to research the topic and try to find a waste compactor that they could use. This I did when I returned to South Africa. I found a suitable design for a waste compactor and sent the information to Misbah via Rabia. During my second trip to Gebel Musa the following year, when I went up the mountain and entered the Bedouins' hut, Misbah greeted me with "Hello, Margaret." I was touched that he remembered my name, because he deals with hundreds of people every week. We discussed the progress of the waste compactor and he agreed that they needed to take some more steps.

By the early afternoon I was ready for the three-hour descent. I walked back down the 700 steps and then rode by camel on the second leg, this time by the Route of Moses. I observed the environment and reflected that from a geological perspective, tremendous tectonic forces must have been at work to form these amazing mountain ranges. Gebel Musa was shaped like a cone with its top sliced off, giving it a unique and imposing appearance. Eventually, by mid-afternoon, we arrived at the foot of the mountain. The camel owners were waiting for their next customers.

I felt close to G-d and sat down in the shadow of the silent mountains to pray and contemplate. I stayed there for two hours, integrating my experiences and spiritual insights. All negativity seemed to have left me and my heart felt softened and opened. When I rose to leave, my heart seemed to be surrounded by light – a feeling that has remained with me until today, giving me security, happiness, and inner strength.

Eventually I was ready to move on. I wanted to go and see the bush that is thought to have been the burning bush where G-d first revealed Himself to Moses, where Moses stood and removed his sandals. This bush reportedly stands today in the outer courtyard of the monastery of St. Catherine's. I wondered if this bush was "the one," and noted that it was of a species of bramble called Rubus Sanctus.

As I stared at the bush, I imagined Moses's experience. A deathly silence falls across the mountainside. Then a bright flash. The whole atmosphere shudders, then with no warning a massive luminous bright fire breaks out. The air around the bush turns orange and yellow. Intense heat fans outwards. This is no familiar sight. The leaves of the bush are burning but not consumed and the downward streaming branches filled with tiny green leaves laugh as they remain unharmed. The crackling fire's colors reflect from the ground.

Shimmering Holy light radiates and suddenly, with a powerful,

I descended from Gebel Musa on a camel by the pathway called the "Route of Moses." |
M Rawicz Trip Photo

awe-inspiring tone, G-d commands Moses to take off his sandals. Moses then perceives the miracle and with intense concentration and amazement kneels in humility. Self-consciously he removes his tough brown leather sandals and prostrates himself completely.

Seconds tick on and Moses looks up again in fearful wonder, and hears his instructions. "Go to the king of Egypt." Moses receives the instruction to lead the Israelites out of their bondage. In the distance his flocks gaze with widened unbelieving eyes at the miracle.

A deep quiet whisper of G-d's voice crescendoes into a gentle boom and then thunders, "I WILL BE WHAT I WILL BE." As G-d's intimate name flows from the fire, Moses cowers in awe. His face reflects the glow, his flimsy flowing robe almost translucent. He recoils, clutching his protective staff firmly, shielding his eyes and leaning away.

I marvelled at this unique moment and then went on to see the nearby well, reputed to have been where Moses was drawing water when he met Jethro's daughter.

I then visited the plain where the Israelites would have camped, where I sat meditating on the Tabernacle, the Ark of the Covenant, and some of the teachings given to the Israelites. These included basic but important principles governing human relations, which remain applicable in our everyday lives. The people received laws about trespassing, stolen goods, borrowed goods, widows and orphans, animal slaughter, perjury, bribery, the return of lost objects, proper worship practices, and many more topics.

However, the overall lesson from Sinai was that we need to strive for unity, peace and perfection.

As I slowly descended from this profoundly spiritual experience, Rabia showed me some of the more mundane aspects of the area. Various types of accommodation for tourists are found at the foot of the mountain, including chalets and huts in a small town. We also passed a five-star hotel and a light-aircraft landing strip. I assumed the latter was for people who want to visit Mount Sinai without travelling through the desert.

Rabia also took me to the local tourist traps. Mostly, these were kiosks selling trinkets and memorabilia, where shopkeepers stood around and called out continually to passers-by, trying to tempt them into buying something. I probably looked like an easy target. A young man sitting in a chair outside his booth beckoned for me to come in and browse. He was dressed in a light-blue kaftan with a dark-blue jacket, and a red head covering. I knew that he – like all Egyptian salespeople – would expect me to haggle, and might be quite insulted if I did not join in his little game of negotiation. However, he didn't count on me having an Egyptian friend that could bargain back just as hard. I got a very good deal, thanks to Rabia. Some shopkeepers tried every trick in the book to tempt me into their kiosks, including asking me to sign their guest book or to help them write a postcard in English or translate a letter from a relative. I was happy to buy a scarf, maps, an ornament featuring the scales of justice (a favorite symbol of the Egyptians), and a few small wooden camels.

When we left the market area, Rabia took me to see an ancient well that is still in use today. Finally, at the end of this rather long and intense day, we went to collect our belongings from the campsite. We had booked into a local hotel for the night.

I updated my log book: "At the camp of Sinai the Israelites were still on a main desert 'highway' which was a trading route, at a place well

A vista of Gebel Musa from the small town at its base. The town has a lot of facilities for the many tourists that come every day. | M Rawicz Trip Photo

known to Moses during his earlier flight from Egypt. The well is still preserved as is the entire history of the site, making it a unique location."

SINAI VILLAGE

On the seventeenth day of my trip, I planned to explore the area around Mount Sinai more thoroughly. I wanted to see if we could find any other sites that are considered holy or archeologically interesting. We began with a trip to the small town at the foot of the mountain. It comprised the Catherine Tourist Village, Daniela Village and Morgenland Village. As in any small town, there was a petrol station, shops, cafés, restaurants, grocery stores, a hardware store, clothes stores, and even a supermarket in the local mall. We passed a bank, a telephone exchange, a post office, a hospital, more than one police station, and a few mosques. The numerous annual visitors to this area can take their pick of three campsites, two "eco lodges," several guesthouses, numerous chalets, and a few hotels: we counted at least four, one of which was five-star. I wanted to have a look inside the five-star hotel, and took the opportunity to ask the receptionist about the town's population.

"At the moment," she told me, "more than four-and-a-half thousand people live in this town. The Egyptian government has plans to develop the area. By 2017, they expect about seventeen thousand people to be living here."

"Who lives here?" I asked. "Where do most of them come from?"

"Three-quarters of the town's population are Gebeliya Bedouin. We also have many Egyptians living here. In the future, we expect that the Bedouin will be in the minority, because there'll be a lot more Egyptians, Greeks, Russians, and even western Europeans."

I was disturbed by this news. The unique nature of this historical site would undoubtedly be marred by commercialization, which went against my belief in conserving the environment.

Rabia also took me to see the Saint Catherine Governmental Cultural House, which functions as a theater, exhibition center, and cultural center. The vibrancy of this little town surprised me. I had always imagined Mount Sinai to be a remote mountain in the middle of a desert. A minibus station and a bus station serviced the area, but the biggest surprise was the small international airport.

We then decided to tour some of the nearby attractions. Rabia took me for tea to the home of his friend Gebeli, who had taken me up the mountain. I was fascinated by the wallpaper in this man's living room. The room was small, with chairs covered in red cloth; across an entire wall was spread a picture of a beautiful palace with lush gardens. The scene differed starkly from the actual external landscape and seemed almost out of place in a desert home. I wondered why they liked it so much. I asked Gebeli about it.

He laughed. "My tribe is well known for the gardens that we plant in the desert. We've been doing this for centuries. We grow many things, including almonds, apples, pears, apricots, peaches, figs, pistachios, dates, grapes, olives, and lots of vegetables. We also grow flowers and medicinal herbs. What we do is find places in the dry wadis, and look for the main water course. Then we build a square or circle of big stone walls – called *shadoof* – that can stand up to the flash floods, which happen very often. The walls keep the soil from being washed away and protect the garden from animals. We also find wells or natural springs for our water supply. If we find a natural spring, we make a dyke called

A vista of Gebel Musa and the St Catherine Tourist Village, Daniela Village and Morgenland Village at its base. | M Rawicz Trip Photo

a *jidda*. We also build small dams and close off small canyons to make reservoirs, and then we channel the water into rock pools, called *birka*. Once the water is pooled we can use it to water our gardens. For hundreds of years we have made narrow channels using flat rocks, and in this way we can move water for many kilometers. Today we use plastic pipes instead, called *khartoom*."

We went out with Gebeli to see some of the gardens and water systems. In nearby wadis we saw the gardens he had spoken about, uniquely beautiful among the mountainous terrain. I also noticed some stone and rock structures that looked like houses, and I asked Gebeli about them.

"We Bedouin traditionally make simple houses," he said. "Mostly these are small stone buildings with cane roofs, which we build inside a garden wall or standing alone a bit further up the wadi, where they won't be hit by flash floods. Sometimes, after a heavy rain we get a flash flood. It doesn't happen often, but when it does, it can damage a lot. Follow me and I will show you something you will like."

Rabia, Gebeli (who helped me climb up Gebel Musa), and myself sitting in the lounge of Gebeli's home, with its mural of a lush palace garden. | M Rawicz Trip Photo

We climbed up a sloping wadi base until we reached a huge boulder.

"Look," Gebeli said, pointing. "Can you see the small house built behind that boulder? That's how we make our houses. We use the natural shelter of a big rock, or we wall up a cave or build a home into a large crack or hole in the ground or mountains. In this way, we protect the house from water, wind, cold and heat. We also build storerooms under boulders. We put up shelves and candle holders inside them. Most people don't even know they're there, because they fit into the nature so well."

Eventually we turned and headed back towards Gebeli's home. As we walked, he pointed out some large boulders with oval marks engraved on their surfaces.

"You'll never guess what these are," he joked.

"I can see it's some kind of symbol," I replied.

"They are marriage offer rocks. A lover draws a line around his foot on the face of the rock, next to his lover's footprint. If the two footprints both fit into the carved oval marks, the wish is allowed and they get married. Here is something else you'll like. It's a wishing rock. It has a flat top, and if you throw a pebble up and it stays on the top, your wish will come true."

Gebeli then took me to see some fascinating natural water features, formed by melted snow running down from the high mountaintops. "The water in one wadi drops into a granite pool, from where it flows down to other pools. Then it disappears under the rock and surfaces again at another place."

He took me to see a thousand-year-old mulberry tree in Wadi Tubug, which is protected by tribal law. Then we visited some other historical, cultural and religious attractions in the area. One was a palace built on a high mountain, called the Jebel Abbas Basha – built by the self-declared Khedive or Viceroy of Egypt and Sudan between 1849 and 1854. The palace had massive two-meter-thick walls of granite blocks and granite sand bricks, but had never been completed. The open quarry was still visible, with huge blocks lying around; kilns for smelting the bricks had been built in nearby valleys.[37]

We passed the ruins of several Byzantine monasteries, churches and monastic settlements, and hermit cells under rocks. It was obvious that through the centuries many religious people have spent time here studying their scriptures and benefiting from the serenity and purity of the environment. We also saw some tombs of sheikhs which have become shrines.

Gebeli said, "Bedouin people come to these tombs to keep *Zuara* or Sheik Day. Most Sinai tribes also come to the tombs of sheiks or in nearby shelters called *mak'ad*, to ask the sheikh to talk with Allah for them."

"What do they pray for?"

"We ask for help with things like getting better from sickness, for good health for the children or pregnant mothers, or to have good crops. Some people even visit the tombs every week to pray."

"I'm glad to know more about the religions and groups in this area," I said. I was especially pleased to have had close contact with the natural environment of this special place. I felt a real bond with Gebeli, and thanked Rabia for having introduced us.

That night I reflected on the day's events, and recalled a lesson that had deeply affected me. After Moses had ascended Mount Sinai, received the Commandments from G-d, and had written them down, he relayed the information to the Israelites. "All that G-d has spoken we will do, and we will understand,"[38] the people replied.

The question asked by scholars is: Why did the Israelites first say that they would do as G-d required and would understand thereafter? Why did they not first understand, and then do? The interpretation that impressed me was that the Israelites immediately undertook to obey all they had been told, but they realized that a full understanding would take place more gradually – over many generations. The great thinkers and prophets during the millennia that were to follow would contribute their divinely inspired insights, and the leaders of congregations would need to assist the ordinary people with interpretations and teachings. Obedience to the Ten Commandments would also require the cooperation of millions of people, each of whom could add a unique gift or ability as imparted by the Creator. In this way, the understanding of the scriptures would unfold continually.

At the end of this wonderful day, I slept at the same hotel again.

Chapter 4

Journeying to Kadesh Barnea – Camps 13–14

GRAVES OF CRAVING –
KIVROTH HATAAVAH

"And they left from the desert of Sinai, and camped at Kivroth Hata-avah."[1]

Kivroth Hataavah means "graves of craving."[2] The prospect of searching for graves of craving sounded ominous and eerie, and I felt slightly anxious as we went forwards. What might we stumble across? Nevertheless, in a spirit of fortitude we set off on the next leg of the car journey, which would be about 60 kilometers. A friend of Rabia's accompanied us as he wanted a lift to visit his family in one of the villages. Sections of the road were tarred, which made for an easier trip.

When we set out, the surrounding landscape was full of yellow sand, but we soon moved into an area that was characterized by sheer dark-grey hills. In parts, the hills had been eroded and appeared almost black, and I had a sense of the mountains closing in on us. For two kilometers a range of even taller mountains was visible, red-grey in color and looming high above, with steep red peaks jutting out occasionally like menacing towers. The plant life was virtually non-existent, but here and there I spotted a lone Acacia tree that had managed to survive the heat, wind and long dry months.

After we dropped off Rabia's friend, Rabia began chatting to me, telling me his life story. He had been born into a typically impoverished Bedouin family and as a young adult he had struggled for years to save money. He had always dreamed of buying a couple of jeeps and running a business as a tour guide, taking people through the desert. The conversation dwelled for a while on the topic of how Bedouin people earn a living. In addition to their traditional pastoral lifestyle, they sell meat, wool and dates to people in the cities, and in exchange buy vital provisions such as grain, which makes up the bulk of their diet. Some Bedouin work in tourism and others become laborers at mines, such as the manganese mines. In the modern world, they depend on settlements for their supplies, but in the desert they have developed extraordinarily sophisticated ways of thriving.

Rabia suddenly said, in an extremely earnest voice, "I want to talk to you like a sister. My mother-in-law Fteha has a message for you. After we left, she sent me a message to say that she loves you, and she cried when we left and wants you to come back. My wife also wants you to come back. We have all been thinking and speaking about it. We would like to invite you to come and live in the Sinai, and we will give you a house in the village."

"Oh, Rabia!" I was overcome with emotion, delighted and yet a little saddened – because the proposal was not feasible. After a while I replied, "I would love to do that, and maybe one day I will be able to. But for now, it can only be a dream." We travelled on in silence.

Suddenly Rabia uttered a grunt of alarm. He was staring ahead, and I followed his gaze and saw smoke streaming from the car bonnet. He brought the car to a shuddering halt and rushed out to lift the cover.

"The engine is overheated," he said, coming over to my window. "We'll have to wait until it cools down."

The heat was sweltering and there were no mountains or Bedouin dwellings in sight.

"How long will we have to wait?" I asked, feeling uncomfortable at the prospect of sitting alone with Rabia for too long.

"Probably a long time," he answered sullenly.

We sat for a few minutes. Then, out of the hazy distance, a lone Bedouin man came riding along on his camel. As he approached, I saw he was wearing a brown kaftan and blue headdress. His camel ambled up to the car.

"I'm Taj. What is the matter?" he asked in Arabic.

Embarrassed, Rabia explained the problem. I gathered that such a thing should not happen to any self-respecting desert driver.

This magnanimous passerby extended his sympathies, and promptly joined us. He and Rabia managed to find a patch of shade from an overhanging rock in which to escape the unforgiving sun, and they lay there together on the soft sand. This prompted me to walk over to a nearby Acacia tree and lie beneath it; I lifted the sand around the plant's roots and let it fall through my fingers. Despite the heat, I had to admit it was pleasant just to lie down. I closed my eyes and listened to the breeze and the silence. *Some people take beach holidays to be able to do this,* I thought. I spread my arms out on the ground and felt a wonderful sense of tranquillity and solidness emanating from the earth.

The lesson of the camp at Sukkot came to mind. "Have faith in G-d's protection, realize that we are dependent on it daily, and find happiness in its shelter and security."

I started to hum, hoping to get myself into a better mood. The men heard me and started to clap in time to the tune, and soon we were creating a merry scene – for stranded tourists. Eventually another solitary wanderer passed by, and I wondered whether we made a bizarre sight. There I was in my blue kaftan and black scarf, sprawled out on the sand while the two men clapped away and we all waited for the car to recover from its ordeal.

Despite my bravado, the idea of finding "graves of craving" still bothered me. The biblical text refers to an incident in which the Israelites became rebellious and angry and complained that they had no meat to eat. They were frustrated by eating manna day after day. The biblical narrative states that "G-d made a wind, and brought quails from the sea, which fell by the camp, in an area as great as a day's journey around it, and two cubits high on the earth."[3] The people stayed up all day and night, greedily gathering the quails. But while the people were devouring the flesh of the birds, G-d became angry and a plague decimated those who had displeased Him. Thousands of people were buried at the camp. The place was named Kivroth Hataavah because "the people that lusted" for meat had been buried there.

After a lengthy hour, Rabia's car's engine had cooled. He started the car and Taj waited around for a moment to ensure that all was well. Then he handed us a bunch of fresh dates and wished us well, and we set off again towards the sandstone plateau that lay ahead. Soon enough we arrived at the large, imposing mountain range of Gebel-el-Gunna, made of hard basalt rock. Here the landscape differed yet again. Chipped red stones were scattered among the sand, and Rabia pointed out some peculiar round structures on a distant hillside.

"I can't see what those things are," I muttered.

Ancient circular tombs from the Stone Age that were built from slabs of red sandstone. The Israelites would have seen these as they were dying after eating too many quails. | M Rawicz Trip Photo

With almost reckless abandon, Rabia veered the car off the road onto a rutted side track. We bounced along it until he brought the vehicle to an abrupt halt in front of the round objects, which I now saw were flat-topped red stone shelters. There were about twenty of them and they covered an area the size of two football fields. It was a remarkable sight, but I still had no idea what they were.

Rabia pointed ahead and said, "*Nawamis*. Look, nawamis! Go and look."

I climbed out of the car and began to make my way over the danger-ously rocky ground.

The side of each structure had been built of flat overlapping slabs of red sandstone or metamorphic cobbles, piled on top of each other extremely tightly to form a circular wall about five meters in diameter. The sturdy walls were about two-and-a-half meters high and supported an absolutely flat red slab roof; the buildings had no windows, and each had a single low square entrance on the western side. They looked sin-ister, standing in this silent place on an isolated hill. I was sure that no one would want to live in such a building or even to set foot in one of them. No wonder Rabia had stayed in the car.

Nawamis are mass graves from some 3500 years ago and are found at the camp site of Kivroth Hataavah. | M Rawicz Trip Photo

A strange-looking man suddenly appeared, startling me. He mumbled and pointed towards the buildings, beckoning me to follow him.

"Nawamis, nawamis," he said repeatedly.

He was joined by another man who was wearing a black uniform and looked quite stern.

"I am Mubid," he said. "What do you want here?"

"Rabia brought me." I pointed to the car where Rabia was waiting.

"Ah," Mubid said, as if this explained everything. "Come with me."

"What does 'nawami' mean?" I asked warily.

"Mosquitoes. Bedouin legend says the tribes of Musa – Moses – built these places to provide shelter from the mosquitoes."

"I'm looking for the place where members of those tribes died after eating too many quails," I said.

"Are you looking for quails?" he asked. "I know about quails. Thousands of quails fly over here. They go from Europe to Central Africa every autumn, and come back in the spring. The birds are often so tired by the long trip that hundreds drop out of the sky over the Sinai. Half dead from tiredness!"

"I've read about that," I commented.

"The Bedouin who live in the Sinai say that the quails sometimes land all on top of each other until there is no more room on the ground. Are you looking for quails?"

"Yes. I suppose so. I know that the Israelites died after eating them."

I could just imagine: a deathly hush falls across the entire camp. It is the hush of a few thousand people suddenly gone quiet as the clatter of pots and murmurings of conversations stop and a gnawing expectation takes hold. A big wind is approaching, although it is strangely intermittent and comes with no warning, for the sky above the western horizon is still blue, unclouded by sand. This is not the familiar whispering of air sweeping across the desert or the rustling of a breeze through acacia leaves. This wind is more a gentle distant clapping. But it is growing louder with every second. Suddenly a shadow descends and the sun is blacked out.

And then the storm hits and they begin to fall, at first just a few landing with a gentle thud and then they are raining down, thousands upon thousands, millions even. People flee to their flimsy tents. But then the realization dawns and fear turns into shouts of jubilation and cries of euphoria for these are little birds falling from the sky, so many that soon the earth is covered as far as the eye can see. These are the answer to our craving for meat. The Lord has answered our plea!

For the rest of the day and all through the night and the next day the people collect the gifts from heaven which lie two cubits deep in places. The birds are laid out to dry in the sun, but many are immediately roasted and the people begin to gluttonize. Later this is followed by people falling and dying like the birds had.

Then I once more heard Mubid's voice, "We Bedouin know that you can't eat these birds, sometimes they've eaten a poisonous fungus in the Nile Valley. So we don't eat them."

"I hadn't read about that. That's very interesting," I answered as I became present once more.

I wondered whether the death of the Israelites after eating the quails could have been attributed to the fungus. An ominous thought flashed through my mind. Maybe these strange buildings were the graves of the Israelites who had died after feasting on the birds, struck down by G-d's anger.

My later research informed me that despite the Bedouin legend, the structures predated the Exodus by hundreds of years. Yet they were indeed graves – mass graves. The doorways were angled to catch the setting sun in various seasons. Furthermore, the westward orientation of the tomb entrances showed that whoever built them shared the Egyptian belief that the soul was spirited away to the west after death.[4]

I bent down and peered in through a doorway and saw a short entrance corridor constructed of upright stone slabs.

"Go in, go in," Mubid insisted. "Go, go go."

Not wanting to be mocked, I braced myself and squatted so that I could get a closer look through the doorway. I felt suspicious of the whole situation.

"Go, go, go!" he urged.

I crawled into the dark narrow entrance. *Was this a mass grave – what am I thinking?* Yet I found myself inching further in, squeezed flat on my stomach, hoping not to see any ghosts. The sound of my own movements made an eerie, hollow muffle as I raised my head and shuffled forwards. The place was completely dark and the air was stuffy. My heart was racing. I stopped for a moment, trying to calm my nerves. Then I pressed a button on my cell phone to generate some light in the hope that I would be able to see something of the interior of the building. I looked up and saw layered stone walls curving inwards towards the top, to form a corbeled roof. Although the outside walls were vertical, the inner walls were beehive-shaped. The roof was too low for me to stand up fully. Satisfied with this taste of feeling trapped in a place of ancient skulls and bones, I crawled out backwards, eager for a breath of fresh air.

Mubid watched me dust myself off.

"These nawamis were not looked at by explorers for hundreds of years," he said. "Then a European traveler called Palmer found them in the nineteenth century. He saw the bones of people lining the inside of the walls. They had been pushed to the side to make room for even more burials. That man also found colored beads and jewelry made from ostrich eggshells, bracelets made of seashells. He found small oil jugs, arrowheads, tools made out of flint or bone or copper, and many other things used by people in their houses. He thought these were for funeral offerings."[5]

Mubid led me around the twenty nawamis for almost half an hour, while I trailed behind him in bewilderment.

Later, I learned that an archaeologist called Ofer Bar-Youssef (of the Hebrew University) and Avner Goren (Archaeological Staff Officer for Sinai) had led an expedition to this area in the early 1970s. They established that the nawamis date back to the middle of the fourth millennium BCE. These structures are the oldest known buildings worldwide that still have intact roofs.[6] The high iron oxide content in the stones has helped to preserve them.

A medical team examined the bones and skeletons found in the nawamis, and concluded that they had belonged to people of a medium to short stature and slender build, with small skulls. These people had dark skin and are known to archaeologists as the Gracile-Mediterranids.[7]

Whoever these people were, their culture was advanced enough that they were capable of constructing these extremely durable and architecturally fascinating buildings in the desert. This made it all the more mysterious. Who exactly had been buried here? These structures could not have been the work of nomadic tribes. Had the people travelled from Egypt or Asia? Did the Israelites have anything to do with these ancient tombs? Surely they would at least have seen them, since they had camped here many years after the tombs had been built. The Bedouin legend that these were built by the tribes of Moses to find shelter from the mosquitoes passed through my mind. To date, these questions remain unanswered.

My visit to this site left an indelible impression on me. I was awed by the fact that I had entered a tomb built some 3500 years ago. But what were the Israelites supposed to have learned at the camp of Kibrothhattaavah? How did everything tie up?

I wandered back to the car, where Rabia was asleep. I reflected on the meaning of "graves of craving." Even if the nawamis had not been Israelite graves (as my later research confirmed), the entire camp where the people had had such a craving for meat had been wiped out. The site of the Kibrothhattaavah camp was one of the most intriguing in my entire journey.

⏏ Addictions and self-destruction

"Moses named the place 'Graves of Craving' (Kivroth HaTaavah), since it was in that place where they buried the people who had these cravings for meat."[8]

The Israelites had been obsessed with their own craving for meat. They were like addicts and could not stop their desire for this scarce food. They had lost control over their desires. In other types of addictions such as smoking or alcohol, addiction can even lead to loss of life.

If an addiction becomes totally extreme, the addict can hit rock bottom. This is often when they have a wakeup call and have to really come to terms that they need to seek help for recovery.

The therapy often involves handing their life over to a higher power or G-d for assistance. This surrender allows them to start on the road to recovery. They can move away from the possibly unconscious desire to do harm to themselves and rather kill the addiction. The craving can hopefully be eradicated and the person is rehabilitated and wiser through the process, according to the teachings of Jacobson.[9]

I wondered whether I would be tested with such a craving, and whether I could cope. I was, however, learning to be satisfied with what little I had on this journey and trust G-d's judgment that I had what I needed, and should not desire more.   ◧

LEPROSY – HAZEROT   CAMP 14

"They left Kivroth Hataavah and camped at Hazerot."[1] *Hazerot* means "courtyards."[2] What could this possibly mean in the middle of a desert? Might it refer to a special type of dwelling, or some sort of unusual building? We set out to find Hazerot. A young Bedouin couple approached the jeep as we were leaving Kivroth Hataavah, asking for a lift. The woman could speak some English and introduced herself, saying "I'm Hanbal, and my husband is Badra."

Rabia agreed to give them a lift and now Hanbal was perched on the seat next to me, talking incessantly. As the day wore on and my fatigue grew, I put my feet up on the opposite seat to relax.

Hanbal complained that she and Badra had been married for two years but still did not have any money. She wanted to set up home with her husband but they had to stay at her mother's home, which made her feel disempowered and unable to determine her own lifestyle. She was worried that this arrangement might continue for years to come. Then she moaned about her father having left home three years ago to work at a manganese mine on the Red Sea coast. The family had subsequently heard that he was having an affair. The news left her mother feeling anxious, dejected and jealous. The family was embarrassed about the alleged affair, and the mother felt guilty and blamed herself.

"My mother is old-fashioned and she is scared of my father who shouts a lot," Hanbal said, in the same complaining tone of voice. "I am not happy with her. I am not going to live scared like she does." A look of disgust crossed her face. "I want to be a modern woman and I want to be freer in my life."

According to Hanbal, her decision to break with tradition had shocked and infuriated her family and had led to enormous tension in the home. The village women had ostracized her.

"I'm bored with our way of life," Hanbal droned on. "The problem is that my community is old-fashioned and now they're angry with me. They have told me they don't like me and I am now alone, but I will not give up."

"What does your husband say?" Rabia asked.

"Oh, he says that all the trouble at home makes him upset. He is mixed up about who is right and who is wrong, and what he must do about it. He has told me that he is not happy about me. He says he still likes me, but this is a problem for him."

On the one hand, I was interested to have this insight into problems that are so similar to other people and not exactly idyllic. On the other hand, Hanbal's incessant talking irritated me. I tried to turn my attention away, but the volume of her voice seemed to rise the further we went. I wanted to appreciate the beauty of the environment and absorb the silence of the desert. I did not have the courage to ask Hanbal to stop spilling out all her problems. Thankfully, within an hour Rabia dropped them off at a cluster of Bedouin homes.

We voyaged on in blissful silence for another eight kilometers. Then Rabia unexpectedly brought the car to a rumbling halt and turned off the track, and we headed towards a large rocky outcrop a few meters away. He stopped the car in front of a solitary rock and said, "Come and look."

I climbed out of the car and strolled over to the rock he was pointing at. To my surprise, I saw a large candelabra etched deeply into the rock face. It was almost double the size of a person.

"This is the Rock of Inscriptions," he said in an earnest tone.

"This is amazing," I whispered.

There, carved into the solid rock, was a huge Jewish menorah in the exact shape described by the Bible: three branches on each side and one

The so called "Rock of Inscriptions," which has an ancient seven-branched Jewish menorah carved into it. | *M Rawicz Trip Photo*

central branch, seven candles in total. The Israelites lit the menorah whenever they worshipped in the Temple. I stared in silent awe.

"The Rock of Inscriptions," Rabia repeated. "We call it *Haggar Maktub*" (the written stone).

Nearby were other carved inscriptions that had been added by people in numerous different languages and eras, during various civilizations – including Nabataean, Greek, Roman, and Byzantine, and from the period of the Crusades. I saw depictions of animals such as camels and ibex. The various writings had been engraved into the rock over many years. I stood there thinking about its long history and the fascinating people that must have passed here and had a desire to leave their inscriptions.[3]

I heard a shout behind me and turned to see two children running towards me. I had no idea where they had suddenly come from. They wanted sweets. To my surprise, the little girl showed me that she wanted to play with my make-up; I was surprised that children living in the desert would know about lipstick. I tried to play with them, but

I stood at the top of a huge canyon and could see the barely visible green speck below, which is the oasis of Ein Hudra or the campsite Hazerot. | M Rawicz Trip Photo

they were interested only in my make-up. Then I noticed a Bedouin woman dressed in a black robe sitting beside a rock. She beckoned me to approach, and held out a cup. I took the cup and sipped the sweet Bedouin tea, made from berries picked from the desert scrub. While I drank the tea, the woman opened up a large multicolored cloth to reveal many pieces of unusual handmade jewelry. Evidently her sales contributed to the children's upkeep.

I examined a necklace made of carved camel bones, with long decorative cream beads that resembled carved ivory. But the necklace that really took my fancy was made of bits of clay painted bright blue, and scarab beetle rings. The scarab beetle served as a symbol of regeneration and creation, conveying ideas of transformation, renewal, and resurrection in Egypt.

DESCENDING THE CANYON

Rabia was standing on a rocky ledge staring into the distance. As I approached, he pointed to a green speck that was barely visible. Between us and the speck there was an extremely steep canyon, and beyond that a kilometer or two of pure desert.

"You must walk to that oasis alone," Rabia said.

I was shocked. Surely he was joking! I stared at the green speck of an oasis, and the canyon that separated me from it.

"I have to drive the long way round to get the jeep there," Rabia said, hurrying towards the vehicle. Then the car door slammed and he was gone.

I stood gulping in terror. The canyon looked far too steep for an amateur like me to climb. How could Rabia have left me alone like this? Then I spotted two men descending the canyon, with three camels. They were already halfway down.

"Help!" I yelled. "Help me!"

The men looked up, startled, but quickly realized I was in distress. One turned back to rescue me. Reassured by their presence, I began to inch my way down the sheer path into the canyon, making every effort not to lose my footing.

"Ah, ah," my rescuer placated.

He drew level with me and began to guide my footsteps, making sure that I did not slip as I cautiously placed one foot in front of the other. My heart was pounding. This was going to be a real struggle. Eventu-

A rebellious camel gives his owner a hard time as they go down the coloured canyon. | M Rawicz Trip Photo

ally we caught up with the camels, which were resisting the descent as much as I was.

"Me, Rushdi," my rescuer said, pointing to himself. "Him, Abid." He gestured to his friend.

Abid was struggling with the rebellious camels, urging them to move forward. Finally, with great persistence and uttering clicks and gurgles that the creatures seemed to understand, the two men got the camels moving. I watched the men's footsteps and carefully followed in their tracks. Each step was critical as I attempted to secure the safest position for each foot before placing my weight on it. Slowly my confidence grew.

Our strange little group paused to rest. I noticed a spectacular array of colored bands in the rock at the sides of the canyon, convoluted stripes of red, yellow, brown, grey and white decorating the cliff in a splendid natural pattern. The beauty inspired me, and from then on the descent seemed more manageable. After an anxious hour of clambering downwards my feet were finally on level ground again.

"Goodbye!" Rushdi and Abid waved farewell cheerfully.

They walked ahead rapidly with their camel caravan. The ships of the desert soon disappeared in the shimmering sand with their intrepid sailors.

I found myself alone at the bottom of the canyon, in a valley at least a kilometer wide and with steep sandstone sides. Exhausted, I plodded towards the oasis in the distance, and walked for two-and-a-half hours. I recalled a recurring dream I had often had, in which I was walking towards an oasis – only this time the dream was real. The sun's heat was fading and the shadows of the valley were lengthening ominously. The air was totally silent except for the sound of my heavy breathing. There was no other soul in sight. For a terrifying moment, I heard a howl. What other sounds would the darkness bring? What was lurking in the desert, and what would happen to me if I did not reach the oasis by sunset?

I thought of Pi-Hahiroth: "Attach yourselves to G-d and acquire the power to transcend your limitations with an Infinite source of energy." I clung to this idea and it became my salvation. At about six o'clock, just before sunset, I reached the outskirts of the oasis that is today known as Ein Hudra. I was most unimpressed with Rabia, but my feet continued to stumble forwards in my effort to find him.

This oasis marked the site of the camp of Hazerot. It has been a stopover point for people traversing the Sinai from west to east for millennia, and the ancient Nabataean, Roman and Byzantine inscriptions on the rock above the canyon were testimony to their passage. Among the many palm trees stood a few Bedouin homes with walls made of hessian cloth and roofs of palm leaves. Again I was reminded of the temporary structures that Jews worldwide build during Sukkoth in remembrance of G-d's protection of the Israelites in the desert. During Sukkoth, people eat and sometimes even sleep in these flimsy structures. But I had not realized how much the present-day abodes of the Sinai desert dwellers still resemble these huts. The festival of Sukkoth took on a whole new meaning for me.

Further into the oasis I found a channel that had been made for camels to quench their thirst. A huge camel was drinking and the scene looked so biblical. A few circular structures had been erected, with pillars of palm-tree trunks supporting a roof of palm leaves, which allowed the air to circulate freely and provided some relief from the daytime heat. I heard voices and walked towards them. I found Rabia sitting with some Bedouin men in front of a typical Bedouin tent. The

The attractive, long, sukkah-like structure that I slept under. | M Rawicz Trip Photo

A Bedouin home is built with walls of hessian cloth and a roof of palm leaves, just like our sukkot structures. | M Rawicz Trip Photo

A long sukkah-like structure had sand floors and coloured woven mats to sleep on. |
M Rawicz Trip Photo

tent was constructed from a single long sheet of colorful woven wool. On the floor were colored woven mats. I glared at Rabia.

He laughed. "You want to understand desert life, so you must learn how to cope alone in the desert sometimes."

He was enjoying a cup of tea. The teapot was simmering away on hot coals on the sand, and Rabia obligingly handed me a cup. The men beckoned me to join them, but I wanted to wash my hands. They pointed to the well. I walked over and found a small water reservoir, a square stone-walled structure with a slightly raised covering of palm leaves, presumably to keep out the sand and other contaminants.

The Bedouin men were making dough to bake in the hot ashes. This would be their supper, along with hard-boiled eggs (from chickens at the oasis), cream cheese (from the goats), dates (from the palms growing here), and more tea. The men sat at a slight distance from me, according to their custom. I tried desperately to understand what they were saying. It was infuriating, as I could only vaguely comprehend some Arabic words that were similar to Hebrew ones. Rabia was too engaged in the conversation to make much effort to translate. I sensed that they were talking about me.

Circular shelters built with palm tree trunks for pillar supports and a roof of palm leaves.
| M Rawicz Trip Photo

A stone-walled was well covered with palm leaves to protect the water. | M Rawicz Trip
Photo

Bedouins were chatting and making tea in the evening. | *M Rawicz Trip Photo*

"Don't be so rude," I told Rabia. "You should translate for me."

He introduced his companions, and explained that they were asking about my background. He then began translating as they spoke. Fayyad asked question after question, and I could see that he was the most intelligent and well-informed of the group on worldly matters. Shihad was more reserved, and just sat and listened with interest, occasionally prompting Fayyad to ask something. Shafeeq eventually joined in, asking questions in a jovial manner as his curiosity was piqued. As the conversation proceeded, I became aware that a strange feeling was developing among my acquaintances. Eventually, Shafeeq nudged Fayyad and muttered something. Fayyad stared at me. Then, evidently lacking the courage to do so himself, he politely but firmly instructed Rabia to ask me something.

"Ah," Rabia said, cautiously. "They want to know why you are coming here alone, and where is your husband? Why are you alone in this desert?"

"I'm following the route taken by the ancient Israelites," I said. "I need to have time in silence and to think alone about what is happening around me, rather than be a companion to my husband."

The men looked surprised and did not seem to fully understand.

My Bedouin hosts discussed the Exodus around the fire until late that night. |
M Rawicz Trip Photo

"She is on the Hajj of Moses, Haj Musa," Rabia explained.

"Ah! Yes, yes. We understand," the men exclaimed.

This seemed to clear the air somewhat. Fayyad nodded approvingly, and Rabia looked positively proud of me. But Shihad just stared at me with an evident mix of prejudice and amusement. Shafeeq was enthralled. More questions followed. Where was I going? How did I know it was the correct route? The Bedouin's oral tradition outlines the route that Moses supposedly walked. My hosts engaged in a heated debate as to whether the route I had planned was correct, compared with the one described in their tradition. This topic and other concerns kept them huddled around the fire until late that night.

I was beginning to realize that these desert dwellers listen intensely when one talks. Maybe they are accustomed to living with vast silence and solitude and listen with real interest. For them, simply encountering another person is a noteworthy event.

I found it magical to meet people who still lived in the places at which biblical events had occurred, leading much the same lifestyles, with their daily lives governed by the same natural conditions. As the night wore on, the mood became more cheerful and ended up in songs and

Sleeping in a sukkah under a camel-hair blanket, where temperatures can drop to 6 degrees, is an experience. | *M Rawicz Trip Photo*

lively clapping around a warm fire. We went to bed late, after unloading my luggage from Rabia's jeep. I began my cumbersome night-time ritual to prepare for the freezing temperatures that set in once the heat of the day dissipated into a cloudless sky. Although the daytime temperature might reach 30° C, the night-time temperature often dropped to 6° C. Sleeping outside required me to wriggle into at least five layers of clothing, including thermal underwear, two pairs of slacks, two sweaters, a long kaftan, and a windbreaker jacket, with two winter head scarves. Only then was I ready to find a spot on the sand to lay down my mat and climb under a thick camel-hair blanket. I positioned my bedding so that I could see the sky. It was totally clear, with millions of stars visible. I could see the entire Milky Way slowly revolving across the sky.

Gazing at the night sky evoked a meditative state as I reflected on my destiny and desire to serve G-d. I felt deeply content and connected to the Infinite as I lay watching the stars for about an hour before drifting off to sleep. At three o' clock I awoke needing to relieve myself, and walked to the edge of the oasis by the light of the stars. Suddenly, a large black thing crossed my path, sending me into a panic. Was it a poisonous snake? I froze, breathless, hoping that the shape would disappear.

Eventually my visual field become one big dark blur, and all I could do was quietly head back to the camp, where I crawled into my sleeping bag in a state of confusion. The warmth of the camel-hair blanket was most welcome. I lay there wondering whether I had just had a bad dream or whether the bad experience was still to come.

By the time I awoke again around eight o'clock, the Bedouin men were engaged in their morning prayers, bowing low towards the ground in the manner of Muslims, while reciting *Allah Hu Akbar*. I followed suit by reciting the Hebrew morning service, *Shacharit*. Our religious practices did not seem to conflict in the slightest, but I wondered how my male hosts really felt about me. I tried not to let the thought bother me.

After breakfast, one of the local women took me to see an ancient spring that still sustains the few local inhabitants and supplies a water reservoir. En route we passed clusters of date palms, and in my mind's eye I could see my ancestors surrounded by the same plants and sights. I could almost feel their presence, and excitement surged through me as I experienced a sense of déjà vu. It was here that Miriam and Aaron had behaved in a less than virtuous manner by slandering their brother Moses. His "crime" was having separated from his wife, the dark-skinned Kushite woman. G-d punished Miriam by allowing her to contract leprosy, and she was ousted from the camp for seven days until she recovered. Here the Israelites learned that if they speak inappropriately as Miriam had, they would suffer harmful consequences and thus undermine their own destiny, much as we may do to ourselves. I resolved to improve my caution when speaking to avoid bad mouthing others.

⮒   Rebelling against our destiny

In a person's life there are times when a rebellious attitude dominates more than one of compliance. This is typically true of teenagers but is present in anyone's life at some point. If the rebellion is against the approach of being faithful to G-d's expectations then it can be detrimental to the path that our lives take. It can even change our destiny negatively. We need to guard against behaviors that work against us fulfilling our mission in life, and choose to act for a positive destiny. According to Jacobson, it requires fine discernment.[4]

I had begun to ease free from the mind-set that accompanies city life, and had been moving closer to my own deep, intuitive awareness – an unlearned "knowing" that is so easily eclipsed. I

I enjoyed the morning in Ein Hudra oasis / Hazerot. | *M Rawicz Trip Photo*

was beginning to feel that I had a different mission in life that would lead to a new destiny. The environment and lifestyles I was currently encountering were bringing me closer to the power of the wilderness, which in turn was allowing me to connect more fully with my own emotions and intuition. My focus on the Israelites' learning experiences and confrontations with their limitations was shaping a new identity in me. I sensed that this journey would reveal that new mission.

I was puzzled by the literal meaning of Hazerot, "courtyards." I searched for anything resembling a courtyard but found no such thing. While I was walking around, I saw that the oasis was shaped like an oblong; towards the northern end was a distinct demarcation, behind which stood a large rock. The rock stood out among the otherwise flat sandy terrain. Within the rock was a hollow. I stared at this natural configuration and realized that the layout of the entire oasis bore some similarities to that of a temple. The temple had comprised an outer courtyard, an inner sanctum, a special area for the priest, and the holy area. The shape of the oasis showed roughly the same pattern, with the rock forming the natural equivalent of the Holy of Holies. Might this explain the name? To date, I have not been able to find any verification of this possibility.

By ten o'clock that Friday morning, we were ready to leave the oasis. We travelled by jeep on the back route that we had used the previous day when exploring Wadi Hudra. The journey was truly hectic – around the valley and through the dunes in a nauseatingly bumpy ride through the sands. But the thrill of it pandered to my adventurous side. Not long afterwards, we arrived at a village where two young men were trying to train a young camel to tolerate a saddle on its back. The sight amused me, as the camel was doing everything in its power to resist the men and was kicking and spitting at them. Rabia, Tolba and their mates then went off to visit their friends, leaving me to observe the desert.

I took a walk through the tiny settlement. At its periphery, I saw a group of camels being loaded onto a truck, with the help of much flogging. One of the animals fell off the ramp and was clearly disorientated when it got back on its feet. I was horrified. The trucks then left, and the poor, tightly packed noisy camels looked like a bouquet of necks and heads. In the middle of this incident, a car drove past, and the driver hooted and leaned out of the window. "Do you want any camel food today?" he yelled. Such fascinating desert sights!

I joined up with Rabia and Tolba again and we were invited to a Bedouin home for tea and food with the family. It was delightful to be with them. After the meal of freshly made bread and salad, I went outside to cuddle a baby goat I had seen earlier, and noticed that a young child who was following me had a wounded foot. I hauled out my emergency medical kit and treated his foot as best I could. Rabia and our Bedouin hosts were still sitting around talking, but I was tired and went to the jeep to catch a welcome snooze.

In the afternoon, Rabia convinced me that we needed to make a slight detour along Wadi Nekheil to visit a special site. The road snaked through magnificent mountains and rugged rock formations until eventually it came out at a cluster of date palms. Rabia turned the car onto a gravel road and soon we arrived at the Coloured Canyon, also called the Rainbow Canyon. This canyon boasts some of the most magnificent rock formations in the world, ranging from sandstone to limestone, and granite with veins of basalt. The vegetation is limited to a few Acacias, green Capparis Tamarisk trees, Willow trees, Sodom Apples and desert pumpkin,[5] but the beautiful geological features make up for the sparse plant life.

We decided to explore the canyon on foot for a couple of hours, accompanied by a local guide. We would spend the night at a nearby camping facility for hikers. The first leg of our hike took us across soft yellow sands, with high rocky walls stretching into the distance the length of the huge canyon – sometimes as high as sixty meters, the equivalent of a twenty-story building. We walked past walls with sandstone layers of red, yellow and light-brown hues. In some sections the rock was almost pink, with tinges of red, and resembled an expressionist painting. My imagination was stimulated and I began to see all manner of human and animal faces in the rocks. I pointed out to Rabia the resemblance of an owl's face, with two large red circles that looked like eyes set against the yellow rockface.

"How did this rock come to look like this?" I wondered aloud as I stood and stared. "What kind of geological process does this?"

"What you see here is sandstone that has been mineralized," our guide replied.

A short distance later we came across yellow rocks bearing fine black stripes, which looked like a Chinese painting of a mountain scene. About 500 meters further on, we saw a pattern in the rock that looked like a "rose" with hundreds of petals of various colors: yellow, orange and red, with a fine grey border outlining each petal. Geological forces had formed the rocks into this magnificent sight. In some places, the rocks radiated crystalline colors. In other areas they had a velvety appearance. We saw beautifully shaped cliffs with layers of pink, purple, silver and gold sandstone.

Other visitors were ambling along, armed with cameras to capture the magic of the scenery. From the start of our hike to the end, I was awed by the sheer range of contrasting textures, colors and sheen.

Our guide told us a bit more about the canyon's structure.

"These rocky walls contain fossilized shells and small phosphorous openings. The walls have been eroded, and if you look very closely you can actually see the tiny shells. Inside the walls, sea creatures have been preserved from ancient times when the canyon lay below sea level. You are actually looking at an ancient ocean when you look at this landscape."

The canyon formed its own unique little universe. We walked on powdery sand through passages as narrow as my shoulders, passing bizarre rock formations. At one point we slid down through a vent where the sides of the canyon almost touched, and a fallen boulder had blocked the way, leaving a narrow opening beneath it. A few steps later we had to swing our bodies around another huge rock that had created an obstacle in the path.

"Do many people visit this area?" I asked.

"It's a popular day trip near Sinai's east coast for tourists staying at resorts at the Red Sea or at camps in Taba, Dahab or Nuweiba. All of these places are extremely popular holiday destinations. And they're fairly close. Local people bring the tourists here by jeep, and then they do a day trip or maybe stay overnight."

The canyon was nearly 800 meters long. We had hiked almost the full length of it, and by the end I was tired.

"I'd like to spend some time alone," I told Rabia.

"Let's go to our overnight camp," he replied.

Once we arrived, I had a sleep and then began to prepare for the Sabbath. In the morning, I recited the Sabbath service on my own as I had done the previous week, and spent the remainder of the day resting. During this time I had the opportunity to appreciate the silence and purity of the environment. I read a little and then went for a walk to explore the Coloured Canyon holiday resort, and found some interesting people to chat to.

Chapter 5

Western Border of Israel – Camps 15–27

CRIMINAL VALLEY –
KADESH BARNEA / RITMA

CAMP 15

"They departed from Hazerot, and pitched in Ritma."[1]

The meaning of *ritmah* is "wasteland" or "smoldering place".[2] This sounded ominous and I felt uneasy about what I might discover at such a site. Would I find the blackened ruin of an ancient building, land that had been scorched in a volcanic outpouring, or would I perhaps find the descendants of a violent tribe? Time would tell, but I set out expecting to find some sort of wasteland or scene of desolation.

Ritma is also known as Kadesh Barnea, a place where the Israelites had camped for possibly thirty-eight years. Thus it was a crucial point in their journey – and in mine.

I planned to visit Ritma and all the campsites that followed, which were in the vicinity of the Egyptian-Israeli border, in the same sequence as the Israelites had followed. I mostly managed to do so, apart from a few places which I could not access because of political boundaries. In this written record, however, I have maintained the right biblical order.

Rabia and I left the Coloured Canyon resort, and headed back to the route that the Israelites would have followed through Wadi Watir before veering northwards to the next camp. The road continued in a north-east direction. This route brought us close to a range of mountains, at which point we turned due north. From here on we were travelling parallel to the border of current-day Israel on the Taba-Rafah road, through Egyptian land. The area is barren desert. It is also a military area, because its proximity to the Israeli border poses a danger in terms of insurgency and terrorism.

The Egyptian army has a military installation at Kadesh Barnea. The Israeli and Egyptian governments have an agreement whereby no person is allowed to enter the zone without special permission, within thirty kilometers of the Israeli border fence. I had applied for a permit to travel through the area and the El-Arish city authorities had promised to get back to me, but I was still waiting. The delay was exasperating because it affected the planning of my routes.

I was almost tempted to give up this challenge, but recalled that one of the lessons the Israelites had learned was the value of persistence. I felt reassured to contemplate that our Creator has endowed us with the strength to face numerous tests and encounters. I desperately wanted to become acquainted with Kadesh Barnea, even if I had to wait.

"I'd like to learn more about Kadesh Barnea," I told Rabia. "Can you help me?"

Rabia started sending out messages using the "desert telegraph" system. This was an ingenious method of getting messages from one place to another by whatever means possible. After two fretful hours, he finally received a positive response.

"A Bedouin man who knows about the history and archaeology of Kadesh Barnea is coming to meet us," he announced.

We hurried along the route and eventually reached a small airfield for light aircraft. Rabia parked the car next to the tiny airstrip and sat around waiting for his contact to arrive.

Before long, a tall man wearing a beige robe approached us. "I am Saadah," he said, stretching out his hand to greet Rabia. His facial expression struck me as intelligent and pleasant. "Salem Aleycum." Turning to me, he said, "I hear you want to learn about Kadesh Barnea."

"Yes," I nodded.

"I'll be happy to tell you what I know. I worked with an archaeologist who worked the site and he taught me a lot about it. Come, let us have tea together." He pointed to a small leisure facility beside the airstrip.

We made our way to the informal lounge and Rabia proceeded to make Bedouin tea. Then, for the next twenty minutes or so, over steaming cups of tea, I briefed Saadah on my mission. I told him what I knew about Kadesh Barnea, and he enthusiastically shared his knowledge of the region I wanted to explore.

"I know that archaeologists disagree about the possible location of

Landscape scene in eastern Sinai of the route the Israelites would have travelled to Kadesh Barnea. | M Rawicz Trip Photo

Kadesh Barnea," I said. "Karl von Raumer and Edward Robinson looked for it in the Jordan Valley in the early nineteenth century, but other archeologists think it might have been at Petra in Jordan."[3]

"Yes, there is some confusion," Saadah agreed.

"Well, I'm looking for a possible site in the eastern Sinai," I said. "I'm following the route described by a book called *The Living Torah*.[4] The maps in this source suggest that Kadesh Barnea was once called Quseima, at a site which is close to the modern Israeli border. From what I've learned, it's about sixty kilometers south of the Gaza-Egyptian border crossing, Rafiah. The sources also showed it as being about eleven kilometers west of the Israeli-Egyptian border, just inside the Egyptian territory."

"Yes, yes," Saadah enthused. "At this place – called Kadesh Barnea – there is a spring, and a desert village called Ein-el-Qudeirat. It's in an area called Quseima."

"Do you know the area well?" I asked.

"I visited Ein-el-Qudeirat when Israel owned that territory after 1967.

It's an important region. It lies at a big crossroad in the northeastern Sinai. Since ancient times, traders and travellers have passed through that area."

"Please tell me about the routes that meet in that area," I said.

"Four important routes come together there. One route, called Darb-esh-Sherif, comes from the southeastern Sinai. People who want to go to Israel after visiting Mount Sinai and Saint Catherine's Monastery have used that route for centuries. It passes through the Nissana border close to Gaza."

"That sounds very direct," I commented.

"The second route is called Darb-el-Ghazza. This route is used by people who want to travel to Gaza from Quseima, travelling northeast along the Mediterranean coast. The third route, Darb-ez-Aaul, takes you from Egypt to the Gaza border post at Rafiah. It runs just north of the Quseima crossroad, and going south it runs from Quseima all the way to the Gulf of Aqaba."

"What's the fourth route?"

"Darb-el-Arish. This route takes you from Quseima to the ancient trading town of El-Arish, travelling north. El-Arish is an Egyptian town on the Mediterranean coast, and in ancient times it was a stopping point between Egypt and the land of Canaan or eastern regions like Persia."

"It sounds like Quseima has been an extremely busy town, for the desert."

"Yes, yes," Saadah said excitedly. "So, at the village of Ein-el-Qudeirat, traders stopped to get water or to rest, or sometimes to recover after a sandstorm. There were many problems in crossing such a huge section of almost completely barren land. They had to travel 175 kilometers from Egypt, moving due east across the Sinai, to reach Taba. Today, Taba is at the Israeli border. Even in modern times, this route is very important."[5]

I could visualise the caravans of Nabataeans and later Arab tribes trekking along the route that Saadah was describing. The camels are covered with colored fabrics and are laden with valuables. Groups of people with their camels saunter through the yellow sands. The animals carry incense, spices, utensils made of earthenware, metals, and other goods.

They are passing through the Sinai, travelling from Persia or the more distant southern Arabia towards Egypt. It is treacherous with howling sandstorms and endless nothingness to be seen. Even today,

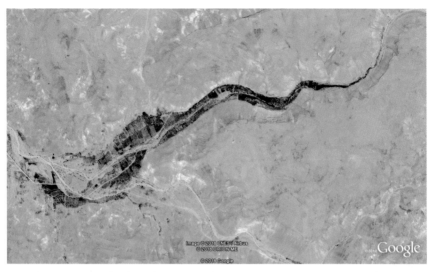

Kadesh Barnea valley (Ein-el Qudeirat), like a green snake in a vast desert. | Google Earth Image

some of these areas can be navigated only by camel; vehicles simply cannot manage.

"To reach Quseima from where we are now," Saadah told Rabia, "you have to drive northwards along the ancient route of Darb-ez-Aaul. After ten kilometers or so you'll see a mountain range to the east."

Rabia listened intently, clearly trying to visualize and remember the route.

Saadah went on, "Those mountains divide the Sinai from the Israeli border, near Eilat. You can't miss the spot. You'll see very high and steep rocky cliffs there, and the rocks have long dark stripes in them."

"That must be granite or basalt that erupted from volcanoes at the bottom of the ocean millions of years ago," I commented.

Saadah nodded briefly, less interested in geological history than modern-day touring. "When you pass the mountains," he said, "You must look out for the white powdery rocks with many colurs in them. You'll see the most incredible colors – you could think you're on the moon! Light-blue, ochre, and dark-red."

"It sounds amazing," I said.

"Then the road becomes a narrow track between the mountains," Saadah continued. "You'll see even more colored stones sticking out of the rock, which is very hard in that area. Keep moving along the dry wadi. Just carry on along that track . . . until you reach a tall Acacia tree."

"Hm," I said, thinking aloud. "Those stones on the track must be breccia from an ancient volcanic lava flow."

Saadah was still more interested in giving Rabia directions than hearing my geological insights. "Then you need to travel north on a track called Taba-al-Quseima," he said. "There is a signpost there. Then you cross many more flat dry wadi tributaries. The whole area looks desolate for about 200 kilometers. Just keep going. Eventually you'll see some sandy hills . . . you have to cross over those. Then, at last, you will arrive at the spring of Ein Qedeis."

Rabia had listened closely to the directions, and I felt confident that he would get me to the spring. But the word "desolate" had registered firmly in my mind. It sounded appropriate for the Kadesh Barnea camp.

We decided to buy something cool to drink and a snack to see us through the next few hours. Rabia rummaged around in the back of the jeep and emerged with bottles of cold water and *shrak* bread, which the Bedouin at Hazerot had wrapped and given us for the trip.

As we sat and ate, Saadah told us about his background. "I am from the Laheiwat Bedouin tribe. Our land is an area of about sixty kilometers stretching from the Eilat border of Israel, west into Sinai. My family, like many others, owned land on the Aqaba Gulf coast but it was sold to investors in the tourist property industry."

"Why?" I asked.

"The Egyptian government decided to sell the land."

"When was that?"

"Hm . . . just before 2000. Anyway, many of us, including some of my family, started to fish to earn a living. But our real love is roaming the land. We're nomads. So, many people in my tribe are unhappy about losing their land. It had been passed down through our families since the fourteenth century."

"Do you have children, Saadah?" I asked.

"Yes, three. They attend schools at the coast. So we're not able to roam much anyway. My kids have grown up living in a small stone house, but we often choose to sleep outside – like our ancestors did."

While we were sitting there chatting, a car suddenly appeared out of nowhere and pulled up close to us before stopping. A stocky Bedouin man dressed in a white keffiyeh and robes, but also wearing a tweed jacket, climbed out of the vehicle.

He greeted us. "As-salam alaykum, hello. I am Ghusun." We nodded in reply, and he looked at me. "I've heard that you would like to go to Quseima and Ein-el-Qudeirat."

"Word gets around," Rabia said.

"I studied archeology at Cairo when I was a young man," Ghusun said. "I can help you."

We welcomed him warmly and he sat down. "Why are you interested in that region?" he asked me.

"It was an integral part of the Israelites' journey," I explained. "They stayed there for at least nineteen years . . . some scholars say it might have been more than thirty years. During that time, the older generation died off. Those were the people who had left Egypt, and they were very rebellious. So G-d allowed that generation to die in the wilderness. It was their children who would enter the Promised Land. The biblical text refers to the place as being eleven days' journey from Horeb, travelling via Mt. Seir."[6]

"That's very interesting," Ghusun said. "Well, I learned about the archaeology of the area, but not about the biblical story."

"I'm interested in the archaeology too," I told him. "At first, archaeologists thought that Ein Qedeis might have been the site of Kadesh Barnea. These days, scholars disagree. Most researchers now think that the settlement north of Ein Qedeis, called Ein-el- Qudeirat, was Kadesh Barnea."

"Oh yes," said Saadah. "I've been there."

"There's a huge amount of water at Ein-el-Qudeirat. We Arabs call it the Holy Fountain," Ghusun said. "Or the Fountain of Omnipotence, or the Fountain of G-d's Power."[7] I later confirmed what he had told us, when I did research on the area.[8]

Saadah then told Rabia which route he should take so that we could continue our journey once we left the spring of Ein Qedeis. We were to travel along a wadi called Umm which ran between some low hills. We would eventually arrive at an intersection, where we should go straight and then continue driving for about six kilometers until we reached two small mountains. "The mountain to the east is Gebel-el-Amrhere," Saadah said. "There's an ancient spring called Muweilih at its foot, and an ancient tel on its top, with the Aharoni fortress. If you go a bit further, you'll come to the village of Quseima." He turned to me and said, "You already know about the large spring there. It gives water to many people."

"That must be Kadesh Barnea," I said.

"No. You have to go a bit further. If you look westwards, down the valley called Wadi-el-Ein, you see it slopes down to the west of the second mountain – called Gebel-el-Ein. The valley looks like a huge green snake crawling through the desert. That's where you'll find Kadesh Barnea. That is the village of Ein-el-Qudeirat, the Fountain of G-d's Power."

Rabia's eyes were gleaming. He was listening intently, and I too was spellbound.

Ghusun interrupted, nodding in agreement with what Saadah had just told us. "Yes," he said. "Many archaeologists think that Ein-el-Qudeirat is the real Kadesh Barnea. It has the largest spring in the Sinai Peninsula – and that's a big attraction. You have to see this spring to believe it! The water gushes out as if from nowhere. When you get closer, you can see the water pouring out of the limestone mountain. That's enough to give water to tens of thousands of people."

"That must be how the Israelites survived for so many years in the desert," I said. "I've read that the water there flows at forty cubic meters per hour."[9]

Ghusun went on: "Well, that area is much drier now than it would have been during the Exodus. In the past, there was more rain and also more underground water. So the spring would have been able to support even more people in those days."

"Is Ein-el-Qudeirat the largest oasis in the Sinai?" I asked.

"Oh yes," Ghusun replied. "Farmers in the valley have put up an irrigation system that covers about two square kilometers. And the area has fertile soil. That's why Wadi-el-Ein looks like a giant green snake."

"What crops do they grow?" I asked.

"Many of the farms grow vegetables, fruit trees, or date palms," Ghusun said. "Wait . . . I have a photo in my car." He went to fetch the photo from his vehicle. When he came back with it, we all crowded around to look at the picture. It showed a fascinating patchwork of colors: light green, dark green and yellow. Tall cypress trees were scattered across the valley, and even the steep slopes at the sides of the valley were intensely cultivated. The area looked beautiful and fertile, exuding abundance. At the edges of the oasis, the sand was poorer and more grainy.

I could imagine thousands of Israelite tents spread along the magnificent valley. The valley itself is bordered by mountains, which have a deep yellow color because of the sand. The solid clusters of tents give

3D close-up satellite image of Kadesh Barnea, showing the magnificent oasis where the Israelites spent the vast majority of their time during the Exodus. The area was not so intensely cultivated then. | Google Earth, Orion-Me, CNES/Airbus

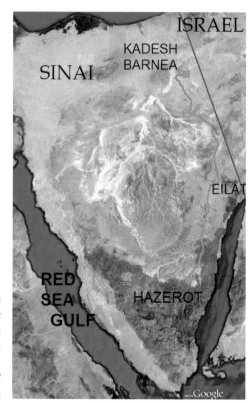

The road from Hazerot to Kadesh Barnea follows exactly the ancient trade route, which is still the main thoroughfare from South to North Sinai today. | Google Earth image edited by M Rawicz

security to the families who live there, adding to a sense of semi-permanent settlement. Along the length of the valley, clusters of evergreen trees are growing, adding a refreshing burst of life. Across the broad, level flood-plain of the valley there are patches of green, some light and others dark.

Ghusun was telling us more about the valley, and the sound of his voice jolted me back to reality. "Rothem trees grow there," he said. "They are a funny shape and look like leafless brooms."

I was aware of the association between the Rothem trees and the name of the camp, Ritma. I opened my bag to search for a note which I had printed at home, before leaving on my trip. I wanted to read it to my guides. I found it and unfolded it. "In 1881," I told my little audience, "an archaeologist called Henry Clay Trumbull described the area like this." I began to read from the note.[10]

"A marvelous sight out from the barren and desolate stretch of the burning desert-waste, and we had come with magical suddenness into an oasis of verdure and beauty, unlooked for and hardly conceivable in such a region. A carpet of grass covered the ground. Fig trees, laden with fruit nearly ripe enough for eating, were along the shelter of the southern hillside. Shrubs and flowers showed themselves in variety and profusion. Running water gurgled under the waving grass. It was quite unlike anything we had seen in the peninsula of Sinai. Bees were humming there, and birds were flitting from tree to tree. Enormous ant hills made of green grass-seed, instead of sand, were numerous. As we came into the wadi we had startled up a rabbit, and had seen larks and quails. It was, in fact, hard to realize that we were in the desert, or even near it.

"Above the gurgling sound of the running stream . . . we found our way through dense shrubbery until we reached the bank of the fountain-basin. There we looked down into a pool . . . a copious stream rushed from out the hillside . . . Its name Ein-el-Qudeirat, the 'Fountain of Omnipotence' or 'Fountain of G-d's Power,' was not inappropriate, in view of its impressiveness, bursting forth there so unexpectedly."

The men looked impressed.

Ghusun said, "When I visited the area, I went to the spring where the water pours onto flat ground and makes a large pond. A square wall has been built around the spring, and small stones have been placed around the pond to mark it off. Quseima has given people water, non-stop, from before Abraham's time."

"I'd really like to go there," I said. "Rabia, do you think we could find it without losing the way? If we got permission, of course."

Rabia looked a little perplexed. He told me that although he knew the desert well, he had never been to that particular area. By this time, it was midday on a Sunday.

"Why don't you come back to my home?" Ghusun suggested. "It's about ten kilometers from here. We can have a meal and rest before carrying on. I'll show you some of the old books that I got from Cairo. Saadah, why don't you come along too?"

SPECTACULAR OASIS VALLEY

Ghusun's home was a simple dwelling made of clay brick. He showed me an old book and I paged through it, gleaning information on the camp I wanted to visit next. Later I did more research, and learned that the Israelites had lived in that area during the Iron Age.[11]

I also learned, after my trip, that Ein Qedeis had been discovered in 1842 by John Rowlands.[12] Many archeologists have commented on this. Rowlands was the first person to suggest a link between the names "Kadesh" (Barnea) and "Kadis."

Much later, in 1905, Nathaniel Schmidt[13] again said that Ein-el-Qudeirat must have been the Exodus encampment of Kadesh Barnea. He reached this conclusion because of its position and the availability of water. In 1914, Woolley and Lawrence agreed that it was Kadesh Barnea, saying that it had the largest springs. Since then, many scholars have accepted this theory.[14]

Ein Qedeis has an ancient tel, with steeply sloping sides. It stands some 140 meters higher than the surrounding plain. From the summit one can see for kilometers in an arc of about 270°, with the campsite of Kadesh Barnea and the spring of Ein Muweilih being clearly visible. In ancient times, the mountain provided a strategically valuable lookout over the routes that crossed the plain below.

On top of the tel stands a fortress. Pottery shards have been found there too, called "Negev ware," made of coarse clay. These remains apparently show that a settlement had existed even before the fortress was built. In fact, excavations have revealed the ruins of three other Iron Age Israelite fortresses, built one on top of the other during different periods. Woolley and Lawrence think that a fortress might already have existed when Moses arrived.

The oldest fortress, from about 950 BCE, was oval-shaped. It might have belonged to a network of fortresses established by King Solomon to protect the trade routes and to secure the southern border of Judah.

After this fortress was destroyed, another one was built in the shape of a rectangle, between the eighth and seventh centuries BCE. It too was destroyed and was later replaced with a fortress that had towers, which was built between the seventh and sixth centuries BCE. This third fortress was also destroyed, apparently by the Edomites, at the time of the conquest of Palestine by the Babylonians.

The archaeologist Cohen did extensive excavations on this fortress.[15] It is believed that the final fortress was built because the site was so important to the Israelites – years after they had conquered Canaan. The mountain possibly had sacred religious associations with the Exodus. It also had the practical purpose of providing water from the spring. The Israelites may therefore have lived together in a single large and well-organized camp, or in smaller camps. They were likely to have claimed ownership of the springs at Ein-el-Qudeirat, Qedeis, Quseima and Muweileh.

The scattered remains of numerous settlements, both temporary and permanent, have been found in the surrounding areas. The earliest were from the Palaeolithic era. Settlements built during the Middle Bronze 1 era were probably built by the Israelites. These settlements had intensively cultivated gardens and orchards.

The bones of domesticated animals have been found, mainly those of goats and sheep, but also asses, cattle, and fowl of various species. Pollen from domesticated cereals suggests that the people living here ate agriculture crops as well as meat. The inhabitants may well have been desert nomads.

The entire area was hugely significant. It seems that the Israelites did indeed live there for many, many years. I was very interested in the findings of the many researchers in this area. I had looked into the works of other archeologists, such as Zeev,[16] Dothan,[17] and Ussishkin,[18] besides those of Woolley and Lawrence,[19] Schmidt,[20] and Cohen[21] that I had already come across, to satisfy my curiosity.

While we sat in the comfort of his home, Ghusun continued to tell me about Kadesh Barnea.

"It's one of the few places in the desert where migrating birds can stop," he said. "Birds flying south for the winter stop there to get some

Major ancient crossroad which is an ISIS centre today
(A) Al Qoseama to Rafah road (Darb-el-Arish)
(B) Taba to Al Kaseema road (Darb-el-Ghazza – Egypt to Gaza)
(C) Al Qoseama to Al Hasna road (Darb-esh-Sherif from St Catherine's)
(D) Road to Kadesh Barnea which is 4 km away

Satellite image showing: Quseima (Al Qosimah) with the main roads that lead to it: Darb-esh-Sherif from Saint Catherine's Monastery, Darb-el-Ghazza, Darb-el-Arish and the track that goes to Kadesh Barnea valley which is 4 kilometers south-east. | Google Earth, Orion-Me

rest and water. Bird conservation societies from all over the world visit Kadesh Barnea, because of this."

He motioned for me to come and eat. I joined him, Rabia, Tolba and Saadah for a meal. We went on talking about the general area, and the men also chatted about their daily lives.

It was very hot and Ghusun suggested that we stay longer so as not to travel in such heat. He invited us to stay for the rest of the day and also to sleep over, so we enjoyed chatting and relaxing before retiring for the night.

The next morning as we were preparing to leave, Ghusun took me aside and whispered a word of caution. "Don't be too hopeful about seeing the sites of Ein-el-Qudeirat, Qedeis, Quseima and Muweileh," he said.

"Oh?" I felt a stab of disappointment.

"I haven't heard of many people getting permission to go to the Kadesh area," he explained. "It's in a military zone."

"I won't give up just yet," I said.

"I've heard that there is a bad element there," he went on. "Some really bad people live in the far-off parts of the desert. They've been living there for a few years already. Actually, I think it might be lucky for you if you can't go there."

I looked at him. I appreciated his concern, but was not convinced.

"Just be happy with what I have taught you," Ghusun said. "Things sometimes work out for the best . . . often. Even if you don't agree."

I wanted to keep an open mind, but I had heard his advice and knew his intentions were good. Rabia was preparing to leave Ghusun's house. While he busied himself around the vehicle, I updated my log book. I wanted to include the information I had just learned about Kadesh Barnea.

The biblical account of Ritma or Kadesh Barnea in Numbers 13 narrates that Moses sent out twelve spies from the site to survey Canaan. On their return, the spies reported that the Canaanites were giant people who lived in walled cities. They said that the Israelites looked like grasshoppers in comparison. Only two of the spies, Joshua and Caleb, felt more positive. These two reported that the land flowed with "milk and honey."

The people became distressed and said, "We should have rather died in Egypt . . . why has G-d brought us [here] to fall by the sword?"

G-d became angry, and decreed that all people older than twenty years would perish in the wilderness. Joshua and Caleb were the only members of the younger generation who would be allowed to enter the Promised Land. The rebels defied G-d, and went to fight the Amalekites and Canaanites. These rebellious Israelites all perished in that battle.[22]

⊡ Slander and evil gossip

According to Hillel, the word "Ritma" denotes desolation and waste: "G-d will punish you with arrows from above and smoldering flame from hell below." Ritma is also derived from the word for "smoldering."[23]

Jacobson writes that "wasteland" refers not only to the desert surrounding Ritma, but also to the events that occurred there. The lesson learned at Ritma was that the fearful gossip of the spies was wrong when they had gone into Israel to scout out the land and had come back with very negative reports. This teaches that one should avoid engaging in bad-mouthing people and unjustly criticizing events or misrepresenting places. However, the name "Kadesh Barnea" had an entirely different meaning. It referred to the "holy place of desert wandering" and it was here that the Israelites spent many years, waiting for the younger generation to mature.[24]

"The scouts betrayed the Promised Land. Whatever their intentions may have been and they were indeed noble and spiritual, they defied the cardinal rule: questioning the very purpose of life because of the difficulties that arose. The spies had said, "We cannot conquer the land because it "consumes its inhabitants." G-d gave us life and charged us with the mission to transform the material land into a sacred place. Our role is to figure out how best – not whether – to fulfill our mission.

"We will face times of resignation in our life when we will be tempted to give up, and even to slander the "Promised Land" and the assurances that we can overcome any challenge. Such moments of self-doubt must be met with ferocious resistance and one should never give up on oneself, on your soul's potential and on G-d who has endowed you with faculties to face any challenge."[25]

Avoiding gossip has long been a principle by which I have lived, and I intended to maintain and strengthen that aspect of my life.

We bid our host farewell as we clambered back into Rabia's jeep. I wondered what drama or joy the rest of the day would bring. I was still waiting for the authorities to contact me about the permit. Ghusun's words, however, lingered in my mind.

We decided to journey further north in the meantime, to a location west of Kadesh Barnea that was outside the military zone. This route would bypass the military zone, but it also meant that we would have to detour via a northwestern route through some remote desert territory.

Rabia said, "Getting the permit may still take a day to two, or even longer . . . maybe never. I want to try this route because I haven't been there before. Let's go today, and see what the roads are like."

We drove for two hours on a remote road. For a long while we sat in silence, and I thought about the huge expanse of desert that we were crossing.

Eventually I spoke. "I'm sure that we all have a dream," I told Rabia, "about feeling calm and quiet, at peace with ourselves."

"Hm?"

"Since I've been in the desert, I seem to have connected with that peacefulness. It's like I've discovered a new way of life, a new way of being in the world – in a quiet space, at peace with myself. I think the silence of the desert brings out an inner truth."

He nodded, and then spoke slowly and with intensity. "Yes, sure, people who come to the desert discover that truth."

"Maybe there's something inside our spirit – I mean the spirit of all people – waiting to be discovered," I said. "Being part of the natural world here somehow allows an inner light to shine inside me. It's not my light, it's G-d's, and I am starting to understand this. It's so real, I don't have to just *believe* in G-d . . . it's as if I *know* and *feel* G-d!"

"Ah yes, many people who come to the desert find peace in their hearts," Rabia said. "The Sinai is a place connected to prophets and spiritual people. You can feel the greatness of Allah here. People say it's like coming home. And when you sleep in the desert at night and see all the stars out there, it's easier to find that star inside you too. That's why I love living here. And I love taking people through the desert."

"You've said it just as I feel it!" I exclaimed. "I've found a star inside myself. It's as if I have really found G-d in the world around me and also a part of Him inside me."

Tolba and I listened intently as Rabia continued, "Yes, that's what brings joy to us. We love the quiet and we connect to each other, even when we're not talking. We *feel* Allah. That's one of the best things about being a Bedouin."

"But your lives aren't easy," I commented.

"No," Rabia agreed. "We work hard to get food, to gather wood for the fire, to plant tomatoes or potatoes . . . but we're never alone. There are always people around you who care about you. Even if I am walking alone in the desert, I know my brothers, uncles and nephews are there for me if I need them. We're a big community in this big desert, and we stick together. People who come here from other places, especially those who live in a city, wish they could feel the same."

I realized how much I enjoyed having Rabia and Tolba as my travelling companions and guides.

As time wore on, the day became desperately hot. Eventually we needed to get out of the car and eat something, but there was virtually

Resting on the desert sand. | M Rawicz Trip Photo

no shade anywhere. The best we could do was a spot between two scraggly thorn trees, where Rabia brought the car to a stop. He picked up a dead log from beneath one of the trees and wedged it at the side of the car, and attached a large piece of material to the roof-rack and tied the other side to the stubby branches. The cloth gave us some much-needed shade.

Tolba showed me another trick: "Look, you can make a fire with this dry camel dung lying here."

To my surprise, the dung burnt well and gave off a lot of heat. Tea was ready in a few moments, and we drank it together with a meal of flat bread.

In the silence, a sudden howl burst forth, followed by yelping.

"What was that?" I asked, alarmed. "I feel as if something is watching us from the mountains."

Rabia shrugged and laughed. "Relax," he said. "There are no lions here, maybe just a few wolves."

As we chatted, I saw another side of this Bedouin man with whom I had already spent so much time. He pulled out a green banknote from his pocket and started folding it into an unusual shape. Then he laughed and showed it to me.

"Look," he said. "We Arabs sometimes joke about Osama Bin Laden and September 11, 2001."

I stared at the folded banknote, and was utterly shocked to see that it resembled the Twin Towers being attacked. Here I was, sitting in the middle of nowhere with someone who could laugh about such a thing. I began to feel extremely vulnerable.

"You should have seen the happiness in some villages the day it happened," Rabia said. He must have noticed my discomfort, because he added, "But you know the people here, they are not educated about the world. They just believe whatever they are told."

I found myself unable to comment.

"They are good people," Rabia assured me. "Don't you worry. You know, in the Sinai we suffered a lot, because the tourists stopped visiting after the attack."

I remained uneasy for a while after we resumed our journey, with only the sight of sand flashing past the car window for company. Eventually I began to relax again, and for the next three hours, we chatted sporadically.

The trip was becoming long and boring. Essentially, we had taken a detour of some 173 kilometers along small roads, passing an occasional tiny Bedouin encampment. The heat was intense, with visible heat-waves sizzling up from the endless bare sand. I fell asleep for part of the journey.

Eventually, we were some fifteen kilometers west of Kadesh Barnea. There, with the help of a lone shepherd, we found a spot with cell phone reception. Rabia called the authorities to try and find out about the permit, but to no avail. We were both feeling irritable and tired. We had reached the Abou Ewaygala road, just north of Al-Oga.

We felt unable to travel any more before sunset, and gratefully accepted the hospitality of a local Bedouin woman who was camping beside the road. She offered us her half-open tent for the night. After a light meal that she generously provided, we debated our plans for the following morning. We sat around our hostess's fire, under a sky brilliant with stars.

Eventually I made up my mind about how to tackle the next stage of my trip. "I want to go to the Nitzana border in the morning," I told Rabia. The Nitzana border post to Israel was just twenty kilometers away from our current spot.

"And then?" he asked.

Saying goodbye to Rabia after having experienced so much together. | *Stopping for a rest in the desert.* | *M Rawicz Trip Photo*

"I'll cross into Israel and see what I can from there. Then I'll come back into Egyptian territory later, once I've heard from the authorities . . . if they give me permission, I mean."

"That sounds like a good plan," he said. "But I think you won't get permission. It's a strange part of the Sinai, which is why I've never been there. Some people say if you go there, you could get shot by the Egyptian patrols. It's very close to the Egyptian and Israeli border. There must be a good reason why people stay away."

The next day we pushed onwards to the Israeli border, where I bid Tolba and Rabia, my Bedouin friends, farewell. It was a sad moment for me. We had established a good comradeship and experienced so much together. I was already missing Fteha, who had earned a special place in my heart, and I felt part of their family. I knew that they would be my friends for a long time to come. Rabia had helped me to learn more about the Exodus as well as initiating me into desert life and introducing me to the modern Bedouin lifestyle. His influence was unforgettable. Tolba had been a quiet but warm companion.

As we parted, I promised to come back again on a future trip. They left me at the Nitzana border post, midway along the fence dividing Sinai and Israel – which was heavily guarded. I later learned that this border post was frequently closed because of Israeli-Palestinian conflict. This point also happened to be part of the route the ancient Israelites took when they left Kadesh Barnea and moved east towards Canaan.

HELLO ISRAEL

At the border, there was a small building on the Egyptian side where passport control was dealt with. The premises were slightly in need of a facelift but the border guards themselves looked smart, with impeccable uniforms and caps. As I arrived, a guard asked for my passport. I searched my handbag and had a moment of panic.

"I think I may have left it in my Bedouin friend's car," I muttered, frantically searching the compartments of my bag. Eventually I found the passport in a small zippered pocket on the side of my handbag. From then on it would stay in one specific place!

I was allowed to cross into the fenced area through a turnstile that led into a strip of no-man's land between the two countries. I then passed through a second fenced area with another turnstile, and finally reached the Israeli border post. The military presence here was noticeable. This border post, unfortunately, had been the target of ongoing incidents of smuggling, with Palestinians trying to take weapons into Gaza. In addition, for many years suicide bombers had terrorized the Israeli population. The feeling of tension and "high alert" security was palpable.

One of the first Israeli soldiers I saw "up close" was a woman, a bombshell beauty with long curly blonde hair cascading over her shoulders, sunglasses hiding her gaze, and close-fitting fatigues underscoring her athletic and attractive body. She carried an M16 rifle diagonally across her chest.

The border post building and its surrounds were clean, organized and carefully arranged. The terminal had palm trees and air-conditioning: a calm and sanitized space. I was led by young, smiling soldiers though the formalities of entering Israeli territory. A short bald man observed me, as he was standing back a little. Then began the unpacking of the contents of my luggage by customs officials. Two chubby women sifted

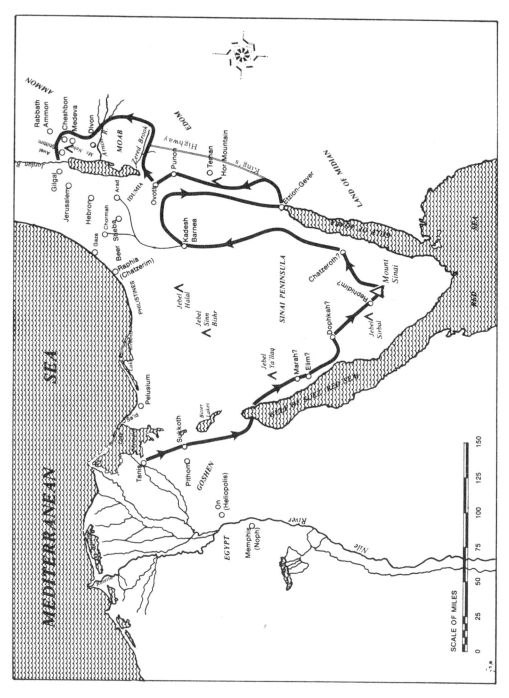

The overall Exodus route from The Living Torah, by Rabbi Aryeh Kaplan, based on Adolf Neubauer, "La Geographie du Talmud", 1868.[1]

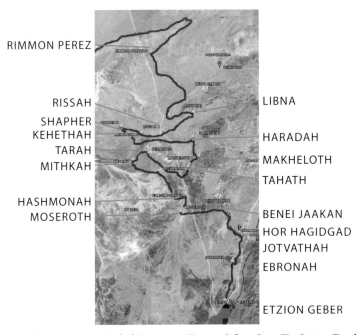

RIMMON PEREZ

RISSAH
SHAPHER
KEHETHAH
TARAH
MITHKAH

HASHMONAH
MOSEROTH

LIBNA

HARADAH
MAKHELOTH
TAHATH

BENEI JAAKAN
HOR HAGIDGAD
JOTVATHAH
EBRONAH

ETZION GEBER

The Exodus route from Kadesh Barnea to Etzion Geber, from The Living Torah, superimposed onto Google Earth map.[3]

through the odd assortment of items, throwing each other amused glances.

The searching and scanning of my luggage was thorough and time-consuming because of the strict security measures. Virtually every item was removed and examined individually. Evidently the officials were not used to seeing a middle-aged Jewish woman travelling through the Arab territories, apparently alone, and entering Israel through the middle of the desert. They seemed surprised. I was taken into an office to be questioned, and sat waiting.

Eventually, a handsome man – quite the lady-killer – arrived. He was about 1.9 meters tall and had huge pectoral muscles.

"What are you doing coming alone to the Sinai?" he asked.

I related my saga. I think my Hebrew name, Malka, was the thing that ultimately saved me from further endless interrogations. I felt great relief at being able to move on after these exhausting procedures.

Although I understood why the border post was a hive of military activity, I was struck by the contrast between the atmosphere in the desert and here. I had become accustomed to the isolation of the desert and the Bedouin people's calm and relaxed attitudes. Now, entering Israel, I was confronted with the sight of soldiers moving around and army tanks parked beneath the palm trees.

As I walked out of the building, I saw an Israeli flag fluttering against the sky above a small bunker. The blue *Magen David* – the Star of David – on its white background filled me with pride. During the relatively short existence of the modern state of Israel, the people have achieved so much.

Although I had entered Israel earlier than planned, the guide I had contacted before leaving South Africa was able to meet me at short notice. His name was Haim. We had called him that morning to explain what had happened; fortunately, he was able to accommodate my new arrangements.

Haim lives in a settlement in the Negev, and his field of expertise is the ecology of the Negev. I had corresponded with him by email before my trip, and he had agreed to guide me through the Israeli leg of it. We met now in person in the border post parking lot.

Haim was in his early forties and greeted me with a pleasant smile, and I could see immediately that he was an energetic, outdoors type who would be happy to have an adventure or two. He introduced me to his 15-year-old son, Michael, who was coming along for the ride and to see parts of Israel that he had not seen before. As we climbed into Haim's jeep, I intuitively knew we would get along well.

"I'm sorry about the sudden change in plan," I said.

"Well, I had to rush to get here in time to meet you," Haim replied, "but luckily my schedule was flexible."

He had come equipped with maps of the area, books on the fauna and flora of the Negev, bottles of water, an Israeli army hat, radio equipment, a copy of the Wayfarer's Prayer, and a gun.

"Let's have coffee in Nitzana," he said. "We can discuss how to spend the next few days."

I agreed, and he drove us straight to Nitzana and parked close to a café. We went in and sat down.

I told him, "While I'm here, I want to visit twelve of the sites where the Israelites camped during the Exodus."

"How long have you been travelling?"

"This is my twenty-third day," I replied, realizing with some surprise that this meant it was my third week.

The Israelites had progressed from being a struggling people, according to Hillel,[26] to a young clan to mature adults, who had made progress in finding their way through life's challenges. They had learned about overcoming doubt, apathy, cynicism and indifference. They had been able to achieve a degree of unity and cohesion among themselves, and had found some inner peace as they had taken control over their own lives. They had surrendered to a Higher Power and were working towards figuring out how best to fulfil their mission.

I too was at a stage of being more adult or mature, with a more cheerful and open approach to life. I felt more settled and in control over my life, and was less driven and task-oriented than before. I was beginning to feel a resonance with the people that I was with and that I met. A sense of inner peace, a new strange – but real and personal – connection to G-d was developing. I had begun to understand that I wanted my life to be one of harmony and connection with people, rather than a bustle of competitiveness.

We agreed that I would first go to Haim's home on Kibbutz Sde Boker, in the Negev desert of southern Israel, to discuss the plans for our forthcoming trip. His family welcomed me. As we chatted I learned that Haim has a Doctorate in Ecology and Animal Behavior from the University of Ben-Gurion, Sde-Boker. He also has seventeen years of teaching experience in the area of nature and desert animals. Some of his hobbies are to photograph desert animals, tour in the Negev Desert, and travel the big deserts of Africa and the world.

The plans had to take into consideration that the Israelites' route had become quite jagged in this area. The first few camps after Ritma (Kadesh Barnea) were in current-day Israeli territory, near the border. The next two, Kehethah and Shapher, were back on the Egyptian side. Then came three more in Israel: Haradah, Makheloth and Tahath. The final four camps were again in Egypt, namely Tarah, Mithkah, Hashmonah and Moseroth.

It would have been impossible for me to try and follow the route in the same sequence. The only two places where a tourist could cross between Israel and Egypt were Nitzana and Taba, the latter of which is

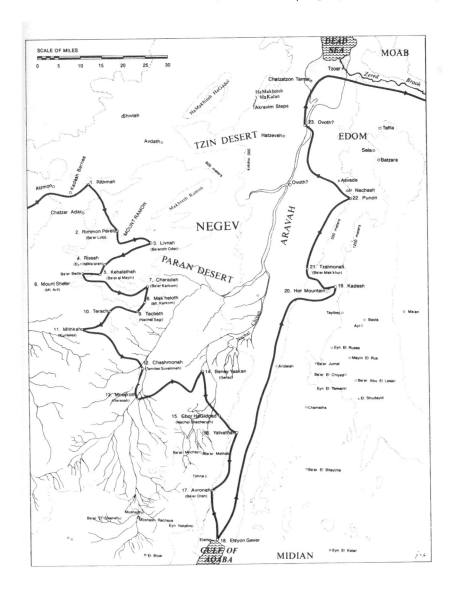

The Exodus route from Kadesh Barnea onwards from The Living Torah, by Rabbi Aryeh Kaplan, based on Adolf Neubauer "La Geographie du Talmud." 1868.[2]

situated at the southernmost point of Israel, in the city of Eilat on the Aqaba Gulf. The only logical option was to visit all of the Israeli camps in a row, and then cross back into the Sinai to explore the remaining camps there. A final trip to Israel would be necessary to visit the last camp, which lay far more to the east than the other Israeli sites. It would have been impossible to cross the border backwards and forwards just to maintain the exact Exodus sequence. In biblical times, the Israelites' zig-zag movements were unimpeded by the political and physical barriers and borders I now faced.

The plan that emerged was that we would use Haim's jeep for most of the way. Where it was possible to hike to view a site close up, we would do so. On such days, Haim would contact a friend of his to come and take care of Haim's jeep while we were hiking. The friend evidently had a son, who – like Haim and his own son – would travel with his father.

Haim offered to take me on a mini tour of the kibbutz and its surroundings. We went to the retirement home of Israel's first Prime Minister, David Ben-Gurion, which is now a museum. Ben-Gurion had moved to this kibbutz to work on his vision of cultivating the arid Negev desert. As we looked around the kibbutz, I learned that it had originally been a large agricultural farm or small village during the 7th to 9th century. It became one of the pioneers of Jewish settlement in the Negev. Although it was comprised of severely degraded sheep grazing land, the Jewish settlers had rejuvenated it into a flourishing community of about eighty families when I visited it in 2003.

We planned our trip before he suggested that I sleep over at a local guest house.

ISRAELI FIRING SQUADS – RIMMON PEREZ   CAMP 16

"And they departed from Ritma, and pitched at Rimmon perez."[1]

"Even though the Israelites were at the brink of the stage of being equivalent to mature adults, many of them had still not broken free from a sense of failure in their progress. Many were still subject to having to depend on the group to feel safe and accepted, even unfortunately being subject to coercion for negative activities, pressure from cynicism and negative criticisms."[2]

"Rimmon perez" refers to a "spreading pomegranate tree" or "heavy-fruited pomegranate."[3] The idea of pomegranate trees was quite different from the things I had been looking out for at the previous camps. I hoped that we would indeed see some of these trees, laden with fruit, at the next camp.

In the morning we journeyed south in Haim's jeep towards the Rimmon perez campsite. We passed the square yellow houses of the Nitzana youth settlement, which runs educational programs to teach immigrants skills in farming vegetables and flowers, as well as agricultural and greenhouse methods.

On the way, Haim chatted about life in Israel. "My friend Ilan lives in a farming settlement where he owns many greenhouses," he told me. "These days life is hard for him as he has to do almost everything himself. Until a few months ago, he had Arab workers helping him, but they had to leave the area."

"Why was that?" I asked.

"We've had so many terrorist attacks from across the Gaza border that the army no longer allows people to move freely between Israel and Gaza. So the farmers are suffering, and their crops are suffering. The Arabs can't get work and the farmers can't get laborers. It's a calamity for both Israelis and Palestinians."

The problems between Israelis and Palestinians are well known, but to hear this personal story from a local was sobering nonetheless.

"We live with great care," Haim continued. "Almost everybody in Israel has lost a family member or friend because of the attacks. One of my wife's best friends was blown up in a bus by a suicide bomber just two weeks ago. The problem is that extremists still get through the border and come and attack the residents here."

I had just spent such a peaceful time in the desert, and Haim's comments were a rude awakening. It was a reminder of the reality that Israelis have to live with every day.

Haim added, "A Kassam missile fired from the Gaza Strip fell two kilometers away from the settlement. Palestinians still manage to get through, despite the constant military presence."

I thought about the lesson from the camp of Ritma, and willed myself to ignore the misgivings that were busy arising in my mind. I wanted to believe that problems were there to be overcome, and that we are endowed with the resources to face any challenges we are given. I would banish my doubts.

We continued to discuss Israeli politics and lifestyles. We were travelling along a military route from which Israel's western border is guarded. The road runs along an ancient wadi from north to south, and the ancient Israelites would have walked this route too.

Not long after we left Nitzana, we reached Tel Nitzana, which stands atop a high sandstone mountain. This was an extremely large fortification built during the first century BCE by the Nabataeans. This may well have been along the spice route with its fortresses that was being

Tel Nitzana a Nabataean fortification atop a high sandstone mountain. The Israelites passed this way after leaving Kadesh Barnea. |
M Rawicz Trip Photo

Remains of the Nitzana ancient fortification from the first century BCE. |
M Rawicz Trip Photo

We examined a map showing the wadi that leads to Gaza and Taba on the ancient Incense Route, probably used by the Israelites. | M Rawicz Trip Photo

investigated by the archaeologist Meshel.[4] Haim, Michael and I braved the howling, freezing winds to walk up to the fortress.

Inside, we found a few inner courtyards with some of the original smooth plaster still in place. From this dizzying height we could see the wadi that led to Gaza, and others leading southwards to Taba; our journey would follow the southern route. I felt awed to be standing in this ancient Nabatean castle from which one could see far and wide in all directions.

Tel Nitzana had been a station on the eastern branch of the ancient Incense Route, serving pilgrims and merchants who travelled from Saudi Arabia to Sinai or central Egypt. The hill itself is no larger than a football field, but its history seemed larger than life. The Israelites, however, would not have seen the fortress. It was built after their time.

We watched some large birds swooping and circling. Haim and Michael drew on their knowledge to tell me about the birds we were looking at.

Haim said, "In this area, we have eagles, but they're close to extinction. There are only eight to ten pairs of Golden Eagles left here – those birds you can see swooping gracefully in circles."

"I hope they'll survive," I said.

"And look – there are two Long-Legged Buzzards, which are birds of prey with long grey streaked wings and light-brown patches around their bellies. Those are the ones that look as if they're scouting the ground for small animals."

As we were leaving Tel Nitzana, we saw a sand-laden whirlwind approaching. We hurried to get back to the car before it hit us; Haim estimated that the whirlwind was between thirty and forty meters high. We jumped into the jeep and drove on, relieved to be safe.

A short while later, we passed a small metal sign shaped like a camel riding on a bicycle.

"What on earth is that?" I asked.

Michael laughed, "It's a humorous demarcation of an old camel track," he said. "These days it's also used as a recreational cycling trail by many local residents and hikers."

Not long after this, we passed a small group of people riding on camels. The saddles on the camels were beautiful: red and elaborately decorated. I also enjoyed the sight of a facility on a nearby hillside, where several camels were housed in an enclosure.

Further along, I noticed that some of the stones at the side of the road bore Nabatean or another ancient script that showed the direction of the camel track. This road had apparently been used as a camel route for over 3000 years. Then I saw a stone structure, and Haim turned the jeep off the trail so that I could investigate it. The structure stood about two meters high and had a rectangular shape, built of square yellow stone blocks. Evidently it had been a Nabatean reservoir, which provided further evidence that this route between Egypt and the empires to the east had been used for thousands of years.

I could picture the merchants with their loaded camels carrying spices and other valuable goods trudging along this track. My mind flashed back and forth, integrating the new information with what I had already known.

Further along on the cycle trail, we passed a small hill called Givat Raglim, meaning "feet." This is a popular Israeli hiking area. On a nearby hill we saw a large guest-house for hikers and cyclists, which looked spacious and well-maintained. We also saw a signpost to the modern-day Ezuz, a small settlement. I was still on the lookout for the location of camp Rimmon Peretz.

We arrived at a small oasis that looked as if it had been a place of

Israeli soldiers training to shoot at an oasis where the Israelites camped. |
M Rawicz Trip Photo

comfort for many years. Although it sported the typical cluster of palm trees, I saw some non-indigenous species too, including pines. Haim parked the jeep and we went for a walk through the cluster of large Tamarisk trees, with dry pine leaves crunching underfoot. I sat on a wooden picnic bench to enjoy the quiet, with just the twitter of birds and rustle of leaves overhead in the faint breeze.

Suddenly we heard loud shouting: *"Aish, aish, aish!"* This means "fire" in Hebrew.

With great curiosity, but also taking great care, we walked through the remaining trees and reached a sandy clearing. Ahead of us, kneeling on their right knees, were at least two dozen Israeli soldiers wearing khaki uniforms and helmets, and aiming ominous-looking Uzis at a target.

One of the soldiers was shouting repeatedly at the top of his voice, "Fire, fire, fire!"

Haim said, "This must be where they train to shoot accurately."

So there they were, training in the hot midday sun. I stared in amaze-

An ancient well with a duct from which livestock were given water. |
M Rawicz Trip Photo

ment. I was glad that we were watching from a safe distance, although I presumed the soldiers were not using live ammunition.

A strapping soldier marched over to us. "I am Rephael," he said. "Please move along now." He cautioned us that onlookers were not welcome.

We walked further into the oasis town. As we walked, I reflected on the sight of the soldiers and the immediacy of the events that Haim had told me about, related to the political tension of the area. Ever since the establishment of the State of Israel in 1948, some Arab League countries have been in conflict with Israel because they hold competing territorial ambitions. Since 1994, the focus of this conflict has been narrowed down to Israeli–Palestinian relations. The current military alert within Israel has resulted from numerous suicide bombings and attacks by the Palestinians, and Israel has established a complicated system of roadblocks and checkpoints around major Palestinian areas in an effort to protect Israeli citizens.

Around the turn of the millennium (2000), Israel slowly undertook a unilateral withdrawal from the Gaza Strip. This was a reversal of the earlier Israeli settler movement. The Israeli government required all

Looking into the ancient well which has been here since biblical times. |
M Rawicz Trip Photo

Jews to leave their homes and businesses in Gaza, sometimes under great duress – and permanently. These Jewish people were helped to resettle within the more central Israeli area. Gaza then officially became Palestinian territory.

When terrorist-linked Hamas seized control of Gaza during a violent civil war with its rival the Fatah party (both parties being Palestinian groups), Israel started to restrict who was allowed to enter Israel freely and who was not. These restrictions on the movement of certain people were put in place at the border between Gaza and Israel. Israel continues to maintain this blockade, in an attempt to limit Palestinian rocket attacks on Israel and the smuggling of weapons capable of hitting Israeli cities. A periodic exchange of rocket and mortar attacks continues between the two countries.

The whole situation distressed me greatly. I resolved again to maintain good relations with everyone I met in person, so that I could do my own small part to keep the peace on an individual level.

Haim, Michael and I stumbled on another surprise. In the middle of an expanse of sand, stood a raised round stone structure surrounded by an iron fence. I went closer and saw that it was an old well, still in good condition. From one side of the structure a duct ran out for about three meters. This must have been where livestock were given water to drink.

I stepped over the iron barrier to examine the well more closely. The bottom of the shaft was in darkness and seemed to be about ten meters below the ground. On one side of the shaft, I was amazed to see a C-shaped chunk carved into the stone. This was where the rope to lift the bucket had run. Over the centuries, the rope had carved into the stone edge of the well during the countless raisings and lowering of the bucket.

As I peered into the dark depth of the well, I suddenly noticed an owl perched on a ladder which descended into the shaft. This was a most unexpected sight! The bird and I stared at each other for several minutes. I was mesmerised by the owl's presence, especially because this species is known to be rarely seen and very shy. My heart pounded with excitement at being so close to this special bird.

I was just as excited when I stepped back from the well and noticed a large plaque beside the stone wall. It read, in Hebrew, "The Well of Aaron."

In 1817 a professor of oriental studies, Mr. Edward Henry Palmer,[5] wrote that two deep wells existed at this site. The wells were built of heavy stones and were surrounded by troughs. One well was dry at the time, but the second provided water for hundreds of camels, goats and horses. The years between 1935 and 1937 were challenging in the Negev, and the British government renovated the well of Moses that was nearby to try and assist the local population.

To my surprise and delight, a flock of indigenous Efroni partridges

A plaque next to the ancient well, which read, in Hebrew, "The Well of Aaron," refers to the Exodus. | M Rawicz Trip Photo

The riverbed that led from Rimmon Perez to the next camp, along which the Israelites may have walked. | *M Rawicz Trip Photo*

came right up to me and milled about my feet. These small birds are known to be fearless, though flightless.

As I turned to leave, I noticed another hill not far off, which contains a cave built of large stones. It is used to shelter sheep, and has been used for this purpose for many centuries.

We drove half a kilometer further, and I looked back to see the terrain. We had been driving along a dry riverbed that led from Rimmon perez to the site of the next camp. This wadi ran between bare, rocky undulating hills, its soft sand and carpet of grey desert scrub providing a stark contrast with the bare surroundings. The wadi would certainly have fulfilled some of the travelling Israelites' needs.

Our journey took us next along a sand road that followed the border between Israel and Sinai, known as Route 171. It is used mainly by the military.

The ancient Israelites had journeyed southwards alongside the present-day Israeli border, following the Nahal Nitzana Wadi, which runs parallel to the road a few hundred meters away. The scene was one of dry rolling scrubland, and held no real interest for the eye. The vegetation was a flat grey groundcover that hugged the earth, with an occasional brush-like Acacia tree.

The village of Ezuz next to the original Rimon Perez campsite. | *M Rawicz Trip Photo*

We went to explore the village of Ezuz, which was inhabited by ten families. The local population included a hermit, an astronomer, a donkey keeper, a farmer of goats (who was also a cheese maker), the owner of a bed-and-breakfast, and military guards. We wanted to buy goat-milk cheese, but the farmer was out of stock. He took me to see the goats. I found it a rather smelly place with a lot of goat noises coming from the wooden pens.

The wild birds, however, seemed to appreciate the settlement of Ezuz. We saw a Black Kite and a Shrike.

Haim said, "When it rains a lot, this area is covered with green groundcover that has beautiful pink, red and white flowers. The flowers stretch out over the ground as far as the eye can see. You'd never think that the area usually looks as barren as it does now!"

He then took me to see an ancient cistern, which had been built by King Solomon and was called the Hehet.

Haim explained, "This cistern was not built in a wadi. They knew that if they built it in the wadi, it would just fill up with silt from all the water during the storms. So, they constructed the channel in a clever way, so that the water would run down from higher ground into a reservoir."

"It seems the Jewish people have always been good at innovation and invention," I commented, and Haim agreed.

On some of the hills nearby, we saw rows of stone walls. "Those are the remains of ancient agricultural terraces," Haim said. "They were built to trap the water and collect the sediment. They're proof of the extensive agriculture that was practised here in the Byzantine period." He went on to tell me that every shallow valley in this area had been cultivated during the Byzantine period. The cultivation in turn improved the condition of the soil in the channels. Today, they are still full of flourishing desert plants.

We drove on. A short distance further, Haim steered the jeep off the road. After a short and slightly bumpy ride, we reached a place where piles of stones had been heaped upon each other to a height of about half a meter. They looked unusual, and we got out of the jeep to examine them.

Haim told me they were called *tumuli* and were ancient tombs. Such tombs are scattered throughout the Negev, but it is uncertain whether they existed when the Israelites passed through. Still, their presence assured me that I was following an ancient route.

An ancient water cistern built by King Solomon on the route that the Israelites would have walked. | M Rawicz Trip Photo

Stone structures called "Tumuli" which are ancient tombs. |
M Rawicz Trip Photo

We climbed back into the jeep and drove on. The vehicle bounced around as we winded our way down a stony, bumpy road to get to the Har Ramon area.

Haim told me about the local ecology and weather. "There are very few plants here, because the rainfall is only about fifty millimeters per year," he said. "The small amount of rain that does fall is blown in during autumn and spring, from the wind that rolls off the Red Sea."

"Does it ever snow here?" I asked.

"Yes, in winter. And then in summer, it all looks very different! Believe it or not, those bare rocky hills are entirely covered in flowers during summer, and the ground looks like a brilliantly colored carpet."

Haim pulled the jeep to a stop right beside a bush, and rolled down his window. He plucked some of the leaves and handed me a few. "This is a Maluach plant," he said. "It's very salty, and goes well with salad. Here, taste it."

I nibbled on one of the leaves. Indeed, it was delicious! Haim promptly picked another big bunch of leaves and gave them to me to snack on.

He drove slowly on, but soon stopped again at a different type of bush. He picked some of these leaves too, and again handed me a sample.

An Atlantic Pistachio tree with leaves coloured red by a chemical injected by wasps when they lay their eggs. | M Rawicz Trip Photo

"Smell these," he said. "They also taste good. You can make it into a tea if you have a sore stomach. The bush is called Artemisia Herba Alba."

I was still busy savoring the fragrance of the leaves, when the silence of the desert was suddenly broken by a strange animal cry. I looked around, startled. I saw nothing at all but the usual bare desert.

"That's the cry of an Asiatic wild ass," Haim said. "It's also called an Onager."

"I've heard of those," I said. "But I'd never heard the sound they make."

"Onagers lived here in the biblical times. But then they nearly went extinct. Now it seems that people have managed to save them from extinction, and they've been reintroduced into this area. So they roam around freely here, just as they would have done centuries ago. If we're lucky, we might get to see one of them – not just hear it."

Michael was delighted by the whole thing. Clearly, he loved the fauna and flora of this area.

"What do the animals in this area eat?" I asked.

"Herbivores, such as Gazelles and Ibexes, mainly eat the plants which grow in the channels," Haim said. "The Onagers also eat bigger shrubs."

Haim pointed out some gently meandering trails, from which stones had been cleared to create a pathway for heavily laden camels. The tracks had existed since ancient times. A short distance later, we came upon a thicket of beautiful old gnarled desert trees. They had lived for so long that the inside of their trunks had been completely hollowed out, and the bark was twisted and knotted all the way up, deep into the light green foliage.

"These are Atlantic Pistachio trees which are very tough," Haim said. "Several hundred of them have survived for centuries in the Negev Highlands. Their brilliant red coloring is not from flowers but leaves that wasps inject with chemicals into which they lay their eggs."

I contemplated the passage of history that these sturdy trunks would have witnessed. They would have been around during Ottoman Turkish rule in the 17th century, when Palestine was a province of Syria. They would have seen the influx of Muslim and Christian Arabs in the 18th century, the start of British rule in 1922, followed by a long period when nomads controlled the Negev, and finally in 1948 the Israeli War of Independence.

Haim made a turn onto a smaller road, and we continued travelling for two kilometers, at which point we passed a sign to Beer Lotz.

"The Beer Lotz are water cisterns from the ancient Israelite period," Haim explained. "They were built about 3000 years ago, when this part of the Negev was a prosperous agricultural area. The cisterns were dug to catch the winter rains and provide drinking water to the people and their animals."

"When did this area stop being inhabited by people?" I asked.

"As far as we know, people lived here until 586 BCE, but then the Israelites were exiled from their land for the first time."

He went on to explain that 3000 years ago, during the time of King Solomon, an attempt was made to settle the lands. He hoped that this would create a barrier between the Israelite territory and the surrounding regions, which were dominated by desert nomads. The cistern that we had just passed was built during the era of King Solomon.

We arrived at a stone structure that had been built to accommodate hikers overnight. It was situated in the middle of nowhere, which allowed guests to spend time in solitude in the desert.

"Some people enjoy coming here," Haim said, as he brought the jeep to a stop and turned off the engine. "You're not the only person who appreciates getting away from the noise and modern civilization for a while."

We walked for about twenty-five meters, and within that short distance saw numerous wells. Seventeen wells have been discovered within a two-square-kilometer area in this region, of which fifteen wells still collect water in the winter months. Some were open pits with side walls made of rocks, but others had been dug straight into the ground. The wells had varying levels of water.

I felt an atmosphere of mystery surrounding these wells. They had endured the passage of so many centuries, and I wondered about all the people that must have benefitted from them. So this was the campsite where the Israelites had stopped. How interesting that modern people also liked to come here to relax! It was a fascinating find.

The air was enjoyably fresh and cool, and I still hoped to find some pomegranate trees. I sat down to ponder the meaning of this camp. *Rimmon* means pomegranates, which in turn are often associated with the Bible.

⊡ Commitment without understanding

The sages noted a correlation between a pomegranate's 613 seeds and the 613 commandments in the Torah that Jewish people are meant to follow. Furthermore, **peretz** means a breakthrough. At this camp the Israelites had a breakthrough in faith when they undertook a commitment to follow G-d's commandments for the sake of Torah without necessarily understanding them.[6]

The profusion of seeds in the pomegranate also represents success, fertility and benevolent endeavors. The Israelites were at the stage when their efforts were yielding positive results. They were able to bring up the new generation, learn and disseminate their knowledge and stimulate each other to greater levels of achievement, as explained by Jacobson.[7] They had begun to deal with reality as mature adults, building their lives and facing the stress of trying to be good human beings.[8]

I, too, had a breakthrough in faith when I realized tangibly how the modern Israeli Jews are protected by the young army conscripts. The presence of that ancient well reinforced this feeling. I accepted that the Divine would eventually intervene and assist people to sort out the military tensions that had such a dire effect on people's lives.   ◧

As we left the site, I noticed a large wild pomegranate tree not far from the wild pistachio trees. I pointed it out to Haim and Michael.

I said, "Maybe the seeds of these trees have fallen to the earth again and again over the years. That would explain why this species has continued to grow here over many centuries."

"That may be the case," Haim replied. "But people in this area do farm pomegranates, so the seeds of this tree might have been planted that way. The people who lived here in ancient times might have farmed pomegranates too. There were many farm terraces lining the hillsides."

Haim received a call that he was needed for family matters. He called a colleague to come and take over for him. In due course, his friend Ehud arrived, accompanied by a younger man – his friend Daniel. Ehud would take over as my guide.

We bid Haim and Michael farewell, and they returned home in Ehud's vehicle.

Ehud was a lanky, tall man in his mid-thirties. He seemed full of energy and very sweet. He had been a tour guide for a few years in the Negev desert.

PISTACHIO TREES – LIBNAH   CAMP 17

"They left Rimmon perez and camped at Libnah."[1]

We set out to follow the route towards the Exodus camp of Libnah, meaning "bricks" or "to build."[2] I wondered what bricks we might find when we eventually located the campsite.

We returned to the main road, which took us past the foot of Mount Ramon, and continued to the western edge of the enormous crater of Makhtesh Rammon. This was part of the Hanan Afriat, an Israel Nature and Parks Authority (INPA) domain. We stopped to view this astounding geological site with its breath-taking view of the crater, which the Israelites would have seen.

Ehud explained, "This crater, called Ramon, is forty kilometers long and varies between two and ten kilometers wide. At its deepest point, it's 500 meters deep. The crater is shaped like an elongated heart. It encompasses a diversity of mountains and rocks, which have fantastic colors and shapes."

It was certainly unlike anything I had seen before.

He continued, "I will explain how the crater is thought to have been formed. Its steeply sloping crater sides have a few strata of six different color rocks. The lowest dark grey level is igneous rocks which was originally the land surface. Then a huge ocean covered this land and the sand and creatures in the ocean sank to the bottom and formed many sedimentary layers. You can see a dark-beige rock layer and then white, orange, brown and red stone – which makes a wavy pattern in the layer above them. Above these are a white layer of limestone and a fantastic red-and-yellow colored clay layer which has millions of tiny spiral ammonite fossils. There is a sixth layer, which is made of a softer whitish chalk. These were all formed by ocean sediment. Then, at some stage, the ocean dried up.

"The earth's surface began to push upwards, and all these layers started to bulge upwards into the hump of the mountain's shape. On a bigger scale, huge tectonic forces were starting to cause the Arava Rift Valley to form. The rivers were starting to change their course and to flow down the hump-shaped mountain, slowly eroding its soft sedimentary rocks. The water and wind carved out this crater."

His description of the geological history had captured my imagination. The enormous size of the crater and its unique colored layers form a stunning and rare landscape.

Ehud told me more: "This crater is one of the natural wonders of Israel. It is our "Grand Canyon." In the desert, the erosion made the crater bottom deeper, and on the walls more ancient rock strata are exposed. The lowest layers of this Ramon Crater are made up of the most ancient rocks. In the far distance there are beautiful table-top black mountains rising at the borders of the crater. They are ancient volcanoes. The mountains are made out of tough volcanic rock that cannot be eroded as easily as the surrounding material. The water that had eroded the ocean floor was unable to erode those black volcanoes. There are also hills made of limestone covered with basalt. Among them is a hill called Karnei Ramon. This is the only place in the world where you can see those strange rectangular 'pipes' on a hill, and they are made of sand. The sand was heated, turned into liquid and formed into rectangular and hexagonal prisms. There is also a spectacular wadi that was gouged out of softer portions of rock. It begins in the northern Sinai, and is seventy kilometers long."

This crater lay along the ancient spice trail, a trade route that had been used by the Nabataeans about 2000 years ago. Traders would spend the night at an inn and allow their camels to rest before continuing to the Gaza port. Animals also gathered here, with Onagers and Ibex (moun-

The panorama of the enormous, breathtaking Rammon Crater with its fascinating coloured rock strata and volcanoes. | M Rawicz Trip Photo

tain goats) coming to drink from the springs. Even today, Ibex clamber up the crater sides or wander along the streets in the town, paying no attention to people.

Ehud bent down and rummaged around in the sand, then stood up, smiling." Look, a shark's tooth! See if you can find one too. Where we are standing was once the sediment at the bottom of an ocean. You can find millions of teeth from all kinds of fish here."

The Israelites passed along this route and they would have seen this entire glorious panorama. I sat enthralled as we continued our journey, which curved around the crater and came out at a flat area near the southern slopes of Har Oded. The road then became a rocky track, extremely perilous to negotiate. It merged onto a hiking trail called Nahal Arod.

At the side of the track I noticed dozens of holes, which Ehud said had been made by porcupines searching for Crocus bulbs. Ehud then gave me a lesson in botany.

"These are unique blossoming desert plants. Some of them grow only in this area, because of the altitude and the relatively high rainfall. Most of these plants bloom during the spring. They have interesting names and include the Sun Rose, which has pink blossoms, and the Lavender Cotton, Yellow Asphodel, Sun's Eye, Oriental Viper's Grass, Lion's Foot, Star of Bethlehem, and even lovely Tulips.

Look here at these large, odd-looking plants called Wild Rhubarb. They are found only in the Har HaNegev Nature Reserve. Each plant can grow as many as three large leaves. After a very rainy winter, the diameter of one leaf can be as much as seventy cm. – a strange sight in the desert! As you can see, the huge circular leaf looks like a little round table. The leaves have deep red veins. When you see the leaves lying next to each other on the ground, it looks like a large tablecloth. In spring, the plant grows red flowers at the center, a huge bunch of flowers with dark green stems and small pink-brown flowers at the top."

It was such an unusual plant that I stood staring at it for a few minutes. Then, to my delight, we spotted an Onager in the distance.

We moved on, travelling parallel to the Arod stream with its large white boulders scattered along the bed. I was looking for the Libnah camp. I asked Ehud to drive slowly.

"There's a hiker's camp not far ahead," he said.

We soon saw a yellow signpost for the camp, which was situated in front of a large mountain. The mountain had large white rock strata running vertically though it. Ehud parked the car and we climbed out. I stood staring in awe. Had this hiker's camp been built right at the ancient campsite? I could imagine a group of modern hikers stopping to refresh themselves here, not realizing that this might be where their forebears had gathered three millennia earlier.

Had I just found the campsite of Libnah – meaning "bricks" and "to build"? Was this the place where boundaries had been marked with building material or bricks? We were travelling along an ancient route, so maybe it really was the right place.

I looked around and saw that we were in a valley between two mountains: the white limestone of Mount Iddo and on the other side, Mount Oded. I wondered whether bricks or stones would be found on either of these mountains. As I stood gazing at the top of Mount Iddo, to my surprise I noticed a huge pile of stones. They had been formed into what looked like a series of sculptures. I looked through my binoculars to try and see more details about these piles of stone.

Daniel, Ehud's young friend, showed me a photo that he had taken when he had visited the top of the same mountain. The sculptures were made up of hundreds of flat round red stones. There were at least twelve piles of stones, each standing three meters high or higher, with the flat stones piled on top of each other to form a narrow tower. At the top of each tower rested a pointed stone. Two towers were connected by what looked like a bridge, and another two towers were piled on top of the bridge. The structure was phenomenal. I asked Ehud if he knew what it had been built for.

"Oh, the hikers pile them up like that," he answered causally. "It's just a local tradition."

I was disappointed. I had thought that the stones might have been related to the bricks or stones of Libnah.

"But there are many shrines in this area," Ehud added. "They are found throughout the Negev, and were built between the sixth and third millennia BCE. The archaeologist Uzi Avner thinks they were built as memorials. Or maybe they were meant to act as a sort of silent witness to the treaties and covenants that were made between people who lived in this area, or the fulfilment of vows. But the shrines might also have been built to commemorate special events, or to show Divine protection for territorial borders."[3]

Ehud told me that we were close to another stone sculpture, called a megalith. "A megalithic site is an enormous circle of at least thirty huge oblong boulders," he said. "The stones stand beside each other on the short sides, pointing upwards. The center of the circle is filled with smaller boulders. So, a megalith is basically a large stone that was used to construct a structure or monument. The people developed an inter-locking system so that the stones would stand firm without mortar or cement."

"What were they used for?" I asked.

"In the Middle East, these structures go back to ancient traditions … such as when Jacob, the grandson of Abraham, poured oil over a stone that he erected after his famous dream about angels climbing up to heaven. Another one was built when Moses erected twelve pillars symbolizing the twelve tribes of Israel."

We then drove on, passing some sparsely-vegetated yellow hills, travelling towards the wadi that is today known as the Nahal–Oded road. The hills sported multicolored strata in shades of beige and yellow, and deep shadows among the cliffs. Gushing floodwaters, during the rare spurts of rain, had cut into the hills over the centuries.

We drove a short distance further and I checked the coordinates for the camp at Libnah. Soon we arrived at the designated point.

One of the ancient Wells of Oded where the Israelites would have camped next to Libnah.
| *M Rawicz Trip Photo*

We had a picnic of Israeli food in the Negev desert. | *M Rawicz Trip Photo*

"These are the Wells of Oded," Ehud said.

In front of us was a large area with ten wells. The mouth of each well was surrounded by large white stones. Ehud parked the car and we walked over to the wells to inspect them.

A metal grate had been placed across the top of each well to prevent anyone from falling in. I looked down the shaft of one well and saw only darkness at first, but as my eyes became accustomed to the dimness I was able to discern water at the bottom. When I dropped a stone into the well, it did not take long before we heard the faint "plop." I was amazed to see that an entire wall of the well had been built of pure white stone all the way down to the bottom.

I thought of the word "Libnah," which comes from the Hebrew root *lavan*, meaning "white." The same word also means "bricks" and "to build." Perhaps these wells could explain the name of the Libnah campsite.

We sat on the ground to have a picnic of Israeli food and to enjoy the cool atmosphere. We discussed these ancient wells.

Ehud explained, "They've been here since ancient times. We know that agricultural settlements existed in this area 3000 years ago. I've read about these wells . . . apparently they were built as part of a grand

The Oded well walls are made of pure white stone till the bottom. | *M Rawicz Trip Photo*

plan to store water in reservoirs. We've only seen a few, but seventeen water pools have been found around here. The ancient people dug them into the chalk rock, and lined the wells with rough-hewn stones – as you've seen."

"How did they get the water into the pools?" I asked.

"The reservoirs were fed by canals, which carried the runoff water from rains and floods. The people devised an ingenious system to gather rainfall in a small bath, so that the sediment could settle out before the water ran into the canals. And you know, what's most amazing is that even today, some 3000 years later, these holes still fill up with rain every year."

"Such ingenuity!" I commented, between mouthfuls of my meal.

"The water holes are evidence that people lived here in ancient times," Ehud added. "As far back as the age of hunters and gatherers, in fact. Further evidence was unearthed with the discovery of flint tools, which would have been used by ancient people in this area."

"The sense of human history in this area is profound," I said. "I feel it everywhere, a sort of living presence. It's quite strange, really."

"Yes," Ehud said. "Not everyone can feel it, though. To some people this is just dead boring desert. But there are many people like you – and me – who are more sensitive. We are the ones who can appreciate the beauty and importance of this area's history."

He went on to tell me that archaeologists have categorized the early settlers as having belonged to the Harifian Civilization, named after the nearby Mount Arif. Small caves have also been found in this area," Ehud added. "They were evidently used to store food for use during the dry summer season."

"I've read about that," I told him. "And we passed those agricultural terraces, where the riverbeds had been closed up to form dams so that crops of grains like wheat and barley could be grown."

"Yes. Fruit trees and other crops were also grown," he said. "Some of the water holes are classified as the Magora type, which means a carved hole under a stone bed that also serves as a ceiling."

"Sounds sophisticated," I commented. "I suppose that when people were living out here in the desert, their minds became obsessed with figuring out ways of storing the water."

"There are also terraces that were built for agriculture. Grain was stored in a granary, which has been found in the area. The remains of indigenous people's dwellings, and even some ceramic pottery, have been found too. And the name of the Lotz Wells might have come from the Ramon Almond trees that grow in this region."

"How so?" I asked.

"*Luz* means 'nut'," Ehud explained.

I remarked, "I've read one line of scholarly argument that says the Bedouins used the Arabic name *lusan,* which suggests unclean water, and called this wadi, Wadi Lutzan. That's similar to the Hebrew name, Nahal Lusan – meaning Lusan stream. The Hebrew root is *listim* – which means thieves."[4]

"That's interesting," Ehud said, smiling. "It's not often that my guests are able to teach me anything about the area!"

"Apparently," I went on, "in the 1950s, wanderers used to pass this way en route from Eilat to El-Arish. And I read somewhere that thieves used to raid the area."[5]

I had time to reflect on the camp's meaning.

There I was, standing in front of an ancient well . . . and the scenes of its history flashed into vivid reality in my mind's eye. The water was nourishing to the hunters and gatherers who had lived in this area many thousands of years ago. Later, enterprising men – who were very strongly built – toiled and dug drainage canals. This would have been about 3000 years ago. They built ten or maybe more wells at the same time.

I could envisage them hewing the chalk rock. Some men were standing head-deep in dirt, struggling and sweating as they hauled sand from deeper and deeper in the ground, trying to reach the hidden precious water.

The strongest men trudged towards them, hauling heavy stones from a distance. Skilled stonemasons, true artists, laid carefully crafted white stones to build the walls of the wells. They chattered and laughed as they worked, trying to lighten their burden in the relentless Negev heat. As the sun set, irritable and exhausted, the men all camped together for the night, hoping that soon their efforts would pay off.

A millennium later, mighty King Solomon's slaves toiled and expanded the wells so that they would form a buffer against marauding desert nomads. Bloody wars were waged, and the wells indeed formed a buffer.

I imagined that in peaceful times, the wells were a haven for people and animals alike. Goats of all colors – black, white, speckled and brown – knelt here and rested after a day of foraging. Flocks of pale woolly sheep trudged here to seek relief from the heat. The dominant sheep would decide where to walk, and the rest followed mindlessly. The sound of bleating and the smell of dung filled the air. Donkeys brayed, and broke into a trot in anticipation of the cool and refreshing water.

Modest, shy but happy women reached down to draw up the water, the liquid gold. Patiently they filled the troughs again and again, and thanked G-d for the gift. The animals, with a cacophony of noise, pushed and shoved to get to the water.

Then came the wild noise of rough traders, in red and brown robes, arriving with their laden camels. The camels broke into a run as they approached water. Thirst is their constant companion. Camels craned their necks to reach the delicious fluid. The sheep panicked from their threat.

This cycle went on for thousands of years.

⊡ Building the future

According to Jacobson, Libnah has been described as a place where the "boundaries were marked with building bricks."[7] The association with "white" also suggests purity.[8] Thus, the campsite at Libnah, whose borders were built of bricks, has been linked with the progress of the human lifecycle of expanding families and building a home accordingly.

I reflected on the stages that I had gone through in building my own family and making a home, with all the hardships and the joys that had entailed. I had, for example, dealt with teenagers with opposing views to mine and the difficulties of meeting their growing needs. I was extremely grateful that I had been able to meet these challenges, and I now resolved to continue to build my home and family life in a constructive manner. I felt a connection to that ancient Israelite community, and a sense of unity with them.   ◀

DODGING MILITARY WATCHTOWERS – RISSAH

CAMP 18

The Bible narrates that the Israelites "left Libnah and camped at Rissah."[1] The word *rissah* means "a well stopped up with stones,"[2] and it also means "ruin" or "to be broke." I wondered about the prospect of finding another well, especially one that was crammed full of stones.

Ehud received a call on his cell phone. Then he said to me, "I have to report to a senior colleague on where I'm taking you. We haven't been travelling on normal tourist routes, and you now want to go into more dangerous territory. So they want a more experienced person to accompany us."

"That seems fair enough," I said.

"My colleague Ohad is also very interested in the Exodus route. I think that's partly why he wants to accompany you further on your journey."

I thought that it might be useful for me to learn from the experience of yet another informed local Israeli. It seemed that my unusual mission was generating a fair deal of interest.

We waited until Ohad caught up with us. Ehud introduced me to this man who was considerably older, in his fifties. Ohad had been involved with geographical, historical and political research in the southern part of Israel for many years.

We all climbed into Ohad's vehicle and continued with the trip. Dan-

Travelling from Libnah to Rissah along an ancient camel trail, which Moses and the Israelites would have used. It passes a paleontological site and a Nabatean cistern. | M Rawicz Trip Photo

iel, Ehud's young friend, headed in the opposite direction with Ehud's vehicle to drive it back home. From this point onwards, Ehud let Ohad lead the way and explain everything to me.

Ohad turned the car away from Libnah as the Israelites had done, and we proceeded south along the Israeli border. This meant travelling back down into the valley before heading west again. We were moving in a general southerly direction. To our right stood the relatively flat ridge of Har Batur, and in the distance to our left was the enormous Har Arif.

Along the way, we stopped so that Ohad could show me a paleontological site. This was situated on an ancient camel trail, and consisted of scattered rocks and the remains of ancient structures. There were patches in the ground that looked as if camels still rested in those spots. According to Ohad, the local Bedouin people did indeed stop to rest here.

I imagined the camels in ancient times also stopping to rest in these places. Man has not changed over the centuries, I thought.

We continued with the drive, but the road was so bumpy that I began

A paleontological site on the ancient Exodus route. | *M Rawicz Trip Photo*

to feel nauseous. Yet my desire to proceed was tenacious. This surprised me a little. It was not a side of me that had ever been pushed to its limits quite as much as now.

Further along, we came to a Nabatean cistern. We stopped the car and climbed out, and I carefully clambered down the steep sides of the cistern and stepped into its large open base. Once again, I could almost feel the presence of people who had been here centuries ago. On my way out, I noticed the paw prints of wolves and a few feces. The wolves evidently came here to drink from the water that collected at the bottom of the cistern.

ANGRY SOLDIERS

We were heading for the border, where the site of the camp of Rissah is thought to have been. We proceeded with extreme caution because we were approaching the Israeli military patrol road and the Egyptian lookout posts in the Sinai. I started taking photos from a distance in case I was prevented from doing so nearer the fence. We brazenly edged forward until we were within 300 meters of the patrol road. Three patrol vehicles came whizzing by, but nobody stopped to interfere with us.

Inside an ancient Nabatean water cistern on the Exodus route. | *M Rawicz Trip Photo*

We could see three radio masts and a few Egyptian military build-ings on the hill across the border, which I found rather exciting. On the other side of the barbed wire fence, some 500 meters inside Sinai, we could see the general location of the campsite of Rissah.

We drove a little closer and stopped again to look across the border. Suddenly some soldiers arrived, and abruptly questioned what I was doing. I explained my quest and what my journey entailed, but they were quite unsympathetic and told me to move on.

"There's a threat of indiscriminate attacks here, if you come across the wrong people," one of the soldiers said.

He launched into a vivid description of a recent incident. As he elab-orated, surprisingly I found myself watching the scene unfold in my mind's eye.

A silver Toyota had been cruising along the border road. The sky was bright blue and the air still. Suddenly there was a burst of rapid bullet-fire and then a loud explosion, followed by a billow of smoke. A horn blasted, and screams rang out. The metal of the car was shattered. Doors were flung open.

Bullets whizzed into the car. Then the killers pounced on the Toyota in person, and dragged their injured victims out to continue butchering them. Blood was dripping from the car seats, and cartridges were scattered on the ground. The bodies of four men lay on the ground, drenched in blood and hacked to pieces. There were also parts of the car lying scattered around.

The killers sped away, and there was deathly silence. Eventually, the grisly scene was discovered by a military patrol.

The soldiers stared at us. The young man continued talking earnestly to me, in a tone of voice that seemed intent on evoking fear.

"We've had incidents of the enemy trying to infiltrate along this border. It's not safe for you to be here. I'm sure you understand our caution."

"I do," I admitted.

"We'll accompany you for a short while, until you are in safer territory," the soldier said.

I accepted the offer gratefully. I had come so far and was not willing to be intimidated into simply abandoning my entire mission at this stage.

"I always consider the risks when I explore a place," I told Ohad and Ehud as we travelled on, escorted by the soldiers. "But there's another side to this. I've seen how fear can provoke problems unnecessarily."

"Oh?" Ohad sounded a little skeptical, but curious.

"I live in South Africa," I explained. "My country has one of the highest rates of violent crime in the world. So, I know what it means when people live in fear. A lot of my friends have left the country because of it. But the work that I've been doing for many years has led me to travel all over the world, and I've gone into areas where my friends and family would never dare to go."

"You sound like a brave lady," Ohad remarked.

"All I'm saying is that my experience of life in South Africa has taught me that living in fear isn't an option. For me, fear means F-E-A-R . . . that is, a False Expectation that Appears Real. So, I've overcome my own fears to a great extent. I'm glad about that. At the same time, I weigh the risks. And right now, I feel comfortable in continuing my journey – if you do too."

Ohad glanced at me in astonishment. He carried on driving in silence for a few minutes, and then we chatted about the meaning and effect of "FEAR" in the Israeli context.

We would, however, need to find another way to achieve my goal of viewing Rissah. It was late in the day, and I wondered aloud where we would stay for the night. I would have to rely on Ohad, who knew the area well enough because of his extensive ecological work.

Farmer's guesthouse where we stayed when seeing the Israelite camp of Rissah. |
M Rawicz Trip Photo

He suggested that we go to a farmer's guesthouse. I agreed, and soon we were being served a delicious meal of kosher meat and Israeli salads. As I was settling in for the night, I wondered about the meaning of "Rissah." What could the name of this place mean, which I had walked and driven so far to find?

Seeing opportunity in failure

I remembered that Jacobson had said that in Hebrew, *rissah* means "to be broken"[3] and in Arabic the same word denotes a [water] well stopped up with stones. The meaning according to Jacobson is that even when life's events lead us to an apparent lack of success, to stagnation or obstruction, we have ways out. Whether we experience failed relationships, endeavors or financial collapse we can still succeed. The word Rissah also means an eyelid and thus, related to vision."[4] We, therefore, have the potential to really examine, think and evaluate the problem. This will lead us to a different perspective and we will be able to see the gift that the situation offers, and the opening up to something good that can be gained.

I had also read that the Hebrew root "r-s-s" means moisture or dew, which could symbolise the people washing their clothes; and according to the biblical sages, this included personal immersion for ritual purification. I understood this to mean that difficult situations lead to personal, emotional or spiritual purification.[5]

My own feeling about this theme of "rissah" was that I might be able to find a new sense of opportunity in certain distressing circumstances, which I had left behind when I had started my journey. I resolved to adopt this positive attitude in the future. It was a comforting thought as I drifted off to sleep.

Early the next morning, we set off to try and view Rissah from a better vantage point. I decided to plan my approach anew, and checked the map again. With a flash of insight, I realized that all the camps from Libnah (the 17th campsite) to Moseroth (the 27th) would probably be visible from a high mountain in this region. I explained this insight to Ohad, and asked if he knew of any mountain that might be high enough.

"Well, there's Har Batur," Ehud said, pointing to a mountain fairly close by. "It's tall, yes, and its slopes are fairly gentle. Still, climbing it won't be easy!"

"I'm not sure I'll manage," I confessed, "but I'd like to try."

When we arrived at the mountain, I gathered my water bottle, camera, binoculars, and lots of enthusiasm. I set out boldly, with Ohad and Ehud following as somewhat more reluctant hiking partners. Within half an hour I was tired, and my footsteps started faltering a little. I knew it would be a great struggle to reach the summit, but now I wanted to prove that I could do it.

At times I felt as if the strong wind would blow me off my feet. I had to keep one hand on my hat and the other holding my dress so that it did not turn into a sail and blow me away. I battled to walk over the sharp stones. At times, my face was blasted with a gust of sand that stung my skin. The sky was grey, but a ray of sun shone through. I willed myself to believe that this was a sign from G-d to encourage me.

Five hours later, after stopping to rest several times and hurting my ankle along the way, I finally reached the summit, exhausted. I was standing 874 meters above sea level. My effort was rewarded with a view of sparsely-vegetated rolling hills along the western side of Israel, all the way to the distant peaks in eastern Sinai. As far as the eye could see, these low rounded hills converged towards the horizon. A few spiky ridges with sharp tops – like the back of a dragon – stood out among them.

From this viewpoint, I could locate the next ten camps of the Exodus route. The vista revealed the northern cliffs of Makhtesh Ramon, Mount Ramon, and Mount Harif. To the east were the Lotz Cliffs; and to the southwest was Mount Hameara, adjacent to Rissah, Camp 18. In the distant background was Mount Sapher, adjacent to Camps 19 and 20, Kehethah and Shapher. To the south was Mount Arif, close to Camp 21, Haradah; rising behind it was Mount Karkom at Makheloth, or Camp 22. To the south-southwest, I could see the distant lowland where Camp 24, Tarah, was located; and in the extreme distance was the general vicinity of Tahath, Camp 23. On the distant southern horizon were the locations of Mithkah, Hashmonah and Moseroth.

I felt deeply gratified to be able to identify the locations of so many of the Exodus sites in such close proximity. They were all within a roughly twenty-kilometer radius of each other.

In my mind's eye, I was transported into the bustle of the Israelites' movement from camp to camp. The scene flashed into vivid reality: roughly 600,000 men were trudging along on foot, and lagging behind them walked roughly the same numbers of women, children, and elderly people. In addition, many non-Israelite people had joined the crowd and were following it at the rear. By some estimates, the number of people was roughly two million in total. Hundreds of animals, the people's livestock, were also part of this Exodus. The entire huge group slowly moved forwards under a stark blue sky.

The large gentle valleys allowed the people to walk in big groups. They trekked easily from one plain to the next in this landscape of rolling hills that were criss-crossed by wadis. The people slowly made their way forward, walking in a snake-like formation and trudging ever onwards along the hot sands. Families clustered in groups, walking about ten people abreast, with noisy livestock following each group. The colorful row of people stretched for more than 160 kilometers. What a massive movement of souls!

I could visualize the families at the front starting to set up their tents and settling into their new surroundings at the campsite where they had just arrived, twenty kilometers away. By the time they arrived, the last of the groups would still be packing their belongings at the previous camp. The time lag between the first and last groups among this enormous mass of people could be as much as two or three days.

The above scenario raises the question of why the Israelites moved around a relatively small area for so long. They covered essentially the same ground over many months, perhaps even years. One explanation is that each camp provided a source of water, and the people moved from one area to the next according to the seasons and the availability of water at each site.[6]

Fascinating information that I later discovered suggests that the availability of water at different times of the year was influenced by the exact soil and wind conditions. I read about Sinai aquifers and understood that depending on the clay or impervious layer of soil and the degree of rain, the various wells and ground water resources would be better at different months. I found it interesting to note that deep under the Negev Desert and the Sinai Peninsula, shared by Egypt and Israel, lies a huge aquifer – a layer of porous rock that holds water. Such an aquifer could be formed in a basin-shaped dip in the crust of the earth; the porous rock that holds the water can be sandwiched between two layers of rock that are more or less waterproof. Water collected in such an aquifer is under high pressure. When it is tapped, either by a natural fault in the overlying rock or by drilling, water spurts to the surface. I had seen a note about Sinai aquifers in the source *Fossil Water under the Sinai-Negev Peninsula* that read: "It has been calculated that the Nubian sandstone aquifer under the Sinai and the Negev holds 200 billion cubic meters of water, 70 billion cubic meters of which is under the Negev."[7]

The availability of ground water and the potential to store rainfall in levees or reservoirs would have been key factors in the location of the Israelite camps. The topography would have been an important aspect of this.

I brought my focus back to Rissah. In the distance ahead we could see a hiking trail in the Sinai. Ohad opened a map, from which we managed to identify the mountains and valleys in the vicinity. We looked through the high barbed-wire border fence that divides Israel from Sinai. We had a clear view of the Israeli patrol road, along which military vehicles trundled from time to time.

From our vantage point, we managed to identify the location of the camp of Rissah. It was in the same valley that we had just travelled, but on the Sinai side. The area was right beside an Egyptian military post.

Ohad told me what he had seen in that area many years earlier, when he was an Israeli soldier. "I patrolled the border, from Taba in southern Israel all the way to Al-Kaseema in the northeast of the Sinai Desert," he said. "I saw a well in that valley, called Wadi Muayn, where scrawny goats and sheep were being watered. I asked the Bedouin about that well."

"What did they say?" I was intrigued.

"They said the well was called Bir-al-Ma'yun, and it's been there since ancient times. It must have given water to hundreds of thirsty – even desperate – desert travellers over the millennia. Ever since I was a young man, I've been interested in archaeology and ecology. So I've always taken an interest in the details of places that I've seen in my travels."

"That area," I said, "the possible campsite of Rissah, was where the Israelites might have washed their clothes and immersed themselves for ritual purification. I wonder whether stones were used to close up the well at some point in history."

Ohad and Ehud looked interested, but soon we turned our minds to how to proceed with the trip.

"I don't think that you want to go any further than this," Ohad said rather firmly. "Behind that fence is an area that you would be better off not seeing. It's been a problem area for many years."

"Why so?" I asked.

"The Israelis and Egyptians have spent years battling a serious drug problem there," Ohad told me. "The Bedouins have been growing drugs in that area, including opium – which they guard with guns. Then they smuggle the stuff out to various places."

"Is that a good reason not to venture in?" I wondered aloud.

"Look, these people are really aggressive," Ohad replied. "I understand that you feel that visiting Rissah is critical for your mission. But you really would not like to run into these types. The Egyptian and Israeli authorities have spent years trying to get these Bedouin smuggling rings under control."

"I see," I said, disappointed.

"There's a cat-and-mouse game being played by the smugglers and the Israeli Defence Force, the IDF," Ohad said. "The IDF even employs Bedouin trackers, who can tell which tribe a man belongs to just by looking at his footprints."

"That sounds like the San Bushmen in southern Africa," I said. "They're also known for their skill as trackers."

"The Bedouin who smuggle drugs have found ways of converting jeeps to look like those used by the IDF," Ohad went on. "They've even stolen a few jeeps from parking lots in Israel. They add a more powerful motor to the vehicle, so that it can drive faster than the soldiers. So, even these elite Israeli tracker units – which include Arabs from the Negev – are in serious danger from the conniving smugglers. To enter this area as a civilian, like yourself, would simply invite trouble."

"Then I guess we really can't go in," I said.

"In any case, this is also a dangerous zone in other ways. The relations between Israel and Egypt have been somewhat stable, but not totally so. People are constantly on the alert. If you go in there, you could be shot at by either side, Egyptians or Israelis. Everyone's watching the border all the time!"

He had convinced me.

AGGRESSIVE CROWD – KEHETHAH   CAMP 19

"And they journeyed from Rissah, and pitched in Kehelathan."[1] *Kehelathan* means "assembly" or "gathering," as in the Hebrew word *kehela* meaning "community," according to Hillel.[2]

I resolved to see any other Exodus sites I could while I was still within the borders of Israel. I also wanted to find out about the places from soldiers who had been posted there before Israel had withdrawn from the Sinai.

Ohad, Ehud and I slaked our thirst with bottled water and then sat in the blazing sun. We scanned the horizon, hoping for a glimpse of the next camp. Eventually, by looking at the map and the landscape around us, we decided to proceed along a major wadi called Wadi Magharah, which skirts the eastern side of a mountain. According to Targum Yonathan, this area was where a dispute had arisen regarding the leadership of Moses.[3] A man called Korach, together with 250 other men who had "assembled or gathered" around him, confronted Moses. They defiantly accused their leader of putting himself and his family above the rest of the people. Dathan and Abiram, who were famous in the congregation, also verbally attacked Moses and his brother Aaron. They accused Moses of reserving the priesthood for his own family.

Shocked, Moses replied that in the morning G-d would make His wishes known. He advised Korach and the entire congregation to wait for this Divine judgment near the "Tent of Meeting."

The biblical narrative says that G-d was extremely angry with the rebels, and He wanted to destroy the whole congregation. However, Moses and Aaron begged Him to spare the people's lives.[4]

Even though the camp of Kehelathan was some distance into Sinai

Looking from Israel across the border into Sinai onto Egyptian security. |
Todayonline.com http://www.todayonline.com/world/usreviewing-sinaipeacekeeper
-missionlooks-automating-jobs

territory, the scene was vividly real to me. I could see the dry wadi where
the camp is thought to have been located, some twelve kilometers west
of Rissah. I was transported in time to that scene where G-d delivered
His judgment.

In a valley between the low hills, a thunderous rumble breaks loose
and the ground begins to shudder. The earth obeys G-d's will as it opens
up into a huge sandy cavern that drops down . . . deep, deep below the
surface of the ground.

Hundreds of men, clad in their long robes with colors of red, blue and
beige, are hurled off their feet. Chaos erupts. The men who had been
standing right at the spot where the earth is busy splitting apart are
flung head-first into the terrifying depths. Other men fall backwards,
clutching vainly at thin air as they disappear into the roaring, shaking
ground. I see a mass of men with arms and legs thrown open, struggling
like feeble insects. Their bodies become mingled with a massive crashing of rocks, and a collective cry is let loose as everything disappears
into the gaping hole in the ground.

The sky is dark, streaked with clouds of red. The sight of it bears witness to G-d's fury.

Korach stands in terror, watching his supporters fall to their deaths. Onlookers panic, and women hurry to pull their children away from the scene, away from the disastrous chaos. One woman is paralyzed by fear and can do nothing but stand and stare. Terrified youngsters are running in all directions away from the chasm, their arms outstretched and pleading for help. A few women crouch down and hide together in a huddle, as if trying to remain invisible. Others run for their lives.

The hills shiver with the force of G-d's anger. Even Korach's followers' tents are swallowed up, disappearing into the abyss as it grows ever wider.

Despite this scene of apparent anarchy, I realize that nature is simply expressing Divine justice. The stench of blood, diseased by the sin of rebellion, pervades the air. Death, the great leveller, rides high in triumph.

The people who had remained faithful to Moses are safe, standing by his side as they all watch the terrible scene unfold. But even these strong men are shaken by anxiety. A group of priests are shaking their fists, raised and clenched in indignation at Korach's audacity. Lightning flashes, splitting through the thick clouds, and the dust rises to meet the storm that is brewing in the skies.

Humbly, Moses lowers his head. As the chaos begins to settle and the screams fall silent, he looks up again in awe, quietly accepting G-d's decree that he should continue to lead the people. In his quiet demeanor, a sense of power and victory shines through.

I came back to present reality with a jolt. Sweat was trickling off my brow, and I took another swig of water from the bottle.

From the position where we were standing, with the help of binoculars, through the shimmering heat we could see hundreds of weirs set up across the wadi for most of its length. Ohad told me that the weirs had been part of the ancient terrace system of farming which we had seen previously. They were cleverly set up to capture the rainfall and retain it for long enough to nurture crops such as wheat. Without the weirs, the water would simply have been sucked up by the sand.

I recalled that Shareef, my Bedouin friend from Dophkah, had told me that he planted wheat whenever he saw an opportunity to do so. It was marvellous to see how ingenious people had been when it came to surviving in such a harsh environment.

Ohad, Ehud and I continued to gaze into the distance. I was delighted to see on the horizon, behind several lower mountains, a high peak called Gebel Araif el Naga. It stands roughly thirteen kilometers to the southeast of Mount Sapher, and the site of Kehelathan is believed to be located just in front of Gebel Araif el Naga. We scanned the rest of the horizon carefully. We knew the coordinates of the place where we were standing and those of the mountain, and used this information to try and pinpoint the campsite. But the entire area simply looked like harsh desert. I could not discern any possible features of a campsite.

I appreciated Ohad's explanation about why we could not physically go and visit that area. He continued telling me about some of the terrible problems in the Sinai area that borders Israel. "It's not just drugs that are a problem in eastern Sinai," he said. "The border is a conduit for the illegal trade of guns and ammunition among countries that don't like Israel. Bedouins in the Sinai will gladly make money from smuggling arms to people who want to attack Israel. Several camps have been established by the Palestinians, by Hezbollah or Hamas."

"People who want to wipe Israel off the map and sweep all Israelis into the sea," I said. Of course, as a Jew, I knew about these political agendas.

Ohad nodded. "The Israeli military have an ongoing problem with smugglers who are backed by Syria and Iran. Various countries are known to provide the weapons that are smuggled into Sinai via Gaza through a network of tunnels. The suppliers include Libya, Sudan, Nairobi, Lebanon, and Iran. Israeli soldiers often intercept large caches of weapons that come flooding into Sinai. They've found surface-to-air missiles, rounds of ammunition, rockets, bomb components, and anti-aircraft guns. Gangs of suspects come in through the desert, but they disappear quickly if they're spotted. Some of them have been ambushed and have left behind the weapons they were carrying.

"During a recent operation," he continued, "the Israeli soldiers reported on the killing or arrest of many arms smugglers, but it seems not even to have dented the smuggling networks. Sometimes the smugglers are simply released. One thing's for sure, though. A ton of weapons are being stored in eastern Sinai, especially anti-aircraft missiles."

"What is Egypt's stance?" I asked. I knew that of all its neighbors, Israel had the most civil terms with Egypt.

"Even the Egyptian Armed Forces can't stop the smugglers," Ohad replied. "Egyptian border guards have been killed and wounded. To stop the smuggling once and for all, a massive military operation would need to be conducted by the Egyptian military and security forces in Sinai. They'd need to deploy troops, tanks, heavy weapons, armored vehicles, and the air force. Everything. Short of that, they just can't get on top of the problem."

He went on to tell me that in some incidents, Palestinian insurgents have thrown grenades at Israeli military patrol vehicles and then fired on the Israeli soldiers. Just the previous week, a car travelling on the Israeli border road had been attacked. Three people were injured and one died.

"The situation is so bad," Ohad concluded, "that the Security Forces are even trying to cooperate with the local Bedouin people."

"It seems that we can't go to Kehelathan either, can we?" I said, disappointed.

"No," Ohad confirmed. "It's like the site of Rissah. Israel's position is very precarious. It's definitely better to view Kehelathan from here and not try to get any closer."

While trying to absorb the information Ohad had given me, I wondered whether the site would have shown any trace of the earth having opened to swallow up a whole lot of people. What exactly had happened to the mob that had ganged up with Korach against Moses? I wondered if one would see any evidence of an earthquake, rock strata having been ripped apart, earth crust movement, or volcanic activity.

It was useless, I would never find out. All I would ever be able to do was wonder and guess.

Some scholars claim that Kivroth Hataavah was the location of the Korach rebellion. Others believe that the rebellion of Korach took place at Hazerot. Because the scholarly opinions vary, I let the matter rest. Perhaps the question would be answered at a later stage.

⊟   Resisting the power of negative coercion and critics

At this camp, the individual Israelites were tested to see whether they would be cautious enough to keep away from the Korach followers who were detractors and denigrators of Moses. They were also given the opportunity to desist and to gather instead as a united, positively supportive community, or "k-h-l," (meaning community in Hebrew). The Israelites were therefore being taught to make decisions based on recognition of the motives of the group.

I reflected on the lesson of Kehelathan. Some scholars are of the opinion that this was the place of Korach's rebellion.[6] Jacobson explains that at certain phases in our lives the members of a group or crowd can encourage or compel us to join them as new recruits. A person must weigh the options before being drawn to comply and not just decide that joining could offer protection and recognition. We must consider whether the underlying motive of the group will lead to a positive or negative outcome.

"One should thus take great care to resist being coerced into supporting any negative activities. We must reflect on other people's motivations for asking us to join a group. If those motivations appear to be personal insecurity, a need to feel right, or a wish to bully others, we should resist.[7]

Groups, for example, that form to promote the study of wisdom and righteous intentions can fulfill the idea of bringing G-dliness into their midst and actions.[8] They can add value to the world. Other groups that have motives of revenge, jealousy, unearned power, self-justification and other damaging outcomes, we should avoid. The core members of such groups may have hidden agendas of personal power. They can impose great negativity in their sphere of influence.

I was also strengthened to think along these lines of being part of a positive group after having been exposed, in discussion, to the negative effects of terrorist group pressure.

If nothing else, the tone of this leg of my journey had forced me to think more deeply than ever before about the negative effects of terrorism. I also resolved to be more alert in avoiding people who might gang up against me, especially when I was innocent. On a more positive note, I loved the idea of people meeting to talk about the Torah (the Bible). I felt a sudden pang of longing to see my friends at home. It would be so good to have a meaningful chat with them about my journey! I realized how important it was to find positive, constructive activities to do together with one's friends.

At this stage, the Israelites had finally become fully mature adults. They had been through the mill and had endured the many stresses that one encounters when building a life.[9] They had developed greater competency and life skills, and were more able now to meet those stresses and deal with them constructively. They had even experienced a breakthrough in their faith. They had re-committed themselves to serving G-d.

What they had learned from the disastrous opening of the earth was that when people gather with a positive intention, to exchange meaningful thoughts, words, wisdom and righteous ideas, such a meeting has far more value than when people gather for negative reasons or give in to negative coercion. Now, after witnessing the disaster that befell Korach and his followers, the surviving Israelites' behavior was more mature and pure.

At this stage of my trip, I also felt more mature. Confronting the harsh reality of what Ohad had told me about the drugs and terrorism had not been easy on me emotionally. I had been most disappointed to hear that the problems were bad enough to stop me from visiting the campsites.

But through this difficult process, I had developed a greater degree of faith in Divine guidance. I also felt that I was developing more of an inclination to avoid negative conversation, and to keep away from negative activities. These inner promptings left me feeling more connected to the Divine, and I intuitively knew that the rest of my trip – and my life – were becoming more meaningful.

From the moment we had encountered the border patrol and their dire warnings of what might happen if we ventured too close to Rissah, I knew that I couldn't allow my entire trip to be derailed by the political forces at play. I had simply come too far, invested too much and had too much still to learn. It was clear that though I need not be intimidated by fear itself, there were realities on the ground beyond my control. Terrorism and drug smuggling had made the region impenetrable. In the Sinai, I had mostly experienced complete freedom of movement and my greatest challenge had been to fit the archaeological and ecological pieces of the puzzle together. I realized that the rules of the game had changed and I would need to rise to the challenge. I couldn't allow myself to be swamped with disappointment in the face of the inevitable obstacles that littered this landscape. In fact it was through these very obstacles that I had discovered gifts of resilience, positivity and patience.

It was when faced with no way to go forward that I had surprisingly come up with one of my most creative insights, travelling upward and finding the highest vantage point from which I had been able to view so many of the camps from a mountaintop. I knew now that I was going to make this journey a success by broadening what my definition of success had been thus far, and utilizing even the dark moments to deepen my connection to G-d, and to refine my character.

DRUGS AND DEATH – SHAPHER   CAMP 20

The Israelites were about to begin the stage of life equivalent to mature middle age with its attendant life crises. They still went through bouts of terror, fear and anxiety. They were also still plagued occasionally with impatience and divisiveness. They had not yet learned sufficiently how to handle the emotions evoked by all these experiences.

"And they went from Kehelathan, and pitched in Mount Shapher."[1] The name of this mountain means "beautiful mountain"[2] in Hebrew. I was faced with a challenge. Among so many mountains, how was I to know which one was the beautiful one? What specific feature would indicate that one mountain was more special than another? The best I could hope for was that either my companions or I would receive some inspiration to guide us to the right place.

Judging from my map, Mount Shapher was located approximately seven kilometers into the Sinai along Wadi Ghawi. The high peak of Gebel Araif el Naga or Urayfan-Naqah or Jabal-Urayf-al-Naghan was about thirteen kilometers to the southeast of Mount Shapher. We saw a smaller mountain called Jabal-Umm-Mafruth close to Mount Shapher. The map also showed that the wadi I was looking at ran around the base of Mount Shapher.

I recalled that, in Hebrew, Shapher also means "shining hill." I mentioned this to Ohad and Ehud and commented, "I wonder why it was given that name?"

"I have a geological map in my pocket," Ohad said. "Let's have a look and see what the mountain is made of."

He took out the map and we examined it. I was amazed and delighted to see that the map showed that this mountain had the same geological structures as those of the Ramon crater. Nowhere else in the vast area included on the map were these types of structures repeated. What an incredible match! Furthermore, Mount Shapher was shaped like a horn. Using the binoculars, I scanned the horizon and noticed a huge hill towering above the surrounding landscape. In contrast to the surrounding dark yellow hills, this mountain seemed to have multicolored strata. I pointed it out to Ohad.

"When I was in the Sinai," he said, "I saw that mountain up close. I had this geological map with me and it showed that the geology of the mountain differed from its surroundings. So I took special note of it. I saw that from the bottom up the layers had the following sequence: whitish limestone at the bottom, then some dark yellow sedimentation, then red and yellow clay, then black basalt, then chunky sandstone of various colors – white, orange, brown and red, then dark beige gypsum, and finally a black igneous rock."

The mountain seemed to be shimmering as I gazed at it. I wondered whether the stifling heat had affected my vision. Perhaps my eyes were deceiving me because of the glare. I had absent-mindedly left my sunglasses in the car. However, Ohad confirmed that the mountain I was staring at was indeed known to take on a shimmering appearance because of the white limestone it contained.

"I read about limestone on the Internet,"[3] I told him. "When the pharaohs built the pyramids, limestone was placed on the surface to give them a spectacular appearance. It was then polished so that it became reflective and visible from vast distances. It must have looked splendid! But over the years the limestone casings were all stolen, except for a few stones, which are now very weathered. They've been so badly eroded by the wind and sand that they look almost the same as normal stones."

Ohad replied, "Yes, Mount Shapher probably resembles the resplendent, ancient surfaces of the pyramids."

I wondered whether this mountain was the jewel referred to in the name of the Israelite camp, which is thought to have been located at the foot of this mountain. Some biblical commentaries regard the "bright mountain" as symbolic of the fire and lightning that accompanied the revelations given at Mount Sinai. In addition, a horn was heard when the Ten Commandments were proclaimed. A horn is called a *shofar* in Hebrew, and the mountain we were looking at was horn-shaped. Thus, Mount Shapher is considered by some to be "Shofar Mountain" at Mount Sinai.[4] Hebrew homiletics allow for this interpretation.

⟐   Appreciating and sharing beauty

During our lives we may visit places of exceptional beauty, either natural or through human endeavors. Instead of keeping the joy, awe and upliftment of our experiences to ourselves, we should share this. We can transmit the beauty and majesty of our experiences to other individuals, communities and even the world to experience, bringing happiness and inspiration to others. It can help to share our appreciation of G-d. By so doing we uplift others and the world. We also overcome selfishness, according to Jacobson.[5]

I enjoyed the idea as I had always had an interest in beauty, especially in nature. I resolved to enjoy and share experiences or photos of beauty as much as possible with my friends.

Ohad turned to me and said, "Even though we cannot see Shapher as close up as you would like, you should consider yourself lucky. Recently, there's been an influx of terrorists into this part of the Sinai. Palestinian support groups have started to use this area as a potential launching pad for attacks on Israel. Israelis are worried that remote places like this are becoming ungovernable. The Egyptian authorities have never asserted strong central control over the Sinai. It's always been seen as a peripheral region. This area is dominated by Bedouins, like a mini-state that is beyond Cairo's control, with Palestinian groups linking up with local Bedouin extremists – and they operate on their own terms. There've been reports of armed groups of unknown origin operating and extremists moving into the Sinai.

"The Sinai Peninsula has been a security challenge. The Israeli Defense Force (IDF) has had to increase its intelligence operations. The violence has dogged the area for some time already and it seems that there's no end in sight. I've heard that even the Egyptian patrol groups don't go in there before getting permission from local tribe members, who escort them. It's too dangerous otherwise. Israel needs to deploy its army to defend from attacks."

Little did I know that in the years to come, this area of the Sinai would become a training base and center for Arab terrorists such as Al-Qaeda, Hamas and others.

I was satisfied to view Mount Shapher from this safe distance. Ohad, Ehud and I were in an isolated area and I was grateful that we did not have to worry about being killed by extremists from an Al-Qaeda training camp. We made our way down the mountain and found a place to stay in the region overnight.

We saw the Israeli Defense Force increase intelligence operations to deal with the influx of terrorists from the Sinai Bedouin extremists over whom Egyptian authorities had not asserted strong central control. | *Rawicz Trip Photo*

EXQUISITE STONES – HARADAH   CAMP 21

"And they removed from Mount Shapher, and encamped in Haradah,"[1] – which means "terror."[2] Now I was really worried. What terror was I seeking out in this bleak wilderness?

Early the following day, we began preparing the next leg of our journey.

The Israelites would have doubled back to travel eastward towards modern-day Israel, through a wadi that passed the mountain called Ras Abu Urjan. This part of our journey was in Israeli territory, so we set off to visit the mountain in question. Usually it is off-limits to the public because it forms part of a practice firing zone for the IDF. But today being a public holiday in Israel, and military activity being suspended, Ohad, Ehud and I were allowed in. As we rumbled over the rough terrain, I saw numerous pieces of missiles and bomb shells scattered along the way. Eventually we arrived at the probable campsite. Here we found a water source and far more lush vegetation than we had seen for many kilometers. The silence was deep and the isolation intense. I wondered why this particular camp might have been called "terror."

At this camp the people journeyed away from their unity, allowed disharmony and animosity to prevail, and destroyed the social cohesion. This was extremely sinful and G-d wanted to punish them. Moses and Aaron tried to secure forgiveness for the offenders. They offered incense and made atonement for the people, but to no avail. G-d sent a plague that decimated a further 14,700 people. The deaths were terrifying to the Israelites. This place of terror, fear and trembling had been named by the people who were confronted by the evil plague.[3]

"You have killed the people of G-d," they moaned.

I delved once again into the biblical text. After the dramatic scene that the Israelites witnessed in which Korach and his men had been swallowed up by the earth, the people fled the area in terror. But instead of resolving to support Moses, they had again complained about him and Aaron.

Facing anxiety and terror; finding solace and vigilance

At Haradah, the Israelites trembled from the terror that they experienced caused by the plague.[4]

There is a possibility that we could experience extreme fear or terror during our lives. Such an experience could cause us to become emotionally frozen. This type of reaction may be from a real event such as hearing of the death of a loved one, but might also be stirred up by imaginary or anticipated events. We should be vigilant to avoid feeling terror from imaginary events. During a real or imaginary experience, things may seem extremely negative. It is worthwhile, however, to remember that positive can emerge even from events of terror. If one maintains an inner strength while one faces the fear with bravery, maintains one's faith and calls on the Divine for assistance, there can be a positive outcome.

Such an event can sharpen one's focus on the crucial things in life, deepen one's appreciation for that which is still good, highlight the value of life itself and lead to one becoming more sensitive to other people. From terror, one can emerge stronger and even heroic. One can also emerge far more connected and appreciative of G-d after having experienced terror.[5]

My resolve to step through fear and proceed boldly was also strengthened.

Hillel also explains that people lose their unity when they are involved in arguments and start to dislike each other. Then they will be "encamped at a lower level." G-d may then punish them for sins that He might have otherwise not considered.[6]   ◄

The silence, isolation and natural beauty of the place where Ohad, Ehud and I now stood provided an extreme contrast to the biblical history of the area. Living and dying seemed intertwined in this place, both historically and as a matter of survival among these semi-desert, bone-dry hills.

PLAGUE AND MISSILES – MAKHELOTH   CAMP 22

"And they removed from Haradah, and pitched in Makheloth."[1] *Makheloth* means "assemblies." Once again, this campsite's name referred to a gathering or congregation,[2] and I wondered what we might find there in these modern times.

We were well inside the IDF firing zone by now, on a clearly-defined hiking trail along a shallow valley through the desert, towards Makheloth. This route from north to south provides access to the famous archaeological site of Har Karkom, at the foot of the mountain Har Shazzar. We passed many Israeli hikers as we trekked through this favorite weekend recreation area. Eventually we reached Har Karkom, which is believed to have been the Makheloth encampment site.

I was waiting in great anticipation to explore the area, after having read about some unique and controversial archaeological findings here. At the base of the steep sandstone and dolomite-shale mountain stood a large blue tent. Through its open side we could see the middle-aged archaeologist whose claims have caused many contentious debates. There sat Professor Anati, poring over his papers.[3]

We explained my mission and requested he spend some time with us. Although he was very busy, he agreed to summarize his views about his findings and conclusions. In short, he had found as many as 1,200 archaeological sites on and around Mount Karkom. These contained 218 rock art sites and more than 40,000 rock engravings, called petroglyphs. In addition, the professor has helped to discover 239 prehistoric sites complete with hut basements, 42 fireplaces, and 55 flint workshops. He had also found 25 sites with large drawings on the ground, called geoglyphs, and 60 standing stones called orthostats, all of which were made of local stone. These findings spanned 40,000 years, according to archaeological dating methods.

He encouraged us to explore the mountain, with its major Palaeolithic cult center, and the surrounding plateau covered with shrines, altars, stone circles and stone pillars. I learned that the peak of religious activity at the site may date back to between 2350 and 2000 BCE, and that the mountain was apparently abandoned after the time of the Exodus, between 1950 and 1000 BCE. Professor Anati claims that this site was Mount Sinai. This claim is hotly contested by numerous other professional archaeologists.

After thanking him, we bade farewell and set off to explore the mountain sites. His contentious claims did not diminish my enthusiasm to examine his findings. After all, the rock engravings and other features found at this site are unlike anything found elsewhere on other mountains across the peninsula or at other rock art sites.

The first of Anati's finds that we came across were two rows of six large rocks each, neatly placed next to each other, which, he claims, represent the twelve tribes of Israel. He maintains that these rocks resemble those which Moses erected at the foot of Mount Sinai. When we arrived, several archaeological students were demarcating a new area close by in the hope of revealing new evidence. A young Israeli named Joshi eagerly explained to us that in the past they had found large flint workshops which may have produced, among other things, flints that the Israelites might have used for circumcision when they were encamped in the large open area at the base of the mountain. The area was indeed extensive enough to accommodate thousands of people.

We left the students to their endeavors and set out to climb the mountain. The stones and rocks were of various shades of red and brown, but every now and then I caught sight of some blackened rocks with carvings, including images of bucks and worshippers. Then we came across a rock depicting two tablets which appeared similar to the tablets brought down from Mount Sinai by Moses. Another rock had images of each of the ten plagues carved into it. What an astounding sight! Further on, lay a rock with a snake and a staff engraved into it, which Anati claims was a symbol of the snake that Moses' rod miraculously turned into when he went to convince the Pharaoh that he had

Examining the archeological remains at Mount Karkom, the Israelite campsite Makheloth. | M Rawicz Trip Photo

been sent by G-d to demand the Israelites' freedom. The engraved snake reminded me of the thin, poisonous Israeli mole viper, *Atractaspis Engaddensis,* which grows up to eighty centimeters long and is endemic to Israel and the Sinai Desert. I hoped that we would not meet any real vipers at this location.

Perhaps the most amazing stone of all bore an image that at first glance appeared to be two figures worshipping a symbol. When I looked more closely, I saw the name of the Israelites' G-d, YHVH, carved in ancient Hebrew script. Later, we saw a carving of a menorah as well as the biblical symbol that represents "the eye of G-d that looks from the rock." This was indeed extraordinary, and I began to appreciate why Anati had made his claims.

The next finding made by Anati was a circle of stones, which he alleges was the site of religious ceremonies. However, some of the stones had the shape of human heads, which would have been a form of idol worship had they been used by the Israelites. A number of such features provided evidence that this place had indeed been extremely important in the ceremonies of an ancient people.

By mid-afternoon, Ohad, Ehud and I were still exploring. The sky suddenly turned black and a violently strong wind whipped up unexpectedly, and the air became thick with red dust. It was impossible for us to scramble down from the mountain quickly enough to escape the storm. With trepidation, we tried to protect ourselves. I dragged myself over rocks to a spot that had a patch of softer sand and buried my face under my arms, lying down flat on the ground.

Ohad yelled to me above the howling noise, "Don't move, just lie down and stay down."

The wind lashed at me, pulling at the protective jacket that I had tucked around my head and body. For a terrifying hour we waited for the wind to subside as blinding rain pelted us. It seemed as if the heavens had opened up in fury. I lay there totally soaked as the water gushed down the mountainside and across our path. It took all my determination and strength to keep still.

A prehistoric engraving called a petroglyph that is found on and around Mount Karkom.
| M Rawicz Trip Photo

After what seemed an eternity, during which I recited as many prayers as I could remember, things calmed down. Slowly and carefully we picked our way over the perilously wet rocks while trying desperately not to slip. Eventually we reached the bottom, to our great relief. When I reached the car, I retrieved a dry set of clothing from my suitcase and found a secluded spot where I could change. Using some clean water that was caught in the hollow of a rock, I succeeded in wiping off much of the mud. I was grateful for a return to some comfort. We also felt lucky to find some hot water still in a flask, which we used to make tea to restore a sense of calm. It was in this restored state that I was able to recall the biblical events that had taken place here.

After the incident when Korach was swallowed up by the earth and the plague that ravaged the people, G-d ordered one man from each tribe to bring Moses a rod with his name written on it. Aaron also gave Moses his rod. This was to settle the issue of leadership and quiet the rebels who had caused the dissent at the previous camp. Moses set the rods before G-d in the Tabernacle of Witness, as he had been commanded to do. Then a miracle occurred and the rod of Aaron, for the Levites, formed buds and then blossomed and produced almonds. This was proof that Aaron was the rightful high priest. "The camp of Kehelathan was the same place where the miracle of Aaron's rod had taken place, when it blossomed."[4]

From that time onwards the rod of Aaron was kept in the golden Ark of the Covenant, below the solid gold cherubim in a special drawer with the tablets next to the Ten Commandments and a symbolic small jug of manna.

Ehud turned to me and said, "That was quite a storm."

I shrugged my shoulders. "Yes, I'm pleased that it's over and that I coped with it. On another note, I'm thinking about what the meaning of this camp was in biblical times."

"Okay, what was the meaning?" he asked.

I explained what I had learned.

✏ Uniting and connecting with others

We may feel the need to join a group that has the same outlook or goal as ourselves during the course of our lives. This could be a sports group, religious community, group for a hobby that interests us, or even professional. Within the group there is unity of purpose and the group could operate in harmony. The group's purpose could be practical or altruistic.

This is what happened to the Israelites at Kehelathan and Makheloth. They gathered in full assemblies and praised G-d. The ultimate transformation of fear is when it leads us to gather together, appreciate and sing in praise of our Divine blessings."[5]

Because the Israelites gathered in harmony they were blessed by G-d. Their ability to create intense connections with each other was pleasing to G-d. There is a teaching that even when two people meet with good intent it brings blessing. Their meeting could be just to support each other in friendship, yet it still brings blessing. If it is to act in gratitude to G-d, blessings will emerge even more.

Jacobson alludes to some of the above concepts and refers to the fact that it is optimum if we can transform our fear and worship in harmony.[6]

My personal experience at this site had been rather nerve-racking with moments of anxiety during the storm. The support of my guide, however, evoked my gratitude. I was inspired to strive for greater unity in my family and personal relationships.

It had been an eventful day with our exploration of the archaeological findings and our encounter with the sudden storm. Now it was time to set up a tent at a local picnic spot and prepare to camp for the night.

SHRINES AND MIRACLES – TAHATH   CAMP 23

"And they removed from Makheloth, and encamped at Tahath"[1] – which means lowlands.[2] The image of lowlands seemed gentler than any of the previous campsite names. Just follow the topography, and surely one would be headed towards the lowlands.

Nonetheless, this campsite was also situated inside the military firing zone, and on normal working days it would have been inaccessible to the public. We followed the route that gradually led downwards from Makheloth, travelling first south and then west. We were surrounded by the biblical Wilderness of Paran, which sweeps in from the Sinai, following along the Nahal Paran, a riverbed that stretches for nearly 160 kilometers – the longest and widest riverbed in the Negev. This is one of the most desolate stretches of desert in the Negev. It was to

Wilderness of Paran. | *M Rawicz Trip Photo*

this parched region that the patriarch Abraham, at the behest of his humiliated wife, Sarah, banished his concubine, Hagar, after she had given birth to Ishmael. Here Hagar had wept for her young son, fearing the arid conditions would destroy him.

After a short while, Ohad, Ehud and I found ourselves moving between magnificent cliffs that form the White Canyon Valley. The shining faces of the white cliffs towered above us as we drove along in the wadi below. The various bands of rock included white limestone, yellowish dolomite, and chalk, all of which reflected the sunlight intensely. This area forms part of the Negev Nature Reserve, which is administered by the Israeli National Park Authority. Its many hiking trails attract nature lovers and students. We met up with one such party, a group of students from the University of Beersheba. They were making this field trip as part of their environmental studies, and their professor was explaining the geological history and rock structures of these fascinating white cliffs, and the local ecology. He gestured to the broad expanse of land around us. "After dusk," he said, "the area suddenly comes alive with hooting owls, bats searching for moths, hyenas, and even an occasional fox prowling in the scrub."

His excitement was contagious. Being a practicing environmental consultant, I was encouraged by the number of nature-conscious youth who wanted to improve their ecological knowledge. After this engaging encounter, Ohad, Ehud and I continued our journey. When we stopped to rest, Ohad showed me some flowers that appeared to be tightly closed but opened up as soon as he placed a drop of water on them. We had a lot of fun doing this.

Luck was on our side when we came across the rare sight of the remains of a carcass that had been mostly consumed by hyenas. We also saw lizards, beetles, and a snake. Further on, we passed a hiker who told us about a poaching incident that he had witnessed the previous day. "We came across a trapped buck with its foot caught in a snare, and immediately contacted the anti-poaching team," the hiker said. "They managed to track down the perpetrators and arrest them."

The fascination of the Negev plants was also revealed to us. These plants last for so long in the desert because dew forms for about four months of the year. The moisture collects on the leaves of trees, then falls onto the bushes and then the ground, supporting the growth of groundcover and small flowers.

Geographically, the campsite was located at a significantly lower level than the previous camp. However, clearly the name Tahath – meaning lowlands – held a deeper meaning.

By now we were hot and tired, so we stopped to refresh ourselves before arriving at Tahath. Our break gave me an opportunity to reflect on the meaning of this camp.

⊟ Low times transformed to peace

Scholars have various interpretations on the meaning of Tahath, including "lowlands"; "then to the lower Makheloth"; "below," or that it refers to a lowly state as Jacobson shows.[3]

Life is like the waves with ups and downs, troughs and crests. At Makheloth the people were unified and on a high. Tahath, however, stands for the low points in life when we feel disconnected. Even in this situation there is some incentive, even serenity in the fact that, with effort, we can each live in harmony. Here the Israelites once again had fallen into a lowly state just as we often do when we move from ups to downs and experience unhappiness. They had learned that this happens when we forsake our unity with others, as Jacobson asserts.[4]

Transforming low times to peace was a foreign concept to me and I thought that it would be worthwhile for me to explore the idea and see if it could work for me. ◀

Birds seemed to talk to us. A Bonelli's eagle with its dark brown wings, white belly and long grey tail soared overhead silently upwards, scanning the ground for its next meal. Another death was imminent. It made a quick dash to grasp its prey from the cover of the foliage of a tree, and we could clearly see its short rounded wings, yellow feet and eyes. Then its fluted call "klu-kluklu-kluee" rang out. Then silence! A final swoop and it flew off towards its nest in a crag, with the poor creature that had just breathed its last breath.

This must be a very favorable spot for wildlife because, as we approached nearer the mountain, a long-legged buzzard hawk soared past on its massive wings of one-and-a-half meters.

The orange tint on his plumage, red tail, pale head, largely white belly, distinctive black carpal patch and dark trailing edge on his wings were clearly visible. It started hovering over one spot and beating its wings at high speed, then dove and flew off with its victim in its large hooked beak.

REFUGEES – TARAH   CAMP 24

"And they departed from Tahath, and pitched at Tarah"[1] – which means "the place of the Ibex."[2] The expectation immediately arose that we would see more of these indigenous buck.

Tarah was located on the Egyptian side, in the Sinai. Evidently we would be able to see it from a high mountain nearby called Arif Anak or Mount Arif.

It takes some effort to negotiate the major challenges of a 4x4 dirt road, but we decided to try and it was a privilege to go. Ohad, Ehud and I went as far as we could by jeep. Then we took a significant hike on the 'green-marked' walking trail, and followed the green lines marked periodically along the rocks, in this military area with very limited access to the public. We walked for one and a half kilometers on a reasonably sloped incline to the top.

Arif Anak is a magnificent reddish mountain with a razor-sharp ridge running along its summit, and an almost lunar quality to its appearance. Standing on this majestic mountain, I searched the horizon for Tarah. In this desolate and isolated part of the Negev, one appreciates the quiet beauty of the darkish black mountains that gaze over the natural splendor of the yellow desert. Only in distant wadis do thin lines of green suggest the presence of water.

From what I knew, Tarah might also be situated close to a water source. In the distance I could see the Israeli–Egyptian border, where a few Israeli soldiers were climbing into a Hummer. Here, too, the ground in Israel was scattered with remnants of missiles and bomb shells from the military practices that took place inside this firing zone. I could also make out a building on the Sinai side with extremely tall steel communication towers.

Ohad explained what he knew from his military days in the Sinai. "Past the mountain known as Jabal Umm Hullaf, there's a large Egyptian military surveillance post. I remember that it had a very thick concrete wall. It was like a fortress surrounded by razor wire, high and dense, behind which I could see large oblong prefab buildings. I guess they were offices and hostels."

Through the binoculars we searched the foot of Mount Jabal Umm Halluf, where the Tarah campsite is thought to have been.

Ohad continued, "I recall there was a large water hole, which would certainly have been used by both people and animals. In ancient times, the shepherds would have brought their flocks there and the locals would have drawn their water. Indigenous animals like Oryx, Ibex and wild asses would also have come there to drink."

✑ Old fool or wise person

I thought about the spiritual meaning of the Tarah campsite again, which is related to the name of the idol worshiper, Terach, Abraham's father. It also relates to the Hebrew word for wait or patience. Jacobson notes that it is connected to the middle-aged point in our lifetimes when we are an example to our offspring. He cites that we can either show our children our well-advised example of being followers of G-d or the ill-advised ways of being worshipers of idols such as materialism. These idols can also be modern or old values that, intrinsically, from a religious point of view, do not have much real value, such as being a celebrity, fashion diva, material status objects. The lesson for the Israelites and ourselves is to learn with patience and acquire wisdom and not be like old fools, like Terach.[3]

I wondered about the future and I hoped that I could gain wisdom before I grew old. It made me decide that I would try to set aside time more regularly to study the wisdom of the sages. The trip was certainly aiding me in being less reliant on material possessions.

"So this is another camp I'll see only from the distance," I commented.

I was frustrated that I could not see the site up close and very disappointed that I would probably not be able to go there in the foreseeable future.

"Well, as you know, Tarah is far from the border," Ohad replied. "If we were to go in there, we could also run into other kinds of criminals! There are impoverished African nations in northeast Africa, like Sudan, Somalia and Eritrea, which have a history of persecuting any political opponents. This has caused thousands of desperate, persecuted refugees to flee through the Sinai Desert. They try to reach the Israeli border and slip through unnoticed. But many of them are kidnapped by Bedouin tribesmen or terrorists. They are then ransomed or suffer horrific torture, rape, electrocution and massive extortion of money. Hundreds of poor families are forced into enormous debt that takes decades to pay off."

None of us knew that in the future this stream of African refugees would turn into a flood.

I said, "I can see why you don't want me to try and get closer to Tarah."

After this interlude, Ohad, Ehud and I continued on our journey, looking out for wildlife. I wondered whether the Israelites had been threatened by wild animals like leopards or hyenas. At one point we stopped the car to take a closer look at the so-called "fat sand rat," a creature that can be as long as seventeen centimeters from head to tail. It studied us for about half a minute before fleeing into a burrow in the shade of a large rock. We saw the chewed stalks of jointed *Anabasis*, which the sand rats had not yet dragged into their burrows to eat in relative safety. We had probably interrupted them.

Then I realized that the rats had another reason to scamper off so quickly. A feathered predator, the desert eagle owl, was sitting upright nearby on a large rock. The bird's mottled light-brown and beige wing feathers, plain beige chest, and two large upright ear tufts revealed its identity, and it stared at us with large, mesmerizing eyes. This intelligent, silent hunter was almost perfectly camouflaged against the reddish mountains. It posed no threat to us humans.

As we ventured further, we stopped periodically. Ohad pointed out the dry stalks of the yellow *Asphodel* and the incredibly beautiful "desert tulips." We could also see the erect stems of the *Danin* fennel, a plant known for its cuplike appearance that is endemic to the western Negev Highlands. Wormwood, a greyish, highly fragrant shrub used by the Bedouin to relieve stomach ache, could be seen almost everywhere.

ASHERAH IDOL AND SWEET WATER – MITHKAH

CAMP 25

"And they removed from Tarah, and pitched in Mithkah,"[1] which means "sweet delight" or "sweetness."[2] I wondered what sweetness could be found in this desert, and the only thing that sprang to mind was drinkable sweet water. That seemed like a reasonable thing to consider.

One would have to travel through the terribly dangerous area of the Sinai to get to Mithkah. The route would follow a wide wadi that skirted the western base of the Jabal Umm Halluf Mountain and run on towards the base of Jawz-al-Mukabirah, where one would find the site considered to be the camp of Mithkah.[3]

Despite using our powerful binoculars and photographic lenses we still could not see these high prominent peaks. Ohad had visited the mountain previously, and we settled down next to our vehicle to have refreshments and to hear him narrate his experience.

"Israel occupied this area between 1967 and 1980," Ohad said. "I was serving in the Israeli army as a young officer, and we went to this hill. As we arrived, I saw a winding path that led to the summit. It looked difficult to climb but I was motivated to try, and on one of our days off I went there with a companion. The drive was hot and dusty. We stopped for a rest, and then we were ready for the challenge. For an hour, we struggled up that steep sandy surface on foot. The ground had been eroded by desert winds, and my feet kept slipping on the uneven surface. A number of times I fell back where the sand was soft and it gave way under my weight. But eventually we reached the summit – what a relief!

"As we stepped onto solid ground at the top, an amazing sight

A view of the Kuntillet 'Ajrud archaeological site | Image excerpted from LaHashem
Teiman VeLeAsherato. *With permission of the Israel Exploration Society.*

greeted us. There was an enormous ancient structure of stone. It looked
as if it had been abandoned centuries ago and never been visited since.
The roof was gone, but the walls of several rooms were still standing,
although some had been quite badly eroded. There were a lot of rooms.

"From this height, we could look out over the vast desert plains below
in all directions. After we had caught our breath, we made our way towards the ruins. There we wandered through a fortress-like main building. We passed through what had clearly been a courtyard and wandered through what looked like a few rooms, where to my surprise I saw
some low benches still standing. I took advantage and sat there resting,
enjoying the shade and wondered about the place that we were at."

I had read a bit about this site and seen pictures on the Internet,
when I was researching the Exodus route. It was used between the late
ninth and seventh centuries BCE according to research by Professor
Gnuse in 1997. It was called Kuntillet Ajrud,[4] an Arabic name meaning

"solitary hill of wells." Water was obtained from several shallow wells at the foot of the hill. The site was excavated by Ze'ev Meshel[5] and a team from the Institute of Archaeology at Tel Aviv University in 1975 and 1976. In 2001, Professor Finkelstein from Tel Aviv University, Neil Asher Silberman,[6] and other historian archaeologists, analyzed the archaeology of Israel in relation to the Bible. They revealed its history and its hidden treasures, which provided a huge amount of information. They concluded that travellers may have stopped for rest and refreshment at this desert roadside station. It is halfway between Beersheba and Eilat and used to be situated at a crossroads between the trade routes. The site overlooks Wadi Geraia, which is really big and runs from southeast to northwest before it joins up with another big wadi, Wadi-El-Arish, in northern Sinai. I noted that a huge watershed drained directly into the site of the encampment and the wadis converged at this point. This was certainly a place where fresh sweet water would have been found.

I told Ohad and Ehud about the website called "Asherah and the G-d of the Early Israelites," which gave a description by Israel Finkelstein and Neil Asher Silberman. The description was fascinating to me. I explained that at Kuntillet Ajrud, Finkelstein and his colleagues found some small jugs and two large water jars in each room. They sent them for instrumental neutron activation analysis. One of the jugs was a pear-shaped storage jar or *pithoi*. It's on display in a museum now. It had a picture of a cow with a suckling calf, which they thought represented the mother goddess, a symbol of fertility and nurturing in various cultures. Other pictures show the Egyptian god Bes, who warded off evil and protected households, especially mothers and children.

I continued, "An image on the storage jar shows two cows standing next to each other. One is female and has breasts, and the other is male. The cows are standing upright like people, with their arms behind their backs, but their faces and feet are those of cows' and they have tails hanging between their legs. They're wearing clothing made of skin decorated with dots, and winged headdresses. The male figure is thought to be Bes – who also represents pleasure – and the female figure is his wife, Beset. Bes has a mane around his face. Now, the oldest pictures of Bes were of a lion rearing up on its hind legs. So the cow figure of Bes has a crown and a beard, and is wearing lion or leopard skin clothing.

"To the right of these images are female representations of Bes playing the harp, sitting on a feline throne with clawed feet and a spotted covering. That's said to be a sign of royalty. Another image on the other

We sat and discussed the amazing ancient fortress, Kuntillet Ajrud.

side of the jug is of the Tree of Life. This is also a symbol for the mother goddess who feeds and sustains life. Two typical caprids, which are a cross between a goat and an antelope, are standing beside the tree eating from it. There's a lion below the tree, and there are also some images of horses. There's an inscription on the jug, above the heads of the figures, overlapping the crown of Bes. One inscription reads, 'Say, say to Yehallelel and to Yoash and . . . I bless you by Yahweh, Shomron (Samaria) and by Ashrth (Asherah).'

"Another jug showed a procession of worshippers and had an inscription that reads 'AmarYau says, speak to my lord, HShLM. I bless you by Yahweh of Teman and by Ashrth (Asherah). May he bless you and observe you and be with my lord.'"

I ended the fascinating review of what I had read, "There were fragments of Hebrew written in black ink and decorated with inscriptions and drawings. The archaeologists also found several bowls bearing the names of petitioners who were asking for blessings."

"I didn't see the jugs," Ohad commented. "I guess they had already been taken from the site and sent to archaeological laboratories."

"The website said that most of the pottery was of Judean origin," I clarified. "But some of the smaller finds were ceramics from Israel, including the northern kingdom. Other ceramics came from the southern littoral of the Levant (Ashdod). The images showed gods and goddesses that were typically drawn in Syria between 1500 and 1300 BCE. They were drawn by different artists, but the basic style was Phoenician or Syrian. The archaeologists were quite surprised to find these items, as they were not related to ancient Egyptian models or to any artifacts of ancient Palestinian art that had been found before.[7] Various populations, such as the Nabataeans, Edomites, Negabites and Midianites in the southern Levant, had used this route from the Negev desert to travel through the Sinai."[8]

"On the day I visited the site," Ohad added, "We walked through the courtyard to an anteroom and then through a waiting room. We also saw two kitchens. We crossed the main courtyard to the other end of the building and saw a large cellar. After this we returned to the ground floor and went outside to see a second structure, which had two long rooms. The remnants of paintings and inscriptions were still visible on the walls. Did you read anything about such a room?" he asked.

I replied, "They found an inscription about Yahweh and Asherah on plaster fragments that had fallen from the walls in the entrance area and doorposts." A biblical command requires the Israelites to write the name of G-d on the doorposts of houses and on the gates, as given in Deuteronomy 6:9. Kathryn Finkelstein[9] and others concluded that the paintings had been done over a long time and that they were painted by several different artists, because they did not form a coherent scene.

"The rooms you saw would have been where people met for strategic and religious purposes. Here the archaeologists came across rare finds. There were artifacts with writing on them, and they realized that the inscriptions showed a surprising mix of religions. Some invoked Yahweh, El and Baal, such as the phrases "Yahweh of Samaria and his Asherah" and "Teman and his Asherah."[10] They concluded that the inhabitants had been invoking the Israelite G-d in connection with a temple in Samaria, which was the capital of Israel at the time, and also the god Teman of Edom.[11] The Asherah was most likely a cultic object."

I allowed myself to imagine this "solitary hill of wells" in its heyday. Women are walking painstakingly in a single line in the stillness with jugs on their heads. They carefully pick their way through the rocky pathway back from the well, carrying the precious liquid. Only their singing breaks the silence. From the sweltering barrenness camels approach. Dusty, dishevelled men, clad in gritty robes, strain at the end of their journey. Their eyes droop with exhaustion.

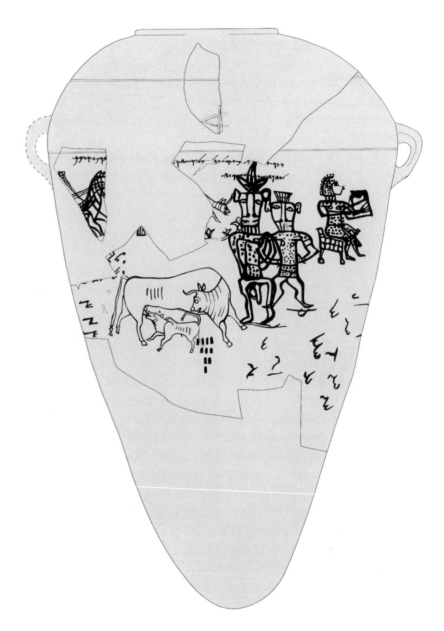

The Egyptian male god Bes who warded off evil and his wife Beset. The lion is rearing on its hind legs and wearing skin clothing. | *Image excerpted from* LaHashem Teiman VeLeAsherato. *With permission of the Israel Exploration Society*

Fortress guards check the visitors, and then money changes hands and all are satisfied. The senior men are escorted through a courtyard, then an anteroom to a waiting room where they gratefully sink on the stone benches.

The burly fort leader beckons them to prayer. They gesticulate in supplication and chant compellingly before the cow god Bes. Women in colorful robes dispense drinks in jugs painted with male and female cows in deference to the gods for the safe journey. From the kitchen two thickset women emerge carrying a lamb stew in a heavy pot, its delicate flavor wafting into the air, reminding the travellers of their hunger. A man emerges from the cellar carrying sustenance. The host entertains his visitors with tales of Nabataeans, Edomites, Negabites and Midianites.

Judith Hadley in the book "The Cult of Asherah in Ancient Israel and Judah: Evidence for a Hebrew Goddess" writes, "The deities mentioned and the location of the place suggest that it was a wayside shrine, and was related to the royal journeys to Elath and Etzion Geber and perhaps also pilgrimages to southern Sinai."[12] The Book of Kings, which was written after the Israelites had settled in the Promised Land, describes a time during the ninth to seventh centuries BCE when the land was divided into two kingdoms, Judah in the south and Israel in the north. There was trade between Phoenicia and Israel, and the Israelites struggled to resist the attraction of pagan gods. The prophets Elijah, Elisha, Amos and Isaiah complained against these transgressions. "At this Kuntillet Ajrud remote desert way station, there was evidence of the mixture of religious practices which had provoked the prophets' fury."[13]

Ohad was interested in hearing the details of the place he had visited so long ago.

"Compared with the fortress at Kadesh Barnea," I continued, "this one at Kuntillet Ajrud seems to have had more art and religious work. The archaeologists found symbols of cows, gods, blessings, Hebrew inscriptions, paintings, and invocations to the gods Yahweh, El and Baal here. It was a wayside shrine for passing pilgrims from 1500 to 1300 BCE and in the ninth to seventh centuries BCE.[14] Kuntillet Ajrud was also a border fort during King Solomon's era."[15] Its uniqueness was that it had numerous rooms on an upper and lower level, still standing even now.

"It's great to understand more about these finds – which shed some light on the early writing, religion and history," Ohad said. "I found it a fascinating and unique place, and I spent four hours there looking around. Before I came down from the mountain, I looked again at the view from that height, and saw the confluence of wadis in the area where the Israelites' camp would have been. The wadis from three large mountains, Jabal Umm Halluf, Mount Seir, and Har Zenifim came together at that point, and the place seemed perfect for human habitation. The location of the fortress also made sense geographically. It's a pity that it's not safe to go in there. I know you'd have loved to see it."

Enjoying the fruits of one's labor

Jacobson explains that spiritually, the camp of Mithkah represents a more mature phase in life when our children are already married and producing their own offspring. We then experience the satisfaction and delight of seeing the next generation and the achievements of our children. We proudly enjoy the results of all the hard work that we have put in over the years. This gives us a reward for the difficulties that we may have endured along the way or "transforms bitterness of life into sweetness."[16] This sense of "sweetness" can also be experienced in other endeavors such as self-development and advancement projects. The lesson is to appreciate the sweet outcome of previous efforts.

This was a profound lesson for me as I had always glossed over my achievements and looked to the next challenge and the next goal. I knew that if I enjoyed the results of all my hard work, my life would be greatly improved.

Families that passed this way with Moses may by now have realized how important it was to avoid idolatry and conquer their fear; they might have been able to appreciate that fearful situations can actually be most empowering. They may have known by now that forces beyond one's control can be handled by surrendering to a higher power, and on a deeper level may be perceived as opportunities. With all that they had been through, these men and women had been given ample opportunities to limit their own slander and aggression, to cope with the low points in life, to work towards peace, and to serve a higher purpose with greater consciousness. They might, by now, have realized the need to become more unified as a people. I envisaged them behaving in a less rebellious manner now that they knew that such rebellion would interfere with their own destiny. Certain individuals might have reached the point of providing inspiration and positive influence for their fellow travellers, encouraging them to think in a positive way. I felt heartened to envisage the families walking through the area as a more mindful flock. I felt as if I, too, had made some progress in absorbing the lessons.

By this time, at this twenty-fifth camp, in summary, the Israelites had learned some of the issues of middle age crisis and had gained greater maturity.[17] They had learned how to harness anxiety and fear and turn them to advantage. They were acting with sharpened wits, focused minds, and avoiding or overcoming the things that made them afraid. They were also acting with greater unity and growing in good deeds and morality and beginning to enjoy the fruits of this labor.

I had developed greater persistence and perception after the trip. I was growing towards and serving a higher purpose. I had feelings of greater gratitude and contentment. I wanted to study more about the practice of good deeds and hopefully bring relief and happiness into the lives of other people.

I was enjoying the routine of travelling with my companions, climbing out of the car to explore on the rough terrain, resting with my bottle of water and a biscuit, and thinking about all the new information, history and archaeology, sights and teachings. I was delighted that I had made the effort to learn about this unique place.

AMBASSADORS – HASHMONAH   CAMP 26

"They left Mithkah and camped at Hashmonah"[1] which means "Ambassador."[2] I could surely not find any diplomat, ambassador or person representing a political group in this distant location.

The Israeli border road was used exclusively by the military and out of bounds to civilians, so Ohad, Ehud and I detoured to a cycle track for some thirty-four kilometers. It ran parallel to the military road before reaching the Paran River, which ran southwest towards the border. With extreme caution, we edged forwards along the rough terrain of the mountain biking track until we were close to the point where it intersected the Paran River in a remote area.

Through our powerful camera lenses, we were able to get another look at the Taba–Al-Kaseema road that ran parallel to the border on the Egyptian side. Looking across the high security fence, the only discernible feature at the Hashmonah camp was a large horse-shaped rise in the ground, which looked unnatural. It might have been the remains of an ancient military outpost, now buried under sand.

The eastern regions of the Sinai were inhabited during the Iron Ages. At various times during the biblical era, the Midianites, Amorites and Edomites had occupied parts of this region, and the Egyptians had conquered other areas. This had been Amalekite country, which was conquered by both King Solomon and King David. It made sense that some form of military defense would have been needed here. Near the point where we now stood was another Egyptian military Sinai border guard. In the distance, we could see a convoy of three large armoured trucks laden with shiny communication equipment installed on the roofs, and machine guns and artillery at the rear, travelling along the border road. "The military tension had hardly changed since the Exodus, but the technology had!" I thought to myself.

For many years the eastern Sinai had been ruled by Bedouins who conducted illegal activities. Now, however, it had become a horrific lawless area. We would have to be satisfied with viewing it from across the border.

✎ Personal leadership skills

The meaning of this camp's name is "ambassador." We can learn from Hashmonah to fulfill with maturity and authority the role of leaders. It teaches us about the position of power we have when guiding others. It also refers to the part we may play as representatives for a specific purpose or as delegates of a group. The Israelites had to learn how to converse, agree to deals, and lead competently, like an ambassador does. They had to learn the art of diplomacy. These could be the skills we acquire in our mature years, as I understood from explanations by Jacobson.[3]

I hoped that my own sojourns with the local Muslims would have added some goodwill to the world and that I had made at least some small, positive impression in terms of personal relationships. I resolved to stop anyone from bad-mouthing either side in my company, when it came to the Israeli–Palestinian conflict.

Sadness filled me and a deep sinking feeling rushed through my chest. When would this animosity cease and peace prevail?   ◨

High in the sky a lone Egyptian vulture, with its black and white plumage and bright yellow-orange face, soared silently towards us. My heart was heavy but the sight of this magnificent bird restored me to feeling better. Certainly, good ambassadors were needed to bring peace to this region.

PUNISHMENT OF REBELS – MOSEROTH   CAMP 27

"And they departed from Hashmonah, and encamped at Moseroth,"[1] which means "chastisement."[2]

I asked myself, "Why all this negativity and punishment? What are we to look for next? Could there not at least be something positive to look forward to?"

Ohad, Ehud and I were moving ten kilometers south along the border to find a point where we could again stop and look into the Sinai for the site at Moseroth. Yet again, disappointingly, we would not be able to visit the actual campsite. It was located in the firing ground and was directly below military airspace.

"During normal work days," Ehud told me, "you can hear the ear-splitting sound of fighter planes here every day. Recently, Israel had a missile attack from its enemies. For about a week, people were fleeing for safety to shelters to get away from the constant shelling. I recall how everybody had to run to avoid missiles coming in at the Sde Boker area at that time."

From this point we hoped to scan the horizon and find the campsite, which was situated about five kilometers from the Egyptian border. With great difficulty, Ohad managed to steer his car over the rocky ground far away enough from the Israeli military road so that we would not get into trouble with the authorities. Although the land was flat, we could not see far enough into the Sinai to see Moseroth. We were unable to get any closer because of the military restrictions on approaching the border. Eventually, we made our way to a large mountain called Har Zenifim, which was slightly deeper into Israeli territory. From its summit, we were able to see the Moseroth site more clearly. We were standing about twenty-two kilometers away from it by now, looking through our binoculars and camera lenses.

The Israelites had journeyed to Moseroth along an extremely broad wadi. Perusing my map it was evident that the wadi was a full kilometer wide, and very flat, with slightly raised mounds at its borders. This wadi was sure to have big trees with wide branches growing along its entire length.

I recalled what I had read, to my surprise, that there was another ancient military fortress at the site of the ancient encampment. It was called the Al Kuntillet, and was part of the chain of fortresses that King Solomon had built to protect the southern border of his kingdom.[3]

About five years after King Solomon's death in 924 BCE, during the reign of the Israelite King Rehoboam, the kingdoms of Israel and Judah were attacked by an Egyptian pharaoh called Shishak. He was an aggressive conqueror and fought with some 12,000 chariots, 60,000 horsemen, and a massive number of troops.[4] Pharaoh Shishak's army managed to defeat and destroy many walled towns of Judah and march on to Jerusalem, where the Israelites lived. He looted many of their treasures and carried home the golden items from their famous temple. Shishak's army also took treasures from King Solomon's royal palace, such as golden shields. Al Kuntillet was just one of King Solomon's fortresses that were looted by Shishak.

However, this fortress would not yet have existed at the time of the Exodus. The location may have had some other special characteristic, possibly military. I thought about that gloomy moment in history when the Israelites had suffered such terrible defeat at the hands of Shishak.[5]

Ohad shared another idea with me. "Al Kuntillet has some similarities to Kuntillet Ajrud as they were both fortresses, however the relics that were found there are not as elaborate. We don't seem to know much about its functioning but more about its demise."

In close proximity to Al Kuntillet was another modern, relatively large military compound, also referred to as a police compound.

We discussed our ideas for a solution to the border problems he had been telling me about. He explained how the IDF had eventually decided to respond to the horrific conditions in the Sinai and the threat it posed to Israel by building a fence along the border, to cut down on the number of people who infiltrated Israel. This step turned out to be a tremendous help in defending the country's southern desert borders. The IDF was also planning laws to allow authorities to detain people who attempted to cross the border illegally, for up to three years without trial. The Ministry of Defense planned a 230 kilometer fortification that would run from the Kerem Shalom crossing at Gaza along the Sinai-Egyptian border, ending just north of the Red Sea resort of Eilat. It would consist of a five to seven meter-high fence, multiple layers of

Israeli border fence and patrol access roads between Israel and Egypt, built to prevent terrorists from attacking Israel. | M Rawicz Trip Photo

barbed wire, patrol paths and access roads. Cameras, radars and other systems would be integrated into the IDF's command-and-control system, allowing for remote surveillance of the vast border area.

I quickly entered into my log book: "Moseroth is the third fortress that we have come across from King Solomon's times. It has many similarities to the one at Mithkah as it is still on the known north–south trade route, still used as a military border patrol route today. Once again, the Israelites would not have seen this fortress."

I wondered how the term "chastisement," the meaning of this camp name, would fit with the characteristics or history of the place. I recalled the biblical account of the death of the high priest, Aaron, brother of Moses, a few camps ahead. The Israelites had mourned Aaron greatly. However, many people had then become disillusioned and rebelled and backtracked as far as Moseroth.[6]

The Canaanite king of Arad, who lived in the Negev, heard that the Israelites were coming. Amalek, who lived in the south, had relocated and now reigned in Arad. Amalek heard that Aaron had died and that G-d's protective pillar of cloud that had accompanied the Israelites since their departure from Egypt, had disappeared. He also knew that the prophetess Miriam was dead, and that the Israelites had rebelled against G-d and returned from Rekem to Moseroth. He went out to wage war on the Israelites and captured many of them.[7]

Thus, the people's uprising resulted in punishment by G-d, and a large number were killed. Evidently, years after the Exodus journey had ended, this site again became a place of anguish when Solomon was defeated.

⌁   Counsel others and offer constructive criticism

> At "Moseroth" the Israelites were experienced, mature and old enough to be in a position of counsel and share their wisdom with members who were in need of this. The level of maturity and stature of those willing to counsel was such that they could confidently chastise or provide reproach that would build up rather than break down the recipient's self-image. This happens in life when a person is already approaching old age and can have a more objective and compassionate approach to life, as I understood from explanations by Jacobson.[8]   ⌁

I was again fascinated by the fortresses and the power of Egypt over the region for years after the Exodus. I was coming to terms with not being able to see a few of the camps up close and benefitting from the wise counsel of my guides.

Again, I reflected on how little had changed. I thought, "Not much has changed here politically for thousands of years. The people of this region still need to learn to live in harmony with each other and their political leadership seems unable to help them do so."

My distress only lessened when I recalled the lesson of the earlier camp of Rissah – from failed relationships and misguided effort, a deeper opportunity can emerge. I could only hope that in the future, greater political resolution would lead to real peace in this region. It was time to move on again. I had now seen the last of the camps in Egypt. We departed from the mountain summit.

Chapter 6

Through the Negev Desert: Camps 28–32

STONE LEOPARDS – BENEI JAAKAN   CAMP 28

"They left the place of Moseroth and pitched at Benei Jaakan."[1] *Benei-Jaakan* means "wells of the narrow path,"or "wells of distress."[2]

The search for wells had by now become familiar. This time, I wondered why the wells had been associated with distress and despair. Would they be similar to the wells we had already seen, or would there be something exceptional about them? Would the name and its location bear any obvious connection at all?

Benei Jaakan was on the same latitude as Moseroth, so we began the trek eastwards and inwards into the heart of the Israeli Negev. I hoped something would be different about this next camp, because Ohad, Ehud and I were about to cross the Israeli desert on the 26th day of my journey. We began the drive around the southern side of the steep Har Zenifim Mountains. From the magnificent peaks of this range, numerous large valleys with abundant vegetation fanned out like fingers into the soft Negev sands, where they formed flat pathways. The Israelites would have walked easily along these valleys.

Ohad stopped the car after a few hours so we could stretch our legs with a brief walk and enjoy the view, but a desert wind suddenly whipped up and was soon strong enough to tear at our clothes and make walking almost impossible. We struggled back to the shelter of the car and went in search of new sights. Following the trail was not always simple, as it passed through the center of an Israeli military practice region. We drove through the desert on ancient tracks called Derech Ha

Arika, which skirted the edges of the military area and were designated mountain cycling routes; they ran from west to east. Ohad pointed out the military zones and related more stories from his past.

"If we were to venture even one kilometer into that area," Ohad said, "we'd be confronted immediately by soldiers in a Hummer with crackling radio static and flashing lights . . . they would surround us, and we would be questioned aggressively about who we were, what we're doing there, and why we were driving on military ground. We would be in danger of imminent arrest. That region is so dangerous! Military maneuvers take place continually, and the public are forbidden access. It's virtually impossible to enter that area or to get permission to do so."

As if to prove the point, as we sat there chatting, we were confronted by six soldiers who jumped off a large truck with their huge Uzi firearms in hand. One of the men approached us and demanded,

"We are patrolling. Where are you going?"

Ohad explained, "All three of us are Jewish and we're making an historical exploration."

The soldiers appeared unmoved. "We have to follow procedures," they said. "Where would we be without them?"

"You're absolutely right," I said, boldly responding to the rhetorical question.

The soldiers displayed a hard attitude, which perturbed me. I began to explain where I was from and to talk about the Jewish community in South Africa and how much they admired the young women and men serving in the Israeli army. Then I spoke about my interest in the Passover holiday. Finally, I began to tell them about the Exodus route that I was following. This captivated their attention, and their attitudes softened. I even dared to ask for a photo, and to my surprise the soldiers agreed. Ohad took a picture of me standing next to a buxom young red-headed soldier, which delighted me. The group then accompanied us for a while.

It was clear that we were traversing extremely dangerous territory, but the seriousness of the situation did not really concern me. Our vehicle rumbled and swayed over the rocky terrain and soft sands, but the soldiers guided us as well as they could, leading us to more stable ground.

Ohad continued telling me about his experiences in this area. "In my early army days, I was in the vicinity of a military training practice area. One day there was a huge noise, and my eardrums felt as if they had burst and my teeth were chattering . . . my whole body was shaking. It was the first time I had been so close to live mortar fire. I felt shattered for quite a while. I had been stationed not far from here, at a large military installation. It has more than twenty hostel complexes, workshops, and huge parking areas for military vehicles and tanks, as well as big sports fields. Almost daily I would see Panzer tanks, with their firing gear pointed ahead as their huge wheels raced and left a mass of yellow dust behind them. This region has many underground facilities, test sites, and firing terrains."

I again lamented the fact that warfare has remained an issue in this region since ancient times.

We approached the Ovda Airport. This is a military and civilian airport, and is the country's second international airport after Tel Aviv. Originally Ovda was built as a military airport but was then modified to accommodate the numerous large aircraft that are unable to use the shorter runway near Eilat. We could see the civilian terminal, which handles flights to European destinations such as Warsaw, Kiev and Helsinki. Ohad stopped the car so that we could watch the planes taking off, and I enjoyed the peaceful sight of a plane launching into the air. When we resumed our journey, we passed a settlement of about forty homes that housed employees of the nearby airport.

The area had a stark beauty, with occasional dry grey bushes. We glimpsed two delicate gazelle grazing between the bushes, their large ears pointing upwards warily as we passed by. Apart from the animals, only the power lines and an occasional station for the underground gas lines broke the emptiness and heat. In the distance we saw deeply eroded gullies in the yellow sandstone mountain, and huge ruts that had caved in. The sun glared off the sand so brightly that it hindered Ohad's driving.

We had reached the eastern side of the Negev and the Bikaat Uvda Valley. The Israelites might have arrived here via a route now known as the Ascend Akof Bypass (Route 19160) or one of several other well-established pathways. They most likely would have passed some ancient wells known as "Gerez Wells." After stopping here, they moved on to the Biq'at Uvda site, which was a few kilometers in a southwest direction.

LEOPARD TEMPLE

Eventually I came across a sign that read "Nahal Ashrun site." Ohad explained that the settlements in this area – an astounding 150 in total – dated back to prehistoric times. This was a temptation not to be missed. The Israelites must surely have seen these settlements, because they predated the Exodus? The people may even have enjoyed the benefits of the resources as they passed through this area. I felt spurred on to explore the ruins. We began walking along a narrow stony path in the direction shown on the sign. We entered an archaeological site measuring 400 square meters which had been almost completely excavated.

Ohad explained, "In the distance, you can see several dozen rounded stone dwellings, each with a diameter of about two to four meters. They are built close together and date from the eighth century BCE. The inhabitants of this Neolithic village were hunters. Hundreds of flint arrowheads and bones of undomesticated animals have been found in the homes. The people also gathered wild grain and ground it up on primitive grindstones that have also been found in the settlements." He referred me to information that he had read.[3]

Enthralled, I walked with him to another site. There we saw an open-air sanctuary from the sixth century BCE. The square courtyard was surrounded by a low stone wall. The corners of this area corresponded to the four points of the compass. In the ritual area were three conical basins where ashes had been found.

We walked from the sanctuary to another site – the "Leopard Temple." It was amazing to see this 9,000 year old site. Stones were embedded into the soil in the form of sixteen mysterious life-size feline figures. Fifteen of these creatures face east. They look like leopards with square heads, huge eyes, four legs, and an upward-curving tail. Only one animal faces west, and has slightly twisted horns and is thought to be an antelope. It is possible that this was a cult site where people asked the shepherd gods to protect their flocks against leopard predators. It was fascinating to see the remains of some cult ritual that had been practiced thousands of years ago.

Ohad explained, "Archaeologists studied the character of temples, but they also found objects from daily life. There were ashes in a hearth, broken bowls with grains of wheat and seals. These things give more information about the people who once lived here. In about 4000 BCE, in the Chalcolithic period, there was an agricultural revolution in this region. People started to grow barley and wheat instead of hunting and gathering wild grain. They also started to domesticate the animals such as herds of goats and sheep. Archaeologists found throughout the valley, small settlements of stone houses and grain silos that had been dug into the ground and lined with stones. They also found sickles of bone or wood, into which toothed flint blades had been inserted. These tools would have been used to harvest the grain. Many grindstones were also found in the homes.[4]

"The site had surprisingly rich soil which had been washed down from the surrounding mountains over the centuries. This would have been prime land for settlements even in prehistoric times. In fact, some researchers think this is one of the oldest agricultural regions in the world. Today, the valley is surrounded by desert, but the ruins suggest this was once a highly fertile area."

I was astounded by the cult stonework and especially the mini altars with stone standing upright in this unique location. It was a highlight of the trip to see such ancient relics completely intact on the soil.

We left the site and drove further. Just south of the temple, about 450 meters from the road, smooth gleaming sand dunes rose up, crisscrossed by numerous hiking trails. We passed a group of five young adult hikers, one of whom called out a greeting. We stopped to chat. His name was Gary and he explained, "We are going to walk to a modern communal settlement in a valley. Although this is a very dry place, it's a favorite hiking trail because it takes you through a magnificent red canyon, which people like to climb. Also, you have a spectacular view from the mountaintops looking over the Negev." I was enthralled by the ancient routes that still exist from those ancient times.

Scholars have discovered that in ancient times, Benei Jaakan had its own wells. The Book of Deuteronomy refers to the "wells of the sons of Yaakan." As mentioned earlier, the name also means the "wells of distress" or "wells of the narrow pass."[5]

When I thought about the route, I realized that we had passed a number of wells along the way, and this campsite had its own wells which might have contributed to the name. With regard to "distress," the high priest Aaron had died not far from this site. When the Israelites grieved, some of them had passed through Benei Jaakan on their way back to Moseroth. Their state of distress may have contributed to the meaning of Benei Jaakan.

At the camp of Benei Jaakan there is a 9000 year old 'Leopard Temple' with life-size feline figures made of stones embedded in sand. | *M Rawicz Trip Photo*

The ancient Leopard Temple has cult stonework with mini altars still intact in the foreground. | *M Rawicz Trip Photo*

⬅ **Dealing with distress**

At Benei Jaakan the distress and confined allusions refer to the time of life of the aged. An aged person can become restricted due to deterioration of bodily energy and functioning, and increasing fragility. This takes place also when muscles and other organs start to reduce their functioning. Possibly medical interventions are needed. Depending on the aged person's outlook, this can be a time of fear, loss of independence, loneliness or insecurity. For the family it can possibly be a time of stress, having to over-extend oneself in caring for an aged person. The family however can rally and make the most of benefitting from the good judgment that age can bring. This can also be a time of increased appreciation and love for the aged.[6]   ⬅

This day was turning out to be much more interesting than I had expected.

BILLIONS OF STARS - HOR HAGIDGAD   CAMP 29

"And they removed from Benei Jaakan, and encamped at Hor hagidgad."[1]

The Hebrew word Hor hagidgad is made up of a few words that are combined. *Hor* is a mountain; *ha* means "the"; *Gidgad* means cleft or hole; *Gad* means "good fortune." Thus, Hor hagidgad means "clefts on the edge of the mountain (or plateau)," according to Jacobson[2] and Hillel.[3]

Was I now supposed to look for mountains and rocks, although they had been part of the entire journey so far? It was a rather strange idea, and I did not know what to expect. Maybe a particularly notable rock or mountain would appear.

The route moved southeast and we were going downhill. Dusk was approaching. The deep shadows of the mountain lengthened and cast darkness over the sand roads. Ohad drove as fast as possible to avoid driving on the rough roads after nightfall. It was imperative to reach the next camp before the sun set, when we would be left in total darkness. Also, it was Friday afternoon and I needed to be at our next place of rest before sunset and the start of the Sabbath. I sat silently staring out of the window and wondering what it must have been like for the Israelites to be here at dusk. There was a sense of loneliness and a fear of what might be lurking when darkness fell. Perhaps hyenas were awaiting their next meal, and would start howling as they set off to hunt by the light of the moon? Or what if a loose stone in the road caused a puncture, and we were stranded out here in the cold night alone? The stony track made for a bumpy ride, which did nothing to allay my anxiety. We needed to push forward if we were to arrive before nightfall.

The terrain became even rougher and the road more unpleasant as the setting sun moved slowly towards the horizon. To lessen my mounting agitation, I recalled the camp of Haradah and thought about its lesson – that fear is part of the journey toward a better state. I struggled to conquer my inner tension, trying to see how my anxiety could be transformed so that I could regain my composure. I sat focusing on this thought until I felt calmer and resolved to accept the situation.

To my utter surprise, a group of people dressed in fancy costumes, one riding a beautiful white horse and all led by a music band, appeared on the road ahead. The band was making a video clip. It was a fascinating yet funny interlude in our journey.

Time dragged on. Eventually, it seemed that we had passed through the worst sections of the road and were approaching an inhabited area. We were now driving uphill on a steep curving road. Suddenly, about halfway up on a rise, Ohad pointed out a wooden pen. Inside the pen were camels, and beyond it we could see a small farmstead. We drove right up to the camels and stopped the car for a quick stretch of the legs and a look around, however brief. There in the pen stood seven camels, quietly chewing their cud,with heads held high and gazing down at us with indifference. I stared up at them in amazement. A tractor was parked in the yard. I walked to a board on which was pinned a large scale map. The details of the map clearly indicated the topography and hiking trails of the surrounding area.

Nearby was a small building. A door opened and a man came rushing out. He greeted us loudly, and introduced himself as Akiva. In the enthusiastic manner typical of Israelis, he babbled something in Hebrew. We eventually realized that he was offering to hire out his camels so that we could hike or tour through the desert. Ohad explained that we were headed for the Hor hagidgad camp. We pointed towards the nearby mountaintop.

A band dressed in fancy costumes and making a video clip passed us on the road to the next Israelite campsite of Hor hagidgad. | M Rawicz Trip Photo

"Oh, oh," Akiva exclaimed. "You want to go to Shaharut hikers' camp site? Yes, I understand. You must travel a bit further on until you come to the top of this rise to get there." We bid him farewell and left.

I was puzzled by his comment, and wondered what Shaharut hikers' camp had to do with the biblical camp of Hor hagidgad.

Dusk had set in as we arrived at the Shaharut hikers' camp. I saw a small brick structure that looked like an administrative building and a second building which appeared to be an ablution block. But what really caught my attention was an extremely large square tent made of multicolored striped material, with a roof of palm leaves and a low stone wall around it.

Ohad was heroically unloading the heavy suitcases. Ehud beckoned me to follow him into the tent. It was dim inside and at first I could not make out what was going on, but as my eyes adjusted to the light, I was amazed to see a huge open sleeping area for at least 120 people. Numerous curtains had been hung to provide privacy for groups that wanted it. Colorful reed and fabric mats covered the entire floor, and a

At the Israelite campsite of Hor hagidgad there was a Shaharut hikers' campsite. |
M Rawicz Trip Photo

huge number of multicolored cushions and warm blankets were piled in the far corner.

Ohad and Ehud found a suitable place for themselves, and I chose a spot at the far end of the tent. It was the most astonishing place I had ever bedded down in. This must be the place that the group of hikers had spoken about. After organizing my baggage and bedding, I hurriedly washed and put on clean clothes and then lit the Sabbath candles. A bit later I wandered outside in search of further pleasant surprises. I was not disappointed. I found myself standing at the edge of a cliff looking down over a huge valley in which thousands of lights were shining, some evidently as far as 100 kilometers away. On the other side of the valley were the distant mountains, now a hulking black silhouette against the darkening sky.

I felt momentarily uneasy as I stood there at the cliff's edge, alone in the dark. But I remained, and gradually the beauty of the quiet night and the stars made themselves felt. The stars continued to appear as the night deepened, at first a few and then in their multitudes and then

Inside the Shaharut shelter, decorated with colorful reed and fabric mats, and curtain partitions. | M Rawicz Trip Photo

a seemingly endless myriad – until the sky was practically ablaze with flickering specks. I marvelled that these orbs of light were so many light years away. The universe and its Creator filled me with reverence. I was entranced by the view and realized the beauty of the universe and creation. It evoked in me a higher spiritual level of connection to the wholeness and unity of everything. My mind finally relaxed after the stress of the day, and my thoughts drifted away in a state of wonder. I don't know how long I stood there, but it must have been at least half an hour. When I eventually returned to the "here and now," the campsite was in complete darkness except for a faint light coming from the huge tent. It was the perfect time to say the evening prayers, in this state of inspiration. Then I carefully picked my way across the stones and slipped inside.

Approximately fifteen campers stood in a queue for food at a long table at the far end of the tent. The delicious smell wafted across and I realized that I was hungry and ready for a hearty hot meal – something I had not had for days. As I took my place in the queue, the lesson of the Sin Desert camp flashed through my mind: "We must do our part, but ultimately we should trust that Divine Providence will sustain us."

The table was laden with some of the many tempting foods that Israelis eat and looked abundant. One could choose hot vegetable soup or a stew made of beans, pumpkin, baby marrow, butternut and sweet potatoes. *Chatzilim* (puree of eggplant and garlic) and mashed potatoes were also being served. Pita bread, falafel, slices of meat, fried chicken-liver cubes, a finely-chopped salad of cucumbers and tomatoes, humus, techina, and cabbage salad added to the feast.

Groups of people were saying the ritual blessings over wine (or grape juice) and the *Challah* bread, as is customary on a Friday evening before the meal. It was an exciting experience of Jewish culture and an example of the sense and spirit of community that is often felt by Jews all over the world. I indulged myself, after having spent so many days in the desert eating sparse, simple meals. We sat in a circle as we ate, relating our stories of adventure and peril. I chatted with a group of young hikers. An Israeli teenager called Sarah told me how much she loved the Negev and its dry rugged landscapes. Her friend, a tough-looking young man called Yossi, said that he spent as much time as he could climbing mountains. We whiled the time away as I got to know more about the Israeli spirit. Eventually, late that night, we retired to our own sections of the tent. The sound of crickets and other night creatures broke the stillness, and I even heard what sounded like the faint baying of wolves in the distance. It was a surreal experience.

Early the next morning, I walked to the edge of the cliff again to see what the vista looked like in daylight. I could see numerous towns and villages in the valley below, with an Israeli kibbutz and the ancient Timna Heritage Reserve occupying the land immediately below the cliff. To the distant west was the Dead Sea. To the far south were the city of Eilat and the sparkling blue Gulf of Aqaba. The light mauve mountains of Jordan formed the backdrop to the valley, and numerous date farms on both sides of the River Jordan looked enticing. The main Israeli national road running from the Dead Sea to Eilat cut across the land, with large settlements and extensive farms scattered along its borders. On the Jordanian side, a main road stretched from the city of Aqaba all the way along the valley to the town of Taphilla.

I realized that the various meanings of words that make up the word Hor hagidgad, such as mountain; cleft or hole; good fortune; and clefts on the edge of the mountain (or "plateau" applied to the entire environment. This name captured the feeling one had looking out over the valley from the edge of this rocky mountain with its clefts and cavities, at the Promised Land gloriously spread out below one's feet. No wonder the name referred to mountains, rocks, and good fortune.

⌐ Acquiring wisdom with age

The camp's meaning is related to the perceptiveness of a person who has reached ripe old age.

At this time it is possible that one has acquired enough knowledge and experience to be able to discern right from wrong with greater clarity. It is possible that the aged can act with more prudence and better judgement.

Here the Israelites had acquired aspects of the wisdom and clear-headedness that is appropriate to ripe old age, as Jacobson explains.[4]

For me it certainly had its own special meaning – one of wonderment, and appreciation. It gave me a vision of the Promised Land and an insight into how extraordinary it is.   ⌐

As I continued to look at the land below, it inspired a connection to the land that became home to many generations of Israelites, including those still to come.

The vast Arabah Valley below me was a marvellous sight. I stood there mesmerized by its beauty and mystique in the soft light of early dawn. Evidently this scene was what set the camp of Hor hagidgad apart from all others.

It was a real privilege and a rare treat for me to be able to spend Shabbat at this particular site, resting and enjoying the view and the companionship of fellow travellers. The experience held a special meaning and charm, which I will always remember.

DELICIOUS DAIRY – JOTVATHAH   CAMP 30

"And they went from Hor hagidgad, and pitched in Jotvathah."[1] This camp is referred to in the biblical commentaries as the "place of pleasantness" or "place with flowing brooks"; a "good, calm place."[2] It also means a "good, rich place."[3]

The steep sand road called the Shaharut Descent which leads from the campsite of Hor hagidgad into into the Arabah Valley. | M Rawicz Trip Photo

This sounded delightful and encouraging.

The morning of my 28th day of exploration was fresh and crisp. Filled with anticipation, I prepared to descend from Hor hagidgad into the Jordan Valley. I decided to walk alone so that I could attune myself more closely to the reality that the Israelites may have experienced. Ohad and Ehud would drive the car down a steep sand road called the Shaharut Descent, which leads from the mountain into the Arabah Valley.

In retrospect, my decision was foolhardy. At eight in the morning I set out on foot, thinking that the walk would take some endurance but nothing I could not manage. Little did I realize what I was doing. At first my interest was focused on a distant building, which I learned later was a school called Ma'ale Shaharut. The landscape was extremely rugged, with huge boulders scattered all the way down the mountain. The rocks lay as they had fallen over thousands of years as the mountainside was slowly eroded by the weather. The vegetation was sparse and the pathway stony. The road wound downwards in a convoluted route to accommodate the steep terrain. Occasionally, I came across a small Acacia tree at the side of the road and would take advantage of the shade to rest beneath it.

My only company was the birds. A brilliant blue bird with red stripes on its wings, called a Wall Creeper, clung to the mountain rock-face and made a loud high-pitched, drawn-out whistle. The bird's cry rose and fell and I was amazed at its ability to perch on the sheer cliff. Then a pair of tawny-colored Griffon Vultures with black feathers at the tips of their wings flapped by, squawking, as I trudged along in the increasing heat.

It felt like I had walked for much longer, but I had been walking for just half an hour. I was carrying a bottle of water and a snack, which should have been enough to sustain me, but were disappearing quickly. I was surrounded by complete silence except for the sound of my feet crunching over the stony road. Another hour passed and the heat intensified. What had started out as a pleasant journey was becoming increasingly uncomfortable as the heat mounted. "Is this what the Israelites experienced during their forty-year expedition?" I thought.

I was wearing a loose kaftan and scarf over my head. The morning heat became so harsh that these garments gave inadequate protection from the sun, so I draped my headscarf over my entire head and face the way the Bedouin people do. The Bedouin cover their faces for good reason, I mused. Had I made a mistake in walking alone? I forced my feet to keep moving ahead, step by step, and took more frequent rests. Any boulder that was large enough at the side of the road became a resting place. My hands were burning and my face felt flushed as the heat became even more intense. My hike was turning out to be lonely and slightly nerve-wracking. My guide in the vehicle would be way ahead by now, waiting for me in the valley below.

I began to regret my decision and even began to wonder if I was in my right mind. As another hour passed, the heat and dust and glare became unbearable. I searched the landscape for an interesting feature, anything that might motivate me to muster up some energy and give me the strength to pull myself forwards. I needed to rest again. I lay down on a patch of dry grass in some shade at the roadside and fell asleep. Fortunately, I awoke feeling slightly better.

I noticed, on the steep downhill stretch, several piles of stones that had been placed conspicuously in a line and built up to form pyramid shapes. Was this a form of communication from previous travellers? Perhaps it was a symbol of something important, or a sign showing directions, or possibly these were even stone shrines similar to those I had seen in the Sinai. At least I had something interesting to think

I had to wear my headscarf over my face, like a Bedouin, for protection from the sun. |
M Rawicz Trip Photo

about now. I traipsed on. I thought about the megaliths and wondered if these stones might have anything to do with them.

Later, Ohad told me that the stones are called *rugum* and might have been placed there by Bedouins who had lived in the area before 1948. "Today," he said, "only one Bedouin family is left in the area." The stones might have been set in place to mark a camel trail, which was more clearly visible further up the slopes. Various types of stone piles were evidently small temples and shrines that were placed along steep dangerous roads. "Travellers set up little shrines or would take their gods with them," Ohad explained, "and would pray to them and ask them to help with the journey. Some of the stones might also have been burial sites for people who died while travelling."

As I continued my long solitary trek, the local birdlife continued to provide me with some distraction and companionship. A light blue-grey Sooty Falcon with its bright yellow beak soared past, presumably in search of prey. Its diet consists mainly of other smaller birds. I wondered whether it would be able to swallow a large dragonfly or another insect as a starter, in mid-flight. Maybe the falcon had chicks hiding in a nest on a ledge or on the rocks somewhere, and it was scouting around

Stone piles called "rugum' are ancient shrines that were placed along dangerous roads. These were found on the route that the Israelites took to the next campsite. |
M Rawicz Trip Photo

for a meal for the babies. These thoughts kept my mind occupied as my feet shuffled forwards. I recalled that this species of falcon migrates all the way to Madagascar in the winter, and sadly is now on the endangered species list, threatened with extinction. The sight of this special bird encouraged me to keep going.

I trudged further onwards under the cloudless sky, slowly roasting like a turkey in an oven. My face was burning and my feet ached as my steps kicked up the dust. Even my hands had started to swell, and my arms hung heavily like logs at the sides of my body. The seething heat was relentless. The yellow pebbled pathway crunched under my shoes. I passed sparse grey desert scrub. In addition to the large white broom bushes that prevail in the area, two big shrubs are quite common: Bladder Senna with its large yellow flowers, and Rhamnus Disperma, a densely tangled shrub with pointy branches. The plants seemed to stare at me, mockingly, as if to say, "You can't survive here. You are not as tough as we are."

It took four long, scorching hours to wend my way down the convoluted mountain pathway. Finally, I came to a slightly wooded area where I was able to find some relief in the denser shade. Walking had become more strenuous, with the stones on the path becoming larger and thus requiring bigger and more careful steps. The lesson of Ritmah urged me forward: "Don't give up!"

As I approached the end of the steep descent, I saw a few buildings in the distance. That must be the camp of Jotvathah – what a relief! After a final rest and having drunk the last few drops of my precious water supply, I arrived at the buildings at the foothills. The lesson of camp Mithkah seemed truly appropriate as I experienced the sweet enjoyment of knowing I had persevered to achieve something important to me. With hindsight, I was pleased that I had decided to walk down alone, even though it had been far more difficult than I had anticipated. It had allowed me to gain insights that I would otherwise have missed. It also allowed me, in a direct and personal way, to appreciate the benevolence shown by G-d to the Israelites as they wandered in the desert. My sojourn was an expression of gratitude for that kindness.

KIBBUTZ AND COWS

I reached the road and a young man was waiting there.

"Hello, what are you doing here?" I enquired.

"I'm hoping to get a lift from a passer-by. My name is Rachmiel and I live at kibbutz Jotvathah." He kindly handed me a bottle of water.

After introducing myself, I exclaimed, "Oh, is Kibbutz Jotvathah named after the biblical camp? The place where the ancient Israelites stopped over during the Exodus? I'd like to see the relics of the biblical Jotvathah that I've read about. I've heard there's an ancient spring there that was also used by one of the early modern Israeli settlements, called Ein Radian."

"I can show you where the spring is. It's next to the kibbutz of Jotvathah." Rachmiel began leading the way. "The kibbutz was built to upgrade and accommodate the people who lived in that settlement."

"The land around there has apparently been an oasis since the Iron Age," I said. "This area has always been used for agriculture, from the Iron Age to the Byzantine period and again today. The springs of Jotvathah have been an important stopover on the north–south road in the Arabah Valley. That was a major trade route in ancient times – even in the biblical era. I saw that road from the top of the mountain earlier today."[4]

Rachmiel nodded. A short distance ahead of us were some palm trees growing at the side of the road, and he seemed to be leading us towards them.

I continued, "From what I've read, at the time of King Solomon, that route was also used for trade with southern kingdoms like Sheba and Arabia.[5] On a hill to the west of Jotvathah, archaeologists found a fortress with tools and other artifacts from copper mines. They were about 3,300 years old. At that time, the Egyptians were mining in this area. The people built a small copper smelting site, and used Acacia trees for charcoal to heat the ovens. They also trapped gazelles in the Acacia groves, for meat. Evidently these activities date back as far as the fourth and third centuries BCE."[6]

Rachmiel commented, "There are Acacia trees growing in an area south of Jotvathah, on the edge of the Salt Flat. It's not far from here. Maybe that was the place."

We continued walking until we reached the palm trees. Rachmiel made a sweeping gesture with his hand and said,

"Ein Radian is actually a whole series of little springs. The water flows out from the ground from various places scattered over half a square kilometer."

I enjoyed looking at this ancient source of water. No wonder the Israelites had made Jotvathah one of their stopping places. I told Rachmiel that I had read that a Roman bath, a Roman fortress, an aquifer, and wells had been found in this vicinity, dating back to 300 CE. To the east of the kibbutz was an Arab fortified resting place that dated back to 700 CE and had been used by travellers on the north–south road.[7]

He said, "Nearby the kibbutz, to the west, are some ruins from the Roman times. They might be the ones that you've read about."

We walked for about 800 meters to examine the remains. On the way back towards Jotvathah he showed me a pool of water enclosed in a stone structure. A nearby noticeboard said – to my astonishment – "Massif Eilat Nature Reserve: Avrona Well." This was an ancient water source, and has been acknowledged by local authorities as having been part of the Exodus route. It seemed appropriate to sample the water, so I splashed my hands and felt gratified to feel it running through my fingers. I contemplated the history that the well had been part of for three and a half thousand years. I would have loved to taste the water but resisted because we were not sure of its quality as drinking water.

Next to the well stood a magnificent old twisted Acacia tree. I sat

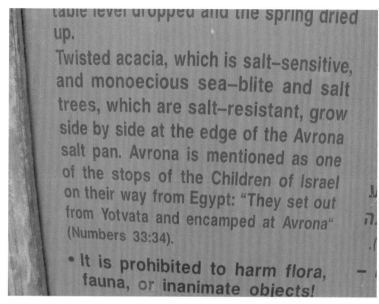

There was an inscription reading that Avrona was one of the stops of the children of Israel. | M Rawicz Trip Photo

I splashed my hands in the well from the days of the Exodus. | M Rawicz Trip Photo

in its shade for a few minutes and listened to the silence broken only by the babbling water. Behind the tree was the soft, level flood plain of the Arabah Valley, which was most likely the route followed by the Israelites to their next encampment.

Noticeboard which read: Massif Eilat Nature Reserve: Avrona Well" -one of the stops of the children of Israel. | M Rawicz Trip Photo

An ancient well that is acknowledged as part of the Exodus route was still in place at the Israelite campsite of Jotvathah. | M Rawicz Trip Photo

"You should go into that shop and taste some of the delicious things made at Kibbutz Jotvathah," Rachmiel suggested.

"Yes, I will, as I'm meeting my travel companions there," I replied. We said farewell and Rachmiel accepted a lift from a passer-by.

There, in the middle of this stretch of desert on the Arabah road, stood a big modern shop and a large restaurant. The red-and-black building was architecturally interesting. At the entrance stood two life-sized statues of cows that had been painted to look very real. I went up to one to touch it, just to be sure that it was not alive. I moved off in search of Ohad and Ehud. Finding them, we settled at a table in the restaurant to enjoy a very welcome meal.

Some Israelis sitting at a nearby table were talking loudly in Hebrew and I assumed that they were probably travelling from north to south on their daily business. There were also casually dressed tourists with cameras. The shop was incredible. I saw many flavors of yogurts, types of hard cheeses and cream cheeses, and flavored milks on display. This geographic area and shop are internationally renowned, especially the

The Jotvathah kibbutz shop has special models of cattle because it is a famous milk production site. | M Rawicz Trip Photo

The modern Jotvathah kibbutz shop and restaurant are at the ancient Israelite camp site of Jotvathah. | M Rawicz Trip Photo

shop for its amazing ice creams and homemade chocolate puddings, sour cream and much more. Tinned products, such as mangos grown on the kibbutz, were also on sale. There was date jam and puree, dried fruits, and a range of other delectable products. It was an extraordinary place.

The restaurant served delicious food and the menu included a wide range of dishes. Naturally, I was ready for a good meal and a drink.

"My son worked as a volunteer student at Jotvathah," I told Ohad and Ehud as we ate. "He spent many hours on top of tall ladders picking dates. He also handled the linens and the washing of other items in the kibbutz laundry. He had the unenviable task of cleaning the large – and often greasy – stoves in their communal kitchen. When he told me this, I was delighted and surprised because when he was a child I could never get him to do anything like that. He got some good hard training at Jotvathah, and it stood him in good stead ever since."

Ehud smiled. A group of young Israeli soldiers were standing in a queue waiting to buy ice cream in cones. Instead of being rugged strong men, however, they were beautiful sexy women, blonde or raven-haired. Each woman carried an Uzi machine gun and they were all dressed in green-and-brown army uniforms. I thought of how much effort the Israelis put into defending their small country, to the extent that even young women were obligated to spend at least a year in the army or associated community service. I felt slightly apprehensive at the sight of their loaded guns, but also felt a sense of pride that these young women were equipped to defend their country.

I chatted with a male soldier who was also dressed in the typical olive-green uniform of shirt and trousers, carrying a green sweater and jacket, and wearing black boots. His green beret had a pin attached to it to identify his rank and was tucked under his left epaulette. He told me about the IDF.

"It's one of Israel's most prominent institutions. The IDF influences everything – the country's economy, our culture, the political scene, and the attitudes among our citizens. Military service is mandatory for all men and women older than 18. Men serve for three years and then become reserves, and continue to do a month of army service for up to a month each year, until they are 43 or 45 years old. While serving, we're not allowed to go anywhere without our weapon, this Uzi gun." He pointed to the ominous weapon hanging against his side.

We bought some treats to eat later on and I also bought presents for my family and friends as well as some giant dates from Jotvathah's palm groves, huge with soft fleshy fruit.

"I'd like to see the kibbutz," I told Ohad. "I want to see where my son lived."

"Let's go and see if they'll let us in," he replied.

It took some delicate negotiating by Ohad before the guard at the gate agreed to let us enter. He directed us to the reception area, where a young man named Ariel greeted us. Ariel had an angular dark-skinned face and a clean-shaven look, with close-cropped black hair; he was wearing lightweight khaki clothing. He showed us around and pointed out various residential buildings, the administrative and production areas, and the kitchen and laundry room. We also saw the dairy and some cowsheds and horse stables. One of the rooms was an art studio. We did not get the opportunity to talk to any other kibbutzniks.

"What's the difference between a kibbutz and a moshav?" I asked Ariel.

"A moshav is a cooperative settlement where individual farmers have their own plots of land. They're like entrepreneurs . . . they buy seeds together and so on, to make their businesses more profitable. They can have core businesses like producing out-of-season crops, partly for export, including vegetables, poultry and flowers. They use highly sophisticated farming techniques and produce is of a very high standard. Some moshavim have hundreds of acres under hothouses.

They have communal recreation and health facilities, shopping and catering facilities. They sell to markets in Europe and America as well as locally. They even have tourism projects, such as rooms to accommodate guests or have health tourism."

"So how does that differ from a kibbutz like this one?" I asked.

"In many ways, they are similar," Ariel replied. "They often include the same activities, but in a kibbutz there are no individual entrepreneurs like you'll find on a moshav. It's not really a settlement, as such. The assets of a kibbutz are owned by the kibbutz members collectively, and the entire kibbutz functions as a single business unit."

We continued looking around the Jotvathah kibbutz. I told Ariel what my journey was all about, and mentioned that this must have been the area of the biblical Jotvathah campsite.

"Oh!" he exclaimed. "My kibbutz was established in 1957 and has more than 700 people. It was set up to secure the road to Eilat and to explore the possibility of establishing permanent settlements in this harsh southern Negev region. Our members have struggled over the last 43 years to prove that settlements can flourish in a water-deprived area and desert climate."

"Yes, it's very impressive," I said.

He proudly continued: "Now, Jotvathah is well known for its dairy. We process milk and produce a wonderful variety of milk products."

"What's your role?"

"I help with the cows. Part-time, I do the finances and accounting."

I left Kibbutz Jotvathah with the impression that it was well-kept and ran along relatively simple lines. The fact that Jotvathah had served the Israelites and their descendants since the time of the Exodus, and today produces such wonderful agricultural products for the international market, became a memory that would often inspire me.

⊟ Transient materialism verses profound peacefulness

The camp Jotvathah is associated with pleasantness: "flowing brooks,"[8] "good, calm place" and "good, rich place."[9]

As a person matures and reaches the beginning of old age, it is possible that he has acquired invaluable knowledge. If the person has studied, then hopefully he has also acquired wisdom from the sages and philosophers. Even just living through the normal experiences of life can make one wise.

This wisdom may have the effect of giving a person perspective and depth to evaluate the everyday dramas. From this perspective, it is possible to avoid being drawn into emotional turmoil, frustration and anxiety. In fact it is possible that the person can remain calm, composed and objective. Life may appear good rather than turbulent. This insight should inspire us to strive for wisdom as we age.

Another perspective of older people is that the prospect of life ending is more present for them than for the young.

This prospect can, however, be balanced by one of understanding that good deeds and a life of virtue leaves something of value to the world even after one has passed on. Each person has the potential to leave some spiritual knowledge for the world that is uniquely their contribution.

At Jotvathah the Israelites experienced a pleasurable, calm place. Besides the beauty of the wonderful environment in which they found themselves, there was also their own peacefulness. This made the camp one of superior pleasantness as Jacobson infers.[10]

It all made perfect sense to me. The pleasant spring of water provided a refreshing contrast to the rather harsh desert journey I had just experienced. A resting point beside the flowing water certainly was a good, calm, quiet place. I felt a sense of peace and hoped that as I grew older the spiritual lesson would help me age gracefully. ◄

DOWN COPPER MINES – EBRONAH   CAMP 31

"And they removed from Jotvathah and ened at Ebronah"[1] *Ebronah* means "river crossing," a "ford."[2] It means to "pass through." I thought to myself that for sure there would be a river crossing at some point, especially in the Jordan Valley.

The Arabah was a gentle valley to walk through, with acacia trees as opposed to the surrounding semi-desert with its scrub vegetation. I walked along the Jordanian border for a few minutes and thought about the strong army of Israelites that passed through here. Perhaps the people had been upset that they could not enter the Promised Land through one of the mountain passes, but rather had to walk all the way down to the Gulf of Aqaba.

The next camp, Ebronah, lay about fifteen kilometers south of Yotvathah, also within the flood plain on the way to the Gulf of Aqaba. Ohad drove the car south for three kilometers along the highway, when we stopped at the Yotvathah Hai-Bar Nature Reserve, where animals mentioned in the Bible and other endangered desert animals are bred. This reserve encompasses various arid habitats, including acacia groves, salt flats, and plain sand. I was intrigued.

An open "safari" area in the reserve is home to herds of desert herbivores. To our delight, we saw several biblical animals including the Addax, a kind of antelope with twisted horns; as well as other types of antelope, gazelle, and roebuck. A single large Wild Ox stood grazing near a few ostriches, who strutted around showing off their feathers and loftily scanned for any approach. Slightly further on, we spotted a few dozen wild asses – the Onager, the predecessor of the domesticated donkey, that I had seen in the wild. One was braying loudly. An Onager looks slightly larger than a donkey, with some equine features,

The Arabah valley down which the Israelites walked, showing the Jordanian mountain in the background. | *M Rawicz Trip Photo*

but its legs are shorter than those of horses. It looks beautiful in its yellow-brown coat in winter and red-brown in summer.

In the southern part of the reserve we saw some enclosures that housed wild animals. A student guide, Shifra, showed us around. The first enclosure contained large predators. I had so often heard wolves howling at night in the desert and now saw some here. Shifra pointed to a cage, saying, "Here you can see a Ruppell's fox, a Blanford's fox, and sand foxes." At the next enclosure we saw striped hyenas yapping loudly. They looked like those we had seen earlier in our journey. The reserve also housed spotted leopards which appeared silent and shy, as well as caracal, and other wild cats. Although we had seen some of these animals in the Sinai and Negev, it was always at a distance. Here, we had an ideal opportunity to study their features more closely.

Shifra, leading us to the section with reptiles, raptors, and rodents, told us that the reserve was home to a variety of creatures that had been found in the desert. We saw poisonous reptiles and birds of prey, some of which I had already seen in the wild. The Griffon vultures were feeding on small pieces of meat.

Finally, Shifra led us to the interesting "dark room" where one could view the night-time activities of nocturnal animals. She pointed out the denizens of the dark room, including tiny mice, a Lesser Egyptian Gerbil, a Wagner's Gerbil, a garden dormouse, a fruit bat and some Sundevall's Jird. The Jird are light-brown mice that live in hot deserts. Their melodious sounds were a delight. Pointing towards them she said, "Those owls over there with grey and black streaked feathers are a pair of Scops Owls, and you can also see those Barn Owls with their mesmerizing stares." It was a relief to learn that none of these were threatened species that may need conservation efforts to ensure their future survival.

A group of young Israeli children were on a fun excursion with their moms. They had much to say about the animals and chatted to each other in Hebrew, some of which I understood. It was a real delight to encounter children again and I enjoyed watching their fresh, sweet youthfulness.

The reserve also maintained a "research and development" farm where they attempted to determine the most suitable crops for the unique conditions of the region. Their efforts focused on winter harvest vegetables, flowers, and fruit, as well as developing the best cultivation methods, especially irrigation. Their work benefitted the local farmers as well as agriculturists in other deserts.

Although my visit to the reserve was a cherished experience, I pondered how unnatural it was for animals to be crowded into such a small space together rather than roaming wild, even if one did not see them as often in their natural habitat. However, I was most encouraged to see the Israeli efforts at conservation. After this interesting interlude, Ohad drove us south towards the next Exodus camp, which was Ebronah. This site is located in the Timna Park Reserve, at the entrance of which stand two supersized statues of Egyptian figures. They looked rather strange in the Israeli setting. "What was this all about?" I mused.

COPPER SLAVES

We entered the park and received a detailed information brochure. A young Israeli archaeological student named Chaya offered to guide us through the park. Not knowing what to expect, we were grateful to have her along.

"Timna Park is some 60 square kilometers. It has areas of geological, natural and historical interest, with a large recreational area that is used by Israelis and tourists," she explained.

An imposing range of high red-and-white sandstone hills and a dazzling display of granite rock formations stood in front of us. The hills had a magnetic energy that seemed to draw me towards them, making me feel uplifted.

"That is the famous rock formation called Solomon's Pillars," Chaya said. "There is another one that looks like a chariot . . . and over there is one that's mushroom shaped. The park also has an ancient Egyptian temple, and many rock engravings."

Chaya asked Ohad to stop the car. Climbing out of the car, she said,

"Here is one of the most ancient Egyptian copper mines, which dates back to before the Exodus. It's been estimated that pharaonic mining expeditions started here during the Late Bronze Age or the First Iron Age."

The era she was referring to lasted from approximately 1318 to 1156 BCE. I now understood why we had seen Egyptian statues at the entrance to the park. My interest was sparked because my quest on this journey was to learn more about those times.

Chaya explained, "Archaeologists have found seals or cartouches of pharaohs at a shrine that was dedicated to the cow goddess, Hathor."

"That sounds familiar," I said, and told her about the shrine we had visited at Serabit, at the camp of Dophkah.

She excitedly added, "Actually, the cartouches found here date back to Pharaohs Seti I, Rameses II, Merneptah and Seti II. They are believed to come from the immediate lineage of the pharaohs that preceded and ruled at the time of the Israelites' Exodus."

I then recalled to the others, that I had read that Seti I was the father of Rameses II, in whose palace Moses had grown up. Also Moses had demanded of the Pharaoh Merneptah that he let the Israelites leave Egypt and it was Merneptah whose army had been destroyed at the Red Sea.

Chaya and I were by now excitedly sharing all that we knew. "Archaeologists believe that the Egyptians mined Timna from the time of Seti I through to Rameses V. Rock inscriptions have been found here that date from the time of Rameses II and Rameses III. The Egyptians not only mined the copper, but also smelted it here," she said.

We moved on to explore other fascinating remains, coming at last to the copper mines, where we peered down one of the ancient shafts. I was shocked to see how narrow the opening to the shaft was.

Suddenly, I visualized hordes of slaves and criminals tortuously wedging themselves one by one underground. An emaciated man was

I peered down the ancient Egyptian copper mine shafts at the Israelite camp of Ebronah.
| M Rawicz Trip Photo

having difficulty breathing and stumbled holding his injured arm.

I saw miners underground hammering against unyielding rock faces with rudimentary tools in precarious spaces. The dust was suffocating, the noise was a horrendous assault on the ears, and the rock movements were unpredictable and lethal.

Suffering souls were squeezing through the many holes from below to deposit the copper ore treasure on the surface. There, a group of men, drenched with sweat, were sorting the bounty with bare hands. There was a constant movement of emaciated bodies, starved, thirsting, straining at the business of bringing up riches from the bowels of the earth. We moved to another horizontal shaft that one could climb into. I wanted to try. I eased myself through the shallow entrance but soon had to drop to my hands and knees as I squeezed through another small hole to get out on the other side. "The men must either have been small," I told Chaya, "or they endured a lot of misery."

Chaya explained, "The work was done by local and foreign workers, mostly in collaboration with the Midianites from across the Red Sea, and the local inhabitants of the Arabah and the Negev."

She took us to see more evidence from the Egyptian geological sur-

I walked into the ancient Egyptian copper mines tunnel, possibly in existence at the time of the Exodus. | M Rawicz Trip Photo

veys and digs. I saw dozens of vertical shafts and horizontal tunnels.

"This must have been a huge operation," I commented.

"Yes," Chaya agreed. "According to an archaeologist named Rothenberg,[3] eleven mining camps were found here. Several of them contain substantial slag heaps of mining waste. These show how intensive the mining activity was."

She took me to see one of the slag heaps, and as we walked through I felt dismayed to see so much waste, knowing how serious a source of pollution it was. However, in ancient days, noxious industry was clearly far more limited than it is today, and the problem would not have been as concerning to them. We also visited the ruins of some workshops and furnaces where copper had been processed into nuggets. These were then shipped through the ancient harbor of Aqaba (next to modern-day Eilat) to the capital cities of Egypt, such as Tanis, Pithom and Rameses.[4] Once it reached the cities, the copper was upgraded to bronze and used for military and technological purposes. I had already seen the cities in question, and was able to picture the whole process quite clearly.

Chaya then told me about a fascinating find.

"A twelve-centimeter-long copper snake with a gilded head was un-

I went down the opening of the ancient Egyptian copper mine shaft and was shocked to see how narrow it is. | *M Rawicz Trip Photo*

earthed at Timna," she said. "It was found by the archaeologist, Benno Rothenberg within a 'sacred precinct,' where a dedication ceremony had been held to honor a bronze serpent. It was similar to the one used by Moses during the Israelites' wanderings."

I told her of the copper serpent that Moses had fashioned at a camp I was still going to visit, when the Israelites had become ill and were dying, in the hope of saving their lives.

G-D'S TABERNACLE

The fascinating history of the area where the Israelite camp of Ebronah had been located enthralled me. However, there was much more to be seen, so Ohad and I moved further into the park. Out of the blue we came across a feature that I will never forget. From a distance it looked like a rectangular area enclosed by silver poles with white material stretched between them. Curious, we approached the structure and were greeted by a middle-aged woman, Miriam, whose job it was to look after the site.

"What is this?" we enquired.

"This is a life-sized model of the Tabernacle that G-d commanded the Israelites to build when they were at Mount Sinai. They carried it with them for the rest of their journey. This is an exact replica of the mobile temple. It was replaced by a much larger temple that they built at Jerusalem after settling in the Promised Land," she replied. Miriam handed us a booklet containing an explanation of the temple structure, and invited us to follow her around.

"This white material, divided by silver pillars and strengthened by ropes attached to pegs in the ground, is the outer structure that surrounded the Tabernacle's outer courtyard. Only priests were allowed to enter beyond these white sheets. Because this is just a replica, we may enter."

I cautiously stepped inside, between the special entrance gates – also made of sheeting material – and stared in wonder. We had stepped into an enclosed courtyard more than a square kilometer wide. Ahead of us was a large bronze-colored block.

"This is an accurate replica of the sacrificial altar," Miriam said. "It was made of acacia wood overlaid with bronze. It was seven-and-a-half square feet from back to front and from side to side, and four-and-a-half feet high. It was raised on stones, and on its corners were horn-shaped bronze protrusions. The priests approached it along this paved path that leads to the altar ramp, and the ramp was raised at an angle, with stones underneath.

"This altar is where the people brought animals to be sacrificed – sheep, rams, goats and bulls. They made the fire under that silver grate you can see at the top. The altar fire was kept burning at all times. The daily sacrifices were offered in the morning and afternoon, and special sacrifices were offered on holy days or when someone made a confession. As you can see, behind the altar stood a large round bronze basin, raised on a central stand. This was the bronze laver that the priests used for washing their hands and for personal purification."

The floor was sand, just as it must have been in the wilderness. The bronze laver was as high as my waist.

"That tent-like structure behind the laver was the inner courtyard of the tabernacle. It was 320 square feet. Only the high priest and his descendants were allowed in there. Please follow me," Miriam said as she ushered us over to the inner courtyard, which looked like a rectangular tent.

Within the courtyard was the inner sanctuary.

A huge sheet of woven fabric had been drawn over the top of the courtyard, with its sides sloping down on each of the rectangle's lengths, so that the fabric could be pegged into the ground. A second fabric, woven in various colors, lined the dark material, with embroidered pictures of angels on its underside. Beneath the walls of this covering we could see the golden walls of the rectangular inner tabernacle. At the entrance was another magnificent, multi-colored woven door.

With trepidation, I entered the inner court of the tabernacle. This would never have been possible had it not been just a replica. "Please come in," Miriam said, pulling the covering aside. The space had a feeling of royalty and majesty. Within its rich fabric walls, an amazing sight greeted us.

On the left stood a large, seven-branched, golden menorah, with three branches splayed out to either side of the central shaft. Its arms were richly decorated with embellished cups and flowers. The seven lamps on top of the branches looked like round saucers with pinched rims, and held the wicks and olive oil.

"In the original temple," Miriam said, "this menorah was made from a single block of gold."

To our right stood a golden table with golden staves by which to lift

A life-sized model of the inner courtyard of the Holy Tabernacle, with the altar and copper washing basin, which the Israelites had built when they were at Mount Sinai. | M Rawicz Trip Photo

it. On the table were twelve flat breads, stacked into two piles, and various golden objects, including a jug and a cup.

"This is the showbread table on which the breads of the temple were placed. It was built of acacia wood and overlaid with solid gold. Twelve loaves of bread were placed on the table each week for the Sabbath, and were replaced by fresh bread the following Sabbath.

Directly ahead of us stood a golden platform: upright, small and square.

"This was the altar for incense," Miriam said. "It held the utensils used for handling the spices." There were ladles, bowls, a pestle and mortar, and jugs. It was three feet high and was also known as the golden altar or the inner altar. This is where the people placed the regular incense offering. Every morning and evening, when tending the light of the menorah, the priests would offer a mixture of eleven spices, with a few extras. These were stacte, onycha, galbanum, myrrh, cassia, spikenard, saffron, costus, aromatic bark, cinnamon, carshina lye, Cyprus wine, Sodom salt, smoke raising herb, and Jordan amber.

The replicas were impressive. Two life-sized models of men had also

Inside the model tabernacle are the menorah, bread table, incense table and high priests, exactly as they are described in the Bible. | M Rawicz Trip Photo

been placed in the room to represent Aaron and another priest. Their presence gave the place an air of dignity.

"As you can see, their clothes are an exact replica of those worn by the priests described in the Bible." Miriam pointed to the first statue. "The high priest is wearing a long white under-robe, with a blue robe on top and gold pomegranates and bell decorations. On his chest he is wearing an ephod woven of blue, purple and scarlet and embroidered with figures of gold. As you can see, he is also wearing a breastplate which has replicas of twelve precious stones set into it in gold. These represent the twelve tribes of Israel. The priest also had two stones which were called the "Urim and Thummim" which would provide a "yes" or "no" answer when he was seeking guidance from G-d.

"On his head, he is wearing a turban with a diadem representing the original that was made of pure thin gold plate. The priest's diadem was engraved with the words, 'Consecrated to the Lord.'[5]

Everything was so real and lifelike that I felt transported to the original tabernacle. Behind the little scene laid out in front of us hung another multicolored curtain woven in red, blue, and gold.

"Inside there is the space of the Holy of Holies," Miriam said softly. "You can go inside, don't be afraid."

A model of the Ark of the Covenant with golden cherubim in the Holy of Holies. |
M Rawicz Trip Photo

I tiptoed in. The inner space was pure gold, along the walls and ceilings. Again, I was in awe and humbled as well. The only object standing in the Holy of Holies was the sacred golden Ark. This, too, had a golden cover on which two golden cherubim stood, one at each end, facing each other. Their gold feathered wings were stretched forwards so that they joined at the tips above the center of the Ark of the Covenant. On the sides of the Ark were two long staves with which to carry it.[8] G-d had commanded the Israelites to make this of gold.

Inside the Ark was a drawer.

Miriam explained, "This drawer contains a model of Aaron's staff that blossomed, a dish with manna, and the two original tablets on which the Ten Commandments were written. The cover that you see on the Ark is called the 'mercy seat.' The high priest sprinkled the blood of the sacrificial goat on that seat seven times on the Day of Atonement. This Ark represents the footstool of G-d's throne."

Miriam continued: "You do understand that the real Ark was made at Mount Sinai, not here? We just keep this model here because Timna is a big recreational area, and many people come to see it. But the original one also passed through this area when the Israelites were advancing

The Ten Commandments, a dish with manna, and Aaron's staff that blossomed, are in the drawer of the model Holy Ark. | HolyLandSites Timna - Ark of the Covenant
http://holyland-sites.blogspot.co.za/2013/04/ark-of-covenant-at-timna.html

to the Promised Land. It would have stood very close to here, if not in this exact spot."

We assured her that we understood.

I had one final look around the area before Ohad and I left. I felt completely uplifted and inspired. So, this was the surprise at Ebronah that I had been waiting for! But how did the location connect to the name of the campsite?

I recalled that Ebronah means "river crossing," a "ford". There is an opinion in *Journeys of the Sons of Israel* by Hillel ben David that "This may be where they crossed the Arabah wadi on the way to Elath" based on Deuteronomy 2:8. My thought that this camp's name might refer to a river crossing may have been correct.

After leaving Yotvathah, they might have walked parallel to the Jordan River as far as Ebronah, after which they would have crossed the river en route to the ancient city of Aqaba. This route appears highly feasible. If the Timna mine exported copper via the Aqaba port – as suggested by archaeologists – then the shortest route to the port would have been to cross the shallow Jordan flood plain at a sandbank ford. This might have been what the Israelites did. Once again, I was astonished by the link between the geography of the place and its biblical name.

⊟ Shortness of life and cultivating virtue

The Israelites attained an understanding of the impermanence and shortness of life. They acquired greater consciousness that we just "pass through" life to another destination. One of the processes to achieve this is to desist from placing excessively high value on material possessions that are of more short term value. According to Jacobson, they learned that we can transform our fleeting lives into a lasting good by cultivating characteristics of virtue.[6] The belief that good deeds are of great value to one's soul even after death underlies this perspective. They learned that through spirituality we can bring goodness into the physical world and achieve greater tranquillity. At Ebronah they were able to encourage each other to aspire to great spiritual heights through good deeds.[7]

I could appreciate the conditions that the slaves had to work under and grasp the shortness and pain of their lives. It made me feel that I should try and do a good deed as often as possible to bring more meaning to each day.

By the time they had reached this camp, the Israelites had experienced much to have grown to a level of maturity that is accompanied with benevolence and giving that may arise in old age. They had achieved a fairly mature position of leadership and influence. They had gained sufficient wisdom to counsel others. They had connected to the deeper aspect of an aging person with wisdom and experience. They had an attitude of pleasantness, calm and peacefulness that accompanies seasoned wisdom. They realized that man's fleeting life should result in a lasting good influence through acts of virtue and kindness.

A summary of my own recent growth was that I had begun to appreciate the value of maturity and benevolence. I wanted to strive for the deeper aspects of wisdom that comes with aging. I had already begun to feel an inner calm and peacefulness. I chose to aspire to undertake more good deeds that would make my contribution to a better world.   ◧

DISCOS AND SHIPS – EZION GEBER   CAMP 32

The Israelites were on the brink of reaching the stage of the human life cycle equivalent to old age with its accompanying infirmities, loss and potential limits to time. They were approaching the stage when people are prone to feeling depressed, irritable and complaining and even lead to unhealthy petulance. Such major transitions challenge people's fundamental commitments which may make their condition meaningless.[1]

"And they departed from Ebronah, and encamped at Etzion Geber"[2] which means "the tower of the cock," "rooster city" or "rooster's crow," or "the giant's backbone."

The idea of searching for a giant's backbone was intriguing. I looked forward to what we might find there.

We travelled along the main highway to Eilat. The Israelites would have walked down the sandy valley on the western side of the river and then along the shoreline, but we had the luxury of a tarred road and modern wheels. Throughout the valley, scattered thorn trees and clumps of palms grew in places where the underground water table was high enough to feed their roots. Their welcome shade must have offered great relief from the blazing sun to the Israelites who, nevertheless, would have been exposed to the winds that swept down the valley carrying clouds of sand. The extremely beautiful surroundings of the entire trip to Etzion Geber may also have cheered them up. The vast mountain range that runs parallel to the Jordan River is colored a gorgeous mix of pale blues and mauves. These mountains, the Abarim range, form a backdrop to the valley, casting a jagged outline against the light-blue sky. The valley itself has its own loveliness, with the thin blue line of the water of the Jordan River streaking along at the foot of the mountains. To this day, travellers walk close to the river to take advantage of its cool refreshing water, and the Israelites probably did the same.

The Jordanian Abarim mountain range, however, formed a formidable barrier all the way down to Aqaba. Many of its slopes were sheer rock. It would have been an impossible and treacherous endeavour for the Israelites. The only places where the mountains could have been crossed into the main lands of Jordan were via two or three steep elongated valleys, which were guarded by the intimidating armies of the Edomites and other nations. Once inside the narrow valleys, the Israelites would have been vulnerable to ambush. The Edomites lived in present-day southern Jordan, the Moabites lived in central Jordan next to the Dead Sea's eastern shores, and the Ammonites lived in Jordan's current capital of Amman, which still bears their name. Each nation's armies stood ready to defend its territories from intruders. The Israelites would have had to choose their route over the Abarim mountain range with great care.

We journeyed southwards, passing date palms and farms. One would be hard pressed not to notice – with joy – the sight and sound of sprinklers on farms. The water sprayed out with a constant hiss as it arced across the crops.

After two hours, we reached Eilat. This is one of Israel's largest cities. It was a dramatic change to be back in a city after having spent so much time in the desert, and I felt something akin to culture shock. The scenery had changed abruptly from sand and palms to billboards, theaters, neon lights, hotels and shopping malls. A visual shock! Bruce Feiler described the feeling well when he wrote that when he arrived in Israel from the Sinai it was like arriving in Disney World from the Middle Ages.[4] Modern Eilat is a bit of everything: a vibrant port, a shopping hub, and an upbeat and exclusive holiday resort. The city is a major tourist attraction and boasts lovely beaches. Although the economic success of Eilat is good news for Israel, I felt uncomfortable at the sudden transition into such hectic surroundings after the peacefulness of the desert.

Eilat is the southernmost city in Israel, and hosts a major military base. It is at the northern tip of the Gulf of Aqaba, and has been an important location for the region for the past 3,000 years, owing to its accessibility to major trade routes and its role as a border crossing point.

We lost no time in booking into one of the modern hotels. It had a classy foyer, elegant lounge and bar areas, air conditioning, and an impressive outdoor patio and swimming pool deck. I was confronted by the sight of porters, computers, televisions, luxurious carpets, suave guests, zippy elevators, fashionable rooms, and sparkling bathrooms with showers. I adjusted rapidly to my new environment. After settling into our rooms and refreshing ourselves, Ohad, Ehud and I went out for an extravagant meal. I savored a substantial meal mainly of meat in a French kosher restaurant. It felt almost decadent after my desert diet. Afterwards, we took a stroll along the beach promenade, where many people were having coffee or looking at goods for sale at the bazaar stalls. It was a Sunday evening and the crowds were quite large. I wanted to learn about the people here, so we engaged with those we encountered around the bazaar.

As I wandered around one of the Judaica stalls I met Chanochi, a religious man. His beard was bushy, his yarmulke (skullcap) was black, and his plain white shirt was neatly buttoned. I asked him how he felt about living in Israel. His smile was warm and quick. He told us about his Zionist ideals and the school for religious study that he had attended.

"I fully support the Israeli army who are doing their work for the entire Jewish nation. Every piece of our land is precious," he said enthusiastically. We chatted and it became clear that he was more interested in the spiritual aspects of life than the material.

When I stopped to buy a drink, a young hitchhiker was also in the queue. She was Tali from Australia and had also just visited a wonderful place.

"I'm interested in nature," she told us, "and I've just done a tour with my friend. We were hiking in the Negev and went to see a landscaped garden in the desert, at the National Park in Zin Valley. The garden was at the grave of Prime Minister David Ben-Gurion. It was very beautiful and had a huge collection of indigenous plants."

It was fun talking to new people after being a bit isolated from the buzz of the city.

Returning to the hotel I sat at the bar adjacent to the lobby, and exchanged stories with other people. I briefly met a young black Ethiopian Jew, a mom with her three kids from Morocco, some Polish Jews, and a young Jewess from Siberia. By the time I had finished sipping my drink, the sun was setting over the Saudi Arabian mountains that were visible across the Gulf of Aqaba. The city of Eilat was ablaze with twinkling neon lights and disco music. Young people were out to amuse themselves, drink, and dance the night away. I was content to settle in for a good sleep on a real bed.

Early the next morning, feeling greatly refreshed, I awoke early and enjoyed the view of the sun rising over Saudi Arabia, the Gulf of Aqaba and the awakening city. Eilat marks the junction of three deserts: the Sinai, the Negev, and the Arabian. The Eilat Airport was visible from my hotel window and I watched nervously as the pilots skillfully landed the early morning aircraft, flying low over the buildings.

The hotel served a typical, generously laid, Israeli breakfast. The table was laden with "Israeli salad," which includes tomatoes, cucumbers, onions, herbs and spices such as parsley and coriander; and a wide assortment of tempting dairy products, including cream cheese made from goat's or cow's milk, numerous yellow cheeses, yogurts, flavored milk, and spiced butters. The eggs had been cooked in various styles and were ready to enjoy. The selection of fish dishes included herrings – prepared in five different ways – smoked salmon, haddock, kippers, and my favorite, carp. There were quiches, tartlets, pies and pastries. The more common breakfast foods such as cereals, fresh bread and toast were also set out. To top all of this, there was a variety of green and black olives, and many delicious-looking fruits. On the sweet side, you could have apple tart, custard pies, carrot cake, ginger cake, croissants, or brownies with the usual coffee, tea, or orange juice. The only food not served was meat, because the kitchen was kosher and catered only for dairy and parve, or neutral, meals. There was a separate kitchen for the preparation of meals which included meat.

What a change from my desert diet!

I was not in any hurry. We took some time to explore the local tourist attractions. We began at the busy beach with its bikini-clad teenagers and refreshment stalls, moved on to Coral Beach Nature Reserve with its famous coral reef, and visited the 3D IMAX cinema at the King's City cultural center, housed in a pyramid-shaped glass building.

At the Nature Reserve, a 25-year-old *sabra* (person born in Israel) offered to show us around. He sported long ginger hair tied up in a pony-tail and surfer glasses, shorts, and a skimpy T-shirt. With a confident, carefree and fun-loving manner so typical of Israeli youth, he led us on a guided tour through the underwater observatory, Marine Park and Dolphin Reef Park, and shared his passion for the sea and its wildlife.

I decided to stay on longer in Eilat. There was so much to do that our stopover lasted two days before I felt ready to return to nature.

We met many Israelis and tourists from numerous countries. Despite the diversity, people interacted in harmony. Watching this, I was reminded of the teaching of the camp of Sinai, which was that the whole Bible was given to us to bring peace to the world, and that people should strive to unite and harmonize their differing yet complementing aspects and thus help lead to the higher, ultimate goal of unity and perfection.

A fitting conclusion towards the end of our stay in Eilat, was the sight of a flock of several hundred flamingos flying along one of the two major bird migration paths between Europe and Africa.

The underwater observatory in Eilat gave us a pleasant break from our routine. |
M Rawicz Trip Photo

CROSSING TO JORDAN

My next goal was to find the camp at Etzion Geber. This marked the end of my journey with Ohad and Ehud. I was sad to part company with them, but felt grateful that they had taught me so much about the desert. They too expressed regret and said that being in my company had stimulated their interest in biblical history, and that they would have been happy to continue to stay with me had it been possible. I thanked them for their warm hospitality in their homeland, and their success at rescuing me from all sorts of trouble. We laughed and agreed to keep in contact and hopefully meet again in the future.

It was also time for me to bid farewell to Israel, and enter Jordanian territory. I wondered whether the experience would prove to be easy or challenging. I left Eilat and caught a taxi to the border, which had simple but unattractive buildings, with a large paved area outside. I had hoped that crossing the border would be relatively quick, but once again I was required to go through the extensive Israeli security system with its in-depth inquiries regarding my tour plans and movements.

A street scene in Eilat, the last place in modern Israel of the Exodus route. |
M Rawicz Trip Photo

An evaluation of my security risk to the country involved unpacking, repacking, X-rays, and computer scanning. I passed all of the tests and walked over to the Jordanian border offices, which were concrete buildings that looked like blocks. Fortunately, I already had my visa and merely had to show my passport and pay the entrance tax. The problem here was inefficiency – a stark contrast to the Israeli "high alert" mentality. The Jordanian officials were laid back and casual. The offices seemed understaffed. The man attending to me insisted on completing the form with the details of my passport himself, instead of giving it to me to fill in, and he was painstakingly slow. I assumed that it would be improper to insist on doing it myself.

I was travelling on a South African passport, not an Israeli one, so no questions were asked about why I was visiting the area. However, even had I owned an Israeli passport, it is possible that I would not have encountered any problems because of the political agreement between Israel and Jordan to cooperate and allow tourists to cross in and out of Jordan.

After this endurance test, l dragged my heavy suitcases over to the parking area where I was expecting to find my Jordanian tour guide. The day was already swelteringly hot, and I could not see anybody who looked remotely like they were there to meet me. My pulse quickened with anxiety as I wondered what new drama awaited me. I stood there considering my next move, running through options in my mind. I could phone the Jordanian tour company which made my booking or I could just stand there and wait to see what would happen next. My anxiety rose steadily. I fumbled to find my cell phone. Just then, a car drove into the parking lot and a dark-skinned man jumped out. Wearing denim jeans and a black checkered shirt, he looked around wildly and then seeing me, waved at me.

"My name is Youseph," he said, hurrying towards me, "I'm so very sorry about the delay!"

I don't remember what his excuse was. I just remember being relieved that he had turned up. His face was long and oval-shaped, his skin had a slight reddish-brown hue; his hair was black, and his eyes were hidden behind large sunglasses. I watched as Youseph strode over to his white Toyota, lugging my suitcases. I wondered what it would be like to be accompanied by this new person. He seemed friendly enough, but only time would tell. Today was just the first step of what was set to be another long journey.

We climbed into the car. A shy young teenager was sitting at the back.

"Don't mind my son coming along, he is very good and quiet. He can hear but can't talk. Something is wrong with him, but he is good with luggage and helping me. I am giving him a treat and my company said it is alright. His name is Makki. Okay! You tell me wherever you want to go, I will take you!" Youseph quickly said.

"Oh, that is okay. It's better that we have someone else coming along," I responded. I briefly described my mission to him. He looked at me incredulously.

My first objective was to explore the city of Aqaba and then attempt to find the camp of Etzion Geber. I had a rough idea of where the campsite was located but would need to refine my search through trial and error. Aqaba is situated right next to the port of Eilat, just across the border. It is the only Jordanian port with direct access to the Red Sea, and remains a strategic location for trade, as it has been for thousands of years.

As we entered the city, the wind was blowing in furiously from the

I crossed the border from Israel into Jordan. | *M Rawicz Trip Photo*

sea and even the large palm trees were bending under its force. Through the car window, I saw that we were passing through large suburbs with square, flat-roofed houses and closely-packed apartments, with yellow being one of the more popular colors. Then we entered a thriving city center with malls, hotels, and a bustling commercial district. I saw sports facilities and the large harbor, where I glimpsed huge passenger liners and a multitude of cargo ships. Many of the ships had been loaded with containers. The city of Aqaba, in addition to its other harbor activities, acts as the chief export point for phosphates mined in Iraq. It is also the gateway for many inland countries, including Iran and Saudi Arabia. It was buzzing with activity.

I needed to prepare for the journey ahead and stock up on necessities. I stopped at a number of small shops and I started to get a feel for the way things are done in Jordan. One of the shopkeepers, realizing that I was a tourist and perhaps an easy target, quoted exorbitant prices, but fortunately, Youseph, proving himself useful, was there to rescue me from the scoundrel.

I had already obtained permission from the Department of Antiqui-

The city of Aqaba is a vibrant gateway for many inland countries. | *M Rawicz Trip Photo*

A glimpse of the Aqaba harbour. | *M Rawicz Trip Photo*

ties to visit the site of Etzion Geber. I had also been granted permission from the military police to enter the relevant zone. I asked Youseph to head in the direction of the shore, because Etzion Geber was almost certainly at the coast. We searched for a while for any indication of archaeological remains, but in vain; we were both feeling frustrated. We saw a group of young adults sitting at the side of the road, and stopped to ask them if they might be able to tell us anything. They directed us to a place called Tel el-Kheleifeh. We found this to be a large open sandy area, a little more than twelve square meters. It looked promising, though it was inconspicuous and at first glance seemed like any of the other surrounding mounds. During the biblical era it must have been on the northern shoreline of the Gulf of Aqaba. However, today the site is roughly 500 meters inland from the shore. The coastline has apparently been advancing outward into the sea as eroded material has been deposited over millennia. It seemed to be located halfway between modern-day Eilat and Aqaba, some six meters east of the fence demarcating the neutral zone between Jordan and Israel.

It was a thrilling moment and I eagerly stepped towards the brown sandy soil to evaluate the place. Was this just a natural mound, or might it be something more substantial? I recalled reading that in the biblical era; the site in question had been a port from which King Solomon had operated a fleet of ships. He had conducted trade between Israel and nearby countries such as Phoenicia, Arabia, Egypt, Sinai, and Greece.[5] From Etzion Geber ships had also set sail on their voyage to the distant Ophir which is thought by some to be near Sri Lanka.[6]

I recalled what I had read in an article by Gary Pratico.[7] "This tel was first surveyed in 1933 by a German explorer named Fritz Frank. He thought the site was the biblical place called Etzion Geber. In November 1937, Nelson Glueck and others from the American School of Oriental Research in Jerusalem[8] conducted a surface survey of what looked like a low mud brick mound. They were able to determine its outlines and a history of who had lived there from the pottery that they found. Glueck suggested that it had been occupied from about the eighth to the sixth century BCE. In addition, water sources were identified near the mound, which was thought to have supplied the local people."

I clambered beneath a wire fence that surrounded the tel so that I could search for the findings I had read about. I saw some large stones, which on closer examination turned out to be the ruins of a wall. These were apparently the remains of a casemate wall, a structure formed by two parallel walls. The area was subdivided into rooms by transverse walls that evidently dated back to the time of King Solomon, when it had been a fortress. The fortress was destroyed during biblical times by the war-mongering pharaoh named Shishak.[9] Within the fortress precinct, archaeologists have uncovered the ruins of rows of industrial workshops that were associated with a nearby smelter. These ruins apparently represent the largest copper refinery ever to have existed in the ancient world and have been linked to the mines at Timna by the pottery remains that have been found here.

The remains of what has been described as a "monumental four-roomed building" were vaguely discernible, if you looked closely. The place had evidently functioned as a citadel. Within this building, the relics of several installations have been found, which could have been hearths.[10] These installations and the pieces of hand-made pottery have led archaeologists to conclude that this ruin was once a smelter. After the destruction of the casemate fortress, another had been built. This in turn had been replaced by a significantly larger settlement with an outer wall and a four-chambered gateway, and "a thin low outside wall, whose purpose was to delay any assailants" according to Glueck. Some of the remains of this later settlement were also visible at the site.

From my reading, I knew that pottery from King Solomon's era had been found here, including "crude, hand-made, friable, smoke-blackened pots most of which had various simple types of horn or ledge-handles, or combinations of both."[11] Pottery made on a potter's wheel had also been found. Other interesting artifacts included a stamped Rhodian jar handle and a bronze trefoil arrowhead, hearths and ovens, a clay stopper, and other pottery shards. All these items had been useful in identifying and dating the site. Glueck attributed this so-called "Negevite" pottery (that is, pottery from the Iron Age) to nomadic and seminomadic dwellers of the Negev and its surrounds. These tribes may have included the Kenites, the Rechabites, and the Yerahmeelites.[12]

The site has been so comprehensively described that I could clearly imagine how the city would have looked and functioned in biblical times. It seems certain that this area was inhabited from as early as 4000 BCE and prospered because of its strategic position at the junction of trade routes between Asia, Africa, and Europe. The early settlements are thought to have been built by the Edomites, and by the Nabataeans in the first century BCE. Visiting the site greatly enhanced my insight into the history and daily life of the inhabitants of Etzion Geber. It seemed that most of the finds had been taken to a museum in Amman, the capital of Jordan. I resolved to visit the museum so that I could view the items in detail. Youseph listened with interest as I told him what I knew, and we explored the site together.

The Israelites who passed this way and camped at the site might have encountered the Edomites, although some of the structures were evidently built after the era of the Exodus.

I still was wondering whether the fortress and the history of this site were related to the meaning of Etzion Geber. The "tower of the cock" might refer to the lookout towers, which were an integral part of the protective walls. The word *geber* comes from the Hebrew word for "strong," which might have described the city fortress.

⊡   Art of perception – discerning between light and darkness

I recalled the different meanings of the camp name such as 'rooster's crow,' 'rooster city,' 'from theroots' meaning strong and tree, 'the tower of the cock' and 'wisdom of the rooster.'[13]

There is a traditional blessing said daily by all religious Jews, "Blessed is He who gave the rooster perception to distinguish between day and night."[14] This analogy of a rooster with wisdom or perception is used because it is able to discern when day begins and night ends and thus, knows when to crow. Similarly a wise person can discern finely between good or light and evil or darkness.[15]

The sages explain that our lives can be a roller coaster with wonderful, happy, connecting times, like day, interspersed with times of trauma, difficulty, sadness, uncertainty and even depression, like night.[16] At this camp, the Israelites learned the art of discernment. Sometimes we can confuse so-called negative events with what we perceive to be positive events. We cannot even recognize the difference in times of confusion. Here they learned to be clearer in their perception. They learned that when negative things occur one should recognize and even allow negative events to run their course and dissipate or deal with them. The ultimate purpose is, however, to acknowledge negative events and strive to make them positive – to transform dark events into light. The quality of discernment gives us the ability to judge the correct attitudes and react at the correct times and take action properly.[17] If we do not handle negative events in the correct way, they may undermine our abilities and strengths.

The Israelites had, in the last few camps, gone through the equivalent of the stages of growth, of age with infirmity and loss when they could have felt dismal, confused, defeated and distressed. They could have questioned everything that they believed in. They had, however, learned to give pain its due and allow it to run its course and developed the sensitivity and timing to discern, be wise, to sanctify G-d's name, and to allow love for others to climb to greater heights.

My journey so far had been full of interesting insights and revelations. Now I was keen to see what lay ahead, as we set out to explore Jordan.

Chapter 7

Through Southern Jordan: Camps 33–37

MIRIAM'S GRAVE – KADESH   CAMP 33

"They left Ezion Gaber and camped in Kadesh in the Zin Desert."[1] The Hebrew word *kadesh* means "sanctuary" and *zin* means "crag" or "to prick." This location is also called Kedem.[2] There is a further reference to this place being in the Zin Desert at the Iron Mount, which is called Rekem.[3] I reflected on what I might find. Would the site contain some type of sanctuary, a rocky crag, or perhaps a mountain containing iron ore?

I left Aqaba and travelled along the other side of the Jordan Valley, also known as Arabah Valley. It was interesting to see Israel from the perspective of Aqaba. The country looked quite different against the backdrop of the hills of the Negev, and I could see the various kibbutzim with groves of palm and other fruit trees bordering the southern part of the Jordan River.

"I've never been to Israel," Youseph commented, "Sometimes I wonder what it looks like on the other side." His words were a reminder to me of the extreme security measures that Israel has put in place.

The valley on the Jordanian side, in contrast, was barren and bare desert for many kilometers. As we went northwards the trees appeared occasionally. To our left was the Jordan River and to our right the mountains. The Abarim Mountains had looked blue from a distance but now took on a more natural brown hue. The distance between the foot of the mountains and the river, which was the border of Jordan, steadily widened; when we set out, the river and mountains were approximately half a kilometer apart but then became more than a kilometer, and eventually twenty kilometers apart, further northwards. Various small to medium-sized gullies and valleys that had been eroded out of the mountain and joined the Jordan River, cut their paths through the road.

We were driving on a tarred road, which had also been an ancient Nabatean trade route and had been used by the Israelites during the Exodus. That the Israelites had trekked all this way saddened me; the area was hot and dusty with very little shade. At one point, we could barely see a few meters ahead as a huge sandstorm passed through the Arava Valley. Occasionally our car shook intensely as whirlwinds of thick sand crossed our path. Keeping the windows closed was obvious in such circumstances and I clung to my seat. I had learned to be less distressed by such storms than I had been earlier in the journey.

Military look-out towers ran alongside the road, perched high on white steel legs: part of the effort to prevent drug dealers crossing into Israel. It was made known that if anyone was seen moving within the 200-meter strip of land beside the border they would be shot on sight. Periodically, to our right, we would see a large telecommunications tower adjacent to a yellow brick building with another lookout tower and the Jordanian flag. Because of the military zone, the landscape was relatively untouched by humans and the magnificent sand dunes looked pristine for many kilometers. Except for a truck and a military vehicle which passed us, and three donkeys at a watering hole, the road was quite deserted.

The first village that we passed was called Katar, which has existed for more than a thousand years. The village has always been supplied by underground water, though in recent times this has been supplemented with water provided by the Jordanian government, lugged into the area weekly in water carts. Now and then we passed through the remains of an ancient settlement.

The second village that we passed was called Rachma, where we filled up with petrol. This village, like many along our route, had small date palms and a few grape farms, but the underground water being salty in places had restricted agricultural activity. Our only entertainment was the interesting Jordanian music that blared from the car radio for about 100 kilometers.

The formidable Abarim mountain range is part of the Great Rift Valley, which runs the entire length of Jordan's western border. To cross the mountains, we would have to travel through one of the few passable gorges that had eroded a valley through the range. Youseph told me that there are many canyons of the huge Jordanian Abarim Mountain range and that we would be seeing some of them.

Eventually, Youseph turned the car onto a road that headed towards the mountains. We started the ascent, which would bring us to the city of Petra. We were driving on a road that had existed since ancient days and was most likely used by the Israelites. At first the incline was gentle, but then became steeper and harder to ascend. As we wove our way along the many curves of the road, we suddenly came across a large herd of goats being tended by young Bedouin people. This was Bedouin territory and the first of many goat herds that we would see. Youseph edged the car forward slowly as the herd moved to the sides of the road to let the vehicle pass.

We snaked our way upwards. The granite and sandstone mountains became visible from various fascinating angles in turn, their bulk looming high into the air with seemingly endless strata of brown, beige, red, purple, and pink rock. The sight was quite fantastic. The hills extended for hundreds of meters ahead of us and rose into the air almost higher than we could see from the car, as we crept along in and out of the shadows of the mountains. The rocks had weathered into amazing shapes. One rock, looking like a huge mushroom, stood at the edge of the road. The late afternoon sun added to the array of colors and interesting shadows.

A white dome rose in the distance through the hazy air, perched on an exceptionally high peak. Youseph said, "That is known as Jebel Aharon."

I realized that we were looking at the tomb of the high priest Aaron, brother of Moses. He had been buried on Mount Hor, according to the Bible. This was extremely exciting. The burial site had later been given its Arabic name by the Muslims.

The birds were swooping and flying in this supremely spectacular place. Along the way, we passed numerous large black Bedouin tents. They had been erected at carefully chosen sites where the ground was level, soft, and secure, and the mountains offered some protection from the wind. These Bedouin tents and the goat herds that we passed gave the area a special, almost biblical character. It took us almost two hours to ascend to the height of the ancient city of Petra.

I began to look for the camp area of Kadesh. I had read that an archeologist named Steve Rudd thought that the biblical site of Kadesh was in the Petra area. Between 1831 and 1916, various archeologists had proposed other sites, but since Rudd's suggestion of Petra in 2005, this has been the accepted location.[4]

MIRIAM'S GRAVE

Kadesh was the area where Moses' sister, Miriam, was supposed to have died.[5]

When we arrived at the summit of the mountain range we set out to look for any trace of a burial site. Enlisting the help of Bedouins, we were directed to one, where we were met by a Bedouin man dressed in a long green robe, sitting on a rock close to his tent. After exchanging greetings he informed us that the gravesite dated back to the Stone Age which testified to the fact that people had found the terrain suitable for habitation. I wondered where Miriam's grave might be, as her death was after the Stone Age era.

Walking further we came upon huge boulders which formed a semi-circular enclosure, within which was a cemetery. The graves seemed recent, but behind this area was an extensive platform, taller than a person. A stone enclosure, sealed with mud, had been built around the platform's base. A second platform rose above the first, also much taller than a man, and again with an enclosed base. As I stood looking at these structures, an Arab man approached me.

"I am from the Jordan Antiquities Department, and I guard this site," he told me.

"Hello," I replied. "I'm looking for the Exodus site of Kadesh, and the place where Miriam was buried."

"As you can see from the notice, this place is very old," he said. "Please, follow me and I will show you some of the oldest graves."

Excitedly, I followed him, making my way carefully between the more recent tombstones. At the very back of the platform he showed me a doorway that had been blocked up with stones.

"This is from a very long time ago, but I don't know who is buried in there. It has always remained sealed."

I had no certainty as to where exactly Miriam was buried, but we were in the general vicinity of the camp of Kadesh. The various ancient graves had to suffice my curiosity since to the best of my knowledge her gravesite is not known.

Without consciously being aware of it, Miriam, Moses and Aaron

Kadesh – an ancient grave site from the Stone Age. | M Rawicz Trip Photo

had been my constant spirit companions on this journey, and now, searching for Miriam's grave and not having found a place to direct my emotions, I realized I felt momentarily bereft. I reflected on the life of what had once been to me a two-dimensional biblical character. From childhood stories of Miriam's role, guarding baby brother Moses in his reed basket on the Nile, I realized that through my efforts at retracing the footsteps of these leaders, Miriam had begun to live within me, and I prayed her lessons would be with me always. From her suffering after speaking against her brother, I hoped my own tongue would not be so quick to utter its judgements against other people. I reflected on what must surely have been the highlight of her life, to have witnessed the splitting of the sea and to have led the women and girls in joyous song and dance. I felt the corners of my mouth lift in a smile, in a recollection of what was now, not an external tale, not an artist's illustration in a children's book, but almost a memory within my own soul. I was elated that Miriam now lived within me, regardless of where her grave might be found. My bond with Miriam, with Aaron, and strongest of all, with Moses, were most unexpected gifts of this trip. It would only be much later, when sitting in the synagogue listening to the Torah portions about these leaders,that I would suddenly find myself overwhelmed with tears; then I knew for certain that I had connected with them in a way I had never expected.

Further along the road we stopped to look at some caves with particularly attractive square entrances. The caves extended across two levels, giving the impression of a two-story building, with separate entrances on each level. Channels had been carved into the huge rock bases in an apparent effort to catch water that ran down the mountain. To my amazement, a large black granite slab stood nearby, with the following inscription: "Umm Qussa. This is an extensive area of Nabataean rock-cut installation quarries, several cisterns (open and roofed), a large pool in the south, one large triclinium in the southeast, rock carvings representing animals and Nabataean graffiti, and numerous steps and channels that span several sandstone outcrops directly to the east of Siq-al-Barid. There are also Neolithic remains in the general area related to the nearby Neolithic village. The installations were reused in the Roman and Byzantine periods.

Back in the car, we continued along the circuitous route around the back of the ancient city of Petra. Eventually, we arrived in the modern part of Petra, and Youseph took me to a modest tourist hotel. It was comfortable enough and served the purpose for the night.The town has many hotels, being an international tourist destination for those wanting to visit ancient Petra and the place where Aaron died. Again, I found it interesting to observe and chat with other visitors and staff, and get to know the Jordanians.

I had set out to find an area of the land that might be called "the sanctuary," and the possible site of Miriam's tomb. Perhaps the ancient cemetery could be regarded as a sanctuary. However, the geology of the area was sandstone, which did not fit with the description, "iron mountain."

✐ Challenge to commitments

At times events take place in our lives that shake our belief in G-d. We may have been steadfast, enthusiastic devotees of the commandments and have vested our faith in His guidance and protection. When catastrophic or tragic events affect us, our confidence in G-d might wane or we may feel let down. We may then weaken in our faith or even abandon it. This was the challenge that the Israelites faced, as Jacobson explains.[6] According to Numbers 20:1, Miriam passed away and her well, that had provided water, ceased.[7] This upset the Israelites and they complained, which affected their degree of devotion. This was a test for them to see if they could overcome their doubts and still be faithful. This is also a test for us in our lives when we face challenging times and a valuable lesson that we must still sanctify G-d in such times. Indeed, to do so can often help us deal with and overcome the difficulties.[8]

I realized that during challenging times it was worthwhile for me to place emphasis on being committed to follow G-d's commandments. If I, for example, continued to help people even when I felt distressed or despondent, these acts of kindness would help me feel better. This would help me feel stronger and make better decisions to overcome my difficulties. ◀

CLIMBING TO AARON'S TOMB –
MOUNT HOR EDOM
CAMP 34

"They left Kadesh and camped at Hor on the border of Edom."[1] Because *Hor* means "mountain of mountains,"[2] I knew that I was going to have to search for a unique mountain among these many mighty peaks.

Kadesh is relatively close to Mount Hor, both being on the border of

Edom.[3] On this thirtieth morning of my journey, we set off to explore
Petra.

EXPLORING PETRA

One of the first things that caught my interest was a bakery shop. I was
drawn in by the sheer variety and beauty of delicacies on display. There
was a shelf bearing platters of appetizing baklava pastries with honey
and different types of nuts such as pistachio. Many were glazed and
shiny. There were trays of pastries and biscuits, decorated with multicolored chocolate sprinkles, plain chocolate coating, cherry jam, white
icing sugar or grated coconut. There were nuts, doughnuts and fudges
in many flavors; the list could go on. *Who would not have been tempted
to sample these enticing treats?* I could not eat them as they were not
kosher so I bought a packet and handed it to Youseph and Makki, and
said, "Enjoy these!"

As I randomly explored, I ventured into a shop selling what looked
like thousands of locally made Bedouin necklaces. A photo of a political
figure wearing military uniform hung on the wall above the jewelry. The
shop itself was small, but it was well lit and had a homely feel. After examining the goods at length, I chose a necklace with matching earrings.
The price was high but after some bartering, we agreed on a price that I
found acceptable. The shopkeeper then placed the items into a bag and
passed it to me saying, with a smile, "Shukran."

I replied, "Shukran – thank you," and left feeling happy with my pur-
chase.

Youseph then took me to a tourist attraction which was a simple and
relatively small structure on a nearby street. We found ourselves in a
small hall with white walls and arched windows. The floor tiles were
light beige, and in the center of the hall was a sunken square pool filled
with water. People were collecting clear water from the pool using buck-
ets or large plastic containers. I watched the children, men, and women
as they came and went. All seemed serious and concentrated on the
activity. The atmosphere was intense.

"This is very special for them," explained Youseph. "This concrete
pond is man-made, but the rock at the end of it is holy to these people."

An elderly man who noticed that I was a foreigner came walking over
to us. He welcomed me, and explained:

"This place is holy and we have many tourists visiting here from all

The building which contains the spring of water associated with Moses. |
M Rawicz Trip Photo

over the world. It's the place where the Israelites that went through the desert with Moses stopped and complained that they had no water. They said they should have stayed in Egypt, rather than die from thirst 'in this evil place.' Moses prayed to his G-d and was told to talk to the rock to get water, but he hit it instead. The water gushed out, but his G-d became angry as Moses had not shown the people that a miracle was possible just by talking. So he was told that he would never enter the Holy Land.[4] According to local tradition, this is the rock that Moses struck and until today, the water flows out constantly. Every day people come to get this water for drinking and for medicinal use."

I was amazed, as this did fit in with the chronology of the Biblical account. I watched with fascination as people collected the water and wondered what it was like some three-and-a-half thousand years back.

My curiosity as an environmentalist led me to examine the geology of the rock from which the spring originated and ascertain the physical cause of the spring. Maybe I could detect an impervious clay layer, but I could not see anything obvious that would reveal the geological origin. For the locals and tourists alike, it had become a sacred place. I felt privileged to be at this legendary place.

Still enthralled about the rock, I walked down a road that winds down the hill towards the site of the ancient city of Petra. From what

The rock that Moses allegedly struck to get water. | *M Rawicz Trip Photo*

I had read, I could look forward to seeing many interesting sights. I found the fact that an entire city had been carved into a mountainside particularly exciting. Just to view something that had been made by the Nabataeans and, according to the pamphlet I was given at the entrance, with contributions to the architecture by the Greeks, Egyptians and Romans, was enthralling. The city is thought to have been built between 100 BCE and 200 CE.

Arriving at the ancient site of Petra, we were confronted by an unexpected and strange entrance to the city: a dim, narrow gorge, hemmed in by brown and beige rocks. A few Bedouin youths, their heads bound with colorful scarves, were riding their donkeys and playing on mouth-organs. This melodious sound echoed throughout the rocky curves of the entrance. I walked down the narrow valley with its sheer cliffs. One of the Bedouin youth introduced himself as Yasar, and offered himself as a guide. Youssef and Makki had seen the area and stayed on to chat with other tour guides.

"The Siq is not a river gorge," Yasar told me. "It was created by underground forces which split the rock in half. Then the waters of the

Wadi Musa flowed in, and the winds blew through and created those rounded edges and smooth curves. Here is an ancient dam that was built to store water for the old city. The entrance road to Petra is narrow and shaped in such a way that only a small number of men would be needed to defend the place against an approaching army. An ancient water channel cut into the rock at the bottom of these sheer cliffs on either side allowed water to flow into the city easily."

The cliffs on both sides rose higher and higher as we penetrated deeper into the heart of the mountain. At one point, the road was just three meters wide and the rocks almost touched overhead. It was cold and dark. Despite the alley being so narrow, horses carrying visitors raced by and horse-drawn buggies carrying older visitors rattled past, on the cobbles.

Yasar continued, "This channel that you see along the cliff wall was cut into the rock so that water could run along it to supply the homes of Petra. Here you can see the remains of the idols that the Nabataeans prayed to, but they have been defaced by other people of religions that believe idols should be destroyed."

Looking at the damaged idols, I was reminded of the teachings from the camp at Tarah. These were about choosing whether to worship idols or not. Here, certain people had chosen to deface the idols left from a bygone era, but I was left wondering how they would have reacted to less obvious idols, such as power, money, or materialism.

Because the road was such a winding one, it was, for quite a distance, not possible to see what lay ahead. Then, all of sudden, the surroundings became brighter.

Yasar shouted, "Look, that is the Siq! The treasury – which you can see at the opening at the end of this valley."

My anticipation had been building as we walked along, and the sudden view of the Siq was dramatic. I stood still, fascinated by the phenomenal beauty and perfect proportions of this exquisite building. The place was enormous and was illuminated by a strip of sunlight. The entire building and all its ornamentation had been carved out of the mountain.

Huge smooth columns, rising some forty meters high, were decorated at the top in a Corinthian foliated style. These upright columns were connected by lintels, with a magnificent thirty-meter wide façade running above them. The rock surface was covered with fine Nabataean engravings depicting mythological figures, dancing Amazons with dou-

The Siq - treasury building carved out of the mountain at Petra. | *M Rawicz Trip Photo*

ble-axes, eagles, horses, and underworld characters, bulls with a solar disc between their horns, and flowers and leaves. Despite the weathering away of some of the details over the past 2000 years, the appearance of the façade remained crisp. Above the façade was a highly decorated triangular tympanum spanning the whole front of the building. And above this, quite unbelievably, was a second story, more magnificent than the first and with even more dazzling architecture; it included two square and one central round decorated pediment. An urn was perched on the topmost part of the entire structure which, surprisingly, had substantial bullet scars. Local folklore attributes these markings to the Bedouins: believing that the Pharaoh of Moses' era had enlisted practitioners of black magic to hide his riches in the urn,[5] the Bedouins apparently shot at the urn in the hope of breaking it so that it would spill its treasures of gold and precious jewels. In reality, I was told, the building was probably used as a temple or a tomb, or both.

An older man approached us and said, "I am Ali, a professional guide for Petra. Let me show you further."

Yasar consented. Apparently they had an agreement to share their customers, because the younger guides could make better money from renting out their donkeys.

Ali proceeded to tell me about the place. "This is the best-preserved building in Petra, and reveals the extent of the former glory of the ancient Nabataean traders. These people had extensive control of the caravan routes, and this was their stronghold at the height of their power. If you walk through this area, you will see the mountains with their fantastic shapes, great chasms, and weathered rocks."[6]

Ali walked beside me. As the circular valley opened up, we could see the inside of Petra, the brilliant red-and-orange mountain into which the city was built. I could hardly believe that such a unique natural setting could house a city of such magnificence and antiquity.

Ali continued: "For centuries this city was forgotten, and became little more than a legend. Several explorers tried to find it, but failed. Then in 1812 an archaeologist named Burckhardt heard the local Bedouin people talking about a city located near the Tomb of Aaron and a valley called the River of Moses.[7] He succeeded in finding it, to the astonishment of those who had been interested in the legend."[8]

I saw houses cut into the rock. Some were two or three stories high, connected by rock staircases. Tiers of streets were visible on several cliff faces. Further on, we saw other great buildings and tombs. After a fairly long walk down one of the central avenues of the city, we arrived at the mountains that encircled the city center on the opposite side. Ali pointed out temples, palaces, baths, and a theater, all cut out of the amazingly colored rocks.

One of the cave-like homes had been transformed into a coffee shop for tourists. The walls were lined with colorful red, yellow, and black carpets and woollen wall-hangings made by the local Bedouin. The stone ceiling was concealed by draped cloths. The floor was strewn with woven Bedouin mats, and I realized how comfortable and attractive this place would have been for the original inhabitants, despite being built into stone. Delicious coffee was served and I sat on a cushion enjoying the convivial atmosphere and chatted with Ali. He was a chubby, round-faced, pleasant man. When we were outside, he wore dark sunglasses which matched his black T-shirt and jeans. Beneath his rugged looks and weathered appearance, however, I found a sensitive soul. He related that he had learned a lot from the thousands of tourists that he had guided over the years, and clearly loved working with people. The biggest surprise was when he started speaking in the most elaborate, visually evocative, poetic manner, which conjured up deep and profound thoughts.

Emerging refreshed from the coffee shop, we explored the valleys spreading out in all directions from the town center towards different neighborhoods, ranging from the humble with small carved out dwelling, to grandiose with large, well-decorated, carved out dwellings. On the very tops of the mountains, the temples were visible. I readily agreed when Ali offered to take me up one of the flights of steps that wound its way up the side of a mountain to the "high places of sacrifice" where offerings had been made, and worship conducted.

We proceeded to the very top of one of the largest mountains, at first by walking up many flights of steep steps. Eventually they became too steep for me, and too uneven; there was no barrier at the outer edge of the narrow ledge on which to steady oneself or to protect one from a fatal fall. I found the situation utterly nerve-wracking.

Ali called a friend, who brought his donkey to carry me up. It still seemed to me that they were asking me to take my life into my hands, and I objected fervently. We wrangled for a few minutes, with Ali countering my objections and rebuking me for my anxiety. His efforts at persuading me were intense and I finally began to consider getting onto the donkey. The teachings of Moseroth came to mind, that "with experience one can counsel others or offer them constructive criticism." Evidently, Ali had the experience, and he was trying to counsel me to trust the donkey. He and his friend continued to reassure me that this donkey had been making the same trip for many years, without incident. Eventually I agreed to take a chance – and trust in fate. As the donkey made its way up those treacherous steps, I looked down the steep cliff and could see the people moving around far below, looking like tiny ants. My heart was thumping in my chest, but I had to carry on. I whispered, "Okay donkey, I trust you!" Then I closed my eyes and hung on for dear life, praying all would be well. I could feel the donkey taking each step as my body rocked to and fro. It was one of those experiences where one needed to tap into one's reserves of courage and trust.

The teachings of the Haradah encampment crossed my mind: when experiences cause us to shudder with fear, that is precisely the time we must not allow fear to consume us, but rather transform it in order to appreciate the Divine and emerge more powerful. I acknowledged the donkey's skill and Ali's assurances and prayed. Nonetheless, I was hugely relieved when we reached the top of the mountain, and I uttered a prayer of thanks.

The view that greeted my eyes, of the vast area of Petra and some of its main features, was worth the traumatic climb. The giant red mountains and vast mausoleums are appreciated as one of the great wonders of the world, and have been declared a world heritage site.[9]

At the High Place of Sacrifice we saw what had once been the most sacred open-air altar. Here, the priests had performed ritual killing of animals. Cut into the rock was a square raised altar with a few steps leading up to it. A central hole had been carved into the top circular sacrificial area to receive the blood, and a channel ran to one side to drain the blood away. The path to the altar included obelisks dedicated to the people's gods, and niches for private worship were cut into the surrounding rock face.

After this, I wanted to return to the lower level of the city to explore another mountain with special architectural features. We descended by another route and met up with the Bedouin youths again. Yasar offered to take me on his donkey to see another marvel of Petra. High on another mountain, we visited the magnificent building known as the Monastery, which has a small altar set into a niche at the back of one of its rooms. The Monastery stands in one of the most elevated positions in the city. From here, the view of Wadi Arabah – some 12,000 meters below – was truly wonderful. The weather was clear and I could see all the way down the valley almost to the Jordan River. The mountains of Israel and Sinai were also visible to the west and south. On the Jordanian side was the enormous Mount Seir range, rising precipitously from the arid plain of the Arabah.

Across the valley, among the Mount Seir peaks, I saw a conspicuous reddish mountain that had a double top, like an extra crown. On the second summit there was a white speck that reflected the light of the sun and shone out in contrast to the red-brown mountains around it. The mountain was approximately 1400 meters high.

Yasar pointed to the mountain and said, "That again is Jebel Haroun, where the prophet Aaron, brother of Moses, is buried. The white building is his mausoleum."

My heart was racing with excitement to be witness to such a famous biblical place. Was that really the gravesite of Aaron, the high priest? Maybe it did fit the description "mountain of mountains" because it looked like a mini-mountain on top of a mountain![10] Had I found the goal of this lap of the journey, to find the unique mountain among so many? I resolved to see it the next day and asked Yasar what the journey would entail.

"If you want to go there," he replied, "you'll have to leave just after sunrise, as it takes up to seven hours to get to the top and you want to get there before the midday sun makes walking too uncomfortable. You would need to drive to the mountain on a small road and then either walk or go up by donkey."

The next day, a Wednesday, Youseph and Makki fetched me from the Petra Hotel and drove me westwards for five kilometers along a winding road outside Petra.

The Bible narrative contains more than one reference to the death of Aaron. In Chapter 20 of Numbers we read:

> Then the Lord spoke to Moses and Aaron at Mount Hor saying, "Aaron will be gathered to his people; for he shall not enter the land which I have given to the sons of Israel, because you rebelled against My command at the waters of Meribah. Take Aaron and his son Elazar and bring them up to Mount Hor; and strip Aaron of his garments and put them on his son Elazar. . . ." Aaron died there on the mountain top. . . . All" the house of Israel wept for Aaron for thirty days.[11]

In Chapter 33 we also read:

> They journeyed from Kadesh and camped at Mount Hor, at the edge of the land of Edom. Then Aaron, the priest went up to Mount Hor

at the command of the Lord, and died there in the fifth month of the fortieth year after the sons of Israel had come from the land of Egypt, on the first day in the fifth month. Aaron was one hundred and twenty-three years old when he died on Mount Hor.

In Deuteronomy, Aaron's passing is referred to again:

> Then he will die on the mountain where you ascend, and be gathered to your people, as Aaron your brother died on Mount Hor and was gathered to his people.[12]

A pamphlet that I found at the hotel had given me some interesting information. There was a reference to research by the ancient historian, Josephus, and also to the archaeologist, Steve Rudd. I learned that the oldest historical record available on the location of Mount Hor is from Josephus, who located it at Petra, on the mountain now called the Jebel Haroun, which literally means Mountain of Aaron.[13] This site was also described to be Mount Hor by Eusebius, the pilgrim, who reported extensively on biblical locations in 325 CE.[14] This location was reported to the western world in 1908 by the archaeologist Robinson.[15]

CLIMBING TO AARON'S GRAVE

We soon left the tourist trail behind. We passed through two Bedouin villages, stopping at the next one to drink tea and check the route. A Bedouin teenager, Alhasan, whom Youseph knew from the village, offered to take me up the mountain by donkey. I gladly accepted, because climbing on foot would have been too strenuous for me. After my experience the previous day, I felt more confident about relying on the strength of a donkey to take me to the mausoleum, which was just a tiny white speck from down below. Nevertheless, even from this distance, I could see the horizontal rock formations of the mountain, stacked in layers all the way from bottom to top. The mountainside offered very little in the way of large vegetation that would provide shade, and looked formidable to ascend.

Alhasan could speak a broken English which made rudimentary communication possible. We trekked by foot up the lower slopes, and did some hectic rock-climbing up a steep dry wadi bank. Then I gratefully got up on the donkey and it walked patiently for about three hours up

View of the mountain range around Mount Hor. | *M Rawicz Trip Photo*

Mausoleum site of Aaron perched on the top of a very high peak. | *M Rawicz Trip Photo*

Mount Hor called Jebel Haroun with white structure, gravesite of Aaron at the top of the distant mountain. | *M Rawicz Trip Photo*

fairly steep pathways that had been worn into the mountainside over the ages. Alhasan told me,

"Not many people go up there, only maybe a few young people, hikers or pilgrims. Most people don't have the time or patience to go up this mountain. You must like adventure." I smiled and said, "Yes, I love it."

Eventually we arrived at level ground, and stopped for a break and to view the magnificent scenery. I rewarded my donkey with treats. We continued on our way, and as we approached the upper levels, I could see that the top comprised two distinct pointed peaks. These are known as the twin peaks. The supposed gravesite of Aaron is a place of great sanctity to the local people, and is perched on the cone of the higher peak. It makes for an extraordinary sight.

Towards the end of the ascent we left the donkeys, as it was customary to walk the final ascent up the higher peak, as the ascent is very steep and it is a sign of respect near the gravesite. As we drew nearer I could see the almost sheer cliff that we would need to navigate to reach the tomb. My guide knew the easiest way up and I followed behind carefully. We climbed through deep crevices and clung to ledges in the rock face. By now I felt very tired and hoped that I could make it to the top. I had to persevere and drew on my last reserves of strength, until finally, with great effort and difficulty, we arrived. We had reached the base of a stone stairway up which we could scramble to access the building. A square stone structure measuring approximately twelve square meters lay ahead, with the white dome above. The ascent had gone relatively well and we had made it to the summit in approximately seven hours. I was hoping that what lay ahead was going to be worth the effort. We rested before exploring the building.

A local Arab, Khalid, was guarding the shrine, which is rarely open. Khalid welcomed us and explained its history: "Religious buildings have stood on this peak since at least as early as the Byzantine era, when Christians recognized the mountain as the site of Aaron's burial. During the 7th century, Greek Christians administered the site. According to local legend, when the Prophet Mohammed was ten years old he visited the shrine with his uncle. It was given its present form of a mosque in 1459. Until recently, the shrine was jealously guarded by the Bedouin people, and non-Muslim travellers were forbidden to ascend this peak."

Khalid invited me to remove my shoes and enter the mausoleum. We stooped low to clamber through the doorway. Inside the white painted rooms, I saw open arches rising to the ceiling. On the floors colorful mats were laid out, and in one corner lay Khalid's few simple possessions. The sun streamed in through an opening, bringing an air of lightness and happiness. The atmosphere evoked prayerfulness, yet I felt some sadness at the memory of Aaron's death after his illustrious life. I could sympathize with the Israelites in their mourning at his passing. I also felt privileged to be at the burial site of this sage.

I entered a second room, and noted a large rectangular structure with a rounded top in one corner of the room. It was covered with a green velvet cloth. Muslim pilgrims often drape shrines with green or white fabric to pay homage to their Prophet.

Khalid said, "Any expedition to Jabal Haroun should be undertaken in the spirit of a pilgrimage, for this is holy ground to the people of Petra."

Then, to my great surprise, I noticed two orthodox Jewish youths standing in another corner of the room. I had not seen any Jews yet in Jordan. They were both wearing black pants and white shirts; both of them were slim built with olive complexions and had neatly trimmed black beards. It seemed they were involved in a solemn, meditative activity. Then I noticed that each young man had rolled up his right-hand shirt sleeve and was busy laying the *tefillin* (phylacteries). *Tefillin* are comprised of two elements, one for the arm and another for the head. The one for the arm consists of a black leather strap that is wound around a man's exposed arm and hand, with a small black box attached to the end of the strap which rests on the upper arm near the heart. This symbolizes the submission of the heart and actions to G-d.

I waited silently, watching unobtrusively. Each man then took another black strap and wound it round his forehead, placing the black box in the center of the forehead. This *tefillin* for the head is similar to the arm and symbolizes the submission of one's mind to the Unity of the One G-d, as well as the rule of intellect over emotion. They started praying from their small red prayer books (*siddurim*). As they swayed slightly in the manner typical of Jews at prayer, the long white strings called *tzitit* could be seen hanging from their shirts. It was such a surprise. These religious youths had been adventurous enough to visit this remote site in Jordan and put on their phylacteries.

I waited until they had finished their ritual. When they looked up, I introduced myself. They looked pensive but thrilled with what they had just done. They told me that their names were Saul and Rachmiel. They were touring religious sites and had decided to perform their religious ritual in this most unconventional location. It is unusual to see orthodox Jews praying at a Muslim shrine and at this remote grave of Aaron. What an amazing encounter!

Then I was told by Khalid that the actual tomb of Aaron was situated at a lower level, in a room built deeper into the mountain. I explained that I was following the Exodus route, which impressed him enough to allow me to go nearer the actual tomb. Visitors are not normally allowed into the lower section. He opened a door and I followed him down the stairs to a chamber closer to where the bones of Aaron lay. This was an extremely special moment. The awesomeness of being near such a righteous giant of the Bible was overwhelming.

Eventually we climbed out onto the roof and stood next to the white dome and the spike with its crescent on top. From here, I looked out over the magnificent beauty of the eastern escarpment and the rift valley. The view, which included the finest rock scenery I have ever seen, was absolutely stunning. The impressive Monastery of Petra was visible from this vantage point just as I had been able to see the mausoleum from Petra. On every side there was a maze of mountains, cliffs, and chasms. Far across the Arabah in the west I could see the relatively small mountains of the Negev, and in the distance to the north I could make out the glistening water of the Dead Sea. The oasis of green close to Ein-el-Weibeh relieved the barrenness of the Arabah to some degree. Eagles, hawks, and vultures flew overhead, screeching. I remained at the top of the shrine for a while, marvelling at the view and praying in gratitude on this beautiful and memorable day. I was also gathering my energy before beginning the descent.

Jacobson explains how when Aaron died all the Israelites mourned for him because he was known for creating peace. He was an expert at fulfilling the commandment of helping to bring peace in the home and in the community.[16] The analogy is made between love that lifts our spirits in happiness and the mountain that rose toward the sky. Aaron's burial place was chosen on a high mountain with an extra high peak above it – a double mountain – to acknowledge his peaceful ways and teachings. Jacobson even explains that the "clouds of glory" that protected the Israelites were present in the merit of Aaron's loving ways. They were temporarily withdrawn when Aaron died. During this time, the Canaanite King of Arad attacked the Israelites.[17]

⊟   Embracing love and handling setbacks

A teaching from this campsite is about love – it's waxing and waning. Often people may feel love for those close to them and even this may dissipate during the interactions and stresses of daily life. Aaron was an inspiration to the community to maintain and spread love on a continuous basis. A positive teaching is that love should be held in the hearts for all people – all creations of G-d. This is often difficult if prejudice exists. Another lesson is that love for dear ones should be maintained as continuously as possible. Often absence makes the heart grow fonder or loss of a loved one can bring out the deeper love. If, however, we can rather try to express love on an ongoing basis when the loved one is present, this is a better way of relating. We should spread love in this world where basically everything is connected. Here the Israelites learned how to allow love to climb to greater heights and enhanced their ability to embrace all human beings.

Another lesson from this camp is how to handle difficulties. It is an easy way out to try to escape from difficulties or even retreat back to a safer known position or place. New challenges can induce fear, anxiety and even be so terrifying that we lose our sense of self-control. The teaching is that it is almost inevitable that major hurdles will be part of our lives. We are advised that even if we undergo setbacks we can dig deeper into the circumstance and find opportunities of value in it. These opportunities can often become one of the possibilities for growth in our lives, as Jacobson explains.[18]

It was deeply touching spiritually to be at such a holy place. I was inspired to express more love to people, especially to my family, as Aaron had encouraged.   ◢

We took a few hours to make our way back to Wadi Musa. I arrived back feeling exhausted but exhilarated, and pleased that I had made the effort that so many others who visit Petra choose not to make.

That evening, the four Bedouin youths, including Yasar, invited me to visit their homes in the village behind Petra. The Bedouins who had inhabited Petra had been relocated when the city was opened to the public many years earlier. I was tired, so I reluctantly accepted. The youths left and said that they would come to see me in the morning.

The hotel guard had seen me talking to the youths, and drew me aside. "They are crooks," he said. "They lure tourists to their village and rob them. Be careful!"

This news came as quite a shock as I had trusted the youths all the time I had been with them. I felt fortunate that nothing bad had happened. I recalled the teaching of the Kehelathan encampment, where groups of individuals had banded together in an aggressive fashion and tried to persuade people to join them. Although the motivation differed, I resolved to act with caution to avoid being taken off the normal tourist route by them in Petra.

SPICE CARAVAN – ZALMONAH   CAMP 35

"They left the Mountain and camped at a place of Zalmonah,"[1] which means "shadiness." It also means "a place of thorns," or "a narrow or squalid place," and is associated with the phrase, "the land of drought and the shadow of death."[2]

I was under the impression that this camp too was situated in a desert landscape, and was surprised at the association with shade. A place

Bedouin who live in Petra. | M Rawicz Trip Photo

of drought and death seemed more likely than a shady place. I set out
once more to establish whether the name reflected the true nature of
the location.

It was a Thursday morning, the thirty-second day of my adventure.
I checked out of the hotel and went to meet Youseph and Makki. To
reach Zalmonah we would have to descend once more into the Arava
Valley, through which the Jordan River runs. This time we used another
ancient road called Ras Namala, meaning "head of an ant." In the past
this road had followed a tortuous track and had been used mainly by
the Bedouins, but it had since been upgraded in modern times. Today,
it looks like a magnificent, huge white snake coiling through the brown
surroundings, winding downwards in myriad curves as far as the eye
can see. The road itself had a magical effect on me. I was elated to use
it and to realize how many generations had travelled along this route
before me; the ancient past seemed to be imprinted in the character
and energy of the road. In some sections we passed green patches of
farmlands or clumps of bushes that were tapping into the extra water
that became available during the rains.

The road's history was verified when we reached the valley below and found stone buildings from the times of the Nabataeans, Romans, and Turks. We moved northwards through seven kilometers of massive, magnificent sand dunes.

Passing a few farms with goats and sheep along the way, I once more saw a Bedouin tent. Outside the tent stood some plastic drums and storage cans – typically used to hold water, goat's milk, and for general household use. Two donkeys were trying to find grass to eat. There was a crude fenced area that seemed to be an enclosure to protect the goats from wolves at night. A short distance away was a second small tent-like structure made from black plastic, its purpose, I could not guess. I asked Youseph if we could visit the tent-dwellers, as I had not spent time with Bedouin people in their tents since leaving the Sinai Desert, and I had missed them. He was delighted. As we approached, we were greeted by an old man with a wizened face; his skin was very dry and one could see the effects of living outdoors written into his features. He introduced himself as Mubarak.

Youseph explained why we had stopped near his tent, and Mubarak immediately welcomed us in for tea. A woman, who appeared to be his

Descending into the Arava Valley along an ancient route called Ras Namala. |
M Rawicz Trip Photo

Yogurt being made in a skin bag that had once been the belly of a goat. |
M Rawicz Trip Photo

wife, sat inside the tent, shaking some type of bag made of skin, up and down in a regular rhythmic movement. A teenage girl sat beside her. After I had partaken of the tea and had followed the usual etiquette, I moved over to the woman.

Smilingly, she said, "Me Nadia, this *maysaa*, we make yogurt."

Evidently, the skin bag had once been the belly of a goat. They had poured milk into it and were shaking it to make the yogurt. I was surprised to see this presumably ancient method still being used in modern Jordan. I was always on the lookout for examples of ancient life and found this aspect of my journey most interesting, so I sat and watched them for a while, enjoying their company. Six smaller children stood and watched us, their body language clearly conveying their delight at having a visitor. They were smiling at Makki.

As we were about to leave, Mubarak's wife rushed toward me, hugged me, and handed me a clay jug containing newly-made yogurt from her goat's milk, as well as a red-beaded Bedouin bracelet. I was taken aback and delightedly thanked her, pressed some money into her hands, and departed with Youseph to continue my adventure.

I did not know the exact location of Zalmonah, and was being guided by what I had read from various archaeologists who had previously studied this route. Archaeologist Aharoni[3] had stated that Zalmonah is possibly at a place known as Khirbat and Bir Madhkur. This is along a caravan route in the Arabah giving it direct access to Petra to the southeast, to Aqaba to the south and to Faynan to the north.[4] I passed this information on to Youseph. He commented that there was a modern village, Bir Madhkur, further ahead. As we approached the area we first saw a few farmers and some border security staff, and a huge telecommunications mast. The area, being prone to drought, had sandbanks built by the locals at the base of the wadis that flowed from this side of the Abarim mountains. In this way they formed small dams to capture the little water that was available and could irrigate the square plots on which they cultivated vegetables and fruit orchards. A building was presumably used by those who looked after this small-scale agricultural project. We asked a local Bedouin man, Anat, if he knew of any of the ancient places in the vicinity of Bir Madhkur. He directed us along a rough road leading towards the Abarim Mountains. We followed his lead, and Youseph's vehicle was jolted and shaken with an intensity that realigned my internal organs and left my mind ungraciously wondering how I would cope! Makki just giggled at my distress of being jostled about like the yogurt making that we had just seen. I traced our route on the map.

I had very little idea of what to expect apart from a few stone remains, but told Youseph what I had read: "It was a caravan station in ancient times. It was occupied by the Nabataeans, and later by other people. It is on the Spice Route that connected the ancient city of Petra with the Mediterranean port of Gaza. It may be near Wadi Namala, which was one of the main routes into Petra." After ten more minutes of rough terrain, we arrived at an historical site, which to my amazement, still had the remains of a huge city. On a hill overlooking the ruins stood a Turkish tower fortress. From the tower, one could see for kilometers and kilometers. Narrow windows had been built into the walls to provide defense during shootouts.

In a site below this, nearer the foot hills of Esh-Shera of the Abarim Mountains, I was surprised to see a major archeological site. This included massive defensive archeological structures and a fortress from the Nabataean and Roman era. It had apparently been a major checkpoint in ancient times.[5]

Bir Madhkur is a major archeological site and had been a major check point on the spice route in ancient times. | M Rawicz Trip Photo

I told Youseph what I recalled about this place. "A contemporary archaeologist named Andrew Smith found remnants of an earlier caravan station and various ancillary structures here. Surrounding these structures, he found signs of old farmhouses and nomadic camps.[6] Smith said that the inhabitants were native people whose economic survival depended on pastoral activities as well as agriculture and trade. They intermingled with non-native people, including pilgrims, merchants and soldiers. This area near Bir Madhkur had been a regional center for social, economic, and cultural interaction and exchange.[7] The archaeologists also found some pieces of pottery from the Nabataean era here.

We continued to explore the site and I later read about what I had seen. There were the remains of large outer defense walls, guard towers, a castellium, and a large army fort that had been built in the late Roman/Byzantine era. There were many ancient structures, several cemeteries, and even some modern buildings. We were amazed to find the original well, which still had an intact water trough for livestock, filled with water. Youseph and I had fun drawing the water and cooling our hands and feet on this hot day as Makki looked on.

As I stood in the midst of this ancient settlement, I wanted to visual-

The original well with an intact water trough for livestock. | *M Rawicz Trip Photo*

ize life here. What I had read about towns and Bir Madhkur provided a framework for my musings.

Above, the sky is light blue and the air mildly filled with dust from the Jordan valley. One could hear the sound of an approaching caravan of traders from the Spice Route. The camels and horses are laden high with merchandise.

They laboriously navigate the last stretch of road to the fortress's towering vertical gates, with its impressive, massive bronze hinges. They tug at reins and stop. There is a hullabaloo as people shout greetings and traders respond with witty replies. The traders jump to the ground and some smile broadly as they stretch their cramped limbs. The guards are sending the news to the elders. The leaders of the traders are ushered into the central administrative building at the main gate. Words are exchanged between the traders and a lead town merchant.

By now the town's folk have been alerted by the approach and a buzz of delight fills the main market road, as they run towards it. Children jump and whoop in anticipation of delights to be savoured. New mechandise in the shops! Clothes, livestock, spices, silks, incense, pulses, wheat, barley! Touching, choosing, coveting, meeting, gossiping, bartering, all add to the excitement. Merchants, craftsmen, cooks,

The town had a large garrison, workshops, livestock quarters and storerooms and many other facilities. | *M Rawicz Trip Photo*

shepherds, older, sterner women, coquettish, younger women balancing pitchers from the nearby well – everyone is there.

I observe the visiting traders being accompanied further down the central road to the major buildings at the top the large hillock. They are greeted by the leader and taken to a large garrison.

Their leaders are escorted on a tour to the bigger, well-constructed stone homes of the wealthy. They admire the collection of dwellings built around its central courtyard. They descend steps going below ground level and enter a room with benches running along the walls. They are then invited to see workshops, a room for the livestock and food storerooms, and cisterns that store rainwater. Then they tour the upper story where the family sleeps.

They are taken on a tour of other parts of the town and walk past a complex of the 600 square meters of modest homes. It is a haphazard, claustrophobic grouping of crowded, tiny family homes with flat roofs and small windows. Everyone knows everyone and there is no privacy. Children play in tiny, dark alleys that reek of cooking and laundry odors. At the back of the town is the bath complex, near a dry wadi.

I imagined myself going out of the town into the surrounding countryside to visit a family at one of the nomadic encampments and to

Government built homes for poor Bedouins. | *M Rawicz Trip Photo*

watch the men work at the agricultural terraces. Most of the town's people live here. They only go within the walls of the town for protection in times of danger.

I drew myself out of my reverie and joined Youseph to look around again.

Near this archeological site there is a complex of beautiful modern homes painted in pink. We wondered to each other why they were located in such a remote area. Later we found out that the homes were built for poor Bedouins by the government, but were not being used. Apparently the Bedouin preferred their own traditional dwellings.

As we were leaving, two middle-aged Bedouin men approached us, looking very aggressive. Youseph spoke to them and was told that they were upset that we were taking photographs. Their tent was nearby, and they did not want us to take any pictures and especially any of the women living there. Youseph apologized and spoke to them in an appeasing manner, and they eventually calmed down. I was shocked at their aggression but respected their views. Maybe they regarded me as an interfering foreigner.

As we were about to leave the area, we noticed that the bark on the trunks of most of the Acacia trees had been stripped. When Youseph asked why, the Bedouins told him that they used it for medicine. I was intrigued.

As we drove off I noticed a sheep's head hanging from the branches of another tree, and enquired of Youseph why it was there. He replied, "The Bedouins put it there as bait for hyenas, and when they come, they shoot them. This is to protect their livestock."

We drove on in silence for a while, and then Youseph said, "They were angry. Sometimes I must be very careful when I talk to Bedouin people. They can sometimes be angry, as their lives are very hard. If a person upsets them they may take all their anger out on you. Maybe someone they know is sick or has no food for days. Maybe the person you talk to is also sick or has no food. You must respect them and talk to them in a good way until you see they like you."

I gained insight into how tough life might be in this remote place and realized how sensitive one should be to people whom one meets on such a journey.

As we drove, we saw little shade except for that cast by a few scraggy bent Acacia trees. This was the place of Zalmonah, the place of thorns, a narrow or squalid place in the land of the Edomites, a part of the land that experienced drought and the shadow of death.[8] The area partly matched my expectations, however the lack of shade may have related to the "place of drought and death."

⏏ Desist from complaining – muster strength

I recalled that at Zalmonah the people had complained again, because "the souls of the people were distressed on account of the way."[9]

As people get older their faculties may start to fail or they may become limited in their movement, for example. They may experience sporadic or continuous pain, loneliness, boredom or lack of motivating activities. This situation may cause the aged to become less agreeable, in that they could complain, be miserable, become depressed, withdraw or blame and lash out at others or at life itself. Some aged may even say that they have lost meaning in life or wish to die. When their family and friends are exposed to this behavior they could be less inclined to want to be with the aged person or not want to visit often. It can be very taxing for the younger generation to cope with the problems of the aged and they may not be able to relate to them. This camp teaches that despite the difficulties of old age it is highly desirable that the aged make a supreme effort to not offload their problems onto their family and friends. They may need real inner strength to overcome their physical or emotional struggles. The better option is for the aged to still be pleasant and not damage their relationships. This could be achieved if they encourage, guide and inspire the younger people with the wisdom that they have acquired, as Jacobson suggests.[10]

At this camp the Israelites were at the equivalent stage of old age, where complaining was creeping in and they needed this lesson.

Quite frankly, I could sympathize with their sentiment. Had I been expected to negotiate the tortuous and extremely rough road of Ras Namala on foot, I might also have complained. The going had been difficult enough in a modern vehicle. I decided, however, to take the challenges of life more in my stride and desist from complaining.

Youseph pointed to an old Bedouin woman walking towards the road. He told me that she was famous in the area, because she remained actively engaged in all normal daily activities. Her outlook was happy and wise, although she was over 100 years old. She was amazing to watch and brought to mind the teaching of the camps of Benei Jaakan and Zalmonah. Benei Jaakan taught me about health issues, infirmity, and the general physical decline associated with aging, and about the agony experienced both by the older person and by his or her family and friends as they saw their loved one waning. Yet, here was this elderly woman, displaying so much positivity and wisdom. I told Youseph about the meanings of the camps and commented that the old lady inspired me.

"Yes," he agreed. "This 100-year-old Bedouin woman is a fine of example of a person who is very old and also is wise."

FIERY SNAKE BITES – PUNON   CAMP 36

"They left Zalmonah and camped at Punon."[1] '*Punon*' means "perplexity."[2] This left me with the task of finding a place where some sort of perplexing event had occurred. Although this was the first camp to be known as Punon, confusing events had happened at so many of the other camps I had already visited. I was intrigued and wanted to explore why this particular place deserved this title.

We left Zalmonah and continued our drive northwards for another hour in the hot sun, through boring flat sands studded with the occasional scrub. In isolated spots, solitary flat-topped Acacia trees stood out. As we moved northwards, these became increasingly more stunted, indicating that the land was becoming ever more arid. The redeeming feature of the landscape, however, was the Jordanian mountain range to our right. From a distance the mountains are a light purple, but travelling along their foothills they once again reveal their fascinating multiple hues, ranging from grey to blue, playing between light and shadow. In places one can see incredibly convoluted geological strata with complex striped patterns. In the upper reaches of the mountains, the curves of deep valleys cast a beautiful jagged outline against the pale blue sky.

At times the road veered away from the mountains and it seemed that the hills looked friendlier. This was, though, a delusion: their impassable slopes had provided an effective defense point for several ancient civilizations. I was fascinated, knowing what lay at their height, and the ancient history beyond. Around the time of the Israelites' journey, this land (stretching from Wadi Zered to Etzion Geber) had belonged to the Edomites,[3] a Semitic group descended from Esau, who worshipped gods such as El, Baal, and Asherah, and the various gods and goddesses of fertility. The Edomites were traders whose caravans traversed along the Incense Route between Egypt, the Levant, Mesopotamia, Southern Arabia and reaching as far away as India. Arable land was scarce, and such trade was vital for survival. They also mined copper in the southern parts of their land. Strong fortresses barred the way on all frontiers even including the formidable natural barriers. The Edomite King was prepared to resist the Israelites' advance with force. However, after the era of the Exodus in the 6th Century BCE, their territory fell to the Nabataeans.[4]

Looking across the Jordan River towards Israel, I felt delighted when I could once again identify several Israeli palm groves in the distance. A little further on, we encountered a road block and were interrogated by the Jordanian police. At first they appeared aggressive and intimidating with their abrupt manner, but Youseph explained to my relief that the police routinely monitor the traffic to prevent drug or arms smuggling across the borders.

As we veered off the main road onto a smaller one, another amazing sight awaited us. In the soft misty haze we saw an enormous group of about thirty magnificent reddish-brown and cream colored camels against the backdrop of the mauve mountains. They moved in a slow procession, grazing as they walked. Ropes tied around their front legs restricted their pace and ensured that the animals would not stray too far from their owner. I jumped out of the car excitedly and walked towards the animals to see them more closely. They were unperturbed and tolerated my presence and even the occasional pat. I felt exhilarated, as I am fascinated by camels. I took note that some of the females had green bags hanging on their rear ends, and wondered why. Suddenly, I noticed a pregnant female, and realized that the bags had probably been put in place to prevent the males from trying to mate with them again. I then also observed that a few of the larger males had a cup-like bag hanging around their genitals – evidently for the same reason. I felt thrilled at being able to approach a heavily pregnant female and give her a little pat on her extended belly with its hidden foetus. Moving forwards with the beautiful camels in these silent, beautiful surroundings had an indelible impact on me. For me it was a rare and exquisite scene.

After some time, Youseph and I moved on. He told me about the Dana Nature Reserve, which we would pass through, near Punon.

He related how exceptionally beautiful it is, surrounded by deep sandstone canyons. The white sandstone is formed into domes and valleys, which are covered with plants and vegetables. In this area, there are apparently some 703 species of plants, including trees like the Red Juniper, Oak, Pistachio, Oleander, Brooms Acacia and Cypress – all originating from the Mediterranean region. There are also as many as 215 species of birds, with the reserve being an important breeding ground for endangered birds. The reserve is also home to about 38 species of mammals.

The Jordanian Society for the Conservation of Nature has set up an active breeding program for the Nubian Ibex, a large wild mountain goat that lives in the gorge. Only a small number remain in the wild, because of widespread illegal hunting. There are also wolves, golden jackals, striped hyenas, red foxes, and badgers in the reserve, and many of these animals are found only in the reserve because they have been hunted out of other areas.

I found it wonderful to hear about such diversity of animal and plant life in what was essentially an arid region. I wondered what terrors the

Israelites might have encountered when such predators had roamed freely.

We decided to make the Reserve the next stop on our journey. I enjoyed seeing large birds of prey such as the beautiful grey-colored Levant Sparrow Hawk, the Lesser Kestrel with its red breast and back, the Bonelli Eagle with its typical fluted call of "klu-kluklu-kluee." I had seen smaller birds such as the Dead Sea Sparrow, the brilliant blue Tristram Starling, and the small bright red-beaked Trumpeter Finch many times on the trip. There were many other birds like the fat-bellied Sand Partridge with its bright orange beak and the noisy Arabian Babbler on the road and also in the Reserve.

This Reserve goes to the top of the Jordanian mountains and people often walk through it to get to plateau above. A shop inside the Reserve sells organically-grown produce from the Dana village gardens, as well as pottery and silver jewelry made by the village women. I had read that the kind and hospitable Ata'ta tribe have made this their home for the past 400 years, and carry on the tradition of settlement in the area that began more than 6000 years ago.

After approximately another thirty kilometers we reached the Punon Valley, where I was to search for the next Exodus camp site. Youseph turned the vehicle onto a reddish sand road and we drove towards the mountains, leaving a huge cloud of red sand behind us, a cloud that would have choked anyone following behind. After half an hour we came to a village where Bedouins were farming guavas and tomatoes. Throughout most of the year, the Arabah is extremely arid and cannot sustain much agriculture. However, the people of this village manage – with the aid of irrigation – to eke out a living by farming close to a seasonal river. Now it was Youseph's turn to be excited. He wanted to buy guavas for a friend who used them medicinally for stomach problems.

After we left the village, we proceeded towards a part of the settlement of Khirbat Faynan that was more modern. This tiny town boasted a small orange painted mosque, serving roughly twenty small, square brick homes. Lots of little children played in the dusty roads. The settlement was dwarfed by the vastness of the desert and the nearby Wadi Ghuweir Canyon and it was not long after leaving the village that huge red-and-black mountain peaks loomed up ahead of us. They looked similar to those we had seen at Timna Park, where the Egyptians had mined copper.

Further on Youseph stopped to ask a local Bedouin for directions to copper mines, cautioning me not to take any photographs so as to avoid offending the man. The man was very thin and had a grey beard, and he pointed up ahead as he spoke to Youseph. More members of his family arrived to greet us.

"Assalamu alaikum," they said, meaning "peace be with you." Youseph returned the greeting. The Bedouin people's smiles conveyed their delight. "We don't see people here often," they observed, Youseph translating the Arabic for me.

An older man said,

"I am Habib, and these are my sons, Jameel and Aladdin. We welcome you!"

He pointed to a tent and indicated that it was his home. Just then, an elderly woman with extremely wrinkled skin looked out of the tent. Habib explained,

"That is my aunt, Ajeebah. We Bedouin like to entertain visitors. We want you to come to our home and have tea and some food."

We were thrilled and gladly followed him to the tent. While enjoying the traditional tea, little kids arrived and happily waved at us and held Makki's hand. Inside the tent, an older family member named Abu greeted us and enquired about our presence in the area.

Ajeebah had first brought the traditional tea, and then followed it with a large gourd full of camel's milk. My companion told me that the milk was very rich, slightly sour, but extremely refreshing, and unlike water, was completely thirst-quenching. I declined, but he really enjoyed it.

Abu enquired in more detail about my journey to this area. Youseph, again in the role of translator, told him what I had read about the history of the region.

"The Arabah Valley has always been important as a transportation route and also because of its copper mines. Ancient traders used to trek through this valley when they were bringing in goods from Africa, Arabia, and India. First the goods were brought on ships and then they were transferred to camel and donkey caravans, and were taken to Syria and other nations to the north. Some of the caravans also passed through Beersheba on a track that ran from east to west."

Abu nodded, "Yes, we know a bit of this history."

"In 1991," I added, "archaeologists came to the Faynan region to see if they could find relics from biblical times. They said that this must have been the Punon area described in the Bible. They found out that

Youseph stopped to ask a local Bedouin for directions to the copper mines.
M Rawicz Trip Photo

people have lived in Faynan ever since 4000 before the Christian era until modern times.[5] The archaeologists found pieces of pottery from the early Bronze Age through to the Early Roman era. One researcher, Schröder, said that this area was very suitable for people from ancient times to live in."[6]

Abu again nodded. "Yes, all around here the land is very dry and barren, but right here the mountains and climate allow us to get water.

Because of this, people are able to farm and the building materials are quite good. So people have been able to survive in this area. That is why we live here . . . and also many generations before us. We survive very nicely here."

I continued: "At Khirbet Faynan, an ancient copper mine was excavated, as well as a settlement."[7] I had read that this was the largest copper mine in ancient times, with an enormous smelter. The area had two hundred and fifty copper mines and adits, or shafts. These copper ore mining features can be found over a twelve-square kilometer area. According to Schröder more than two hundred and fifty thousand tons of ancient copper slag can be seen on the surface. The region still contains roughly twenty million metric tons of copper.

Abu, an intelligent and knowledgeable person who took a keen interest in his environment, confirmed that he knew of some archeologists who had worked in the area many years earlier and who had made some significant finds, including tools such as axes and chisels, ceramic castings, molds for ingots, crucible pieces, and a few furnace remains.[8]

When we finished our tea, Abu directed Youseph to our destination, gesturing and waving his arms up and down as he spoke. We thanked him and climbed into the car and followed his directions to a mining site from which copper had been extracted. As we approached the site, we saw huge piles of black slag, the remnants of smelting. I was keen to explore the ancient slag heaps. I walked along the blacked hills, noticing that they were positioned right next to a large wadi. This agitated me, as it had at the mines in Timna in Israel; I was concerned to see slag piled next to a watercourse. This is strictly prohibited as an environmental management practice. Unfortunately, people of old would not have been concerned with such matters. On the wadi the remains of two huge ancient dams could be seen, where water would have been stored for the processing of ore. I wondered whether the people had been affected by polluted water.

We all climbed back into the car and rattled our way over the extremely rocky wadi. Youseph pointed to a stone ruin and said, "There is also a Roman fort called Calamona in the Orat-al-Salmoneh Wadi, which must have been built here because of the mining."[9]

We decided to examine the fortress near Wadi Ghuweir. Thousands of stones were lying in piles; the sheer quantity of rocks giving the impression of the remains of a small town. I wondered whether the place

Huge piles of black slag from ancient mines. | *M Rawicz Trip Photo*

had perhaps been demolished by an earthquake. We could still see the remains of Roman arches.

Following Abu's instructions meant that we had to drive up a large hill at about 45 degrees, with boulders strewn across the path and hardly any visible track, and then down the other side. By a supreme effort, Youssef navigated over this awful path, but it left his arms and shoulders aching. When we stopped, he followed some exercises I suggested which offered some relief. We then proceeded on foot. Makki was delighted when he noticed a few stones with ancient pictures chiseled into them.

A few meters ahead we came across a magnificent tunnel, high enough for a person to walk through. Its entire entrance shone with the green hue of copper ore. I was drawn in but hesitated.

With trepidation, I recalled the story of the copper snake to Youseph. "In the biblical account, the Israelites who camped here had an incident with snakes biting them. The people had complained about G-d and Moses having brought them out of Egypt to die in this wilderness without bread and water, as they were tired of eating manna. G-d then sent fiery serpents to bite the people, and many of them died. Then they came to Moses and said, 'We have sinned. Please ask G-d to take

Entrance to the copper mine. | *M Rawicz Trip Photo*

away the serpents.' G-d told Moses to make a copper serpent and put it on a pole. G-d said that 'everyone who is bitten, when he looks at it, will live.' So Moses made a serpent out of copper. The healing process did start, as the people looked upwards and remembered their allegiance to G-d by looking towards heaven. G-d saved anyone who had been bitten by a snake and looked at the sculpture for healing."

This brought to my mind the caduceus and the rod of Asclepius which are used as symbols of modern medicine.

I ventured into the tunnel cautiously.

Suddenly, a scene of the Israelites being attacked by snakes became vivid in my mind's eye. Long, thin, black and yellow dotted, venomous, rear-fanged "Tchernov's chainling," slithering between the people's feet and some injecting poisonous venom. Men and women who had been bitten were crawling away, in agony.

A huge red and white patterned Russell's Viper was writhing over its victim, a prostrate young man. More ominous creatures were hissing at a crowd.

I imagined a mother cradling her crying infants. Her daughter was lurching forward, holding her arms up in useless pleas for help. In the distance, a group of women were clinging to each other in fear as

A magnificent tunnel entrance to an ancient copper mine, with the green hue of copper ore. | M Rawicz Trip Photo

I ventured into the ancient copper mine tunnel. | M Rawicz Trip Photo

agonizing screams rang out. A thin Narrow-striped Dwarf snake, with black, grey, white and beige strips running top to tail, had just attacked one of them. A small boy lay limp as a black and orange Sand Boa slithered away from him. Even strong, heavily-built men lay prostrate as silent killers mocked them victoriously. Snakes were the agents of G-d's wrath for the Israelites' ingratitude. The dark sky portrayed His mood.

Then I saw Moses raise the tall rod with the massive copper snake, silhouetted again the black and grey clouds in a red sky. The rod cast a long shadow like a protective symbol over the swooning hordes. People started yelling, "Look up, look up, look up," and started crawling to the upheld copper image looking to heaven for relief. Their gesture was as if in repentant prayer.

I imagined the miraculous change of Moses' imposing and dramatic healing gesture. In the distance, patches of white cloud appeared suggesting relief.

I became aware that I was still in the tunnel. I was shaken by the image and walked forward slowly for about fifteen meters, then crawled a further five meters before the darkness became too intense without a torch.

During the Roman period, criminals and Christians were sent to these mines as forced labor.[10] I thought about these miners who must have been scared working inside such shafts for long hours, but for me, exploring the tunnel was exciting.

The reality of G-d's punishment of sins seemed very real in my mind. I was afraid of the pain and even the death snakes might cause me if I was bitten. I did not go as far as my adventurous spirit would have liked.

Eventually I emerged, unhurt and gratefully so. I collected some of the hundreds of green ore stones scattered around the site. It was one of the highlights of my adventure to find this remote mine at the site of the place where Moses had made the serpent and to see the beauty of the rock and the ancient mine workings.

Youseph then pointed out a large vertical shaft that linked into the horizontal one, which had probably been used for lifting the ore to the surface. I thought that the shafts had poor ventilation for an area with such a hot climate. Once again, from the perspective of my professional background in mine safety, it bothered me that the work conditions had been so dangerous and even cruel.

▣ Disease, death and healing

As I reflected on the meaning of "perplexity" associated with this site, it started to make more sense. It may have been associated with the many deaths.

Jacobson discusses the paradox that the serpent caused the dying, and yet an image of them resulted in the healing of those that had been stricken and had not died yet .When the people looked at the high pole they remembered to pray and this contributed to G-d healing them. The lesson from this camp is the value of prayer at times of illness.[11] The power of prayer to cause events to be changed or reversed is awesome and inestimable. The choice is ours. This lesson was particularly pertinent to the Israelites as they were at a stage of old age and susceptible to disease and the potential approach of death, as Jacobson relates.[12]

Prayer was already something I enjoyed, but its power was reinforced and I decided to be more consistent in praying.　　　　　◄▮

On our way back from the site, we saw Abu again. He invited us to return to his abode, but I wanted to keep moving as we still had a lot to do, so we bade him farewell. As we continued driving along the road, I looked towards the old settlement of Faynan and noticed a large number of sheep and goats, perhaps 500 in all, walking along a high sheer cliff. The animals walked in two rows and looked like so many little ants.

FREEZING MOUNTAIN NIGHT

It was late in the afternoon and we needed to rest. Youseph began to search the landscape for a resting spot and taught me how to find one: the spot had to be not too windy or too steep, away from people and away from a wadi that carried water, flat ground that was not eroded and had no plants, away from any noisy road, away from cliffs, and not too rocky. At first we looked in the mountainous area. We found a place next to a Bedouin cemetery but decided not to use it.The next spot we found was at the side of a hill, however across a shallow valley was a large black Bedouin tent.

"I had better talk to them so as to be polite neighbors and be respectful," Youseph said. We drove over to the tent.

A large vertical shaft of the ancient copper mine. | *M Rawicz Trip Photo*

A Bedouin woman dressed in black and two children were feeding their goats and sheep. Youseph asked for her permission to use the site. She became angry.

"The desert is big enough," she snapped. "Why do you want to be so close to me? My husband is not here and I don't want you around." She shouted, waving her arms as if to chase us away.

A large black Bedouin tent in the Jordanian mountains. | *M Rawicz Trip Photo*

Youseph meekly drove the vehicle away from her tent.

"She is afraid," he told me.

I understood her response. We continued searching, and passed many suitable ledges and open spaces, but they were all occupied by the same type of large black Bedouin tent. At one tent, the head of the household invited us to stay over in an empty tent of his. He also invited us to have supper with him. Youseph thanked him, but declined as he thought we might be better off away from people, as we had to leave early the next morning.

We approached yet another tent to ask if the inhabitants could tell us where to find a suitable spot to rest. The Bedouin man who greeted us seemed to be in a bit of a huff, but beckoned us to follow him. He led the way to an enclosed area that housed a large goat. The goat looked most uncomfortable – and then, in front of our eyes, she began to give birth. For me the experience was a thrill, as I don't see this miraculous experience much, but the Bedouin man looked relieved when the ordeal was over. The goat began licking her baby to clean off the mucus that still clung to its tiny body. The kid was trying without success to stand.

A car arrived and three Bedouin men joined us.

"*Allah hu Akbar* – Praise to Allah!" they said, congratulating each other on the birth.

Shortly after this, the owner took the goat and her baby and put them next to his bed for the night. The other Bedouins gave Youseph some guidance as to where we could find an appropriate place to rest. He drove us over to the sand dunes and over the 45-degree slopes, up and down, like a surfer on high waves. Inevitably, we got stuck a few times and Youseph had to reverse the vehicle to extricate its wheels from the sand. I endured the roller-coaster ride in dead silence, not wanting to interrupt Youseph's concentration. It took nearly 90 minutes to find a suitable spot, but it had some litter from previous campers or Bedouin nomads. I dutifully walked around picking up the trash, and Makki dug a hole in which to bury it.

Youseph and Makki were to sleep on a mattress in the back of his jeep, exposed to the elements, as they were accustomed. However, Youseph handed me a small red tent and showed me how to erect it. He was very particular about the exact location and direction, saying that the door must face in such a way as to ensure both safety and privacy. Then Makki walked around looking for bits of wood so that he could make a fire. He unpacked some old foam mattresses from his jeep and formed them into a windscreen beside the vehicle, to shelter the fire. Then, together we lifted down boxes of food from the storage racks on the vehicle's roof.

Once the moving and carrying were done, the most important first step was to make tea. This calmed our slightly frayed nerves and thereafter the work of preparing the evening meal could begin. Supper consisted of pita bread filled with freshly cut tomato, onions, and cucumber, with humus, cream cheese, tinned tuna (from Israel), and boiled eggs . . . and more hot tea with lots of sugar.

Before the evening became too dark and cold, I took my "shower." The procedure entailed advising Youseph of my intentions so that he could ensure that nobody would interrupt my privacy. Earlier, he had filled an empty plastic bottle with water and warmed it beside the fire. Now I filled a small basin with the warm water, and added some cold water from the big yellow plastic container. I fetched my soap and face-cloth and towel, and disappeared behind a large rock. First, I washed my lower body while keeping on my long skirt, and then dressed in fresh clothing that would see me through the night and following day. I

Youseph and Makki slept in the jeep. I had a tent. | *M Rawicz Trip Photo*

put on clean underwear, three pairs of thick winter pants, and two pairs of thick socks. Next I stripped my upper body and washed myself, and donned four thick tops, a thick jacket, and a long coat. I brushed my hair, pulled on a balaclava, a warm outer cap, and a thick green Bedouin scarf that I had borrowed from Youseph. After brushing my teeth and spraying myself with lovely deodorant, I felt shiny and clean. I knew that I would not be able to change my clothing until about ten-thirty the following morning; before that, the air would be too cold even to consider it.

The night was drawing in, so we sat down to eat beside the fire. I wrapped a warm blanket around myself. As we relished the delicious food, Youseph and I chatted. He had a unique English dialect that I followed easily, and my Hebrew helped me to understand a bit of his Arabic; we managed to exchange views on our respective religions, our families' local history, the environment we were in, and tourists. We even joked a bit. The atmosphere was adventurous, with a shared interest in the natural wild environment. Youseph had never finished his formal schooling, but his years of experience had made him a wise man.

Youseph preparing tea and pita bread for the evening meal. | *M Rawicz Trip Photo*

Finally, I became sleepy and retreated to my little red tent, zipping up the entrance once I was inside. I covered myself with a sleeping bag and a thick blanket, and placed a plastic hood over my headscarves for extra warmth and for protection against any trace of the wind. I was ready to face the freezing cold night. Sleep came easily, despite the fact that my thin camping mattress was lying on hard ground. The excitement of the day's adventures made any other concerns seem insignificant.

JERUSALEM THORN – OBOTH   CAMP 37

"They left Punon and camped at Oboth," as stated in Numbers 33:43.[1] *Oboth* means "the people became enemies of G-d" as well as "place of sorcery" or "necromancy."[2] This is a form of magic in which the practitioner seeks to summon the spirit of a deceased person, either as an apparition or ghost or to raise them "bodily" for the purpose of divination. It sounded ominous and sent a chill down my spine. The drama of my journey seemed never-ending as we set off to look for this bewitched place.

I kept warm wrapped in a blanket, beside the fire, in the freezing night. |
M Rawicz Trip Photo

The actual campsite was situated in Israel, across the border. I had visited it before entering Jordan so that I would not have to keep crisscrossing the border. At that time, I had travelled along the road that runs parallel to the Jordan River on the Israeli side. As my narrative follows the Exodus sequence, I am first discussing this campsite here. From the Israeli side I had visited Ir Ovot ('the city of Ovot'), where there is an extensive archaeological complex known as Tamar Fortress or Hatzeva Fortress, dating back to the tenth century BCE. What a sight! The enormity and extent of the excavations impressed me. A large signboard noted that the site had been excavated under the auspices of the Blossoming Rose, Israeli Antiquities Authority, and the local Tamar Regional Council. Had this been the camp of Oboth? The board showed the entire layout of all the archeological diggings. It highlighted the location of the Edomite shrine 7th- 6th century BCE, the gate of the middle fortress from the Israelite period (First Temple period), a courtyard house from the Israelite period, the Roman remain and its military bathhouse and aqueduct and trough, and the remains from the British mandate period.

The city with its fortress was located on a trade route. The biblical town named Oboth seemed so similar to Ir Ovot (city of Oboth in Hebrew), that it was logical to me that they would be the same place.

The Ir Ovot excavations descended as deep as eight "digging strata," or layers, as depicted on the sign. There was a gigantic square fortress wall, with perfect rows of clean-cut, rectangular, pale yellow stones piled one upon the other. The site had an Iron Age fortification surrounded by a casemate wall suggesting a very large city. The fortified area extended to 10,000 square meters – four times larger than other fortified Negev cities. The excavations revealed many of the building walls and large pathways. An attractive wooden bridge with wooden sides and palm leaf shade cover had been built over a section of the excavations. The ancient Israelites must have drawn water from its vast underground water reservoirs. As I stood at a massive, deep well, peering into its depths I imagined the multitudes that had quenched their thirst here.

At the lowest levels, the red-brown stones had weathered into rounded shapes. These stones were from a fortress that had been built during King Solomon's reign. It resembled other Negev plateau fortresses from that era, such as the one at Tel Kadesh Barnea and Tel-el-Kheleifeh at Aqaba with the large pillar at the entrance gates, thick

My little red tent in the massive Jordanian mountains. | M Rawicz Trip Photo

A massive, deep well at ancient Ir Ovot. | M Rawicz Trip Photo

double-walled perimeter fortifications, and guard towers along the walls at periodic intervals. A later fortress dated back to the biblical times of Jehoshaphat, Hezekiah, and Josiah; still later ruins, which were associated with the Nabatean, Edomite, Early and Late Roman, Byzantine, Islamic, and finally British Mandate periods, were also visible. The differences between these various fortresses and stones was clearly distinguishable. I saw some large wheat grinding stones with the grinder stone still lying in the hollowed-out stone that held the wheat. Many shards of multi-colored pottery were also scattered around.

I was enthralled to find a modern army bunker on the edges of the site. The location was still valuable as a military outpost to the Israelis.

Archaeologists have been very interested in Oboth because of the extensive nature of the remaining ancient structures, and there is much evidence of that interest. They have, however, been unable to agree on the location. The diverse opinions are presented in the text of "East of Jordan Territories and Sites of the Hebrew Scriptures,"[3] and others.[4] I have accepted the location of Oboth on the Israeli side of the Jordan, in the vicinity of Ir Ovot, as I was following the route depicted by the Talmud scholar, Adolf Neubauer.

I also followed the opinions of archaeologists Davies and Glueck.

At Ir Ovot we saw some of the eight "digging strata" excavations. | *M Rawicz Trip Photo*

Davies believed Oboth to have been in the Arabah Valley, in the general vicinity of Ir Ovot. Glueck maintained that it was on a Nabataean caravan route (which this site is), while Musil considered Oboth to be at the oasis called Al-Webeh (not far away from Ir Ovot) in the Araba valley in Jordan at the crossroads of routes to Aqaba and Petra in the south and Gaza. In the northwest he had first identified this site as Oboth in 1902, and later in 1932 had identified a Roman fortress there. Michael Avi-Yonah had found pottery from the time of the first biblical temple in the area. Aharoni and Rudolph Cohen also conducted some excavations. An alternative opinion was expressed by Bartlett who postulated that Oboth was located near Punon between Dana and Wadi-al-Hasa, also in Jordan, and thus in Moabite territory.

There was an enormous Paliurus spina-christi (Jujuba) tree, also known as the Jerusalem Thorn in the center of the entire complex. It was reportedly 1,000 years old and the largest tree in Israel. It had stood there for a third of the time period that had passed between the Exodus and my own lifetime. The tree had witnessed the lives of past generations and I also felt connected with those lives.

I wondered about the name "place of sorcery" or "necromancy." Where exactly was this ominous place of magic in which one might call

Excavations revealed remains from the Nabatean, Edomite, Early and Late Roman, Byzantine, Islamic, and British Mandate periods at Ir Ovot. | M Rawicz Trip Photo

An enormous 1,000 year old tree called Paliurus spina-christi (Jujuba- Jerusalem Thorn). | M Rawicz Trip Photo

up the apparitions of spirits or ghosts to assist them in divination? Had anyone actually called up the spirits? Had I unknowingly seen the bewitching place, or had I somehow missed it? Or was I looking in the wrong place entirely? These questions remain unresolved for me.

⬦ Anger, courage and strength

> I took a moment to reflect on the meaning of Oboth, namely that "the people became enemies of G-d in this place after all their wearying travels through the wilderness."[5] In terms of Jacobson's writings, the place was called Oboth because of the sorcerers who lived there, as "ovos" are mediums involved in necromancy.[6]
>
> Sometimes in life, events occur that are too much for us to bear: possibly a major community catastrophe; a tragedy of severe proportions; or a personal event that strikes very deeply. We become entrenched in our agony and grief. The emotional turmoil or defeat that we suffer makes us turn away from G-d and regard Him as an adversary, not a guardian. We, however, cannot just resign, but need to find the inner will to continue with our lives and progress bit by bit until we are functional again. Here, the Israelites had to learn to find the boldness to continue the journey, as understood from Jacobson.[7]
>
> This surprised me as Oboth looked like a lovely, ancient city. I felt that the tree had witnessed the lives of the past generations and through it I also felt connected to them.
>
> I resolved that I would remember to deal with anger in a more meaningful way. I would dig deep to access faith to help me deal with whatever issue I might be facing and move on.   ◀

To follow in the Israelites' footsteps, I would have to go further north in this flat Arabah Valley, to the southernmost part of the Dead Sea. I drove for three and a half kilometers eastwards to the edges of the Arabah Valley. There I saw Aeolian erosion cliffs from the many years of the Jordan River eroding its banks. This is where the Israelites had crossed back over the Jordan to continue to the southernmost end of the Dead Sea. I could not cross the border between Israel and Jordan here, as there is no official border crossing now.

Chapter 8

Through Northern Jordan: Camp 38

"They left Oboth and camped at Iyay Ha'avarim on the border of Moab."[1] This next camp that I was to visit lay further to the north, but within Jordan. *Iyay Ha'avarim* means various things: "passage of the fords," "desolate passes," "crossing fords," and "desolate mounds."[2] *Iyay* means "ruins," whereas *Ha'avarim* derives from the word for sin, meaning spiritual displacement. Thus, *Iyay Ha'avarim* can be translated as "the ruins of sin" or "the ruins of displacement." The phrase has even been said to mean "the ruins of those who copulate," thus alluding to a specific sin.[3]

I thought about the meaning of this camp's name and felt a sense of desolation. What sort of challenge did I face now in looking for some desolation, ruin, displacement or place of sin? At times, the meanings of the names of the camps just seemed to become more dire as my journey progressed! I braced myself for whatever tragedy I might find.

Youseph, Makki and I continued our journey together. As we set out to find Iyay Ha'avarim, I recalled the biblical text: "The children of Israel set forward, and pitched camp at Iyay Ha'varim, in the wilderness which is before Moab, toward the sun rising.[4] From there they removed, and pitched in the valley of Zered."[5] In another section of the Bible, the narrative recounts that Moses and the people journeyed west of Edom until they reached the Zered Valley skirting around Moab. A bit later the text states that the people travelled along an ancient desert caravan track.

We travelled for about an hour on the tarred road that runs parallel to the Jordan River. This had been the ancient desert caravan track. By mid-afternoon that Friday, we arrived in Fifa, a mid-sized town which is a service center for the numerous farms that are scattered throughout the Jordan Valley. The farmlands interested me after having been travelling in the desert with only bushes, so we took a detour and drove down a dirt road between some farms. I was checking the topography of the mountains and the location of the valley that meandered between its steep rocky slopes because I wanted to identify where people might have walked down the mountains and through the valley to then cross over into what is today Israeli territory. I had read about an ancient road that crosses from the Jordan side to the Israel side of the river at the southernmost point of the Dead Sea, and wanted to see if I could locate it. I asked Youseph to weave down through the valley via criss-crossing farm tracks.

When I thought we might have arrived at the correct conjunction, I asked Youseph to stop the car. The jeep was now parked at the edge of a large tomato field, with a man nearby hoeing his crops. We had stopped behind some tall trees. I walked forward, uncertain about whether I had made correct assumptions about the local geography. But as I reached the end of the row of trees, I was amazed to see a large hill of soil about seventy meters away that appeared as if it might be an ancient tel. The farmer came over and introduced himself as Ghanim.

"What is that large soil mound?" I asked, and Youseph translated.

Ghanim waved his arms in the air and said, "This has been here for many years ... ever since my family has owned this land, which has been many generations. We don't know what it is. I think it must be very old."

With great excitement and expectation, I walked to the mound and began climbing the rough ground. I reached the top, and saw that it indeed was a typical tel, complete with stones that looked as if they might be the remnants of ancient walls. I also saw some shards of pottery. I was delighted to have found it – and at the exact point of conjunction with a large wadi that ran down from the Jordan mountains. I had read about the biblical town called Zoar and was convinced that I had located it correctly. Evidently, I had managed to locate the site of the ancient town on an ancient established route. Youseph was astonished and Ghanim delighted. He felt proud that I was on his farm when I explained what it might be.

I found an ancient tel of the biblical town of Zoar, to which Lot fled, in a farmer's field. |
M Rawicz Trip Photo

Later I did more research and found out that this town was associated with the cities of the Plain or Valley of Siddim,[7] the city to which Lot had escaped after leaving Sodom. Zoar was situated in the hot, barren valley at the end of the Dead Sea, and is thought to have been an important station on the trade route between Aqabah and Jericho, at the base of the mountains of Moab.[8] I must admit that I was chuffed with myself for having found it.

I wrote in my log-book: "Before we found Iyay Ha'avarim we came across a unique tel at the town of Fifa that links Israel and Jordan on the fourth major north-to-south route and the major east-to-west route."

We went back to the town of Fifa before continuing on towards our goal of Iyay Ha'avarim, and stopped at a roadside café for something to drink, where we were immediately surrounded by flies. The sheer number of farms in this region and the industry of packing and discarding tomatoes, means that thousands of flies are attracted to the area. Sitting at a table outside the café was a stately-looking man, to whom we introduced ourselves. He informed us that he was the head of the local Bedouin tribe. His companion found my project of great interest, and I fell into a conversation with him about archaeology.

After we left the café, to my surprise, Youseph reprimanded me severely.

"You must not tell any strange person what you are doing here!" he said. "They might think you're a tourist looking for gold. You know some people won't believe stories like yours and they can think that you are here for more money-making reasons."

I was shocked. However, later I uncovered that Youseph's anger was fuelled partly by the fact that I had spoken directly to the Bedouin men myself, and had not granted him greater authority to converse on my behalf. He felt that I had not followed protocol, because he was supposed to be my local guide. I was amazed to learn this unexpected side of his character.

His anger passed in time, and to ease the tension between us he recounted an anecdote.

"Did you know that if a fly falls into the tea of a Bedouin person, we drink it because it's considered good luck?"

All I was able to reply was, "Wow."

Youseph then pointed to the dark brown Jordanian mountains to our right. He exclaimed,

"Oh! That reminds me. I must take you to see the memorial to Lot, the man in the Bible who survived the destruction of Sodom and Gomorrah. I hope you don't mind if we go a few kilometers northwards and then return to your Exodus route. His wife turned to salt when she looked back, after she was told not to. On the side of this mountain is the cave believed to be the one Lot fled to with his daughters. Pilgrims go and stand to pray outside the cave."

I was fascinated to see the dark rocks that led to the cave. Youseph pointed out one of the more unusual rocks on the mountainside, which looked like an extremely tall person.

"Our local tradition says that that was Lot's wife."

The tall stone was indeed most unusual. I climbed up to the cave and peered into its dark entrance.

It was becoming overcast and a haze descended over the Dead Sea. Youseph and I decided to hurry towards Iyay Ha'avarim in the rugged western escarpment of the ancient Moabite plateau (today known as the Jordan Mountains) called Abarim.

Five kilometers from the village of Fifa, on the banks of the river that flows down the Jordanian mountains from the Wadi-al-Hasa canyon, we came to the site believed by Glueck and others who obtained their information from an ancient Madaba map to be Iyay Ha'avarim.[9] I was disappointed because as far as we could establish there was nothing of note at this place.

Just as the exact location of Ovot is disputed, there are various theories about where Iyay Ha'avarim is. Several Talmudic scholars believe that Iyay Ha'avarim is closer to the next major river that flows down the mountains in Wadi-Al-Karak. Also Iyay Ha'avarim is regarded as a general area rather than a specific site, because the phrase can be translated as "the ruins on the other side."

Youseph and I thus continued along the same road towards the next potential site. This area borders the Dead Sea to the south of which are 30-kilometer-long salt pans filled with extremely salty and chemically rich water. The ground, saturated with salts, is unsuitable for agriculture. Even in biblical days, I assumed it would have been considered a barren wasteland. I began to wonder if the "desolation, ruin, and displacement" might have referred to this salty wasteland.

Youseph took the opportunity to boast about some of his country's achievements.

"We have many industries that work with this salty water," he told me. "The water has more than thirty-five different minerals. They are very good for one's health and body, even skincare. Our factories use magnesium, calcium, potassium, bromine, sulphur, and iodine to made creams and salts that help heal many illnesses."

"Like what?" I asked.

"Oh, many diseases, like arthritis, rheumatism, psoriasis, eczema, headaches and foot-ache. Other creams are made to feed and soften the skin. Jordan is well known for its Dead Sea bath salts and makeup."[10.]

"Of course," I said.

He continued: "In the tourist season, I am kept busy because everyone wants to visit the Dead Sea. Visitors come here from all over the world because it is the lowest point on earth, 423 meters below sea level. I heard that some interest groups even want this sea to be made into one of the world's wonders. This is the second most salty lake in the world; many factories want our salts for new products. If you look ahead along the road, you can see the fences with the salt pans behind that are being mined. There are many kinds of factories, from food to microchips and cell phones. Sick people also come here to breathe the clear, fresh air and bathe in the healing water and see what it is like to float."[11]

We set off to cover the next nine kilometers and find the river thought to be the Zered Brook of the Bible, which today flows at Wadi-Al-Karak. Two kilometers before we reached the town of Ghar Mazara, Youseph turned to me and said,

"I think that what you are looking for is nearby. Let me take you there."

He veered the jeep off the main road and after half a kilometer we arrived at an archaeological site.

"This is what people say are the remains of the city of Sodom and Gomorrah," he declared.

The large site of four hectares comprised a couple of large hills made up of light yellow sand, with brown rocks strewn around. I set out to explore, and could clearly make out the remains of a wide ancient city wall with gates and the remnants of towers built out of massive stones. Large yellow-brown rocks, once square, now rounded after decades of erosion, had been used to demarcate the presence of an important city. According to the archeologist Walter, layers of ash had also been found, as well as the remains of numerous homes that had collapsed, burying their inhabitants alive. These bore testimony to a fire that had swept through the city, destroying large parts and killing nearly 1,000 people.

The site is known as Bab-edh-Dhra, and is one of the candidates for the possible location of the so-called "city of sin," Sodom.[12] Viewing the ruins sent shivers down my spine. I reflected on the meaning of Iyay Ha'avarim, and recalled that Ha'avarim derives from the word for sin, namely "spiritual displacement," and that some of the more specific connotations are "ruins of displacement" and "ruins of those who copulate." Wanton copulation was exactly what the story of Sodom and Gomorrah had been about.

In my imagination, I saw myself at Sodom during its fiery destruction. A fireball of terror ignited against the black clouds as the heavens raged. The bloody sky shifted from the fury of red to purple. Then black hot rain showered the city. Buildings crashed down with loud rumbles, crushing the people below and massive dust clouds exploded.

A blast of hot air blew clothes off bodies and naked, burnt men and women sprawled across pathways. The huge crowds fled, pushing each other to escape in desperate hopelessness. A terror stricken woman struggled to run while her screaming children clung to her.

The ancient important city of Bab-edh-Dhra spread over four hectares. |
M Rawicz Trip Photo

G-d was meting out His just reward to those who had reveled in their drunken sinfulness.

Some perverted men stood wide-eyed as unsavory women lay dying in shame. The fire swept through, destroying everything in its path. Chaos reigned.

There, then, was Lot fleeing with his family from the seething mass of the damned.

I looked at the surroundings and the sight of such tangible evidence of the whole disaster left me feeling shocked and weak at the knees as I stared at the blackened stones in front of me.

Burial areas had been demarcated with stones. Archaeologists had found the tombs of roughly 20,000 families, which together would have had the capacity to hold approximately half a million people – even though only 1,000 inhabitants were thought to have lived here. Thus, the theory is that these dolmens (mounds or graves) might have served as a central cemetery for the whole region. With great interest and a little trepidation, due to the history of the site and its vastness, I walked around the site and observed some of the dolmens. My exploration was brought to an abrupt halt when three large wild dogs barked

A huge circular stone was possibly used for grinding wheat. | *M Rawicz Trip Photo*

Archaeologists found a regional burial site with thousands of tombs at Bab-edh-Dhra. |
M Rawicz Trip Photo

down at me from the top of one of the large mounds and began making their way toward me. I was disappointed to have to stop my search, but turned and ran back towards the jeep. At least these were real wild dogs rather than the ghosts of ancient people!

I wondered whether the dolmens might have been the "desolate mounds" referred to in the phrase "Iyay Ha'avarim," and whether this site had been near one of the Exodus encampments. Overall, I had found it a fascinating but unsettling experience because of the vastness and many graves. As we left, I contemplated the meaning of this place and some insights that scholars have provided.

◧   Finding purpose when life appears meaningless

There are times in our lives when whatever we attempt seems to fail, nothing happens as it is expected to, and we feel that as time passes we are going nowhere. Times like this may also have the added complication of making one feel isolated, cut off and alienated from people. One may perceive that others are succeeding and one is not part of the general progress.

During such distressing times it is possible for one to lose confidence, hope and a sense of a future. Life can appear to be purposeless and useless. One lives from day to day in a state of drifting and feels defeated.

This is the condition that the Israelites experienced at Iyay Ha'avarim. They felt that they were wandering aimlessly and endlessly. The remedy was that they had to make an effort to feel connected to each other, other people, and the world in general. The raising of their consciousness to the indisputable reality would help them. In our lives a similar process can make us feel more connected as well as being unique participants, as Jacobson expounds.[13]

Further, the place evoked a sense that danger and desolation would follow upon lives lived in an immoral, evil way. It reinforced how important it is for us to be connected, caring and ethical towards each other.   ◧

Looking out over a sharp cliff on one side of the road, we were presented with the magnificent lower reaches of Wadi-Al-Karak leading up to the

At the lower reaches of Wadi-Al-Karak one can see the Jordan valley. |
M Rawicz Trip Photo

Jordanian mountains. Lush vegetation grew along the banks. Clearly, the proximity to this passageway between the mountains had given the location its importance. The beauty of the valley soothed away all sense of disappointment and fear that I had been feeling.

We returned to the main road that runs parallel to the Jordan River. I was hot, dusty, hungry, and thirsty, and gathered that Youseph and Makki were feeling the same way. We headed towards Al-Mazraa, a nearby village, to stock up on our provisions.

Thereafter, Youseph began the search for a place to sleep overnight. I was greatly relieved to be closing this chapter of my journey, as the day was wearing on and I did not want to be on the road as the Sabbath approached. Youseph decided to take me to Ma'in Hot Springs, a special place, with hot water gushing from the mountain and magnificent vegetation, frequented by hiking groups. As the sun sank lower in the deep red sky, our jeep slowly climbed the enormous mountains and we enjoyed the breath-taking view. Finally, we arrived at a small campsite located between the high walls of the Wadi Bin Hammad canyons.

The walls were covered with hanging gardens that sprouted among the spaces between the rocks. In places, the entire vegetation resembled the innards of a vast, complex living machine, with woody components entangled to form a strange live entanglement. I saw Palms, Cassia, Erythrinas, MassiveIvoko, Sapele, and Poinsettia trees with parasitic succulents growing high up on their trunks. The sight, which evoked a legendary world, was stunning.

We all unpacked, and took turns to enjoy a most welcome and refreshing hot shower from the natural spring that gushed from the rocky walls. We gathered for supper and I made the customary Friday night blessing on the grape juice and bread. We ate bread with tomato, onion, and cucumber salad, and tea and chatted like old friends.

Youseph told me about the canyon. "In the rainy times, it has water running down its middle that can reach your knees, and at one special place there are very beautiful stalactite rocks. Along a lot of the canyon you can see hanging gardens like this one."

Feeling weary, I shifted to my tent to relax. It seemed a reasonable place to spend Friday night, but I wondered how I would fare spending the entire next day here too. Jewish law prohibits observant people from driving on the Sabbath.

The next day, feeling peaceful and refreshed on waking, I stepped into the lovely sunshine. A welcome coolness lingered in the canyon. This was my thirty-fourth day of the journey and my fourth Sabbath away from home. It turned out to be an unusually interesting one, but for now I indulged in the pleasure of the surrounding quiet and solitude.

"During the spring," Youseph told me, "you'll see a great sight here . . . hundreds of geese flying in the sky, high up. Many, many other birds also fly past this area to a nature reserve that gives them a good stopping point. This region – and parts of Israel – are on an international flight path for migrating birds. Every year these birds fly along the Rift Valley between Africa and northeast Europe."

I knew from my reading that the species of migratory birds that pass over the Middle East include White Storks, Black Storks, Buzzards, Levant Sparrow Hawks, and Eurasian Griffons.

Youseph, Makki and I spent the rest of the day chatting and reflecting on the journey that lay ahead. I told them what I knew about the remainder of the Exodus. "The next few legs of the Israelites' journey involved crossing the huge Jordan Mountains and reaching the plateau above. They started their uphill climb at Zered Brook, at the southern end of the Dead Sea."

"Which canyon did they go up?" Youssef asked.

"Well, many Talmudic scholars believe that their route to the next camp followed Wadi-Al-Karak, as Kaplan shows in his book,[14] and Neubauer on his map.[15] But major archaeologists like Gleuck, Simons, Abel, Aharoni, and Lemaire maintain that the route went through Wadi-Al-Hasa[16] and the ancient Madaba map identifies the Zered Brook with Wadi-Al-Hasa.

"Yes, I think it must have been Wadi-Al-Hasa," Youseph said, nodding his head. You won't get far if you try to go through Wadi-Al-Karak."

I thought about this, and then laughingly said, "I'm sorry to tell you this, but we're going to have to at least *try* to go up Wadi-Al-Karak."

"Oh," he said, looking not altogether surprised. "Why do you want to do that?"

"I'm tracing the route depicted in a book called *The Living Torah*," I replied. "The map in there shows that the Israelites probably walked up Wadi-Al-Karak."

But Youseph spoke from personal experience.

"It usually takes ten hours for a strong young man or woman to hike downwards through Wadi-Al-Karak," he told me as politely as he could. "You want to hike upwards! And you're a much older person. It would take you at least two days to hike up the whole wadi."

"Really?"

"Definitely. And in some places, the path is very difficult to find. But you don't have to believe me. You can see for yourself."

In the end, we agreed that we would make a partial exploration of Wadi-Al-Karak, attempting to see how far up we could get before we decided what to do next. I felt that my route needed to remain consistent with the one shown in my source book.

Youseph assured me that he felt at home in the wilderness of rocks, precipices, cliffs, waterfalls, and hidden valleys of Jordan's canyons. My trust in him gave me the confidence to decide to hike up the wadi, although I anticipated that it might be a treacherous journey. Youseph was also associated with a reputable Jordanian touring company and required to report on our progress and whereabouts daily. I was further reassured by this backup support system. So, with some trepidation, I decided to risk the adventure because it was important to me to follow the route as closely as possible.

That evening, we took stock of whether we were ready to start the hike in morning. Youseph had some supplies but we would need to replenish them with additional fruit, vegetables, and eggs, water and flour to make bread. I still had some tins of fish from Israel. Youseph had a large backpack in which he would carry the tents, camping equipment, and provisions. I had waterproof hiking shoes, and Youseph had a wet-suit and life jacket. Makki had his equipment and would come along to assist with carrying and organizing things. That evening, I packed the minimum that I might need for the next couple of nights, with the idea of travelling light. Youseph arranged for a local acquaintance of his, Zayed, to take charge of his jeep.

CANYON CLIMBING

In the morning we returned by jeep to the now familiar main road that runs parallel to the Jordan River and shopped at the Al-Mazraa agricul-tural settlement before picking up Zayed. We drove past the lush fields surrounding the settlement and on past another small farming village before reaching the foot of the mountains. We wanted to find the Zered Brook, where "the children of Israel pitched in the valley of Zered," and from where they headed up into the mountains. We were greeted with the sight of the lower end of Wadi-Al-Karak.

Youseph said, "I hope you are ready for this hard trek along the river and through the gorges."

Zayed bade us farewell, saying, "I hope you have a good time. If you manage to get to the top, call me to meet you there. I'll drive up the easy way, on Route 50." He chuckled and drove away, leaving us standing there with our backpacks.

With a broad smile, Youseph turned to me and Makki and said, "Let's start the walking and climbing!"

I was excited at the prospect of what lay ahead. We set off up the trail, chatting as we proceeded.

Youseph remarked, "Wadi-Al-Karak is one of the largest wadis of Jordan that goes up from the Jordan Valley to the high plateau at the top of the mountains. This climb follows a very tough route up until it meets the ancient King's Highway. This ancient road runs next to the modern main road that goes from north to south along the plateau."

For the first couple of kilometers, our hike was an easy and pleasant walk beside the bubbling stream, or sometimes right through the wa-ter. I savoured the beautiful scenery: wonderful plants growing in the nooks and crannies of rocks, and magnificent riverine vegetation along the sides of the wadi. The ecology differed dramatically from the dryness of the desert in the Jordan Valley, and this area displayed amazing biodiversity. What impressed me was the beauty and peacefulness in the wadi. We stopped periodically to rest, and the silence was broken by delightful bird calls.

For a while the route wound its way through low hills, but then entered a steep valley in a narrow winding gorge, which eventually opened into an even steeper and densely vegetated V-shaped valley. The cliffs became wider apart and smaller valleys led off here and there, revealing secret pools and cascading waterfalls.

I was relieved when it was lunchtime. After eating, we rested and dozed before continuing. Soon after we had started walking again, we saw a slender animal with long legs and short brown fur, about the size of a dog, with a short tail and long black-and-white ear-tufts. It was visible between the rocks of the canyon, and looked as if it was stalking something as it slowly moved forwards on its belly. Suddenly it leapt forward, sprinted, and pounced, grabbing its prey with powerful jaws. It slinked off among the rocks with a hissing sound. I stood transfixed.

Youseph and Makki laughed at my surprise, and Youseph said, "That's a large wild cat called the Caracal. It's a very strong and fast hunter, and has just caught a bird."

By late afternoon, we needed a tea break. l felt hot, sticky, and dusty, and my legs and rear were aching from all the walking. I felt somewhat revitalized by the tea, water and biscuits, but when the time came for us to set off again my body yelled at me, "No! No more!" The shadows were lengthening, and the deeply rutted cliffs of Wadi-Al-Karak were beginning to cast their darkness across our path. The idea of setting up camp in the dark did not appeal to me in the slightest, and I was genuinely tired.

To my relief, Youseph agreed to stop for the day.

"Ok," he said. "I'll find some open ground above the wadi floor where I can put up the two tents. That way, even if a flash flood happens in the night, we won't get wet in the water."

We found a spot, and while Makki pitched the tents, I stepped behind the bushes to wash and change. We then prepared supper. Youseph got a fire going after a lot of patience and much puffing. Makki balanced a pot of water on a circle of rocks that had been placed around the fire and boiled some Bedouin tea. I improvised by roasting potatoes, onions, tomatoes, and butternut over the fire, and opened a tin of tuna.

Dusk had fallen and the nightlife was beginning to stir. At first it was limited to a couple of beetles and moths. We sat close to the fire and it cast a protective smoke screen around the area; any insects that flew too close were incinerated in the glowing flames. Suddenly, a dark creature flew out of the night and flapped around in front of me, casting a huge shadow on the side of the tent.

"A bat," said Youseph, as it fluttered past my head.

By now, the sun had set and the mountains were silhouetted against a deep red sky that was slowly fading to a dark orange. As the night wore on, huge buzzing insects emerged from every crack and crevice and made an intense noise.

"It's time for me to get some sleep," I announced.

Youseph and Makki bade me goodnight. "Oh, and don't worry about creatures like scorpions or poisonous insects," he added. "You should be safe in the tent."

I felt anxious and my mind started playing tricks as the shadows of the vegetation outside seemed to take on the shapes of wild beasts. A palm tree mutated into a huge animal pawing the ground, ready to charge. Another tree became a camel, which would bow its head lightly every time the wind blew. It was difficult for me to remain rational when I was exhausted!

In the morning we prepared to set out early as we hoped to hike to the top of the wadi. Before leaving, I spread liberal doses of insect repellent over my arms and neck, followed by sun block, working on the theory that if I got sunburnt the last thing I wanted was insect bites as well. Now I felt ready for a happy day of walking. But I was in for a surprise which presented itself before long. Our path was completely blocked by a huge waterfall.

Youseph laughed and said,

"That waterfall is thirty meters high, but I know how to climb it."

I stared in shock.

"I have a rope that we can use to scale it," he kindly offered.

I replied, "Not a chance."

He volunteered, "I can wind the rope around to make a sort of rope chair. Then you can sit in it while I hoist you up."

"No, no," I retorted. "Really, not to worry. If I can't get up there on my own, how would the Israelites have been able to do so with all their animals, the old people, and little children?"

"Hm," he said.

The stream in Wadi Al Hasa flows through a narrow gorge of spectacular red, grey, and white sandstone. | M Rawicz Trip Photo

"Ok. I've seen the route. We must go back to Wadi-Al-Hasa." I felt sad about the prospect; Makki and Youssef were supportive.

We spent the next few hours retracing our tracks. Youseph contacted Zayed and asked him to meet us at the point where we had started.

Youseph had tried to warn me about Wadi-Al-Karak. At least I had attempted to traverse the route suggested by the Talmud and as depicted in *The Living Torah*. That night we prepared to set out again, this time in another direction, to explore Wadi-Al-Hasa.

Wadi-Al-Hasa has been identified as the biblical Zered River based on the depiction on the ancient mosaic map of Madaba. Several scholars have objected to the theory that the Exodus route would have included Wadi-Al-Karak, and so have several prominent archeologists.[17]

I had a slight preference for Wadi-Al-Karak because of the suggestions of the Talmud scholars, but was also just eager to ascend one of these canyons to have some experience of what the Israelites may have gone through.

Zayed once again saw us off at the entrance to the Wadi-Al-Hasa, close to the small village of Safi that we had visited earlier. Youseph looked at the old sports shoes I was wearing.

"No special equipment or abseiling skills are needed for this one," he commented. "Young men take eight hours to hike down the wadi. Let's see how many days it takes us to get to the top."

This canyon was quite different from the previous one. Above the narrow entrance to the gorge, the sheer cliffs rose some fifty meters high. I was struck by the incredible sight of a large spherical boulder suspended above us, between the cliffs. Along its lower course, the wadi cut through spectacular red sandstone. On the first day, we walked part of the way in ankle-deep water and passed some magnificent rock structures. The cliffs exhibited bands of red, grey, and white rocks that had been carved into flowing, rounded shapes by years of exposure to the water. The wadi changed shapes and colors along the way. We walked through narrow gorges in some places, but in others the vista opened up and the path was wide. Once again magnificent hanging gardens were evident, and even a rare tropical tree growing in the bed of the wadi, called Dalbergia Sissoo. This species is not seen anywhere else in Jordan. All three of us enjoyed spotting animals and pointing them out to each other. Youseph glimpsed two mongooses, welcome companions to view for a moment.

As the day wore on and the sun turned red, and despite the wonder-

The sheer cliffs of Wadi Al Hasa which have a large spherical boulder suspended between the cliffs. | M Rawicz Trip Photo

ful wildlife and natural surroundings, I secretly began to wish that this uphill journey would end soon. I wanted some luxury again – enough with roughing it! Maybe that explained the Israelites as a rebellious and complaining bunch of "stiff-necked people," as G-d had referred to them in Exodus 32:9. They had my full sympathy. We rested briefly in the late afternoon and set off again for the last stint of hiking before evening. We stopped to cook supper, pitch the tents. We chatted about the many wadis that we had seen together as well as some that I had seen on the earlier leg of my journey.

Youseph reminisced, "As you've seen, the wadis of Jordan provide many extraordinary recreation areas for hikers and nature lovers. East of the Dead Sea going southwards we crossed Wadi Manshala, then Wadi Zarqa Main, Wadi Hidan and Wadi Mujib, the largest and widest where we saw people farming high up on the steep banks. South of that we had fun at Wadi ibn Hammad, with its warm spring and spectacular hanging gardens. South of the Dead Sea I take people for camel safaris along some of the wadis like Wadi-Al-Hasa, Wadi Ghuweir with the fantastic red sandstone. The smaller wadis further south like Wadi-Al-Farasa, Wadi Saqra, and Wadi Siyagh are also great to visit if you like silence."

I had also seen Wadi Feinan, with its old copper mines, and Wadi Musa at Petra.

While we were talking, insects skittered everywhere. We were pestered by the insects running onto and over our hands and legs and retreated to the tents. After thoroughly securing myself inside, determined to keep the insects out, I fell asleep, only to succumb to nightmares about insects.

The next day was magical, with easy walking. Every 100 meters or so, we came across a hot water pool or a flowing stream. Some of the water that enters the canyon emerges from hot springs, with the highest temperature among these being roughly 54°C. At other points we found cold streams that yielded drinkable water. In one place, a tributary entered the wadi in the form of a beautiful waterfall, with water spouting out from behind a massive boulder that had crashed down the mountain and lodged between the walls of the gorge.

Lunch was spent beside a welcoming green oasis, and I caught up on a little sleep. By now I had learned to fall asleep almost anywhere.

I found a smooth, well-positioned rock in some shade, and spread out my sleeping bag . . . and awoke some twenty minutes later feeling quite energized. I stood near the water's edge, splashed my face with cold water, and felt refreshed. A large array of magnificent indigenous birds looked on approvingly.

We continued walking an hour in Wadi-Al-Hasa and then spent the night in a sheltered area of the canyon. Over supper we talked about the people in this region of the Middle East: Jews, Muslims, and Bedouins. It was interesting to realize how many customs they all had in common. It made me feel uneasy that there were still religious wars. I want to promote tolerance and acceptance between old enemies by encouraging good communication on an individual level.

Just before I disappeared into my tent, Youseph said, "If you hear any animals around the tent at night, don't worry. They can't see you, only smell you. Even if you think it sounds like a dangerous animal, just stay quiet."

My heart skipped a beat. Wow! Youseph was getting really good at scaring me just before bedtime.

He continued: "You will, for sure, hear noises in the night, because animals always come sniffing around a tent looking for food. But everything is packed away, so it will be fine. If you need to relieve yourself during the night, first check carefully that there are no snakes on the ground before you step out. Goodnight!"

With that cheery comment, he vanished into their tent, leaving me standing there in shock. I zipped myself into the tent and must have fallen asleep quite quickly. I awoke in the middle of the night to the sound of a loud noise outside. I sat up, trying to make out what it was. I was rigid with worry for the next half hour before the sound became fainter and I realized that whatever was outside must have moved on. My heart was still beating fast and my knees were a bit shaky when I eventually lay down again.

I awoke in the morning feeling somewhat strained, and walked over to the fireplace where Youseph was sitting. He had already prepared breakfast.

"Whatever that was that came visiting last night," he said, "left us in peace. I hope you were okay."

"I just kept silent when it was here," I replied.

This day, the scenery was different. The upper reaches of the canyon were white limestone, through which the river had carved its way, creating a playground of giant grey and white boulders and potholes. Later in the day we saw a mountain village in the distance, its tilled lands visible on the slopes between the natural vegetation and boulders. Our passage became more difficult and we had to clamber around boulders that had fallen from the rocky walls of the wadi and now lay at the edge of the steam.

Gradually, the scenery changed again as we started the steep ascent to the top of the wadi. We saw cultivated terraces, tree plantations, groves of plants, sheep and goats grazing and a twisting road running along the mountainside. Sweet music of people in prayer rang out as Muslim congregants praised G-d from a mosque situated high among the cliffs. We walked on for another couple of hours until we reached the confluence of the Wadi-Ofra and Wadi-Al-Hasa. In the upper reaches off Wadi-Al-Hasa, a prominent hill supported the ruins of a Nabataean temple, Khirbet Tannur.

Reaching the top of the wadi, we saw attractive square houses painted white or blue. From here we had a view for roughly twenty-five kilometers along the valley. The barely visible river curled like a black snake as it wound its way from this tremendous height to the distant valley. The weather was clear, and we could see all the way to the Dead Sea and across it to the Mount of Olives, which borders Jerusalem. What a magnificent scene! And what a feeling of achievement for having climbed all the way up.

I had just endured a similar experience to that of the Israelites when they ascended the border between the ancient Moab and Edom kingdoms. They had conquered these rugged, lofty and otherwise impassable Jordanian mountains. I felt connected with their energy during this climb and was satisfied that I had explored both possible alternatives proposed for the Exodus route. I hoped that the Israelites, too, had felt rewarded by the beauty all around.

At last, we were greeted by Zayed and the delightful sight of Youseph's vehicle on a road called the R35 that crosses the valley. Then we bid farewell to Zayed before proceeding with our usual quest: finding somewhere to sleep. We drove twenty kilometers northward to Karak City along the R35. The city has been inhabited since at least the Iron Age, and was an important city for the Moabites. Youseph knew of a hotel that was reasonably priced, and took us there.

While managing our booking, the receptionist said, "You are lucky, as Tuesday is not a busy night. Often we are booked to capacity with

From the top of the Jordanian mountains at Wadi Al Karak the view extends for twenty five kilometres down towards Jerusalem. | *M Rawicz Trip Photo*

tourists coming to see Karak and its fantastic fortress, which was built in 1132 under the reign of King Fulk, the Crusader king of Jerusalem."

The Karak hotel was pleasant: the rooms were clean, hot water was provided, and the staff was friendly. But to me, the greatest luxury was being able to sleep on a bed inside a brick room again after the nights in a tent. Tomorrow would be the 38th day of my trip, and we would be heading into the Eastern Desert on a long journey. The prospect was formidable.

In the morning, we first visited Karak City Center. We needed to stock up on food, water, and general provisions, and draw cash. The main shopping street on King's Highway was a curious place: classical Middle Eastern architecture mixed with small modern offices, a few fruit and vegetable shops and other consumer shops, and the bustle of busy citizens. I was intrigued by the idea that this main road, which was called the King's Highway even in previous eras, had once been the ancient north–south route that ran through Edom and Moab, and also one that the Israelites may have used. Today, the road runs all the way from the Gulf of Aqaba for 335 kilometers before ascending gradually to Petra and thereon to northern Jordan. The modern road still winds its way close to the edge of the Eastern Desert, passing Nabataean temples and the Wadis Hasa and Karak. It crosses the Wadi Mujib–Arnon valley, which in biblical times was the canyon that divided Edomite and Moabite territories. The road then winds through the picturesque, shallow valley of Wadi Wala and continues northwards through modern-day Dhiban, Madaba, and Amman. In places where the modern route departs slightly from the original road, one still sees the ancient tracks, some five meters wide, consisting of paving stones and larger stones marking the edge, running through nearby fields.

I told Youseph, "The next major encampment of the Israelites was Dibongad. After they had crossed the mountains they moved northwards to the northern shore of the Dead Sea. The first area they passed through belonged to the Edomites. After that, they would have to cross the Moabite territory further north. This would have involved a journey of at least forty kilometers."

TERRIFYING WASTELAND

Moses wanted to follow the King's Highway from the wadi that the Israelites had ascended to the point where they would enter the Promised Land. It would have been the easiest route. He assumed that the Edomites would consent.[18] But the Edomites refused them passage and forced them to detour, travelling on the Way of the Wilderness, through the Eastern Desert.[19]

I checked the biblical text to see if it mentioned specific features to note.[20] I read: "The children of Israel went to Beer, . . . and from the wilderness they went to Mattanah . . . to Nahaliel . . . and to Bamoth . . . in the valley that is in the country of Moab.[21] Israel dwelt in all the cities of the Amorites, in Heshbon, and in all the villages thereof."

My journey would thus take me away from the King's Highway through the settlements of Ar, Beer, Mattanah, Nahaliel, Bamoth, and Heshbon before arriving at Dibon and the subsequent Exodus encampments. All this travelling for about fifty kilometers would be challenging in the difficult desert environment, but I was determined to complete the task I had set for myself.

We set off northwards, in the direction of the desert highway of ancient times. The Route 15 highway links Jordan to Syria and Iran. Large trucks carrying goods use this route, but Youseph, Makki and I saw very few vehicles.

At first I took note of the change in landscape, but soon realized that the scenery would remain relentlessly similar for kilometer after kilometer, the only significant feature being black basalt boulders. These rocks formed a blanket over the ground, known as "desert pavement." In the inhospitable harshness of this region, one quickly learns respect for the environment and does not take chances. There were no signs of human habitation. Occasional small slopes in the otherwise flat landscape had been formed by basalt lava flow and volcanic cone eruptions in ancient times.

Youseph told me about the area. "This huge Eastern Desert, the Badia Region, covers more than fifty percent of Jordan. It also goes into Syria, Iraq, and Saudi Arabia in what is known as the North Arab Desert. On the far horizon to the east is the hilly limestone plateau, behind that is the Iraqi border. For the few Bedouin people who move around this area, life is hard. For strangers, it can seem like a living death. The climate is extreme, with very big changes in temperature between day and night. Daytime summer temperatures can go up to 40 degrees centigrade, but at night in winter, it's nearly freezing – and dry and windy. The rainfall in a year is less than 50 millimeters. There are three groundwater aquifers under eastern Badia but people have

In the eastern desert for kilometer after kilometer the scene is mostly black basalt boulders. | M Rawicz Trip Photo

only been accessing the underground water relatively recently."

I felt like crying at the thought that the Israelites had been forced to walk this way – after all the trials that they had already endured! However, I drew solace from reflecting on the teachings of the Sukkot camp: we depend on G-d, and His presence and protection during our journeys can help us to cope and find a new inner strength. As strangers passing through this land it must have been very difficult.

The only sign of life was the sparse hardy groundcover with plants the size of a fist. During the cooler months, the groundcover survives on small amounts of atmospheric humidity. Sizzling, shimmering heat waves bounced off the ground and made the desert look as if on fire. There was no place to hide, no shade from the glaring sun, and when we stopped to stretch our legs, the only sign that life had once existed here was the skeleton of a sheep lying half buried in the soil. It could have lain there for years. The sight was heartbreaking and my sympathy for the Israelites increased all the more.

Eventually, in the vast emptiness, we found a small roadside lodge

In the sizzling desert, the only sign of life was the skeleton of a sheep in the soil. |
M Rawicz Trip Photo

and shop for truck drivers. It had been built to cool without the use of electricity, fans, or fridges. A large central room was surrounded by a narrow unroofed courtyard, off which several smaller rooms led. The walls were made of earth and chopped straw, keeping the interior relatively cool. A tall earthenware pot – designed to let moisture condense through its porous sides – provided guests with chilled water. Each bedroom had two narrow beds, a chair, and a dressing table.

In the ablutions facility, hot and weary travellers were able to take a shower. The shower apparatus consisted of a steel bucket suspended from a hook in the ceiling, and by using a handle attached to the bucket, one could control the flow of water through holes in the bucket's base. The bucket was empty when I went in to investigate. One had to ask at reception before using the shower, and each person was allowed to use only one bucketful. We took turns refreshing ourselves and then bought some cold drinking water. Afterwards, we drove on into the empty silence. Travelling through this desert made me feel isolated and insignificant. I had the persistent, nagging feeling that the center of

I wandered down a wadi which the Israelites may have traversed. | *M Rawicz Trip Photo*

the desert was travelling with us and that we would never escape from it. Crossing the immense Ard-as-Sawwan Desert was no mere Sunday afternoon jaunt.

I spotted a wadi which seemed the type along which the Israelites may have walked, as it had interesting vegetation, and I wanted to examine it. Youseph stopped the car patiently. "Please wait here for me, it's hot and I will be back very quickly," I said, as I set off. I walked for about a hundred meters. Suddenly, it struck me that if Youseph and Makki had for some reason decided to drive off, I would have been left alone in the middle of nowhere. I experienced a moment of panic and turned around to go back.

Perhaps Youseph sensed my anxiety, because I saw his car making its way towards me over the sand. It was bumping and lurching over the rutted surface, corrugations, pits and gullies, and soft sandy patches. The wheels bounced and the car came to a standstill in a ditch. Youseph emerged and said, "We have a puncture." He began to crank the car up on a jack. "I think something else has also been damaged," he moaned, as he slithered upside down into the space under the vehicle. "At least

I'm in shade here," he called. "You're going to roast up there!" Makki slipped under the car too.

The temperature was over forty degrees centigrade. The hot dry southerly Sirocco wind was blowing. I wondered what would become of us if we got caught in a sudden sandstorm. The vehicle repair process seemed painfully slow. Youseph was right; I was burning up in the heat and was starting to experience sunstroke. In desperation, I took a mattress out of the car and placed it on the sand. I lay down and threw bedding over myself to try and hide from the sun. A problem with a car in the desert immediately destroyed the sense of invulnerability that I may have felt as an occupant. Youseph and Makki took the better part of an hour to finish the repairs and by the end of it they were angry, hot, and sweaty. Youseph blew on his fingers, which had blistered from working with the hot car parts. At last we were ready to set off once more. Behind us, we left a churned-up mess of footprints and tire marks, which bore witness to how easily the desert could swallow up people who momentarily lapsed into over-confidence.

My guides were also a stimulus for my spiritual growth, as I practiced staying calm while they were provocatively angry.

Many more boring, flat, and featureless kilometers passed. Suddenly, a curious rock became visible, pocked and shattered like broken nutshells by the constant hammering of fire and ice throughout the desert days and nights. I was hungry.

"Let's stop and get the food out," I said. "I wish there was a river we could picnic beside."

Youseph replied, "I've got an even better idea. If there was a river nearby, we could get right into the water and eat our lunch there!"

The route that the Israelites took must have approached Lejjun via the Lejjun tributary that eventually joins Wadi Mujib. Along the way, we gradually began to see signs of previous habitation, including ruins of desert castles. Their presence added to the sense of forlorn emptiness. Such castles were built by the Umayyads between 661 and 750 CE during an era when Muslim Arabs had succeeded in transforming the fringes of the desert into watered settlements. We passed by two castles.

Youseph explained, "You can see castles like the strange Qasr Kharanah and a Roman fort that was changed into an Umayade palace at Qasr-el-Hallabat. Further north, there is a massive brick vaulted castle called Qasr Mushatta, which was so large it was never completed.

It is thought to have been commissioned by Caliph Al-Walid II whose reign was too short to have completed it before the Abbasid dynasty came to power and moved the capital from Damascus. There's also a black basalt medieval Islamic fort at Azraq, and a huge fire-baked brick fort called Qasr Tuba that was also unfinished. Some of the castles have Arabic names that might seem strange to you, like Mahattat Suwaqa, Al- Muwaggar, and Hammam Assarah. They were built in the Ottoman times."[23]

I commented, "These castles were built long after the Israelites passed through here, so they wouldn't have seen them. They are not of major relevance to me now."

Many more kilometers of depressing barrenness followed. The teaching of the camp of Iyay Ha'avarim helped me, as I realized that feeling disconnected and lost in this environment could be counteracted by making an effort to find purpose even under such desolate conditions.

Makki had fallen asleep. Out of the blue, Youseph said:

"You know, I really like women very much. It would be nice to have many in my life."

My heart missed a beat. "What are you taking about?" I thought. There we were, far from civilization, and my guide was talking about "having" women. I felt vulnerable. What on earth would I do if he decided I was his next target? He rambled on about his love of women.

Eventually, I turned to him and said as assertively as I could, "Youseph, my religious beliefs forbid a woman to touch any man other than her husband. Will you please stop talking to me about a way of life that is totally out of keeping with mine?"

He fell silent. After a long while, he looked at me meekly and apologized profusely.

He added, "You have taught me something. I will try to act with better morality in my own life also."

I was surprised by his comment but breathed a sigh of relief. We drove on without speaking further.

We eventually arrived at the upper reaches of Wadi Mujib, the Arnon River of the Bible. The wadi plunges to the banks of the river below and carves a massive valley for some twenty-five kilometers, down to the Dead Sea. This had been an important boundary between the Edomite and the Moabite territories. We stopped to view the landscape from a bridge where the valley was five kilometers wide and almost a kilometer deep. The canyon stretched westwards towards the Jordan River and some twenty kilometers eastwards toward the inlands of Jordan. I stared down at the valley with a sense of awe, thinking that this would be a terrible place from which to fall. I clung tightly to the rails. The valley's steep sides were covered in dense vegetation, and the river flowing along its floor was barely visible. The enormity of the Arnon Valley was breathtaking.

Historically, this valley also played a significant role. I could visualize the Moabites and Amorites clashing along its banks. At this site, a tremendous miracle had taken place. According to the Midrash, the Amorites had hidden themselves in the caves high up in the mountains, waiting to dislodge huge boulders that would crash down on the Israelites as they ventured into the valley. However, as the Amorites waited, G-d caused the mountainsides to cave in, and it was the Amorites who were crushed to death instead. I scanned the horizon with my binoculars to see if there were any ancient burial sites, but nothing obvious stood out. Today, the Jordanian army maintains a military camp in the area.

I wandered over to a makeshift coffee shop at the roadside, set up by an enterprising young man. I asked him if he knew of any burial grounds in the area.

He pointed to the valley and said, "There are two cemeteries in this valley, both about 2,000 years old. They're near the river, where the water flows."

Not long before my visit, a dam wall had been completed and now formed a large lake. I admired the incredible view and could see why this valley had formed a natural boundary between two opposing nations.

In the Bible, the route is described in Numbers 21:13–15 as: "They pitched . . . on the other side of Arnon . . . [at] the stream of the brooks that goes down to the dwelling of Ar, and lies upon the border of Moab from the other side of Arnon." The Arnon is widely acknowledged as Wadi-al-Mujib.[24] We followed one of the routes recommended by an archaeologist to get to a village where Wadi-al-Lejjun flows into Wadi-al-Mujib. On the river banks I saw an agricultural settlement that might have been Ar,[25] but I could not identify any significant archaeological features.

The Israelites had conquered all the lands of the Amorites, including villages and cities, when they came out of Egypt. Nations that came out to them with swords and would not allow them to pass peacefully were met with battle. Echoes of these vicious battles and the conquests of the Israelites under the guardianship of G-d seemed to rise up from the ground itself, and I could visualize the clashing of swords and throwing of spears as the Israelites mowed down the huge armies that attacked them. I could also imagine their cries of victory. I felt proud of their success, especially because the people had picked themselves up after a generation of miserable slavery and had built up a powerful army to defend themselves against oppressors.

Next we proceeded to search for Beer, "the well of which G-d spoke to Moses."[26] A wadi called Wadi-ath-Thamad has been suggested as the possible location, but because Beer means "well" it might have been any one of the wells in this entire region. Bearing this in mind, we abandoned the search fairly soon.[27] I decided that we should move on to look for the next place mentioned, Mattanah. The route took us into a bleak, sandy desert with an eerily howling wind which blew sand into the jeep. For two kilometers we followed a wadi along which only tiny, scrawny bushes grew. We were by now midway between the ancient Desert Highway, which is the modern R15 route, and the King's Highway, which is next to the modern R35.

The chain of events that followed would have seriously tested the resilience of even the hardiest of trekkers. Initially, the ground of the wadi was reasonably solid, but the sand became steadily looser and more difficult to navigate. To make matters worse, a little sandstorm had obliterated any tracks made by vehicles travelling earlier. Suddenly Youseph's jeep came to rest with a soft crunch which sounded from beneath the car. The wheels had left solid ground and were buried deep in the sand. As Youseph tried to pull off again, the rear wheels spun powerlessly.

"We need to dig the car out," Youseph apologized. "We will also have to take everything out of the car so that there is a better chance of getting out of the sand."

We had no spade. Makki and I started by emptying the car, and then we sat down, beside the rear wheels, and started digging the sand with tin plates used for our meals. The feeling of being forsaken in this desolate, uninhabited desert was eerie, to say the least. Every time I felt panic rising, I called to mind the teaching from the camp of Rephadim, where the Israelites had experienced a crisis of faith at having no water. I tried to muster up my faith that we would somehow get out of the current situation intact. I tried to feel more secure within myself in this rather desperate moment.

The heat became suffocating as it wrapped itself around me like a huge unwelcome electric blanket. The desert can exert a strange influence in moments like these, prompting one to take ill-advised action which could prove fatal. My skin was burning in the heat, and I was starting to think in a completely illogical way. I was imagining unrealistic ways of handling the problem, like just pushing it forwards. But finally, we had removed enough sand and through a combined effort, freed the jeep.

"It will be fine," said Youseph, turning the wheel.

We were exhausted and dripping with sweat, but still had to reload the car before we could go on.

I could completely understand that the Israelites had become weary, felt that they had been wandering aimlessly and endlessly. Having gone through the Eastern Desert I also felt at times that time passes and we were going nowhere. I could really empathize with their feelings of being lost, having no confidence, hope or a sense of a future. I could easily grasp that they had felt that they were just drifting and were defeated with no purpose.

BATTLES OF KINGS

By now we were well into the territory that had been ruled by the biblical Sihon, King of the Amorites, who would not let the Israelites pass through his lands but had "gathered all his people together, and went out against Israel into the wilderness."[28] He had brought his army to Jahaz and had initiated a battle in which the Israelites had "smote him with the edge of the sword, and possessed his land from Arnon to Jabbok."

We stopped to look at a gigantic sand dune on which a large structure, using rectangular blocks hewn out of desert stone, had been built in ancient times. The structure was approximately twenty-five meters long and stood two meters high. Small dark-green bushes were visible growing out of the cracks between the stones. This site had once been Khirbat-al-Mudayna, a Moabite city, one of a series of fortified sites along Wadi-ath-Thamad on the southern side of the Madaba Plateau.[29] Several archaeologists have said that this is the possible site of Jahaz, where the Israelites conquered Sihon the Amorite. Professor Michèle Daviau, who excavated here in 1999, said that the site was similar to others from the Iron Age, having a fortified wall and a six-chambered gate complex. The excavators were amazed to find a small temple with limestone altars, a limestone statue, and several objects depicting a person's high status. They also found some buildings used for making textiles in which there were remnants of yarn, loom weights, and textile tools.[30]

Daviau had found an ancient house dating back to roughly 600 BCE. In a large domestic area, he found many fascinating objects including three small black earthenware vessels, one of which had triangles carved into it. There were also three cosmetic containers and their mortar; two faience bottles; two alabaster vessels; one basalt bowl. The alabaster and faience containers had the influence of Egypt and Assyria, the two superpowers in the region at that time. Other unusual objects were found in the same room, including a forty-centimeter high statue of a man, with red paint preserved on his left leg and hands. These objects may have come from Egypt or Phoenicia. Such rare relics have not been found anywhere else in Jordan, and are today displayed at the archaeological museum in the nearby town of Madaba.

Daviau[31] also found a Neolithic village, a Nabataean villa, and an early Roman-period reservoir in the surrounding region. It seems possible that Wadi-ath-Thamad might have provided a west-to-east route link between the two major north–south axes of the ancient Desert Highway and the King's Highway. Traders moving between the west and east might have been responsible for the foreign influences represented by the rare objects found.

Apparently, few tourists visit this area and we were lucky to have found it. I was spellbound to have come across a site alleged to be of such significance in biblical history. The Israelites would have fought their memorable battle here; for the duration of my visit, the sounds of their fighting and eventual triumph echoed through my mind.

"And from Mattanah the children of Israel went to Nahaliel."[32]

In Hebrew, *Nahaliel* means "valley of G-d," which has led several archaeologists[33] to identify the site as a spring in the upper reaches of the Arnon River. The distance between Mattanah to Nahaliel was approximately ten kilometers, thus the Israelites could have reached Nahaliel by walking along the convoluted wadi.

When we arrived at Nahaliel, I was astounded to see hot mineral springs gushing forth. We had arrived at Wadi Zarqa Ma'in via a dry, hot desert road, and the presence of the abundant springs seemed quite miraculous. By now, I was also feeling excited and fulfilled at having personally seen so much of the land described in the Bible. I had driven along the very road referred to in the words, "Israel sent messengers unto Sihon, king of the Amorites, saying . . . we will not turn into the fields, or into the vineyards; we will not drink of the waters of the well: but we will go along by the king's highway."[34] I had also visited the fortified desert city from which Sihon had fought against Israel, at Jahaz, and where Israel had taken his land extending from Arnon to Jabbok and to Ammon. I had passed through the region of Ar and the mighty Arnon-Wadi Mujib and seen the area where Israel had taken all the cities of the Amorites, including Heshbon, and all the villages.

I looked forward with great anticipation to journey on through lands where people's blood had drenched the ground as the Israelites had conquered the kings of city states demarcated by high walls, as well as numerous local unwalled towns. This was a section of the exodus in which the Israelites had been victorious against powerful enemies and which is mentioned in the Jewish daily prayers. I hoped to pass Heshbon, Dibon, the biblical Chemosh, Nophah, land of the mighty King Og of Bashan, the land of the Amorites and the Edrei battlefield.[35]

Clearly, the Israelites had been helped by G-d not only during their journey but also in conquering the Moabites, Amorites, and Ammonites, and acquiring land that had once belonged to these ancient peoples.

The Israelites, by this time, had gone through the stage of life's cycle when age with its infirmities and loss had taught them lessons. They had developed even greater sensitivity to transform dark experiences into light experiences. They had improved more in their ability to embrace human beings and give love. They found mature strength and aging had brought opportunities to guide and inspire the next generation. They had accessed the power to handle disease and death and appreciate the value of health and life as a gift that should not be taken for granted. They had become more deeply connected in life, even in conditions that appeared to be meaningless.

I had gained further insight into the life stage of age with its infirmities and loss. I was learning to transform my own dark experiences into light. I looked forward to embracing all human beings and to loving people more. I anticipated that I might also guide or inspire others. I hoped that I was on a pathway of transforming my life with clarity, optimism and joy, even when confronted by negative experiences. I wanted to sanctify G-d's name in times of light and dark circumstances.

The Israelites had now completed the stage of life's cycle equivalent to old age and were about to experience the equivalent of great old age, a stage preceding death.[36]

Chapter 9

Bloody Battles: Camps 39–42

MOSQUES AND FLOWERS - DIBONGAD CAMP 39

"They left Iyay Ha'avarim and camped at Dibongad."[1] *Gad* means "good fortune" and *Dibongad* means "the place of fortune."[2] I hoped that this next campsite would be interesting, as it was not situated at a wadi, oasis, tel, mountain spring, or ancient mining site.

We arrived at the modern town of Dhiban, the place referred to in the Bible as Dibongad. Its position on the King's Highway, in part, explains why settlements have repeatedly been built at this location over the centuries. I had read that Dibon/Dhiban had been occupied intermittently over the last five millennia.

Today, the town has a thriving community of approximately 15,000 people. I anticipated some difficulty in identifying exactly where the Israelites would have lived, as the town contains numerous diverse features such as new suburbs and commercial areas. The town had developed hugely over the millennia and I had no idea whether there were any ancient remains. We entered the town's main road from the outskirts, and I began searching for signs of any tel. In the distance, down one of the side streets, I caught a glimpse of what looked like a large, rocky hill. I asked Youseph to drive us closer. As we approached, I saw some remnants of walls indicating a tel. I became excited at the possibility that I might have come upon the mound of the ancient ruins of the location of Dibongad so soon.

At the end of the little road, we drove onto a field where Youseph parked. Goats were grazing, a young boy sat on a donkey, and three young children were playing with a soccer ball. On the edges of the field were family homes. The children joined me enthusiastically to explore the tel. Having the children accompany me and listening to their chatter, made me miss my own family.

I explored the excavated parts of the tel. Carefully I stepped into a deep, wide pit, and then gingerly made my way down the slope, hoping that the soil would not give way beneath my feet. The pit led into a large cavern that may have been a room in some bygone era. I stooped low to enter it. The place was dark, but I could make out an opening at the far end. As I stood peering into the dimness, to my utter astonishment I heard a cell phone ringing from deep inside the room.

I called out in surprise, "Hey, hello hello."

A young teenager crawled out, looking sheepish. He had some blue and white beads in one hand, and a sifter in the other. He guiltily put out his hand and pointed to some beads that he had just dug up. I was interested in examining the beads. My impression was that it was a local game to dig up artifacts from the ruins. I shook my head and said "no" to indicate that he should not tamper with archaeological artifacts. I felt disconcerted that the children should casually rummage through this potentially historically valuable site that an archaeologist might want to still investigate.

Inside the cavern there were some sheep bones, perhaps left over from a recent barbeque and discarded as trash. When I emerged from the cavern, the children were waiting for me and happily accompanied me out. I then saw a noticeboard providing some archaeological information. This was indeed the site of the ancient Dibongad!

In 1868, the Mesha Inscription was found at Dibongad. This was a stone which bore carvings in an early script very similar to Hebrew, inscriptions which validated the existence of King David in its reference to the "House of David." This stela also connected Dhiban with the biblical Dibon and revealed that Dibongad had been the capital of Mesha, a prominent Iron Age Moabite kingdom. The Moabite king subsequently expelled the Israelites, who had previously captured the city.[3] The defeat of Dibongad had caused huge bloodshed.[4] After reclaiming the area, the Moabite king rebuilt ancient Dibongad as an important settlement, and enlarged it. The new architectural features included a grand citadel, monumental city walls, towers, and gates. He restored the town's water supply and required every household to have its own cistern. He also built a palace for himself and an altar for his god Chemosh.

I was thrilled to explore the huge tel of Dhiban. | *M Rawicz Trip Photo*

As the news of this discovery spread, a steady trickle of research-ers, visitors, tourists, and scholars began to arrive in Dhibon.[5] In the mid-twentieth century, archaeologists continued with excavations on the fifteen-hectare tel which unearthed structures from the Early Bronze Age (third millennium BCE), parts of a Moabite fortress from the Iron Age (ninth century BCE), a Nabataean temple, Roman fortifi-

At a large cavern children were searching for archeological remains. |
M Rawicz Trip Photo

Ancient Dibongad included a grand citadel, monumental city walls, towers, and gates and
many other city features. | M Rawicz Trip Photo

cations with a tower, a Byzantine church, and Islamic settlements.[6] The fascinating history from Moabite times through the sixteenth century has been revealed.[7] It is still a vibrant, active archaeological dig site.[8] Throughout its long history, the town has been a center for agricultural and pastoral activities and was well known for its farming of sheep, goats, wheat, and barley. Excavations indicated that crafts were also important, various waves of residents having produced objects in ceramic, stone, metal, and glass.

Once again, I heard the clashing of swords, the jangling of shields and cries of the defeated inhabitants as the Israelites stormed the city and vanquished it. I saw brave, strong men, the descendants of those who had died in the desert. The bearers of the banners of the twelve tribes and the Levites carrying the Ark of the Covenant were marching with confidence as G-d helped them vanquish everything "from Heshbon even unto Dibon."

I was thrilled to have found this well-preserved site that had been located on the Exodus route – and I had even interacted with some of the modern-day locals. But as I climbed into the car, I saw that Youseph was sitting there with a deep frown.

"What's the matter?" I asked.

"The police came," he said. "They asked what you are doing, and if you have permission to be here. One of the neighbors had phoned them. It took a lot of persuading from me to convince them that they had nothing to worry about."

At first I was shocked, as I took it as malice from the neighbors to call the police, but then I focused on the fact that we were just passing by and were leaving. I quickly forgot about the incident as we continued our journey.

⬕ Good fortune, celebration and charity

According to Jacobson, the Israelites had survived the harsh desert condition from the last section of their journey and were in a mood of rejoicing.[9] In addition, the word "gad" refers to a charitable outlook on life when people support those who do not have and are in an unfortunate, poverty-stricken state. This benevolent outlook makes not only the giver but also the recipient happy.

There are times in a person's life when they have gone through difficulties, such as lack of money, health, good fortune or have endured great difficulties. When this stage is over and they see that they are "out of the woods," there is cause for celebration. This is what happened at Dibongad, as presented by Jacobson.[10]

Times of difficulty are stressful but as we overcome the challenges we learn new skills, acquire new character traits and prevail. This also is cause for celebration.

At Dibongad, the Israelites had truly found a place of fortune. They had coped with the terrible Eastern Desert and recognized the importance of acknowledging the blessings of good fortune. They recognized the gifts that are acquired in life.

I, too, had enjoyed the feeling of being again in a really positive environment, and had enjoyed the feeling of emerging from the desert and re-entering city life. I felt a great sense of gratitude for the gift of life, and acknowledgment of the many wonderful things that constantly sustain me.

By now the Israelites were at a stage of life equivalent to approaching the end, close to death and what lay beyond death.[11]

Youseph asked me if I minded going to visit some of his family that lived in the area, especially since Makki had not seen them for a long time. I was delighted. We were shown into a modest home on a small side street. The lady of the household, Hala, was his aunt. She offered me some tea. It was the best I had ever tasted. Hala, it turned out had won the accolade of making the best tasting tea at an international commercial fair held in a large European town. She would not tell me her secret recipe however. Hala pleaded with us to stay overnight. Youseph could share a room with one of his family members and I could have the guest room. We had been through a tough day in the desert and gratefully accepted her offer.

As a guest in her home, and while enjoying her hospitality, I recalled the teaching of Dibongad and felt grateful for my good fortune and pleasure. These were particularly welcome gifts after our rough and long journey through the barrenness of the wilderness.

After a quiet night, we arose early in the morning to a pleasant breakfast of delicious fruit. Then we headed back to the center of town. After the endless silence of the desert we were assaulted by the noisy traffic, vehicles trying to pass around the scene of a car accident, and police and traffic officers trying to deal with the congestion. There were

I was introduced to a local family in Dhiban. | M Rawicz Trip Photo

squeals of tires, horns, roaring motors, exhaust fumes, and sudden braking as drivers swerved to avoid the pile-up. Above the general din came the sound, from first one loudspeaker, then another, and then more, of a muezzin calling people to morning prayer. Just as suddenly as it had started, all the noise calmed down.

We made our way further into Dhiban, which was abuzz with activity. Shops lined the main road and everywhere people were going about their business as they had for centuries. Fumes from the traffic mixed with the more ancient odor of farm animals, making for a curious atmosphere. Donkeys and camels, laden with villagers and merchandise, drank from water containers. Most fare, appealing to either a cityslicker or a country bumpkin, was on sale here. There were plastic chairs, braziers, kettles, pans for frying *falafel* and *kibbeh*, crates of *pita*, pots of *hummus*, olives and pickles, and shelves lined with cigarettes, lighters, tins of meat and beans, oranges, avocados, and tomatoes. Men sat around small cafés, chatting. Further on, we passed some children running out of front doors to play in the street. On the front porch of a house, a young girl was kneeling in front of an old woman so that her

It was a delight to see the colourful market stall at Dhiban. | *M Rawicz Trip Photo*

long hair could be plaited and oiled. It was Thursday and many women were shopping. People were getting ready for the *Jumu'ah* midday prayer on Friday. Outside the local mosque, white-robed men sat in the shade of the trees and studied the Koran. I respected their devotion.

FLOWERS AND FRUITS

We drove beyond the town's limits into a green and lush landscape with fields of wheat and vegetables and meadows full of grazing cows, goats, and sheep. The open fields had either been cultivated or were covered with beautiful, yellow wild flowers as far as the eye could see. As I gazed at the scenery, I thought of Ruth the Moabite. This had been her homeland before she loyally followed Naomi, her mother-in-law, into Israel. The fertility, productivity, and lushness around Dibongad provided such a contrast to the desert we had recently emerged from, that the change seemed almost unbelievable.

The villages of white houses with red tiled roofs seemed pinned to the hilltop, creating a picture of uniform cubes and blocks. Satellite dishes were visible on many homes and the side of a steep hill was terraced and dotted with olive trees. In the valley of a tributary of the distant Jordan River, shrubs and shoots were green and plentiful, grass and

weeds sprouted from the banks, and livestock munched on the plants
in easy contentment. The sun was deliciously warm rather than blazing
hot. The entire scene was so idyllic and most inviting that I decided to
go for a walk to get a better feel for the surroundings.

I found a sheep track that broadened into a lane and followed it up
a gently rising hill. Leaving the lane, I proceeded upwards and quickly
found myself on a narrow trail, wide enough for only one step at a time.
The path weaved between the bushes and jagged rocks. Half an hour
later I reached the top and saw the brow of yet another rise.

There were endless kilometers of incredibly rich agricultural lands
bearing crops and vineyards. I understood why Moses had tried to persuade the Edomite king to allow access to this highway by agreeing not
to encroach on the fields or vineyards.

Then, unexpectedly, the benign atmosphere shifted as the sky turned
from light-blue to a mass of low, dark clouds and the wind gathered
strength. The grass was swept low against the land, and the barley
plants twisted and rustled as the storm approached. Before I had time
to make my way back to the car, the rain started falling and quickly
became a deluge. I hurried to a large olive tree for shelter and waited
there for the storm to pass. Despite being soaked to the skin, all I could
think of was what a blessing the rain was, and how different this area
was from the desert.

Dhiban city was abuzz with activity. | *M Rawicz Trip Photo*

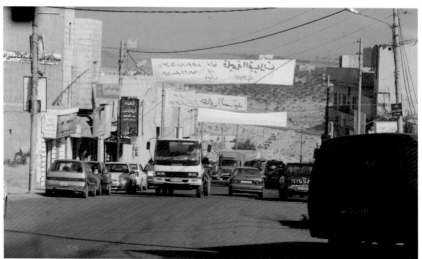

As we left, I wrote in my log book: "Dibongad. This tel was unique in that the Israelites lived here after the Exodus period. The place also shows evidence of all the levels of intermittent occupation over the last five millennia. Its uniqueness is the fact that it has extensive very fertile agricultural surroundings, showing that we were in Moabite territory. The tel is in the middle of the vibrant modern-day town of the same name."

We were ready to explore the next camp.

ALMONDS AND KINGS' BATTLES – ALMON DIVLATHAYMAH

CAMP 40

"And they removed from Dibongad, and encamped in Almon Divlathaymah. And they removed from Almon Divlathaymah, and pitched in the mountains of Abarim, before Nebo."[1]

Almon divlathaymah means "cake of pressed figs" or "double cake of figs." This sounded quite different from what I had become used to searching for, no wells or ruins. The phrase evoked more positive associations than many of the earlier camps. *Almon divlathaymah* can also be translated as "hidden sweetness," and one interpretation gives the meaning of this camp's name as "the place where the well was concealed from them because they forsook the words of the Torah law, which is compared to sweet pressed figs."[2] Some scholars say that this place had many streams where chestnuts and figs grew.[3] The idea of figs seemed an enticing interpretation and added to my sense of anticipation.

We continued in the footsteps of my forebears as we went further northwards. In the distance, the hills rolled in curves under a never-ending sky. I was amazed at the beauty and stared in awe, and I just wanted to be still and enjoy the landscape. I asked Youseph to stop the car and I found a cluster of rocks where I could sit for a moment to relish the sight of the flowers which I thought looked like buttercups. Their stems yielded in the soft breeze and their little petals fluttered and twisted gently. Beside me, a single flower shuddered as gentle gusts of wind rippled the grass, and I sat happily whiling away ten minutes watching the field and its fragile beauty, thinking of nothing, engrossed in the breeze and the yellow flowers that seemed to go on and on. I shut my eyes, breathing in air laden with the fresh smell of soil and grass. The joyfulness and fruitfulness of this environment was just wonderful after the enormously harsh desert.

Youseph began to sing some Jordanian songs. I managed to grasp the tune and some of the words. In this happy atmosphere we drove north towards the major town of Madaba. Ten kilometers before Madaba, we came to a settlement surrounded by agricultural lands, including groves of fig trees. The place was called Khirbat ad-Deleilat al-Gharbiyeh. I recalled reading that Almon Divlathaymah[4] might have been located close to the modern-day towns of Khirbat-ad-Deleilat al-Gharbiyya and Khirbat-ad-Deleilat ash-Shargiyya.

We stopped to ask for directions, first from an old man and then from a teenager, and finally a middle-aged man walking along the road. Each time, we were directed to the eastern edge of the settlement where we were told we would find some old stone structures. To my utter surprise and delight we found the remains of an enormous ancient town. The ruins stood within a vast field that now was surrounded by modern homes. I saw enormous piles of stones and rubble, and several ancient stone doorways still standing, some arched and some square.

I walked towards the ruins, wanting to explore them. Suddenly, a truck pulled up next to me and two tall, strong Jordanian men stepped out and hurried towards me, addressing me in Arabic. I was taken aback and wondered whether I was once again contravening a local convention. Youseph quickly came to my side.

The men turned to him, and without asking any other questions, said:

"Would you like to come and have tea with us? We live nearby. Welcome to the neighborhood!"

Youseph translated for me, and my initial reaction of surprise was quickly followed by delight at their positive attitude. It was a contrast to the neighbours at Dhiban. We thanked them but did not go as we had lots to do.

I had imagined that Almon Divlathaymah (Almon diblathaim)was only a small center but we were looking at the remains of a huge town. It had an important history in the Israelites' conquests during the Exodus.

We were standing at the site on the way that the Israelites had "gone up by the way of Bashan"[5] to where "Og the king of Bashan who lived in Ashtaroth and Edrei"[6] had dwelt; where Og, as Amorite king, had set out to do battle against the Israelites; where "The Israelites had smitten him, his sons, and all his people, until there were none left alive. Then they possessed his land."[7] The Bible narrates that the Israelites had

I wandered through the remains of an enormous ancient town at Almon Divalthaymah. |
M Rawicz Trip Photo

"laid them waste even to Nophah, which reaches to Madaba,"[8] and that
they had also defeated Sihon, the king of the Amorites, who lived in
Heshbon.

Indeed, several archeologists believe that this was on the route that
the Israelites took to their victorious conquest over King Og of Bashan.[9]

I spent a couple of hours exploring the fascinating ruins and even
discovered that figs really do grow in the area.

⬛ Transcending loneliness – feeling connected to G-d

I thought about the meaning of Almon Divlathaymah. The literal
interpretations of "cake of pressed figs" and "double cake of figs" as
well as the connotation of "hidden sweetness" all made immediate
sense. In addition to the beauty of the area, the fields were productive and even today still yielded chestnuts and figs. But at a deeper
level, Almon Divlathaymah means a state of concealment.

Jacobson discusses the idea that when we feel all alone it is just
a result of our misperception. The fact that we cannot literally see
G-d, does not mean that He is not with us. He is in concealment. In

I spent a couple of hours exploring the fascinating ruins with various chambers. |
M Rawicz Trip Photo

It was interesting to examine the ruins in the vicinity where Og king of Bashan and Sihon
king of the Amorites had passed. | *M Rawicz Trip Photo*

*A huge stone, which was used possibly for grinding wheat, still lay on the ground. |
M Rawicz Trip Photo*

fact, He is always with us and therefore we are not alone.[10]

At times a person may have endeavored to reach a goal for a very long time. It is possible that even when they are nearly there or have almost achieved what they want, they lose faith that they will never see the end. They could be misled by their own misperceptions and become depressed and gloomy. Their state of mind hides the endpoint journey or the achievement of the goal. In such a situation one should attempt to continue to believe that it is achievable and stay committed. Even if it seems implausible, one should still apply one's efforts and hope that in the bigger picture things will materialize for the best. It is possible that if this attitude is adopted, the person will be able to access more resources and will eventually receive the final reward. Through faith they will press onward and achieve what they set out to accomplish.

This camp addresses the great challenge that the Israelites faced toward the latter stages of their journey. Here they had to fight battles against a few powerful kings. They had to access their resources, resist fear, keep their faith intact to prevail, overcome any sense of being alone, avoid being distressed, and make sure that they prayed for success to continue until the end. This stage of their journey was equivalent to advancing age, as I understood from Jacobson's explanation.[11] This is possibly a state of mind that people of advanced age also have to deal with. With a positive attitude we can bring more goodness into the world, according to the sage Arizal.[12]

I thought I am also never alone as G-d is also helping me all the way. This gave me enormous inner strength and a wonderful serenity that has stayed with me since.

The experience of enjoying the field of flowers, and now witnessing the productive town, showed me that at the end of a long desert trip there was a sweet ending. I now fully appreciated the meaning of the camp. However, the less obvious interpretation of the name – "the place where the well was concealed from them because they forsook the words of the Torah law which is compared to sweet pressed figs" – remained unclear to me.

We left Almon Divlathaymah, and continued retracing the Israelites journey along the King's Highway.

After travelling for seven kilometers, we approached the ancient and yet still very vibrant town of Madaba which is mentioned in the Bible in the narrative of the Israelites' conquest of Sihon, the king of the Amorites. The Israelites took over the land as far as the town of Madaba, and I decided to make a short detour to visit this biblical site.

Youseph explained that the town is famous for its mosaics, and attracts many tourists. "I will take you to see something called The Map of Madaba," he said. "It's in one of the buildings where they found the best ancient mosaic."

Entering a small building, we met Salsabeel, a tour guide who offered to show us around. He explained, "This town has a very long history and was once a Moabite border city. It dates back to the Middle Bronze Age, and has been inhabited continuously ever since that time. The Ammonites conquered Madaba in 165 BCE and later gave the city to the Nabataeans. Eventually, it became a Roman provincial town."

"I'd like to hear about the mosaics," I said.

"In 1896, Giuseppe Manfred discovered a magnificent map from the sixth century, probably about 560 CE. The map was made out of two million pieces of colored mosaics that had been almost perfectly preserved. The town has been famous for its mosaics since then."

The ancient and yet vibrant town of Madaba still keeps its name from Biblical days. |
M Rawicz Trip Photo

We walked into a room where the map was on display. It covered the entire floor, and showed the world as it had once been, extending all the way from Egypt to Asia. Individual features – hills and valleys, villages and towns, roads and waterways – were clearly depicted in small pieces of mosaic.

Salsabeel continued, "This map is an important link in the archaeological understanding of the geography of biblical times. The mosaic was originally composed of over 2.5 million pieces, and measured a staggering twenty-five meters by five meters. Historians have been able to get an understanding of what the region looked like and have correlated what the map shows with other sources and findings. All of this has vastly improved our knowledge of history."

Madaba has been called the "City of Mosaics." Hundreds of mosaics have been found here and are now being carefully preserved. In addition to the building that Salsabeel showed us, a 3,000-year-old Iron Age temple was discovered in 2010 at Khirbat Ataroz, which is near Madaba.[13] Today it houses several figurines of ancient deities and cir-

The famous ancient Madaba mosaic map shows the layout from Egypt to Asia. |
M Rawicz Trip Photo

cular clay vessels that were used in Moabite religious rituals, and has contributed to Madaba being a key tourist destination in Jordan. Every year, hundreds of international visitors flock to these sites.

I gazed at the mosaic map for a full hour, taking in every detail of Israel and its surrounds. I was interested to see how the people of old had viewed their world, compared with the extremely accurate maps of today. Their understanding of borders and the orientation of countries relative to each other was obviously less realistic than modern knowledge allows, but I could identify many places that still exist. Seeing this map certainly added to the richness of my trip.

The next station that the Israelites passed was Bamoth. "And from Nahaliel the children of Israel went to Bamoth."[14]

This place is thought to be either a village called the Dolmen sites, or the villages of Khirbat-al-Queiqiyeh and Maslubiye, which contain ancient sacred sites.[15] These two villages are situated roughly five kilometers from Madaba on the road running northwest towards Mount Nebo, near the village of Mukhayat. No distinguishing features caught my attention as we drove through a flat area with a multitude of farms that produce citrus, tomatoes, cucumbers, olives, strawberries, and pitted soft fruits. Sheep, poultry, and dairy cattle are also farmed. This region clearly forms part of the "breadbasket" of modern Jordan.

MOSES' SANCTUARY – ABARIM   CAMP 41

"And from Bamoth in the valley, that is in the country of Moab, [they journeyed] to the top of Pisgah, which looked toward Jeshimon."[1] I had read that the Israelites left the direction of "Almon Divlathaymah and camped in the Abarim camp in front of Nebo."[2]

Abarim[3] can be translated as "heights beyond" or "distant heights."[4] The mountains of Abarim are widely thought to have been the mountain range along the Dead Sea, extending possibly as far as the Arabian Desert in the south.[5] In biblical times, these mountains fell into the northern Moabite territory (now known as Pisgah) and the southern Ammonite territory to the north of Heshbon. G-d told Moses to go up this mountain in the Abarim Range.[6] Mount Nebo is one of the highest peaks, and from here Moses viewed the Promised Land.[7]

After traversing the attractive rolling hills of the territory of Moab, we passed a village called Faysaliyah, roughly seven kilometers west of Madaba. We headed for Nebo, which had been visited as early as 325 CE as a pilgrimage site.[8] The actual Mount Nebo was six kilometers further, a significant Iron Age ruin in the Mount Nebo region. It is described in the Mesha Inscription as a city in Moab that Israel had once occupied, and is known to have been a desert village in the fifth century CE.[9] A short distance away we arrived at the Peaks of Siyagha which is part of the majestic Abarim mountain range. Ras-es-Siyagha was visible, towering to a height of 710 meters. To its west, I spotted an even higher peak at 790 meters, called el-Mukhayyat or the famous Mount Nebo.

These mountains are celebrated as the place where Moses spent his last days, as described in moving words in Deuteronomy. According to the scriptures, G-d instructed Moses to ascend the Abarim Mountains and go up Mount Nebo. There, before he died, he was to look out over the stretch of land that G-d was about to give the Israelites as their inheritance. The Bible narrative states "And Moses went up from the plains of Moab to Mount Nebo, to the top of Pisgah which is opposite Jericho"[10] so that he could prepare to die." After he died, his body "was buried in Moab, in the valley opposite Beth-peor," which has long been

The view of Mount Nebo from a distance. | M Rawicz Trip Photo

associated with the site known today as Ayun Musa (Springs of Moses), a small lush valley northeast of Mount Nebo. The exact location of his tomb remains unknown to this day.

As I gazed at Mount Pisgah, I thought about the biblical account of the Moabite King Balak who had sent Balaam, a prophet, to curse the Israelites. According to the Babylonian Talmud,[11] Balaam's advice was to "ensnare the children of Israel" by using their preference for linen against them. They were trapped by old women selling linen outside tents, but would then be lured by younger women who were prostitutes. After a time the men would be drunk and succumb to having sex and bowing to a foreign god. In the same narrative a man and a woman had fornicated in front of the people of Israel and Phineas, an Israelite priest, killed them by piercing his spear through both of them.

We approached Mount Nebo from the south, driving up a gently spiralling road towards the upper levels. One had to walk the last stretch to the top along a broad paved path that was lined with pine trees. At the entrance to the Nebo site stood an impressive gate and a beige marble slab, shaped like one of the tablets on which the Ten Commandments

This is part of the view of the Promised Land that Moses saw from Mount Nebo. |
M Rawicz Trip Photo

had been inscribed. The stone tablet was standing upright and bore the words: "Mount Nebo, Memorial to Moses."

At the top of the mountain we arrived at an interesting structure, built in a modest yet elegant style and with an air of sanctity about it. At the far end of a large paved area stood a low wall with an imposing metal sculpture. This was a modern sculpture of Moses' staff with a serpent climbing it, symbolizing the bronze serpent created by Moses in the wilderness at Punon. It was similar to the symbol used in the Western world to designate the medical profession – which is itself based on Moses' serpentine sculpture. There was another slab of stone, into which a map had been carved to show the vista that Moses would have looked out over before his death, a panorama of cities, lakes, and regions in Israel. The stone map intrigued me, and since it was a very clear day, l sat down on the wall to check what I was seeing against the map.

In the distant south were the biblical deserts of Judea and Samaria, now known as the Negev. I could identify Hebron on the West Bank and

Bethlehem, and discern the single cone of Herod's fortress at Herodium. Looking straight ahead, I could make out the entire Dead Sea, the Qumran area, and Jericho. On the horizon were the towers and buildings of Jerusalem and the Mount of Olives. North of Jerusalem was Ramallah, and to the extreme north, the seas of Galilee and Tiberius were just visible. Moses had certainly seen most of the Promised Land from this lofty height and yet was forbidden from entering.

A group of religious tourists arrived and stood in a circle holding hands and singing psalms of praise. Listening to their voices and watching their expressions of religious zeal moved me profoundly, and I was reminded of the teachings of Makheloth on the state of unity that can be achieved when we feel connected to others. Together, we can serve a higher purpose.

After some time savoring the experience, I wandered over to the opposite side to see the Pisgah Mountains, the plains of Abarim, and the place from which Balaam had blessed the Jewish people instead of cursing them, when he said the words that G-d commanded him to say.

The view over Jordan includes the King's Highway that leads to the city of Karak at the top of the wadi that we had ascended in the Jordan Desert, and the distant sandy wastes of Saudi Arabia. To the north, the seven hills surrounding Amman were visible in the distance, as were the steep sides of the plateau of Hesban and the mountain of Mushaqar. I could also see a number of places that have interesting names such as Shunet Nimrin and some dams. The edges of the plateau and the hilly spurs were also visible.

Next, I entered the simple but beautiful, yellow stone Memorial Building of Moses. When I stepped inside I was surprised by the sanc-

Tourists come from all over the world to celebrate the life of Moses throughout the year. | M Rawicz Trip Photo

tity of the atmosphere. An official, Bashshar, dutifully offered to inform me about the building.

"The contents of two tombs that an archaeologist called Ripamonti found in the 1960s illustrate the history of Nebo during the Iron Age," he said.[12] "In the fourth century CE, this sanctuary was built to honor Moses – and it might have been built on the site of an even older structure.[13] Prior to that, the Pilgrim Egeria from the sixth century had seen "a slightly raised place about the size of a normal tomb," which was a representation of the fact that Moses died in this place.[14] In the sixth century, the building was enlarged, and many of the floor mosaics that are still visible date from that time. Not long afterwards the site became the heart of a large monastery and many pilgrims came to see it. That's how the place remained for nearly six centuries, and it thrived. However, by 1564 the site had been abandoned, and for several centuries it remained neglected. Finally, in 1993, it was purchased by Franciscan monks, who excavated and restored the area. As you see, today Mount Nebo is a popular stop for pilgrims and tourists."

Bashshar led me into the interior of the stone building. The simple roof was made of attractive wooden beams placed across pillars of various sizes that flanked the central aisle. Light streamed in through beautiful stained-glass windows with red, blue, and yellow patterns, and rows of wooden benches were arranged on either side of the aisle. On the floor were a few rows of reed mats adorned with magnificent pictures of red and blue peacocks.

Just inside the entrance, to the left, Bashshar pointed out a room containing an amazing mosaic on the floor, protected by a railing.

"It dates back to 531 CE and is in remarkably pristine condition, because another mosaic was laid over it just a few decades later, in 597. The underlying mosaic remained hidden for nearly 1,400 years. It was discovered in 1976 when the mosaic on top was removed for restoration. The second one now hangs on that wall at the back of the room."

The older mosaic showed a large square divided into four strips by a border with a chain-like design. The scenes showed men and animals, a shepherd fighting a lion, a soldier fighting a lioness, and two hunters on horseback defeating a bear and wild boar. Trees were also depicted in fine detail. Below this were pastoral scenes with a touch of the exotic: a shepherd watching his goat and sheep grazing in the shade of trees; an ostrich on a leash held by a dark-skinned man; and a boy holding the

Inside the Memorial Building of Moses one finds beautiful wooden beams, and stained-glass windows. | *M Rawicz Trip Photo*

leashes of a zebra and a spotted animal that looked much like a camel but represented a giraffe. I was captivated to see this rare art.[15]

We moved into an eastern room with a floor that was also decorated with a mosaic, this one depicting animals and flowers, with a rich multicolor geometrical frame running around the pictures. The western room was graced with geometrical motifs and an altar, above which were positioned two bulls and gazelles. In the far right-hand corner, I noticed a small mosaic bearing the greeting, "Peace to all."[16]

Bashshar continued to explain, "Six tombs of unknown people were found hollowed out from the natural rock beneath the mosaic-covered floor. Regarding the actual burial place of Moses, the valley in the region of ancient Moab, called Ayun-Musa, is considered the most likely place."

"The Spring of Moses," I commented.

"Yes. It's north of the mountain ridge where Ras es-Siyagah is located."

On one side of the room candles were burning in memory of Moses.

Stone interior of Memorial Building of Moses. | *M Rawicz Trip Photo*

An amazing mosaic floor from 531 C.E. | *M Rawicz Trip Photo*

People light candles in memory of Moses. | *M Rawicz Trip Photo*

I felt compelled to light one myself. As I did so, I was overcome with an intense feeling of love for this patriarch in whose footsteps I had walked for so many weeks.

I walked outside, and returned to gaze at the panorama below. I suddenly had the strangest experience. I felt an electric current pass through my whole body from my feet to my head; it was as if a white light somehow flashed through my entire being. It happened so fast that I just stood there in total shock. Gradually, my normal awareness returned. As I sat down to regain my composure, I wondered if this unusual experience might have had something to do with a mystical connection to Moses.

I have thought about my unique and intense experience often since then. I will never forget it, and each time I recall it, I reach the same conclusion about its meaning. It symbolized the very strong connection that I had developed to Moses and his link to me from his heavenly abode.

Looking out at the view in contemplation, I was transported back to the days when Moses was here.

I visualized a lone, tall, powerful, righteous man aged 120, with a long white beard walking up the gentle slope of Mount Nebo. He was dressed in a long robe and heavy sandals. He moved briskly. His unique power and authority radiated from his gait.

This was the man who had brought so much righteousness into the world. He was walking confidently and enthusiastically, coming to die, as G-d had commanded him.

Moses was more than the prince of Egypt, slayer of an Egyptian, shepherd in the desert, leader of a nation, agent of miracles, prophet, the man who had direct communication with G-d – he was also a simple, humble servant of G-d who would never enter the Promised Land. Being the servant of G-d was his most precious mission that has influenced the world since his lifetime! All was silent, just a few swallows flying past.

I imagined him arriving at this very place seeing this panorama of the land promised to Abraham many years ago. He was composed as he considered G-d's harsh decree, but knowing that it was both his and his people's sin that had led to this moment. He heard G-d saying, "It is My decree that you should not pass over." Such a bittersweet moment!

I visualized G-d in all His inconceivable grace, coming from the highest heavens to receive Moses' soul.

I imagined angels surrounding Moses as he sat down, Michael at his right, Gabriel at his left, and Zagzagel at his feet. G-d in His Divine Majesty was at Moses' head.

Moses was sanctifying himself with his quiet serenity to the will of G-d as he prepared to die here.

I could imagine G-d gently commanding him: "Cross your feet. Fold your hands and put them on your breast." . . . Then G-d whispering, "My servant, I have given you one hundred and twenty years in this body. Now come back with me as I take you to the highest heaven. Come to rest near in my palace."

Moses closed his eyes. G-d kissed him like a mother kisses a child to sleep. G-d whisked his body away to his secret burial place. The ministering angels mourned.

I was crying. I often cry now when I think of Moses. The thought of him opens my heart.

I rejoined Youseph and Makki, and we drove down a route on the northern side of the mountain. I looked back seeing Mount Nebo as one of the last peaks of the Abarim range. Although we were driving on a modern road, I could see signs of the wadi that would have been used by the Israelites and other people to descend the mountains.

As we drove, I had the opportunity to reflect on the meaning of Mount Nebo, the name of which means "passing through." Moses had climbed the mountain[17] and looked at the Promised Land[18] and had then passed through his final transition.

◰ Transitions in life and death

From this encampment, we learn about the final journey of our lives: We learn about the last moments before a person dies. Even though the people who continue in life can't relate physically to the deceased, there is still solace. If one believes that the soul lives on in the spiritual realm and continues on another journey, the experience is not so final. One can conceptualize that the soul is still able to have knowledge of the events of the temporal, human world. At this camp Moses' death symbolizes that "other world" or the "world to come." This gives us the ability to think about our own death and passing into the next world and the potential state in the world of souls. We understand that our material possessions are left to others, but also the deeds and memories that we created live on in the minds and hearts of those still alive. These can be known for generations in some cases. The legacy of Moses continues around the world for generations, as we know.[19] In our own case we can strive to leave both material gifts to our children and memories that they will be happy to think about or follow. This is a great motivation to live a principled and virtuous life. ◲

Since then I have not feared death.

Looking back over some of the ground we had covered, I could visualize the Israelites in their multitudes walking along the same route, and I could summarize the many ways in which they had been emotionally and spiritually changed at their recent camps. By now, many people would have developed greater leadership ability and the community would have been more aware than before that each person could make a valuable and unique contribution to the group. This awareness itself was a contrast to the previous slave mentality. Many would have come to understand that even though life may be brief and ephemeral, each person has his or her own divine purpose. Individuals who had achieved deep levels of understanding would be giving others their constructive criticism and advice.

The Israelites' experiences would also have taught them to acknowledge G-d through the offering of daily blessings. They were learning to sanctify His name even when facing tough challenges, and that their prayer could lead to healing. They were getting an inkling of the idea that striving toward unconditional love could help to keep one's enemies at bay, and their ability to curb their anger towards G-d might also have been improving. I felt inspired by the thought that the congregation that had finally reached the point that I now looked out on, had been greatly improved and refined, both the adults and children who walked together.

Reflecting on my own inner development during the journey I had made so far, I felt that I, too, had already improved; the time spent reflecting on the valuable teachings of the Exodus had helped me to mature spiritually and in my relations with others.

It was getting late and we took a detour to find a hotel in Amman for the evening. As the 39th day of my journey drew to a close, I was filled with sadness almost to the point of tears that I would be leaving the route that Moses had followed. I felt that he had become my companion on this journey, and my heart ached at the thought of him leaving me. I sat in silent mourning for a long while.

I was consoled by the teaching from Yotvathah. This camp had shown that seasoned wisdom can result in a deep sense of calmness, and that "the minds of elderly scholars become wise, settled in their aged years." I gazed out of the car window, half hoping to see a small lush valley northeast of Mount Nebo, called Ayun Musa. My thoughts lingered on the exemplary nature of Moses' life. I recalled, too, the teaching from Avrona on the transience of the material universe and how ephemeral human life is. Through acts of virtue and kindness, we have the power to transform our fleeting moments into something more lasting by leaving a trail of good deeds behind, whose effects can last forever.

DELICIOUS FRUIT AND BLOODY BATTLES: CAMP 42
B'ARVOS MOAB

"They left the Abarim mountains and camped b'Arvos (in the West Plains of) Moab on the Jericho opposite Jordan. There they camped along the Jordan from Beth HaYeshimoth to Abel-Shittim on the West Plains of Moab."[1]

The meaning of the individual words in the original Hebrew text of Numbers 33:49 are very interesting: *b'arvos* can mean either "darkness" or "sweetness,"[2] *moab* means "mother's father," *jordan* means "descending from the judge" or "channel," *beth yeshimoth* means "house of desolation" or "wasteland," *abel* means "meadow," "flatlands," or "desolate plains," *shittim* are "Acacia trees,"[3] and *jericho* means "across from the moon."[4]

This seemed like an amazing combination of words. In my simplicity I could associate features of the landscape with the words channel, flatland, wasteland, desolate plain and meadow of Acacias. These also bore some connection with the words darkness and across from the moon. To me, the words associated with lineage were "mother's father," "descending from the judge," and "house of desolation." The word "sweetness" seemed different. This gave me a lot to consider in the search for features at the camp site.

On this final leg of the journey, we once again followed the route of my ancestors. We were traversing the area between Amman and Nebo to access the plains. We journeyed through lands that had once belonged to the Amorites.

Then we stopped at a field where again the Israelites had slaughtered their enemy and destroyed the cities, as expressed in Deuteronomy 2:32–34, "And the Lord our G-d delivered him before us; and we smote him, and his sons, and all his people. And we took all his cities at that time, and utterly destroyed the men, and the women, and the little ones, of every city we left none to remain."[5]

Despite the calmness that now prevailed through the area, images jostled for attention in my mind.

There I was, at the battle ground of the Amorites, watching them charging at the Israelites. Masses of soldiers roared as they surged forward to attack. The well-organized Israelite army, in formations according to their tribes, was ready. Thousands of arrows from long-range bows whizzed though the air from the Israelites. A hailstorm of hundreds of stones followed.

A cry of agony rose from the Amorites. Blood started to flow. Spears flew across the space between them as the Amorites responded. The men were falling over each other by now. A constant thud was heard as heads or chests hit the ground. There was a rhythmic thump as more groups from the Israelite army followed their fallen comrades into battle. Their large, sharpened, wooden spears gave the appearance of a forest of tall trees. The Israelites attacked again with greater vigor as their leaders loudly sounded the horns. The Israelites fought bravely as a far greater hoard continued with the charge. A darkened sky looked ominous.

The atmosphere was charged with yells of anger and aggression from the Amorites. Israelites began to fall as casualties. Vanquished, prostrate men lay with arms spread out. The enemy reserves approached. A low-pitched 'Nuuuuuurrr' sound of camels accompanied by high pitched moans, groans and deep loud roars of men rent the air. The Amorites camel battalion had arrived. The agitated beasts were gnashing their teeth. From their open mouths, skewed teeth stuck out. The Israelites responded in kind, with troops similarly mounted on camels joining the battlefield. The cacophony increased. The Israelites large beasts moaned, screamed and roared with throaty bellows. The opposing racing camels, with thick dark ruffled fur and legs shooting outward and forwards, clashed. Mounted soldiers pulled out knives. Others threw stones with slings as they held onto their leather shields. The sky filled with huge rocks being hurled high above the heads of the foot soldiers. The smell of sweat and fear filled the air. Wounded soldiers cried out as many men from both sides perished in agony. These are the horrible ravages of battle.

Leaders yelled to foster heroism and bravery. After many hours, the Israelites emerged victorious. G-d had helped them once again, even though they had also suffered losses.

Even though the fields I now viewed were calm, I felt a sense of consternation at the thought of the historical events. Looking back, however, from the distance of time, I could see the logic of the destiny of the region and the various peoples from biblical days.

We left the site of the battle and headed for a hotel in Amman for the night.

In the morning, before setting off to find b'Arvos, we visited the Amman Museum. Negevite pottery from the Iron Age, which numerous archeologists have commented on, was on display. The displays indicated the era and place in which they had been found and some comments on the use of the pottery. I was fascinated to see so many idols from the ancient days peering out of their glass cabinets. One of them looked like a square slab of stone with the face of a man on it. I wondered how the attraction of idol worship had been so strong in those days. I also saw idols that were used by the Nabataeans, Ammonites, Canaanites, Edomites, Moabites and even the Asherahs idols.

After briefly seeing some of the highlights of Amman, we resumed our trip on the main road. We passed large commercial farms, each boasting a huge mansion presumably belonging to the owner. There were thousands of rows of palm trees interspersed by fields of densely planted vegetables as well as Acacia and Cypress woodlands. A little further on, the topography changed to rolling hills, surrounding the fields. The boundaries between farms were demarcated by low white walls built of stones taken from the hillsides.

We passed through a little village that had just been deluged by heavy rains which caused a traffic jam after the central street was flooded. Some cars were partly submerged, halfway up their tires. I was thoroughly enjoying the rain, though I pitied the townsfolk. Youseph knew the area well and drove through the residential area along narrow side streets and tiny alleyways to avoid the water and the traffic.

This detour proved to be interesting, as it gave me a close glimpse into the locals' living conditions and lifestyles, on a rainy day. The muddy roads were lined with double-story apartment buildings interspersed with simple square cement-brick homes. The wooden shutters had been drawn closed across the windows, and children's toys lay strewn about the street, a sign of the haste with which the storm had arrived and the children had fled for shelter. Washing that had been hung out to dry was soaked. A poor little donkey, abandoned by its owner, was still hitched to its cart, which was laden with fruit for sale. A couple of old cars stood forlornly, mud clogging up around their wheels.

After this short detour, we rejoined the main road. Descending from the mountainous height on which Amman is built, the road curved sharply to the left and later to the right as it negotiated the relatively steep drop into the Jordan Valley. Through a soft mist, I could see far into the valley below, and noticed another extensive patchwork of fertile fields.

After half an hour, we came upon a food stall at the side of the road that looked so enticing that I asked Youseph to stop. It offered an enormous variety in terms of color and product. There were almonds; dark red, bright orange, and grey colored spices; squares of dried fruit; beans of red, green, and brown; jams of all colors and flavors; and fresh fruit including apples, pineapples, plums, melons, figs, grapes, oranges, and

We made a detour into a local village of Jordan during a storm. | *M Rawicz Trip Photo*

pears. We feasted our eyes on delicious salads and vegetable produce, both fresh and pickled, including lettuce, tomatoes, cucumbers, onions, celery, red and green cabbages, eggplants, fresh olives, sweet peppers and carrots. The array of goods was a real treat after the barrenness of the Eastern Desert. Naturally, I was keen to indulge and bought some treats for Makki and fruit for us all.

A young Muslim woman, Jamilah, dressed in a light-blue *abaya*, served me. Her tiny baby, Nora, was carried by an older girl – evidently Jamilah's daughter. After I had made my selection, Jamilah smilingly agreed to let me hold her baby. The infant's face was beautiful, very peaceful and happy. It was an absolute pleasure to have such a soft, young and vulnerable child in my arms after having travelled through many varied and often harsh landscapes for forty days. I peered into her deep brown eyes, relishing the moment. As I said good-bye to Jamilah and her girls, I remembered the lesson of Mount Hor: the efforts we invest in loving each other and bringing love into this world are what carry us forward in our life's journey.

We continued towards the plains opposite Jericho. Just before the

It was a treat to behold the fertile fields of the Jordan Valley. | *M Rawicz Trip Photo*

slopes levelled out and the land became flat and arable, I could see the wide floor of the Jordan Valley east of the Jordan River, along the northeast Dead Sea Plain. I was looking at what had once been the plains of Moab. The Israelites had camped between two villages, Beth HaYeshimoth and Abel-Shittim, and I needed to find them to confirm the route we would take. The manager of the Amman Museum had directed us to a turn-off to the Kaffrein Dam.

We arrived at the dam mid-morning, ready to look for Abel-Shittim or "the place of Shittim." This village was at the southeastern edge of the Israelites' encampment and, according to the Bible, was just north of the Dead Sea, beside the east bank of the Jordan River. After finding it, we looked next for Tel-el-Hammam. This was on the south side of Wadi El-Meq Taa, which was the eastern extension of the larger Wadi Al-Keffrein. As we approached the location I saw a prominent yellow hill, which we later learned from the locals was Tel-el-Hammam. The hill appeared to be located precisely at the geographical point identified as the biblical "Cities of the Jordan Plain" by the famous archaeologist, Glueck.[6]

The colourful food stall selling Jordan valley produce was a tribute to its productivity. |
M Rawicz Trip Photo

I recalled reading that Tel-el-Hammam was the most outstanding and impressive city in the entire area known as the Plains of Moab. It was more than a kilometer long from east to west and had a circumference of three to four kilometers, making it one of the largest cities at the time in the Near East. It was clear from our spectacular view and from archeological information that this was strategically positioned as it commanded a broad view of the Jordan Valley. In biblical times, the people who lived in this city had the power to control the flow of merchandise moving in a northern and southern direction along the main trade route on the precious Jordan River and the eastern shore of the Dead Sea. The community was also able to control the eastern and western trade from the direction of Cisjordan, Jericho, and the Transjordan Highlands. The city was, thus, a crucial point on two major highways. This regional importance meant that the city grew to be quite large. Its growth was supported by the fertile farming lands and the permanently plentiful water supply from the Jordan River, numerous springs, and seasonal wadi flows. This abundance continues to yield quality produce even in modern times.[7]

With great difficulty, we climbed up the extremely steep sides of Tel-el-Hammam and entered the archaeological site through a wire gate. From this vantage point, I could appreciate even more how sprawling and impressive the city must have been in times of old. An understanding of this city's influence was key to understanding the developments that had taken place in this part of Jordan.

In Jordan there had been at least fourteen named archaeological sites and many others which have not been formally named. Of all these sites, Tel-el-Hammad is the largest. The tel had been the flourishing epicenter of a major city-state, and numerous satellite towns, villages, or hamlets had sprung up around it. These smaller locations continued to exist well after the biblical era, into the Bronze Age, and remains from almost every period have been found, including the ruins of a very large and strongly-built fortress from the Iron Age, surrounded by three-meter-thick city walls and a four-chambered gateway flanked by separate huge towers.[8]

Some mounds have been identified as dating from the biblical era. Pottery shards from the same era are preserved in the Amman Museum.[9] One of the relics was a beautifully shaped clay jar with two han-

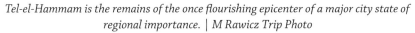

Tel-el-Hammam is the remains of the once flourishing epicenter of a major city state of regional importance. | *M Rawicz Trip Photo*

Archeological remains including a strongly-built fortress to guard the confluence of major trade routes. | M Rawicz Trip Photo

dles, a diamond base, and an oblong neck, colored in hues of red and yellow. Another was a pale grey jar with a ball-shaped body and short narrow neck with a delicate spout.[10]

Abel-Shittim must have been a welcome place for the Israelites to stop and rest after having spent so long in the wilderness. Perhaps that was the reason it had been named "Meadow of the Acacias."[11] A forest of trees among the hills would certainly have provided a refreshing place of rest and rejuvenation, and this would have been the ideal spot for the Israelites to prepare for the next crucial leg of the journey. Indeed there were Acacias in the area and possibly the area had "sweetness" for the people and their livestock.

The other meaning of Shittim, namely "a flatland" and "plain," was also evident in the broadness of the Jordan Valley. Perhaps "channel' was associated with the Jordan River. I was delighted once again to have found such physical evidence of an encampment's name.

To complete the exploration of this campsite, we went another ten kilometers to the east, to Beth-HaYeshimoth, close to the Dead Sea. This bare, desolate, sterile, salt-saturated terrain was such a contrast to the fertility of the valley. The lack of agriculture in the area was well

We saw archeological relics including red clay jars at the excavations site on the top of the tel. | M Rawicz Trip Photo

described by the Hebrew word *jeshimon,* meaning "wasteland,"[12] and Beth HaYeshimoth means "house of desolation." Beth HaYeshimoth had been a Moabite frontier town that G-d promised to destroy in a prophecy recorded in the Book of Ezekiel. The biblical town is today associated with the ancient remains at Khirbat Suwayma or Tel Azeimeh, Jeshimon.

However, I still wondered if I would find any clues as to why the camp name referred to Moab, Jordan, and Jericho. This encampment was the last stop the Israelites made before crossing the Jordan River into the land of Canaan.[13]

At this camp G-d had commanded Moses in Numbers 33:50–55, about the Canaanites, telling him to speak to the children of the One who will rule as G-d, and to say to them that when they cross they must drive out all the inhabitants of the land of Canaan.

Youseph and I chatted about the Canaanites. I told him what I had read about them.

"I know that they were immoral, and that their practices were horrific. The Canaanites were among the earliest practitioners of demon-worship, occultism, child sacrifice, and cannibalism.[14] By Jewish standards, their worship rituals involved extreme immorality. They sacrificed children to their god Molech, by burning the child in a fire made in the belly of an idol.[15] At first, the things I read about the Canaanites were so bad that I thought they must be exaggerated. It seemed too far-fetched that the Canaanites also built the walls of their houses out of the bodies of live children, because they believed that this would make the walls stronger.[16] But as I read more, I found that one source after the next all said the same thing. Those people really were that bad! They were among the earliest practitioners of sinful wicked worship. They are referred to in the Bible as abominations. I saw some of their idols that had been described by Mullins in the museum at Amman."[17]

Youseph said, "I've also heard about the idols and occult rites of the ancient Canaanites. I've heard some other really terrible things, too, like sex – or even marriage – between a person and their uncle or aunt, or between a man and his daughter-in-law or sister-in-law, mother, or daughters, and sleeping with women during their period. They condoned adultery and even mated with animals. I know these acts are forbidden in the Bible, but they were part of the Canaanites' religion! They participated in prostitution, sodomy, and even the male priests slept with male worshippers. That is how immoral they were. It was deep into their way of life."

I felt quite sick at the thought of it all. "No wonder G-d had warned the Israelites against them," I said.

He carried on, "If you think that was bad, they also did sorcery and witchcraft. During their worship, they danced wildly and cut themselves with knives and whips. They cut off the private parts of men in honor of a goddess. They also killed and ate each other! Even the other people that lived around the area were sickened by the Canaanite ways."

The scenario was repulsive. "I now understand the commandments G-d gave to Moses," I said, as I opened my Bible and read about the Canaanites and others in the pertinent verses. "Destroy all their carved images and their cast idols, and demolish all their high places"[18] . . . "You shall not bow down to their gods, nor serve them, nor do after their works"[19] . . . "but you shall utterly overthrow them, and break down their images"[20] . . . "And when the Lord your G-d delivers them before you; you shall smite them, and utterly destroy them" . . . "You shall make no covenant with them, nor show mercy to them"[21] . . . "For my Angel shall go before you, and bring you in to the Amorites, and the Hittites, and the Perizzites, and the Canaanites, the Hivites, and the Jebusites: and I will cut them off."[22]

⊟ Transforming life from dark to light

Here the Israelites learned about passing through the final period of life, before the final transition to death. The lesson that death is a portal to the life after earthly life and that the journey continues was emphasised. They recognized that the end of one life stage leads to the birth of another even at the very end, to a spiritual world yet to come. This part of the journey was the final, harshest, and most difficult of all the journeys in the wilderness.[23]

My experience with the "spirit" of Moses made me aware of his transition through death to the world of souls. Even though I could not see him, I felt his presence and it was like a channel opened momentarily for me to the energy of the world of souls and I could subtly sense his presence. ◀

I was still trying to assimilate all the meanings of the camp's names. Linking them together, they could be read in a rather absurd manner: "In the darkness or sweetness, here on the plains of the mother's father, the Israelites camped along the 'descending from the judge' or 'channel' from the 'house of the desolations' or 'wasteland', to the 'flatland', 'meadow of the Acacias' or 'desolate plain' across from the 'moon place.'" How strange! What could this possibly mean?

I had read Jacobson's[24] explanation and understood the meaning: Moab, the land on the eastern side of the Jordan, represents the end of the long journey of the Exodus – the exile and time of difficulty – at which point we must aspire to new levels of spiritual understanding. As we grow, we are overcoming our limitation-constriction, leaving our inner Egypt, "the land of narrowness" or "land of constraint" on an ongoing basis.

As we grow we move from levels of inner darkness or bitterness to greater levels of inner light or sweetness. "In Hebrew 'b'Arvos' indicates that a change had occurred from darkness to light or from bitterness to sweetness."[25]

We, thereby, grow in our self-actualization, step by step, camp by camp. As we transform and behave differently we also transform the world around us, our personal domain or the greater reality. We come closer to G-d. The world also acquires more light and goodness.

The Jordan River represents the place and time of transition.

The land across the Jordan, on the western side where Jericho is in Israel, represents the new "Promised Land," the future. If we make choices based on good judgment, the future will be better. If we, however, are negligent and choose evil ways, the future will be appropriately negative. Moab, which translates as "from a father," can have a dual meaning spiritually. A father in the positive sense can be a source of sanctity, or in a negative sense a father of evil. The Israelites had to follow G-d's commandment to destroy the Canaanites with their evil ways, and bring new G-dly spirituality to the Promised Land.

They were about to cross from the "wasteland" to the Promised Land. Jericho lay across the flatland and was to be the first stop in the Promised Land. Thus, this town would provide the Israelites' first real exposure to Canaanite idol worship, and there was a danger that these practices might take a hold on them.

They had learned many lessons and grown as a people, yet still needed much encouragement to continue forward and succeed. They needed to integrate the insights they had received time and again under various circumstances so that they could move ever upwards, spiritually, in an ongoing positive spiral.

The Promised Land is potentially the land of a better future, for each of us, the next generation and destiny of the world. This is a greater meaning for life itself.

It was incredible to see the wonder of the Promised Land and the point at which the Israelites would have crossed over. Looking over the Jordan was like looking into the new world to come. Where once there had been the evil of the Canaanites, there would now be a land of sanctity, after the Israelites had conquered it.

I could envisage a large mass of strong people camped on the huge area that we were looking at. By now they would have matured greatly in their outlook.

By this stage, many adults would have the sensitivity to feel the constant, comforting presence of G-d and not succumb to feeling emotionally alone. Those men and women who had matured in years would have learned that despite any physical distress, their contribution and wisdom was valuable; hopefully, they would have been able to integrate the deeper sense of peace that can come with age, and would be guided by the knowledge that the soul is immortal.

I wanted to follow this path of the revelation of light, of spiritual improvement. Just as the Israelites had learned, I also wanted to recognize and confront my desires so that I could acknowledge my humanity and strive towards holiness.[26] I also wanted to incorporate spirituality into the physical world and into my consciousness. I wanted as well to learn how to bring harmony between body and soul.

We completed our tour of the site and then chatted about what to do next. Youseph suggested that I rest for the remainder of the day at an attractive hotel at the edge of the Dead Sea, just three kilometers from Beth HaYeshimoth and I agreed.

It was a Friday, the 40th day of my journey. I had taken forty days to do what the Israelites had done in forty years. The synchronicity of the numbers amazed and delighted me.

After a refreshing cold drink, it was time to bid farewell to Youseph and Makki. I would be catching a bus across the Israeli border alone so that I could enter the Promised Land.

Finale

Being in a relaxed environment allowed me to reflect on the astonishing time I had been through for the last forty days. I had thought that I would learn a lot when I left South Africa, but never imagined that I would have such profound experiences.

I had traversed the massive Nile River Delta, arid sand and stone deserts, oases, springs, mountains and cliffs, coastlines and beaches, river gorges and flood plains, salt marshes, and fertile highland plains. As an environmentalist, I had learned a great deal about the varied and beautiful terrain, geology, topography, and habitats.

The Israelites, too, must have appreciated all the variety offered along the route. Their journey had not been a monotonous one of boring, endless sand for forty years, as I had previously imagined. I understood that they had wandered but not that they had been exposed to such a variety of places and peoples.

In my flora and fauna log book I had recorded many species of canines, cats, ruminants and other mammals. My guides and I had recognized some of the thousands of species of birds including those that frequent these regions during their migration times. We had also come across hundreds of insects, including bees, beetles, ants, and plant species in various ecosystems. The Israelites would have moved at a much slower pace than I did, taking forty years and maintaining far closer contact with the ground. They would have been able to identify far more animal and plant species than I had, and one has to wonder how the journey might have enhanced their ecological insight and knowledge. Surely, in addition to having witnessed several miracles and receiving a thorough spiritual education, they would have developed a profound appreciation of G-d's wondrous creation.

I had seen the camps and learned to my astonishment that they had included six ancient cities, two major trading city ports, a town in the center of a vibrant modern city with the same name, an epicenter of a major ancient city-state, three ancient Nabataean centers, at least five military fortresses – three from King Solomon's time, as well as two others. Camps included also a desert pharaonic temple, at least three oases, a Neolithic settlement, two small copper smelting sites and a huge copper mining and handling site. I had found astounding archaeology on the way.

The routes had included four main west–east Sinai routes used very commonly, including by the powerful Nabataean traders, military borders including four major known routes from north to south and an immensely strategic location between countries, and on the north–south Jordan and east–west Cisjordan/Jericho/Transjordan route. The Israelites had thus interacted with many cultures along their way.

I had first-hand experience of the places where Joseph, Jacob and his family had settled in the Land of Goshen and their Egyptian surroundings. I witnessed the place where Moses had been placed into the Nile River and saw the pyramids. I had lived, slept and eaten like the Bedouin and managed through the bitterly cold nights and blazing hot days as we journeyed through the sites. In this way, I had, perhaps, experienced something of the austere conditions the Israelites would have endured. I had a more realistic understanding of the miracle of the splitting of the Red Sea and an appreciation of the setting in which the Ten Commandments had been given to the Israelites. I had seen the fascinating and treacherous pathways of Sinai, the dangerous Edomite and Moabite territories, and places where vicious battles had been fought and won. I had a more realistic understanding of the tribes and cultures with which the Israelites had interacted. Biblical history was a greater and more meaningful reality to me in terms of the suffering, trials and miracles. For me the Israelites' experiences in Egypt, Sinai Desert, Israel and Jordan were authenticated.

⛊ Insight and transformation

I gained enormous insight into my religion as a whole. The festival of Passover, a milestone in the Jewish people's faith and survival, now had incredible meaning. I understood why the Exodus is an important part of the stories recollected by the three main monotheistic religions of the world – Judaism, Christianity, and Islam. It is a model of liberation under difficult circumstances.

I had come to the end of my trip and, in a manner, had been exposed to experiences similar to that of great old age. I recognized the great blessings to which I had been exposed; and the gift of life and of G-d who constantly sustained me. I tangibly understood that G-d was ever-present and a comfort and that G-d surrounded me and was in me, through the life he was breathing into me, my soul that He sustained from moment to moment during every second of my life.

I now live daily in a state of semi-contemplation and gratitude on an ongoing basis. I can feel a great inner reserve of light and resources that sustain me on a higher level of consciousness. It feels as if I have gotten to know experientially the presence of G-d. I do not have to rely on believing in G-d. It was a fantastic revelation and inner illumination. I have a great optimism in my future. It is like life after life . . . .

My heart was open and I resolved to try to keep it open. I know that G-d will always protect and watch over me. I know that I can pray easily and live in gratitude. I get on with people and have much better relationships. I have a better balance between work and living. After my enthralling adventure I have satisfaction, serenity and peace as a constant state.

I had been rejuvenated and transformed emotionally and spiritually. I sought personal transformation. I wanted to move beyond my limitations, my inner Egypt – the "land of narrowness." I was ready to face my desert in the hope that it would give me renewed energy and a new perspective on life. Besides gaining experience in the Israelite transformation from downtrodden slaves into a strong, uplifted nation, I had been transformed as well. The wonderful people that I had met along the way would be a lifelong memory. I would now live with trust in people that I meet and not with the fear that I had been used to in South Africa. ⛊

The Temple Mount – Western Wall. | M Rawicz Trip Photo

My epic journey through the wilderness was finally reaching its end.

A new journey was about to begin. I would continue learning the tradition and teachings that Moses received and that I had received through the generations. But now I felt that he and the Israelites had become a much more permanent part of me, something that I would take forward into the rest of my life. I was inspired and uplifted and felt that I could live on a new level of awareness just as the Israelites had when they proceeded forward with Joshua across the Jordan and into the Promised Land.

I had gained a new mission in life. Career and success in the secular world were less important. I now understood more clearly that living in the presence of G-d and helping people and fulfilling the commandments of G-d were supremely important for happiness. I resolved to pass this on to others along the daily life trip ahead . . . my life has never been the same since.

The Promised Land is potentially the land of a better future, for each of us, the next generation, and the destiny of the world.

Bibliography

One of the many pleasures of spending so much time immersed in researching this subject was sampling the extensive literature on life in the biblical world. My research, while comprehensive, was in no way definitive. Instead, 1 tried to read as widely as possible and seek out experts who might further guide me. I used footnotes with particular attention to books that I found most helpful or that might be of interest to those curious about further study.

First a few words on fundamentals. English translations of the Bible vary in style, substance, and purpose. For the sake of consistency, all quotations in the text come from the Torah. I also consulted the Revised Standard Version, the New International Version, and the King James Version.

In keeping with long-standing academic custom and recent trends in popular writing, the non-sectarian terms CE and BCE were used.

The key references for the meaning of the names of the camps and the spiritual meaning and lessons are from:

HILLEL BEN DAVID (Greg Killian), *The Journeys of the Sons of Israel*; http://www.betemunah.org/stages.html

JACOBSON, SIMON, *42 Journeys*. 2008, Meaningful Life Center. www.meaningfullife.com

Many references were consulted for the routes taken for the Exodus. The route in this book is from the following:

Rabbi Kaplan, Aryeh. *The Living Torah: A New Translation Based on Traditional Jewish Sources (The Five Books of Moses)*; New York / Jerusalem: Maznaim Publishing Corporation, June 1, 1981.

Neubauer, Adolf. *La Geographie du Talmud (La Geographie du Talmud: Memoire Couronne par l'Academie des Inscriptions et Belles-Lettres)*. Paris: Michel Levy Freres, 1868.

Endnotes

All references, including archaeological, historical, biblical, and other information come from the following references, listed by camp number:

CHAPTER 1

INTRODUCTION

1   Rabbi Kaplan, Aryeh.*The Living Torah: A New Translation Based On Traditional Jewish Sources (The Five Books of Moses);* New York /Jerusalem: Maznaim Publishing Corporation, June 1, 1981.

2   Neubauer, Adolf. *La Geographie du Talmud (La Geographie du Talmud; Memoire Couronne par l'Academie des Inscriptions et Belles-Lettres);* Paris: Michel Levy Freres, 1868.

3   Maps from Suez United Arab Republic. Sheet NH 36-10. Scale: 1:250,000. Washington, D.C.: 1970.

4   Ismailia United Arab Republic. Sheet NH 36-6. Scale: 1:250,000. Map of Wadi Tumilat; Washington D.C.: Survey of Israel, 1970.

5   Map: Israel. Agaf ha-medidot, South Sinai Map of Attractions – 1:250,000; Survey of Israel, 1994.

6   Map: World travel map, Israel with Jordan scale 1:350,000; Edinburgh: Bartholomew, 1971.

7   Map: Israel Touring Map including maps of Jerusalem, Tel Aviv, Jaffa Haifa. Scale: 1:400,000; Israel: Israel ministry of Tourism: Survey of Israel, 2002.

8   The Holy Land Satellite Atlas Volume 2, 1:530,000; Rohr productions, January 1, 1999.

9   Map: Luma Khalaf-Nahhas; Markaz al-Jughrāfī al-Malakī al-Urdunī, Jordan- Sunrise of the New Millennium – Map of Jordan; Amman: Jordan Tourism Board, 1998.

10 Map: Egypt, Globetrotter travel map. 1: 2,000,000 ; 3rd; New Holland (Publishers) Ltd, 2002.

11 Walker, Jenny. *Jordan, Lonely Planet*; July 1, 2012.

12 Siliotti, Alberrto. *Guide to the Exploration of the Sinai*; White Star Publishers, Inc., 2003.

13 Satellite maps, from Google earth.

14 Mattfeld y de la Torre, Walter Reinhold Warttig. *The Route of the Exodus*; Internet prophetess.lstc.edu/~rklein/Documents/theexodus.htm

15 Yohanan Aharoni, Michael Avi-Yonah, Anson F. Rainey and Ze'ev Safrai. *The MacMillan Bible Atlas, 3rd Edition*; New York/Toronto: MacMillan, March 3, 1993.

16 Yohanan Aharoni, Michael Avi-Yonah, Anson F. Rainey and Ze'ev Safrai. *The MacMillan Bible Atlas, 3rd Edition;* New York/Toronto: MacMillan, *March 3, 1993.*

17 Tourist map of Jordan, English version new edition; .Jordan: Royal Jordanian Geographic Centre, 1994.

18 The Gods and Goddesses of Ancient Egypt. British Science Museum, http://www.ancientegypt.co.uk/gods/home.html. Accessed 2011.

19 "Hathor," Wikipedia, http://en.wikipedia.org/wiki/Hathor. Accessed 2010.

20 Mattfeld y de la Torre, Walter Reinhold Warttig. *The Route of the Exodus: Proposals for Yam Suph (Lake Timsah), Etham/Shur (Tumilat/Timsah/Abu Suwayr)*. http://www.bibleorigins.net/YamSuphTimsahElimAyunMusa .html.

21 Mattfeld y de la Torre, Walter Reinhold Warttig. *Exodus Memories of Southern Sinai* (Linking the Archaeological Data to the Biblical Narratives). http://www.bibleorigins.net/ExodusTimnaSerabitelKhadim.html

CHAPTER 2

GOSHEN AND TANIS

1 "Geography of Egypt," Wikipedia, http://en.wikipedia.org/wiki/Geography of Egypt.

2 Hoffmeier, James K. *Ancient Israel in Sinai, The Evidence for the Authenticity of the Wilderness Tradition;* New York & Oxford: The Oxford University Press, 2005.

3 Mattfeld y de la Torre, Walter Reinhold Warttig. *Dating the Pentateuch: Rameses (tell el-Qantir) and the Fields of Zo'an (San el-Hagar, Egypt)*; http://www.bibleorigins.net/Zoananachronisms.html. August 2004.

4 Redford, Donald B. Zoan, *The Anchor Bible Dictionary*; N.Y.: Doubleday, 1992. (p.1106, Vol. 6).

5 "Heliopolis (ancient)," Wikipedia. http://en.wikipedia.org/wiki/Heliopolis _(ancient)

6 Exodus 1:11.

7   Grimal, Nicolas. *The Oxford History of Ancient Egypt*; Blackwell, Oxford Illustrated Histories, 1994.

8   Montet, Pierre. *Lives of the Pharaohs*; Spring, Weidenfeld and Nicolson, the University of Michigan, January 1, 1968.

9   Naville, Edouard. *The Store City of Pithom and the Route of the Exodus;* Second edition; London: Messrs Trübner & co. Egypt Exploration Fund, 1885. http://digi.ub.uni-heidelberg.de/diglit/naville1888a. Accessed 2009.

10 Redford, Donald B. Zoan, *The Anchor Bible Dictionary*; N.Y: Doubleday, 1992. (p.1106, Vol. 6).

11 Montet, Jean Pierre Marie. *La Necropole Royale de Tanis*, 3 vols. Fouilles de Tanis; 1947; Paris: 1960.

BURIED CITY – RAMESES: CAMP 1

1   Numbers 33:3.

2   Jacobson, Simon. *42 Journeys*. 2008, Meaningful Life Center, Genesis 47:11 www.meaningfullife.com, https://www.meaningfullife.com/behaalotcho-42-journeys-part-1.

3   Salkow, Robyn and Angel, Sheri. *A Time to Actualise: Journey into Ever Expanding Consciousness*; South Africa-Johannesburg: unpublished.

4   Bietak, Manfred. *Avaris, The Capital of the Hyksos, Recent Excavations at Tell el-Dab'a*; London: British Museum Press, 1996.

5   Montet, Pierre. *Lives of the Pharaohs*; Spring, Weidenfeld and Nicolson, the University of Michigan, January 1, 1968.

6   Clayton, Peter A. *Chronicle of the Pharaohs. The Reign-By-Reign Record of the Rulers and Dynasties of Ancient Egypt*; Thames and Hudson, December, 1994.
    Bietak, Manfred. *Avaris, The Capital of the Hyksos, Recent Excavations at Tell el-Dab'a*; London: British Museum Press, 1996.

7   Bietak, Manfred. *Avaris, The Capital of the Hyksos, Recent Excavations at Tell el-Dab'a*; London: British Museum Press, 1996.
    Bietak, Manfred. *Avaris, The Capital of the Hyksos, Recent Excavations at Tell el-Dab'a*; London: British Museum Press, 1996.

10 Naville, Edouard. *The Store City of Pithom and the Route of the Exodus*; Second edition, London: Messrs Trübner & co. Egypt Exploration Fund, 1885.http://digi.ub.uni-heidelberg.de/diglit/naville1888a. Accessed 2009.

11 Exodus 1:11.

12 Hillel ben David (Greg Killian). *The Journeys of the Sons of Israel*; http://www.betemunah.org/stages.html. Sotah 11a.

13 Hillel ben David (Greg Killian), *The Journeys of the Sons of Israel*; http://www.betemunah.org/stages.html. Avot 5:21.

14 Jacobson, Simon. *42 Journeys*; 2008, Meaningful Life Center, www.meaningfullife.com.

15 Salkow, Robyn and Angel, Sheri. *A Time to Actualise: Journey into Ever Expanding Consciousness*; South Africa-Johannesburg: unpublished.

MYSTERIOUS TEL & MIRACULOUS CLOUDS SUKKOT: CAMP 2

1   Exodus 13:20.
2   Numbers 33:5.
3   Hillel ben David (Greg Killian). *The Journeys of the Sons of Israel*;
    http://www.betemunah.org/stages.html.
4   Woolley, C. Leonard and Lawrence, T. E. *The Wilderness of Zin*; Chapter IV,
    Ain Kadeis and Kossaima; 1914-1915. http://www.bible.ca/archeology/bible
    -archeology-exodus-kadesh-barnea-woolley-lawrence-the-wilderness-of
    -zin-1914-1915ad.htm. Accessed 2009.
5   Deutsch, Yoseph. *Let My People Go*; Feldheim Publishers.
6   Rav Bin Nun, Yoel. Parashat Beshalach – "The Meaning of the Prohibition
    Against Returning to Egypt;" Yeshivat Har Etzion, The Israel Koschitzky
    Virtual Beit Midrash, http://etzion.org.il/en/meaning-prohibition-against
    -returning-egypt.
7   Exodus 13:17.
8   Hirsch, Emil G., König, Eduard, Schechter, Solomon, and Broydé, Isaac.
    "Ephraim," Biblical Data, Jewish Encyclopedia.com (The unedited full-text
    of the 1906 Jewish Encyclopedia). http://www.jewishencyclopedia.com
    /articles/5793-ephraim.
9   Jacobson, Simon. *42 Journeys*; 2008, Meaningful Life Center,
    www.meaningfullife.com.
    Yalkut Shimoni, Midrash HaChefetz, Tosephot & Rashi, Ralbag. Accessed
    2008.
10 Mattfeld y de la Torre, Walter Reinhold Warttig. *The Route of the Exodus
    as Envisioned by the 562 BCE Exilic Narrator* (Augmented by Archaeological
    Investigations); http://www.bibleorigins.net/RouteOfTheExodus.html.
    Accessed 2009.
11 Exodus 40:38.
12 Exodus 13:21.
13 Mattfeld y de la Torre, Walter Reinhold Warttig. *The Route of the Exodus*;
    Internet prophetess.lstc.edu/~rklein/Documents/theexodus.htm,
    Accessed 2009.
14 Bietak, Manfred. *Avaris, The Capital of the Hyksos, Recent Excavations at Tell
    el-Dab'a*; London: British Museum Press, 1996.
15 Goedicke, Hans. *Pi(ankh)y in Egypt*; Baltimore Maryland: Halco, Inc.
    December 1, 1998.
16 Mattfeld y de la Torre, Walter Reinhold Warttig. *The Route of the Exodus*.
    Internet prophetess.lstc.edu/~rklein/Documents/theexodus.htm.
    Accessed 2009.
17 Living Waters: A Hebrew Roots Fellowship. *Torah Commentary Beshalach:
    Exodus 13:17 – 17:16*. http://www.yourlivingwaters.com/Exodus/Beshalach
    -Commentary-2009.pdf.

18 Josephus, Flavius. *The Antiquities of the Jews, A History of the Jewish Wars,* and *Life of Flavius Josephus*; AD 93. http://sacred-texts.com/jud/josephus/, Accessed 2007.

19 Josephus, Flavius. *The Antiquities of the Jews, A History of the Jewish Wars,* and, *Life of Flavius Josephus*; AD 93. http://sacred-texts.com/jud/josephus/, Accessed 2007.

20 Josephus, Flavius. *The Antiquities of the Jews, A History of the Jewish Wars,* and, *Life of Flavius Josephus*; AD 93. http://sacred-texts.com/jud/josephus/. Accessed 2007.

21 Naville, Edouard. *The Store City of Pithom and the Route of the Exodus,* Second edition; London: Messrs Trübner & co. Egypt Exploration Fund, 1885.

22 Jacobson, Simon. *42 Journeys*; 2008, Meaningful Life Center, www.meaningfullife.com Baal Shem Tov. Accessed 2008.

23 Hillel ben David (Greg Killian). *The Journeys of the Sons of Israel*; http://www.betemunah.org/stages.html – Avot 5:21.

24 "Suez Canal," Wikipedia. http://en.wikipedia.org/wiki/Suez_Canal. Accessed 2010.

25 Montet, Jean Pierre Marie. *La Necropole Royale de Tanis*, 3 vols. Fouilles de Tanis; 1947; Paris: 1960.

TASTE OF DESERT & ARAB REVOLUTION – ETHAM DESERT: CAMP 3

1 Numbers 33:6.

2 Exodus 13:20.

3 Hillel ben David (Greg Killian). *The Journeys of the Sons of Israel*; http://www.betemunah.org/stages.html.

4 Mattfeld y de la Torre, Walter Reinhold Warttig. *The Route of the Exodus;* Exodus sites on internet.

5 Jacobson, Simon. *42 Journeys*; 2008, Meaningful Life Center, www.meaningfullife.com. Accessed 2008.

GREAT IDOL AND RED SEA SPLITTING – PI-HAHIROTH AND MIGDOL: CAMP 4

1 Exodus 14:2.

2 Hillel ben David (Greg Killian). *The Journeys of the Sons of Israel*; http://www.betemunah.org/stages.html.

3 Numbers 33:7.

4 Deutsch, Yoseph. *Let My Nation Go;* Feldheim Publishers.

5 Hillel ben David (Greg Killian). *The Journeys of the Sons of Israel*; http://www.betemunah.org/stages.html.

6 Mattfeld y de la Torre, Walter Reinhold Warttig. *The Route of the Exodus*; Internet prophetess.
    Hillel ben David (Greg Killian). *The Journeys of the Sons of Israel*; http://www.betemunah.org/stages.html.

8 Exodus 14:2-4.

9 Hoffmeier, James K. *Ancient Israel in Sinai, The Evidence for the Authenticity of the Wilderness Tradition*; New York & Oxford: The Oxford University Press, 2005.

10 Numbers 33:7.

11 Numbers 14:2.

12 Exodus 14:3-4.

13 Talmud Arachim.

14 Rav. Alcide, PhilJ. Parashat Beshalach, Study Guide 16. https://es-la.facebook.com/notes/philj-alcide/parashat-beshalach, 2014, 11:00.

15 Robinson, E. *Biblical Researches in Palestine, Mount Sinai and Arabia Petraea*; New York: Arno. Reprint of 1841 edition.

16 Salkow, Robyn and Angel, Sheri. *A Time to Actualise: Journey into Ever Expanding Consciousness*; South Africa, Johannesburg: unpublished.

17 Gaine, Hugh, *The Holy Bible, Containing the Old and New Testaments*: translated out of the original tongues; and with the former translations diligently compared and revised. New-York: Printed and sold by Hugh Gaine, at his Book-store and printing-office, at the Bible, in Hanover-Square, M, DCC, XCII. [1792] , https://books.google.co.za/books.

18 Aish.com, Breslov.org, Chabad.org, Kabbalaonline.org, OU.oorg, Torah.org. YashaNet, Questions and Concepts for Parsha Beshalach, www.yashanet.com/shabbat/parsha/beshalach.htm. Accessed 2011.

19 Deutsch, Yoseph. *Let My Nation Go;* Feldheim Publishers.

20 Exodus 14:1-29.

21 Exodus 15.

22 Talmud Arachim.

23 Jacobson, Simon. *42 Journeys*; 2008, Meaningful Life Center www.meaningfullife.com.
The Midrash Mechilta on Exodus 13:18. Accessed 2008.

24 Exodus 14:15.

25 Jacobson, Simon. *42 Journeys*; 2008, Meaningful Life Center www.meaningfullife.com.
The Midrash Mechilta on Exodus 13:18. Accessed 2008.

26 Rabbi Scherman, Nosson. *The Stone Edition Chumash The Torah, Haftaros, and Five Megillos with a Commentary from Rabbinic Writings*; ArtScroll Mesorah Publications, 1993.

27 Hillel ben David (Greg Killian). *The Journeys of the Sons of Israel*; http://www.betemunah.org/stages.html – Avot 5:21.

28 Jacobson, Simon. *42 Journeys*; 2008 ,Meaningful Life Center www.meaningfullife.com.
The Midrash Mechilta on Exodus 13:18. Accessed 2009. (Ohr HaTorah Massei p.1383).

29 Exodus 15: 20-21.

30 Rabbi Kaplan, Aryeh.*The Living Torah: A New Translation Based On Traditional Jewish Sources (The Five Books of Moses);* New York /Jerusalem: Maznaim Publishing Corporation, June 1, 1981.

31 Smith, William. *A Dictionary of the Bible*; Grand Rapids: Zondervan Publishing House, 1948.

32 Mattfeld y de la Torre, Walter Reinhold Warttig. *The Route of the Exodus*; Internet prophetess.lstc.edu/~rklein/Documents/theexodus.htm. Accessed 2009.

33 "Suez," Wikipedia. http://en.wikipedia.org/wiki/Suez. Accessed 2010.

34 Naville, Edouard. *The Store City of Pithom and the Route of the Exodus*, Second edition; London: Messrs Trübner & co. Egypt Exploration Fund, 1885. http://www.archive.org/stream/storecityofpitho01navi. Accessed 2009.

35 "Red Sea," Wikipedia. http://en.wikipedia.org/wiki/Red_Sea. Accessed 2010.

36 Prof. Dr. Nazeer, Ahmed. *Egypt and the Suez Canal*; *History of Islam*: An Encyclopedia of Islamic History; http://historyofislam.com/contents /onset-of-the-colonial-age/egypt-and-the-suez-canal. Accessed 2010.

37 Woolley, C. Leonard and Lawrence, T.E. *The Wilderness of Zin*, Chapter IV, Ain Kadeis and Kossaima; 1914-1915.http://www.bible.ca/archeology/bible -archeology-exodus-kadesh-barnea-woolley-lawrence-the-wilderness-of -zin-1914-1915ad.htm. Accessed 2009.

38 "Suez," Wikipedia. http://en.wikipedia.org/wiki/Suez. Accessed 2010.

39 "Suez," Wikipedia. http://en.wikipedia.org/wiki/Suez. Accessed 2010.

40 "Suez Canal Company," Wikipedia. http://en.wikipedia.org/wiki/Suez _Canal_Company. Accessed 2010.

41 "Suez Canal Company," Wikipedia. http://en.wikipedia.org/wiki/Suez _Canal_Company. Accessed 2010.

42 Rabbi Scherman, Nosson. *The Stone Edition Chumash: The Torah, Haftaros, and Five Megillos with a Commentary from Rabbinic Writings*; ArtScroll Mesorah Publications, 1993.

BITTER WATER – MARRAH: CAMP 5

1 Numbers: 33: 8.

2 Hillel ben David (Greg Killian). *The Journeys of the Sons of Israel*; http:// www.betemunah.org/stages.html

3 Exodus 15:23-25.

4 Mattfeld y de la Torre, Walter Reinhold Warttig. *The Route of the Exodus*; http://www.bibleorigins.net/EthamShurYamSuphMarahElimMusa.htm. Accessed 2007.

5 Zahran M.A. and Willis, A.J. *The Vegetation of Egypt*; Springer Science & Business Media. https://books.google.co.za/books?id=5AnoCAAAQBAJ& dq=plants+Frankenia+sinai+desert.

6 Jacobson, Simon. *42 Journeys*; 2008, Meaningful Life Center, www.meaningfullife.com. Accessed 2008.

7 Hillel ben David (Greg Killian). *The Journeys of the Sons of Israel*; http://www.betemunah.org/stages.html – Avot 5:21.

8   Hillel ben David (Greg Killian). *The Journeys of the Sons of Israel*; http://www.betemunah.org/stages.html – Baba Kamma 82a.
9   Hillel ben David (Greg Killian). *The Journeys of the Sons of Israel*; http://www.betemunah.org/stages.html – Sanhedrin 56b.
10 Hillel ben David (Greg Killian). *The Journeys of the Sons of Israel*; http://www.betemunah.org/stages.html.
11 Salkow, Robyn and Angel, Sheri. *A Time to Actualise: Journey into Ever Expanding Consciousness*; South Africa-Johannesburg: unpublished.

RECUPERATION OASIS – ELIM: CAMP 6

1   Exodus 15:27.
2   Numbers 33:9.
3   Hillel ben David (Greg Killian). *The Journeys of the Sons of Israel*; http://www.betemunah.org/stages.html – Hakham Shlomo Riskin,. Accessed 2008.
4   Mumford, Gregory D. *S.E.P.E. Survey and Excavation Projects in Egypt*; 2002. http://www.bibleorigins.net/YamSuphTimsahElimAyunMusa.html and http://www.deltasinai.com/sinai-01.htm. Accessed 2010.
5   Jacobson, Simon. *42 Journeys*; 2008, Meaningful Life Center, www.meaningfullife.com. (The Maggid of Mezritch – Ohr Torah Massei. Explained in Ohr HaTorah Massei pp. 1378-1393. See Degel Machne Efraim). https://theshtiebel.files.wordpress.com/2011/07/42journeys.pdf.
6   Salkow, Robyn and Angel, Sheri. *A Time to Actualise: Journey into Ever Expanding Consciousness*; South Africa-Johannesburg: unpublished.
7   Hillel ben David (Greg Killian). *The Journeys of the Sons of Israel*; http://www.betemunah.org/stages.html.

CHAPTER 3

BEACH PICNIC – RED SEA: CAMP 7

1   Numbers 33:10.
2   Hillel ben David (Greg Killian). *The Journeys of the Sons of Israel*; http://www.betemunah.org/stages.html -Targum Pseudo Jonathan for B'midbar; Numbers 33:10.
3   Hillel ben David (Greg Killian). *The Journeys of the Sons of Israel*; http://www.betemunah.org/stages.html – Soncino Zohar, Shemoth, Section 2, Page 50a.
4   Jacobson, Simon. *42 Journeys*; 2008, Meaningful Life Center. www.meaningfullife.com. Accessed 2008.

BUYING FOOD FOR THE DESERT – WILDERNESS OF SIN: CAMP 8

1   Numbers 33:11.
2   Exodus 16:1.

3   Hillel ben David (Greg Killian). *The Journeys of the Sons of Israel*; http://www.betemunah.org/stages.html.

4   Jacobson, Simon. *42 Journeys*; 2008, Meaningful Life Center. www.meaningfullife.com. Accessed 2008.

5   Hillel ben David (Greg Killian). *The Journeys of the Sons of Israel*; http://www.betemunah.org/stages.html.

6   Jacobson, Simon. *42 Journeys*; 2008, Meaningful Life Center. www.meaningfullife.com.

TEARS, GOLDEN CALF FRIENDS, DÉJÀ VU AND A MARRIAGE PROPOSAL – DOPHKA: CAMP 9

1   Numbers: 33:12.

2   Hillel ben David (Greg Killian). *The Journeys of the Sons of Israel*; http://www.betemunah.org/stages.html.

3   Siliotti, Alberto. *Guide to the Exploration of the Sinai*; White Star, April 12, 2001.

4   Zorn, Moses Jeffrey R. *The Anchor Bible Dictionary: Dophka;* Doubleday: New York 1992. Accessed 2007.

5   Exodus 12:38.

6   Montet, Jean Pierre Marie. *La Necropole Royale de Tanis;*3 vols. Fouilles de Tanis: 1947; Paris: 1960.

7   Moorey, Peter Roger Stuart. *Ancient Mesopotamian Materials and Industries: The Archaeological Evidence*; Eisenbrauns, 1999.

8   Moorey, Peter Roger Stuart. *Ancient Mesopotamian Materials and Industries: The Archaeological Evidence*; Eisenbrauns, 1999.

9   Mattfeld y de la Torre, Walter Reinhold Warttig. *The Route of the Exodus*; http://www.bibleorigins.net/YamSuphTimsahElimAyunMusa.html. Mattfeld y de la Torre, Walter Reinhold Warttig. *The Route of the Exodus*; Internet prophetess.lstc.edu/~rklein/Documents/theexodus.htm. Accessed 2009(1).

10 Mattfeld y de la Torre, Walter Reinhold Warttig. *Israel's Golden Calf Worship is a Recollection of Egyptian Solar Cults at Serabit el Khadim in the Sinai*; http://www.bibleorigins.net/GoldenCalfHathorReliefs.html. 05 Oct 2004.

11 Ions, Veronica. *The Creation of the World, Egyptian Mythology*; Feltham, Middlesex: Paul Hamlyn Ltd, 1965, 1968. (p.24)

12 Mattfeld y de la Torre, Walter Reinhold Warttig. *The Route of the Exodus: Proposals for Yam Suph (Lake Timsah), Etham/Shur (Tumilat/Timsah/ Abu Suwayr), Marah/LXX: Merrah The Bitter Lakes (Murrah), Elim (Ayun Musa's 12 Springs) Wilderness of Sin.* http://www.bibleorigins.net /YamSuphTimsahElimAyunMusa.html. Accessed 2009.

13 Mattfeld y de la Torre, Walter Reinhold Warttig. *Exodus Memories of Southern Sinai*; Vol.3, p.289, Mumford. "Sinai." http://www.bibleorigins.net /ExodusTimnaSerabitelKhadim.html. Accessed 2009.

14 Jacobson, Simon. *42 Journeys*; 2008, Meaningful Life Center www.meaningfullife.com. *Baal HaTurim.* Accessed 2008.

15 Jacobson, Simon. *42 Journeys*; 2008, Meaningful Life Center www.meaningfullife.com. Accessed 2008.

16 Jacobson, Simon. *42 Journeys*; 2008, Meaningful Life Center www.meaningfullife.com. Accessed 2008.

17 Hillel ben David (Greg Killian). *The Journeys of the Sons of Israel*; http://www.betemunah.org/stages.html- Avot 5:21.

18 Hillel ben David (Greg Killian). *The Journeys of the Sons of Israel*; http://www.betemunah.org/stages.html- Avot 5:21.

MANNA VALLEY – ALUSH: CAMP 10

1   Numbers 33:13.

2   Hillel ben David (Greg Killian). *The Journeys of the Sons of Israel*; http://www.betemunah.org/stages.html.

3   Sinai: Emilo travel. http://www.emiliotravel.com/travel/safari_sinai.htm

4   Beit-Arieh, Itzhaq. *Canaanites and Egyptians at Serabit el-Khadim*; Anson F. Rainey, editor. *Egypt, Israel, Sinai; Archaeological and Historical Relationships in the Biblical Period* ; Tel Aviv, Israel: Tel Aviv University, 1987.

5   Rainey, Anson F. *Egypt, Israel, Sinai; Archaeological and Historical Relationships in the Biblical Period;* Tel Aviv, Israel: Tel Aviv University, 1987.

6   Mattfeld y de la Torre, Walter Reinhold Warttig. *The Route of the Exodus;* http://www.bibleorigins.net/ExodusTimnaSerabitelKhadim.html. Accessed 2009.

7   Mattfeld y de la Torre, Walter Reinhold Warttig. *The Route of the Exodus;* http://www.bibleorigins.net/ExodusTimnaSerabitelKhadim.html. Accessed 2009.

8.1 Albright, William Foxwell. *The Proto-Sinaitic Inscriptions and Their Decipherment;* Cambridge: Harvard University Press, 1966. (p. 65)

8.2 *The Origins and Emergence of West Semitic Alphabetic Scripts: An Introduction to J. R. Harris, D. W Hone And To Old Negev. The Old Negev Script & Proto-Canaanite Language.* http://net.lib.byu.edu/imaging/negev/Origins.html.

9   Mattfeld y de la Torre, Walter Reinhold Warttig. *Exodus Memories of Southern Sinai*; Vol.3, p.289, Mumford. "Sinai." http://www.bibleorigins.net /ExodusTimnaSerabitelKhadim.html. Accessed 2009.

10 Exodus 16:13-15.

11 Exodus 16:31.

11.1 Golding, Louis. *In the Steps of Moses the Lawgiver*; Great Britain: Rich & Cowan, London.

12 Exodus 16:23.

13 Exodus 16:4.

14 Parshat Beshalach, chabad .org. http://www.chabad.org/parshah/in-depth /default_cdo/aid/36138/jewish/Beshalach-In-Depth.htm. Accessed 2010.

15 Parshat Beshalach, chabad .org. http://www.chabad.org/parshah/in-depth /default_cdo/aid/36138/jewish/Beshalach-In-Depth.htm. Accessed 2010.

16 Salkow, Robyn and Angel, Sheri. *A Time to Actualise: Journey into Ever Expanding Consciousness;* South Africa-Johannesburg: unpublished.

17   Jacobson, Simon. *42 Journeys*; 2008, Meaningful Life Center
       www.meaningfullife.com. Accessed 2008.
18   Hillel ben David (Greg Killian). *The Journeys of the Sons of Israel*;
       http://www.betemunah.org/stages.html- Avot 5:21.

AMALEKITES WAR – REPHADIM: CAMP 11

1   Hillel ben David (Greg Killian). *The Journeys of the Sons of Israel*;
       http://www.betemunah.org/stages.html- Avot 5: 21
2   Numbers 33:14.
3   Hillel ben David (Greg Killian). *The Journeys of the Sons of Israel*;
       http://www.betemunah.org/stages.html.
4   Exodus 17:1.
5   "Nabataeans." Wikipedia. http://en.wikipedia.org/wiki/Nabataeans.
       Accessed 2013.
6   Exodus 17.
7   Hillel ben David (Greg Killian). *The Journeys of the Sons of Israel*;
       http://www.betemunah.org/stages.html.
8   Mattfeld y de la Torre, Walter Reinhold Warttig. *Is Mount Horeb (Mt. Sinai)
       Jebel 'Arribeh by St. Catherine's or Mount Timna'*. 13 October 2002
       http://fontes.lstc.edu/~rklein/Documents/MountSinai-Horeb-Timah.htm.
       Accessed 2003.
9   Exodus 17:1.
10   Rohl, David. *From Eden to Exile: The Epic History of the People of the Bible*;
       London: Arrow Books Ltd. 2003.
11   Exodus 17:13.
12   Exodus 17:14.
13   Deuteronomy 25-19.
14   Exodus 17:14.
15   Hillel ben David (Greg Killian). *The Journeys of the Sons of Israel*;
       http://www.betemunah.org/stages.html.
16   Jacobson, Simon, *42 Journeys*; 2008, Meaningful Life Center
       www.meaningfullife.com. Accessed 2008.
17   Exodus 17:8.
18   Jacobson, Simon. *42 Journeys*; 2008, Meaningful Life Center
       www.meaningfullife.com. Accessed 2008.

MOONLIGHT TREK UP MOUNT SINAI: CAMP 12

1   Numbers 33:15.
2   Hillel ben David (Greg Killian). *The Journeys of the Sons of Israel*;
       http://www.betemunah.org/stages.html.
3   Mattfeld y de la Torre, Walter Reinhold Warttig. Various Site Proposals for
       the Location of Biblical Mount Sinai or Mount Horeb. Is Jebel Suna on the
       north side of the plain of er-Rahah. "The Mountain of the Law" in Arabic,
       Mount Sinai?: http://www.bibleorigins.net/MountSinaiVariousProposals
       .html, Accessed 2009.

4   Rabbi Kaplan, Aryeh. *The Living Torah: A New Translation Based on Traditional Jewish Sources (The Five Books of Moses)*; New York /Jerusalem: Maznaim Publishing Corporation, June 1, 1981.

5   Jarvis, C. S. *Yesterday and Today in Sinai*; London: W. Blackwood & Sons, 1938.

6   Burckhardt, Lewis John. *Travels in Syria and the Holy Land*; published by Authority of the Association for the Promoting the Discovery of the Interior of Africa; London: John Murray, Albemarle Street, 1822.

7   Sir Petrie, William Matthew Flinders. *Researches in Sinai*; London; John Murray, 1906.

8   Mattfeld y de la Torre, Walter Reinhold Warttig. *The Route of the Exodus*; http://www.bibleorigins.net/MountSinaiVariousProposals.html. Accessed 2012.

9   Aharoni, Yohanan. *The Land of the Bible in Bible Times: A Historical Geography*; Philadelphia: Pennsylvania, The West Minister Press, January 1962.

10 Eusebius of Caesarea. *The Onomasticon & the Exodus Route (Dictionary of Places)*; 325 AD. Pilgrim nun Egeria.

11 Palmer, E. H. *The Desert of the Exodus*; New York: Harper & Brothers, 1872.

12 Robinson, Edward. *Biblical Researches in Palestine and in the Adjacent Regions*; London: Boston, Crocker and Brewster, 1856.

13 Kitchen, Kenneth A. *On the Reliability of the Old Testament*; Grand Rapids, Michigan: William B. Eerdmans, 2003.

14 Professor Anati, Emannuel. *Har Karkom: 20 Years of Biblical Archaeology*; http://www.harkarkom.com/History.php?more=all, Accessed 2009.

15 Beke, Charles H. *Sinai in Arabia and of Midian*; London: Trubner & Co, 1878.

16 Lucas, A. *The Route of the Exodus of the Israelites from Egypt*; Edward Arnold & Co, 1938.

17 Nielsen, Ditlef. *The Site of the Biblical Mount Sinai: A Claim for Petra*; Copenhagen, 1928.

18 Cornuke, Robert and Halbrook, David. *In Search of the Mountain of God: The Discovery of the Real Mt. Sinai;* Broadman & Holman Publishers, June 2000.

19 "Saint Catherine, Egypt," Wikipedia.http://en.wikipedia.org/wiki/Saint _Catherine,_Egypt. Accessed 2010.

20 Siliotti, Alberto. *Guide to the Exploration of the Sinai*; White Star, April 12, 2001.

21 Exodus 19:11.

22 Exodus 19:16.

23 Exodus 19:20.

24 Exodus 24:18.

25 Exodus 24:16.

26 Exodus 20:1.

27 Exodus 24, 1-11.

28 Jacobson, Simon. *42 Journeys*; 2008, Meaningful Life Center www.meaningfullife.com. Accessed 2008.

29 Hillel ben David (Greg Killian). *The Journeys of the Sons of Israel*; http://www.betemunah.org/stages.html.

30 Salkow, Robyn and Angel, Sheri. *A Time to Actualise: Journey into Ever Expanding Consciousness;* South Africa-Johannesburg: unpublished.

31 Hillel ben David (Greg Killian). *The Journeys of the Sons of Israel*; http://www.betemunah.org/stages.html.

32 Hillel ben David (Greg Killian). *The Journeys of the Sons of Israel*; http://www.betemunah.org/stages.html.

33 Salkow, Robyn and Angel, Sheri. *A Time to Actualise: Journey into Ever Expanding Consciousness;* South Africa-Johannesburg: unpublished.

34 Numbers 10:11.

35 Exodus 33.

36 Exodus 32.

37 "Saint Catherine, Egypt," Wikipedia http://en.wikipedia.org/wiki/Saint _Catherine,_Egypt. Accessed 2010.

38 Exodus 19.

CHAPTER 4

GRAVES OF CRAVING – KIVROTH HATAAVAH: CAMP 13

1 Numbers 33:16.

2 Hillel ben David (Greg Killian). *The Journeys of the Sons of Israel*; http://www.betemunah.org/stages.html.

3 Numbers 11: 31.

4 Loveridge, Emma. *The Nawamis of The Sinai Desert*; October 08, 2009. http://ezinearticles.com/?The-Nawamis-Of-The-Sinai-Desert&id=5120062, Accessed 2009.

5 Loveridge, Emma. *The Nawamis of The Sinai Desert*; October 08, 2009. http://ezinearticles.com/?The-Nawamis-Of-The-Sinai-Desert&id=5120062, Accessed 2009.

6 Feiler, Bruce. *Walking the Bible Journey by Land Through the Five Books of Moses*; Harper Collins 2001.

7 Beit-Arieh, Itzhaq. *Fifteen_Years_in_Sinai;* Tel Aviv University School of Medicine, Jul/Aug_1984. http://cojs.org/cojswiki/Fifteen_Years_in_Sinai ,_Itzhaq_Beit-Arieh,_BAR_10:04, Accessed 2009.

8 Numbers 11:34.

9 Jacobson, Simon. *42 Journeys*; 2008, Meaningful Life Center www.meaningfullife.com.

HAZEROT: CAMP 14

1 Numbers 33:17.

2 Hillel ben David (Greg Killian). *The Journeys of the Sons of Israel*; http://www.betemunah.org/stages.html.

3   Gohary, Professor Said and Dr. Jocelyn. *Report on Cultural Heritage Sites in South Sinai*; http://st-katherine.net/downloads/Cultural%20Heritage %20Sites.pdf, Accessed 2011.

4   Jacobson, Simon. *42 Journeys*; 2008, Meaningful Life Center www .meaningfullife.com.

5   Tawfik, Dina. *Coloured Canyon*; http://www.allsinai.info/sites/sites /ColouredCanyon.htm, Accessed 2011.

CHAPTER 5

CRIMINAL VALLEY – KADESH BARNEA / RITMA: CAMP 15

1   Numbers 33:18.

2   Hillel ben David (Greg Killian). *The Journeys of the Sons of Israel*; http://www.betemunah.org/stages.html.

3   Rudd, Steve. *Chronological History of the Search for Kadesh: Kadesh is Located at Ancient El Beidha in Petra: 2000 BC – 2013 AD*; http://www.bible .ca/archeology/bible-archeology-exodus-kadesh-barnea-historical-search .htm.

4   Rabbi Kaplan, Aryeh. *The Living Torah: A New Translation Based On Traditional Jewish Sources (The Five Books of Moses)*; Maznaim Publishing Corp, June 1, 1981.

5   The Nabataeans; http://nabataea.net/index.html. Accessed 2009.

6   Deuteronomy 1:2.

7   *Ein El Qedeis: "Piltdown Kadesh"*; The Interactive Bible. http://www.bible.ca /archeology/bible-archeology-exodus-kadesh-barnea-fortresses-ein-qedeis .htm. Accessed 2009.

8   Ortloff, Charles R. *The Water Supply and Distribution System of the Nabataean City of Petra (Jordan), 300 BC- AD 300*; 2005: Cambridge Archaeological Journal, The McDonald Institute for Archaeological Research. http://www.bible.ca/archeology/bible-archeology-exodus -kadesh-barnea.htm. Nabataea.net, 15:1:93-109. Accessed 2009.

9   Ortloff, Charles R. *The Water Supply and Distribution System of the Nabataean City of Petra (Jordan), 300 BC- AD 300*; 2005: Cambridge Archaeological Journal, The McDonald Institute for Archaeological Research. http://www.bible.ca/archeology/bible-archeology-exodus -kadesh-barnea.htm. Nabataea.net, 15:1:93-109. Accessed 2009.

10   *Ein El Qedeis: "Piltdown Kadesh"*; The Interactive Bible. http://www.bible.ca /archeology/bible-archeology-exodus-kadesh-barnea-fortresses-ein-qedeis .htm. Accessed 2009.

11   *Ein El Qedeis: "Piltdown Kadesh"*; The Interactive Bible. http://www.bible.ca /archeology/bible-archeology-exodus-kadesh-barnea-fortresses-ein-qedeis .htm. Accessed 2009.

12   *Ein El Qedeis: "Piltdown Kadesh"*; The Interactive Bible. http://www.bible.ca /archeology/bible-archeology-exodus-kadesh-barnea-fortresses-ein-qedeis .htm, Accessed 2009.

13   Schmidt, Nathaniel. *"Barnea"; Journal of Biblical Literature*, Vol 29, no 1, 1910. http://www.bible.ca/archeology/bible-archeology-exodus-kadesh -barnea-petra-nathan-schmidt-kadesh-barnea-journal-of-biblical-literature -vol-29-no-1-1910ad.htm. Accessed 2009. (pp. 75-76)

14   Woolley, C. Leonard and Lawrence, T.E. *The Wilderness of Zin*, Chapter IV, Ain Kadeis and Kossaima; 1914-1915.http://www.bible.ca/archeology/bible -archeology-exodus-kadesh-barnea-woolley-lawrence-the-wilderness-of -zin-1914-1915ad.htm, Accessed 2009.

15   Cohen, Rudolph. *The Iron Age Fortresses in the Central Negev*; Bulletin of the American Schools of Oriental Research 236, Fall 1979, Department of Antiquities and Museums, Jerusalem, Israel, 1979. www.bible.ca/ . . ./bible- archeology-exodus-kadesh-barnea-iron-age-fortress, Accessed 2011.

16   Meshel, Zeev. *The "Aharoni Fortress" Near Quseima and the "Israelite Fortresses" in the Negev*; Tel Aviv, Israel: Bulletin of the American Schools of Oriental Research, No. 294. Institute of Archaeology, Tel Aviv University, May, 1994. http://www.bible.ca/archeology/bible-archeology-exodus -kadesh-barnea-aharoni-fortress-near-quseima-israelite-fortresses-in -negev-zeev-meshel 1994ad.htm. Accessed 2009.

17   Dothan, M. *The Fortress at Kadesh-Barnea, Ein el-Qudeirat 1965 AD*; Israel Exploration Journal, 1965. http://www.bible.ca/archeology/bible -archeology-exodus-kadesh-barnea-ein-el-qudeirat-fortress-at-kadesh -barnea-dothan-1965ad.htm. Accessed 2009.

18   David, Ussishkin. *The Rectangular Fortress at Kadesh Barnea*; Tel Aviv: University Israel Exploration Journal 45, 1995. http://www.academia.edu /3167528/The_Rectangular_Fortress_at_Kadesh-Barnea_-_Notes_on_the _Excavation_Conclusions_of_R._Cohen, (pp. 118-27). Accessed 2009.

19   Woolley, C. Leonard and Lawrence, T.E. *The Wilderness of Zin*, Chapter IV, Ain Kadeis and Kossaima; 1914-1915. http://www.bible.ca/archeology/bible -archeology-exodus-kadesh-barnea-woolley-lawrence-the-wilderness-of -zin-1914-1915ad.htm. Accessed 2009.

20   Schmidt, Nathan. *Kadesh Barnea – Kadesh at Petra*; Journal of Biblical Literature, Vol 29, No 1, 1910. http://www.bible.ca/archeology/bible -archeology-exodus-kadesh-barnea-petra-nathan-schmidt-kadesh-barnea -journal-of-biblical-literature-vol-29-no-1-1910ad.htm. Accessed 2009.

21   Cohen, Rudolph. *The Iron Age Fortresses in the Central Negev*; Bulletin of the American Schools of Oriental Research 236, Fall 1979, Department of Antiquities and Museums, Jerusalem, Israel, 1979. www.bible.ca/ . . ./bible- archeology-exodus-kadesh-barnea-iron-age-fortress. Accessed 2011.

22   Numbers 13:1–14:31.

23   Hillel ben David (Greg Killian). *The Journeys of the Sons of Israel*; http://www.betemunah.org/stages.html.

24   Deuteronomy 1:2; 2:14.

25   Jacobson, Simon. *42 Journeys*; 2008,Meaningful Life Center www.meaningfullife.com.

26 Hillel ben David (Greg Killian). *The Journeys of the Sons of Israel*; http://www.betemunah.org/stages.html. Avot 5:21.

ISRAELI FIRING SQUADS – RIMMON PEREZ: CAMP 16

1 Numbers 33:19.
2 Hillel ben David (Greg Killian). *The Journeys of the Sons of Israel*; http://www.betemunah.org/stages.html Avot 5, Mishna 21.
3 Hillel ben David (Greg Killian). *The Journeys of the Sons of Israel* http://www.betemunah.org/stages.html.
4 Meshel, Zeev. *The "Aharoni Fortress" Near Quseima and the "Israelite Fortresses" in the Negev*; Tel Aviv, Israel: Bulletin of the American Schools of Oriental Research, No. 294., Institute of Archaeology, Tel Aviv University, May, 1994.
5 Palmer, Edward Henry. *The Desert of the Exodus: Journeys on Foot in the Wilderness of the Forty Years' Wanderings*; Cambridge: Deighton, 1871.
6 Jacobson, Simon. *42 Journeys*; 2008, Meaningful Life Center www.meaningfullife.com.
    Targum Pseudo Jonathan (for Numbers 33:19).
7 Jacobson, Simon. *42 Journeys*; 2008, Meaningful Life Center www.meaningfullife.com.
8 Hillel ben David (Greg Killian).*The Journeys of the Sons of Israel*; http://www.betemunah.org/stages.html Avot 5:21.

PISTACHIO TREES – LIBNAH: CAMP 17

1 Numbers 33:20.
2 Jacobson, Simon. *42 Journeys*; 2008, Meaningful Life Center www.meaningfullife.com.
3 Avner, Uzi. *Sacred Stones in the Desert*; BAR 27:03, May/Jun 2001. http://members.bib-arch.org/publication.asp?PubID=BSBA&Volume=27&Issue=3&ArticleID=2. Accessed 2010.
4 "Borot Lutz," *Travelling in Israel, Tiuli*; http://www.tiuli.com/track_info.asp?lng=eng&track_id=119.
5 "Borot Lutz," *Travelling in Israel, Tiuli*; http://www.tiuli.com/track_info.asp?lng=eng&track_id=119.
6 Jacobson, Simon. *42 Journeys*; 2008, Meaningful Life Center www.meaningfullife.com.
7 Jacobson, Simon. *42 Journeys; 2008*, Meaningful Life Center www.meaningfullife.com – Targum Yonatan for Bamidbar, Numbers 33:20.
8 Hillel ben David (Greg Killian). *The Journeys of the Sons of Israel*; http://www.betemunah.org/stages.htm.

DODGING MILITARY WATCHTOWERS – RISSAH: CAMP 18

1 Numbers 33:21.
2 Jacobson, Simon. *42 Journeys*; 2008, Meaningful Life Center www.meaningfullife.com.

3   Jacobson, Simon. *42 Journeys*; 2008, Meaningful Life Center
     www.meaningfullife.com – Heichel HaBracha Kamarna.
4   Jacobson, Simon. *42 Journeys*; 2008, Meaningful Life Center
     www.meaningfullife.com.
5   Hillel ben David (Greg Killian). *The Journeys of the Sons of Israel*;
     http://www.betemunah.org/stages.html. – Targum Pseudo Yonathan for
     Numbers 33:21.
6   Hillel ben David (Greg Killian). *The Journeys of the Sons of Israel*;
     http://www.betemunah.org/stages.html – Rashi.
7   Pielke Sr, Roger, Climate Science: pielkeclimatesci, July 13, 2013 · 2:09 pm,
     https://pielkeclimatesci.wordpress.com/ ref to "Issar, A, 1985: Fossil Water
     under the Sinai-Negev Peninsula." Scientific American, Vol. 253, No. 1, p
     104-110, July, 1985.

AGGRESSIVE CROWD – KEHETHAH: CAMP 19

1   Numbers 33:22.
2   Hillel ben David (Greg Killian). *The Journeys of the Sons of Israel*;
     http://www.betemunah.org/stages.html.
3   Hillel ben David (Greg Killian). *The Journeys of the Sons of Israel*;
     http://www.betemunah.org/stages.html.
4   Numbers 16:31-35.
5   Chabad, Parsha In-Depth – Chabad.org http://www.chabad.org/parshah/in
     -depth/plainBody_cdo/AID/3014 .- Rashi Deuteronomy 1:1.
6   Jacobson, Simon. *42 Journeys*; 2008, Meaningful Life Center
     www.meaningfullife.com – Targum Yonathan. Baal HaTurim. Rokeach.
7   Jacobson, Simon, *42 Journeys*; 2008, Meaningful Life Center
     www.meaningfullife.com. Avot 3.
8   Jacobson, Simon, *42 Journeys*; 2008, Meaningful Life Center
     www.meaningfullife.com. Avot 3:2.
9   Hillel ben David (Greg Killian). *The Journeys of the Sons of Israel*;
     http://www.betemunah.org/stages.html Avot 5: 21.

DRUGS AND DEATH – SHAPHER: CAMP 20

1   Numbers 33:23.
2   Hillel ben David (Greg Killian). The Journeys of the Sons of Israel;
     http://www.betemunah.org/stages.html-Septuagint.
3   Miller, Nathaniel. *What Would Make Pyramid Limestone Casings Shine?*,
     http://www.ehow.com/info_7783051_would-pyramid-limestone-casings
     -shine.html#ixzz1GwG3cuGW. Accessed 2009.
4   Hillel ben David (Greg Killian). *The Journeys of the Sons of Israel*;
     http://www.betemunah.org/stages.html.
5   Jacobson, Simon. *42 Journeys*; 2008, Meaningful Life Center
     www.meaningfullife.com-Targum Yonathan.

EXQUISITE STONES – HARADAH: CAMP 21

1   Numbers 33:24.
2   Hillel ben David (Greg Killian). *The Journeys of the Sons of Israel*; http://www.betemunah.org/stages.html.
3   Hillel ben David (Greg Killian). *The Journeys of the Sons of Israel*; http://www.betemunah.org/stages.html – Targum Pseudo Yonathan for Numbers 33:24.
4   Hillel ben David (Greg Killian). *The Journeys of the Sons of Israel*; http://www.betemunah.org/stages.html.
5   Jacobson, Simon. *42 Journeys*. 2008, Meaningful Life Center www.meaningfullife.com.
6   Hillel ben David (Greg Killian). *The Journeys of the Sons of Israel*; http://www.betemunah.org/stages.html.

PLAGUE AND MISSILES – MAKHELOTH: CAMP 22

1   Numbers 33:25.
2   Hillel ben David (Greg Killian). *The Journeys of the Sons of Israel*; http://www.betemunah.org/stages.html.
3   Anati, Emmanuel. *Har Karkom: 20 Years of Biblical Archaeology*: http://www.harkarkom.com/HKsurveyRockArt.php.
4   Hillel ben David (Greg Killian). *The Journeys of the Sons of Israel*. http://www.betemunah.org/stages.html.
5   Jacobson, Simon,, *42 Journeys*; 2008, Meaningful Life Center www.meaningfullife.com. Baal HaTurim.
6   Jacobson, Simon. *42 Journeys*; 2008, Meaningful Life Center www.meaningfullife.com.

SHRINES AND MIRACLES – TAHATH: CAMP 23

1   Numbers 33:26.
2   Hillel ben David (Greg Killian). *The Journeys of the Sons of Israel*; http://www.betemunah.org/stages.html.
3   Jacobson, Simon, *42 Journeys*; 2008, Meaningful Life Center www.meaningfullife.com – Targum Yonathan.
4   Jacobson, Simon, *42 Journeys*; 2008, Meaningful Life Center www.meaningfullife.com.

REFUGEES –TARAH: CAMP 24

1   Numbers 33:27.
2   Hillel ben David (Greg Killian). *The Journeys of the Sons of Israel*;. http://www.betemunah.org/stages.html.
3   Jacobson, Simon, *42 Journeys*; 2008, Meaningful Life Center www.meaningfullife.com – Yalkut Midrashei Teiman.

ASHERAH IDOL AND SWEET WATER – MITHKAH: CAMP 25

1 Numbers 33:28.
2 Hillel ben David (Greg Killian). *The Journeys of the Sons of Israel*; http://www.betemunah.org/stages.html.
3 Rabbi Kaplan, Aryeh. *The Living Torah: A New Translation Based on Traditional Jewish Sources (The Five Books of Moses)*; Moznaim Publishing Corp, June 1, 1981.
4 Gnuse, Robert Karl. *No Other Gods: Emergent Monotheism in Israel*; Sheffield Academic Press, 1997 pp. 69-70.
5 QannaYahu, Kathryn (Based on Ze'ev Meshel). *Kuntillet 'Ajrud Inscriptions*; The Institute of Archaeology of Tel Aviv University, 1975–76. http://www.lebtahor.com/Archaeology/inscriptions/kuntillet, Accessed 2009.
6 Silberman, Neil Asher and Finkelstein, Israel, *The Bible Unearthed: Archaeology's New Vision of Ancient Israel and the Origin of Its Sacred Texts*; Touchstone, June 11, 2002. Accessed 2010.
7 Blogspot, Documenta: Kuntillet Ajrud, Jan 29, 2012, http://documenta-akermariano.blogspot.co.za/2012/01/kuntillet-ajrud.html- reference to Keel, Othmar and Uehlinger, Christophe. *Gods, Goddesses, and Images of God in Ancient Israel*; Fortress Press, 1998.
8 Gunneweg, Jan. Gunneweg's Publications and Abstracts, Archaeometry at Institute of Archaeology, The Hebrew University, Jerusalem, Israel, December 2000, http://pluto.mscc.huji.ac.il/~msjan/abstract.html- reference to Asaro, F., Mommsen, H., Gunneweg, J., Perlman, I. and Meshel, Z. *A Provenience Study on Pithoi from Kuntillet 'Ajrud*; Israel Exploration Journal, Vol 35, 1985. pp. 270-283.
9 QannaYahu, Kathryn (based on Ze'ev Meshel). *Kuntillet 'Ajrud Inscriptions*; The Institute of Archaeology of Tel Aviv University, 1975–76. http://www.lebtahor.com/Archaeology/inscriptions/kuntillet. Accessed 2009.
10 Bonanno, Anthony. *Archaeology and Fertility Cult in the Ancient Mediterranean*; First International Conference on Archaeology of the Ancient Mediterranean University of Malta, 2-5 September 1985. http://books.google.co.za/books?, Accessed 2009. (pp. 238ff.)
11 Keel, Othamar and Uehlinger, Christophe. *Gods, Goddesses, and Images of God in Ancient Israel*; Fortress Press, 1998. (pp. 210ff.).
12 Hadley, Judith M. *The Cult of Asherah in Ancient Israel and Judah: Evidence for a Hebrew Goddess*; University of Cambridge Oriental Publications, 57. Cambridge, UK: Cambridge University Press, 2000, xv, 262. http://www.jhsonline.org/cocoon/JHS/r056.html. Accessed 2010.
13 Asherah. Wikipedia, http://en.wikipedia.org/wiki/Asherah, Accessed 2013.
14 QannaYahu, Kathryn. *Kuntillet 'Ajrud Inscriptions*; The Institute of Archaeology of Tel Aviv University, 1975–76. http://www.lebtahor.com/Archaeology/inscriptions/kuntillet.htm.
15 Hadley, Judith M. *The Cult of Asherah in Ancient Israel and Judah: Evidence for a Hebrew Goddess*; University of Cambridge Oriental Publications, 57;

Cambridge, UK: Cambridge University Press, 2000. http://www.jhsonline
.org/cocoon/JHS/r056.html . Accessed 2010.

16 Jacobson, Simon. *42 Journeys*; 2008, Meaningful Life Center
www.meaningfullife.com.

17 Hillel ben David (Greg Killian). *The Journeys of the Sons of Israel*;
http://www.betemunah.org/stages.html Avot 5:21.

AMBASSADORS – HASHMONAH: CAMP 26

1 Numbers 33:29.

2 Hillel ben David (Greg Killian), *The Journeys of the Sons of Israel*;
http://www.betemunah.org/stages.html.

3 Jacobson, Simon. *42 Journeys*; 2008, Meaningful Life Center
www.meaningfullife.com.

PUNISHMENT OF REBELS – MOSEROTH: CAMP 27

1 Numbers 33:30.

2 Hillel ben David (Greg Killian), *The Journeys of the Sons of Israel*;
http://www.betemunah.org/stages.html.

3 Cohen, Rudolph. "The Iron Age Fortresses in the Central Negev"; *Bulletin of
the American Schools of Oriental Research*, No. 236. Autumn, 1979.

4 2 Chronicles 12:1–12.

5 Cohen, Rudolph. *The Fortresses King Solomon Built to Protect His Southern
Border: String of Desert Fortresses Uncovered in Central Negev*; May/June
1985. http://www.bible.ca/archeology/fortresses-king-solomon-built-to
-protect-his-southern-border-rudolph-cohen-1985ad.html Accessed 2009.

6 Jacobson, Simon. *42 Journeys*; 2008, Meaningful Life Center
www.meaningfullife.com.

7 Numbers 33:40.

8 Jacobson, Simon. *42 Journeys*; 2008 ,Meaningful Life Center
www.meaningfullife.com.

CHAPTER 6

STONE LEOPARDS – BENEI JAAKAN: CAMP 28

1 Numbers 33:31.

2 Hillel ben David (Greg Killian), *The Journeys of the Sons of Israel*;
http://www.betemunah.org/stages.html.

3 Cohen, Rudolph. "The Iron Age Fortresses in the Central Negev"; *Bulletin of
the American Schools of Oriental Research*, No. 236. Autumn, 1979.
http://www.bible.ca/archeology/bible-archeology-exodus-kadesh-barnea
-iron-age-fortresses-central-negev-rudolph-cohen-1979ad.html. Accessed
2009. (pp. 61–79)

4 Cohen, Rudolph. *The Fortresses King Solomon Built to Protect His Southern Border: String of Desert Fortresses Uncovered in Central Negev;* May/June 1985. http://www.bible.ca/archeology/fortresses-king-solomon-built-to -protect-his-southern-border-rudolph-cohen-1985ad.html Accessed 2009.

5 Hillel ben David (Greg Killian). *The Journeys of the Sons of Israel;* http://www.betemunah.org/stages.html.

6 Jacobson, Simon. *42 journeys;* 2008, Meaningful Life Center www.meaningfullife.com.

BILLIONS OF STARS – HOR HAGIDGAD: CAMP 29

1 Numbers 33:32.2   Jacobson, Simon. *42 Journeys;* 2008, Meaningful Life Center www.meaningfullife.com

3 Hillel ben David (Greg Killian), *The Journeys of the Sons of Israel;* http://www.betemunah.org/stages.html

4 Jacobson, Simon. *42 Journeys;* 2008, Meaningful Life Center www.meaningfullife.com-Genesis 30:11.

DELICIOUS DAIRY – JOTVATHAH: CAMP 30

1 Numbers 33:33

2 Hillel ben David (Greg Killian). *The Journeys of the Sons of Israel;* http://.www.betemunah.org/stages.html.

3 Hillel ben David (Greg Killian). *The Journeys of the Sons of Israel;* http://.www.betemunah.org/stages.html

4 Rothenberg, Beno. "Timna", *The New Encyclopedia of Archaeological Excavations in the Holy Land.* Simon & Schuster 1993. Ephraim Stern, Editor. vol.4, p.1475, 1485. http://www.bibleplaces.com/tabernaclemore .html Accessed 2009.

5 I Kings 10.

6 Mattfeld y de la Torre, Walter Reinhold Warttig. *The Route of the Exodus;* Internet prophetess.lstc.edu/~rklein/Documents/theexodus.html

7 *Yotvata.* BibleWalks.com, http://www.biblewalks.com/Sites/Yotvata.html. Accessed 2011.

8 Hillel ben David (Greg Killian). *The Journeys of the Sons of Israel;* http://www.betemunah.org/stages.html

9 Jacobson, Simon. *42 Journeys;* 2008, Meaningful Life Center www.meaningfullife.com

10 Jacobson, Simon. *42 Journeys;* 2008, Meaningful Life Center www.meaningfullife.com.

DOWN COPPER MINES – EBRONAH: CAMP 31

1 Numbers 33:34.

2 Hillel ben David (Greg Killian). *The Journeys of the Sons of Israel;* http://.www.betemunah.org/stages.html.

3   Rothenberg, Beno. "Timna", *The New Encyclopedia of Archaeological Excavations in the Holy Land*. Simon & Schuster 1993. http://www.bibleorigins.net/ExodusTimnaSerabitelKhadim.html. Accessed 2009.

4   Mattfeld y de la Torre, Walter Reinhold Warttig. *The Route of the Exodus*; Internet prophetess.lstc.edu/~rklein/Documents/theexodus.html, Accessed 2009.

5   Exodus. 28:36-38; 39:30-31.

6   Jacobson, Simon. *42 Journeys*; 2008, Meaningful Life Center www.meaningfullife.com.

7   Jacobson, Simon. *42 Journeys*; 2008, Meaningful Life Center www.meaningfullife.com – Pri Megadim, responsa 1:3.

8   *Tabernacle Replica*; bibleplaces.com;http://www.bibleplaces.com/tabernaclemore.htm. Accessed 2010.

DISCOS AND SHIPS – EZION GEBER: CAMP 32

1   Hillel ben David (Greg Killian). *The Journeys of the Sons of Israel*; http://www.betemunah.org/stages.html – Avot 5:21.

2   Numbers 33:35.

3   Hillel ben David (Greg Killian). *The Journeys of the Sons of Israel*; http://www.betemunah.org/stages.html.

4   Feiler, Bruce. *Walking the Bible Journey by Land Through the Five Books of Moses*; Harper Collins 2001.

5   1 Kings 9:26, 22:48; 2 Chronicles 8:17.

6   Rajasingham, K.T. *Locating Ophir – The Search for El Dorado*; http://k.t.rajasingam.tripod.com/doro.htm.

7   Pratico, Gary D. *Nelson Glueck's 1938-1940 Excavations at Tell el-Kheleifeh: A Reappraisal*; The Semitic Museum: Harvard University, 1985. http://www.bible.ca/archeology/bible-archeology-exodus-kadesh-barnea -ezion-geber-nelson-gluecks-1938-1940-excavations-tell-el-kheleifeh -reappraisal-gary-pratico-1985ad.htm (Glueck 1938a: 14).

8   Pratico, Gary D. *Nelson Glueck's 1938-1940 Excavations at Tell el-Kheleifeh: A Reappraisal*; The Semitic Museum: Harvard University, 1985. http://www.bible.ca/archeology/bible-archeology-exodus-kadesh-barnea -ezion-geber-nelson-gluecks-1938-1940-excavations-tell-el-kheleifeh -reappraisal-gary-pratico-1985ad.htm (Glueck 1938a: 14).

9   Pratico, Gary D. *Nelson Glueck's 1938-1940 Excavations at Tell el-Kheleifeh: A Reappraisal*; The Semitic Museum: Harvard University, 1985. http://www.bible.ca/archeology/bible-archeology-exodus-kadesh-barnea -ezion-geber-nelson-gluecks-1938-1940-excavations-tell-el-kheleifeh -reappraisal-gary-pratico-1985ad.htm (Glueck 1938a: 14).

10 Pratico, Gary D. *Nelson Glueck's 1938-1940 Excavations at Tell el-Kheleifeh: A Reappraisal*; The Semitic Museum: Harvard University, 1985. http://www.bible.ca/archeology/bible-archeology-exodus-kadesh-barnea -ezion-geber-nelson-gluecks-1938-1940-excavations-tell-el-kheleifeh -reappraisal-gary-pratico-1985ad.htm (Glueck 1938a: 14).

11 Pratico, Gary D. *Nelson Glueck's 1938-1940 Excavations at Tell el-Kheleifeh: A Reappraisal*; The Semitic Museum: Harvard University, 1985. http://www.bible.ca/archeology/bible-archeology-exodus-kadesh-barnea -ezion-geber-nelson-gluecks-1938-1940-excavations-tell-el-kheleifeh -reappraisal-gary-pratico-1985ad.htm (Glueck 1938a: 14).

12 Pratico, Gary D. *Nelson Glueck's 1938-1940 Excavations at Tell el-Kheleifeh: A Reappraisal*; The Semitic Museum: Harvard University, 1985. http://www.bible.ca/archeology/bible-archeology-exodus-kadesh-barnea -ezion-geber-nelson-gluecks-1938-1940-excavations-tell-el-kheleifeh -reappraisal-gary-pratico-1985ad.htm (Glueck 1938a: 14).

13 Hillel ben David (Greg Killian), *The Journeys of the Sons of Israel*. http://www.betemunah.org/stages.html.

14 Jacobson, Simon. *42 Journeys*; 2008, Meaningful Life Center www.meaningfullife.com Berachos 60b.

15 Jacobson, Simon. *42 Journeys*; 2008, Meaningful Life Center www.meaningfullife.com Tzioni. Rokeach.

16 Jacobson, Simon. *42 Journeys*; 2008, Meaningful Life Center www.meaningfullife.com The Ohr HaTorah, Massei.

17 Jacobson, Simon. *42 Journeys*; 2008, Meaningful Life Center www.meaningfullife.com The Ohr HaTorah, Massei.

CHAPTER 7

MIRIAM'S GRAVE – KADESH: CAMP 33

1 Numbers 33:36.

2 Hillel ben David (Greg Killian). *The Journeys of the Sons of Israel*; http://www.betemunah.org/stages.html -Targum.

3 Hillel ben David (Greg Killian). *The Journeys of the Sons of Israel*; http://www.betemunah.org/stages.html. Targum Pseudo Yonathan for Numbers 33:36.

4 Rudd, Steve. *They're Digging in the Wrong Places: The Search for Kadesh*; http://www.bible.ca/archeology/bible-archeology-exodus-kadesh-barnea -petra-mt-hor-jebel-haroun.htm Accessed 2009.

5 Numbers 20:1.

6 Jacobson, Simon. *42 Journeys*; 2008, Meaningful Life Center www.meaningfullife.com. Talmud Shabbos 89a.

7 Numbers 20:1.

8 Jacobson, Simon. *42 Journeys*; 2008, Meaningful Life Center www.meaningfullife.com.

CLIMBING TO AARON'S TOMB – MOUNT HOR: CAMP 34

1 Numbers 33:38.

2 Hillel ben David (Greg Killian), *The Journeys of the Sons of Israel*; http://www.betemunah.org/stages.html.

3   Numbers 33:37.

4   Numbers 20.

5   *Petra,Jordan: Atlas Tours .Net* Petra Map & Monuments, http://www.atlastours.net/jordan/petra_map.html.

6   *Petra – A Brief History*. http://almashriq.hiof.no/jordan/900/930/petra/jda /petra.html.

7   Rudd, Steve. *Mt. Hor, Moserah: Aaron's Mountain (Jebel Haroun) at Petra*;http://www.bible.ca/archeology/bible-archeology-exodus-kadesh -barnea-petra-mt-hor-jebel-haroun.htm, Accessed 2009.

8   Burckhardt, John Lewis. *Travels in Arabia: Comprehending an Account of those Territories in Hedjaz which the Mohammedans Regard as Sacred*; published by Authority of the Association for Promoting the Discovery of the Interior of Africa. London: Henry Colburn, New Burlington Street 1829, 1784-1817.

9   *Petra – A Brief History*. http://almashriq.hiof.no/jordan/900/930/petra/jda /petra.html.

10   Hillel ben David (Greg Killian). *The Journeys of the Sons of Israel*; http://www.betemunah.org/stages.html. Bamidbar Rabba 19:16, Numbers 20:22, 26; 21:4; 34:6.

11   Numbers 20:23-29.

12   Deuteronomy 32:50.

13   Rudd, Steve. *Mt. Hor, Moserah: Aaron's Mountain (Jebel Haroun) at Petra*; http://www.bible.ca/archeology/bible-archeology-exodus-kadesh-barnea -petra-mt-hor-jebel-haroun.htm, Accessed 2009.

14   Schmidt, Nathaniel. "Barnea"; *Journal of Biblical Literature*, Vol 29, no. 1, 1910. http://www.bible.ca/archeology/bible-archeology-exodus-kadesh -barnea-petra-nathan-schmidt-kadesh-barnea-journal-of-biblical-literature -vol-29-no-1-1910ad.htm. (pp.75-76).

15   Robinson, George L "The True Mount Hor:Jebel Maderah"; *The Biblical World*, Vol. 31, No. 2. Feb,1908. http://www.bible.ca/archeology/bible -archeology-exodus-kadesh-barnea-true-mount-hor-the-biblical-world -george-l-robinson-1908ad.htm. (pp. 86-100)

16   Jacobson, Simon. *42 Journeys*: 2008, Meaningful Life Center www.meaningfullife.com – Rashi 20:29.

17   Jacobson, Simon. *42 Journeys*; 2008, Meaningful Life Center www.meaningfullife.com – Rashi Numbers 21:1; 33:40.

18   Jacobson, Simon. *42 Journeys*; 2008, Meaningful Life Center www.meaningfullife.com.

SPICE CARAVAN – ZALMONAH: CAMP 35

1   Numbers 33:41.

2   Jacobson, Simon. *42 Journeys*; 2008, Meaningful Life Center www.meaningfullife.com.

3   MacDonald, Burton. *East of Jordan Territories and Sites of the Hebrew Scriptures*, ASOR Books Vol 6. American School of Oriental Research,

Boston MA, Victor Mathews, editor. http://www.bu.edu/asor/pubs/books
-monographs/macdonald.pdf), Accessed 2011. Aharoni (1979:202)

4   *Biblical Jordan: AtlasTours*. http://www.atlastours.net/jordan/exodus
_stations.html. Accessed 2011.

5   MacDonald, Burton. *East of Jordan Territories and Sites of the Hebrew
Scriptures*, ASOR Books Vol 6. American School of Oriental Research,
Boston MA, Victor Mathews, editor. http://www.bu.edu/asor/pubs/books
-monographs/macdonald.pdf), Accessed 2011.

6   Dr. Smith, Andrew M II. The Site of Bir Madhkur.
http://home.gwu.edu/~amsii/wadiarabaproject/bmp/birmadhkur.html.
Accessed 2010.

7   Smith, Andrew M II. The Site of Bir Madhkur;
http://home.gwu.edu/~amsii /wadiarabaproject /bmp/bir madhkur.html
and http://cnelc.columbian.gwu.edu/andrew-m-smith-ii and
http://wadiaraba.tripod.com/madhkur.htm. Accessed 2012.

8   Jacobson, Simon. *42 Journeys*; 2008, Meaningful Life Center
www.meaningfullife.com.

9   Jacobson, Simon. *42 Journeys*; 2008, Meaningful Life Center
www.meaningfullife.com – Targum Yonathan. Rokeach.

10 Jacobson, Simon. *42 Journeys*; 2008, Meaningful Life Center
www.meaningfullife.com – Ramban Numbers 33:41.

FIERY SNAKE BITES – PUNON: CAMP 36

1   Numbers 33:42.

2   Hillel ben David (Greg Killian). *The Journeys of the Sons of Israel*.
http://www.betemunah.org/stages.html.

3   Smith, Mark S. *The Origins of Biblical Monotheism: Israel's Polytheistic
Background and the Ugaritic Texts*; Oxford University Press, 2001. (pp.
140–145)

4   Glueck, Nelson. "The Civilization of the Edomites," *The Biblical
Archaeologist*, Vol. 10, No. 4, Dec 1947. http://www.bible.ca/archeology
/bible-archeology-exodus-kadesh-barnea-civilization-of-the-edomites
-nelson-glueck-1947ad.htm, Accessed 2010. (pp. 77-84)

5   MacDonald, Burton. *East of Jordan Territories and Sites of the Hebrew
Scriptures*, ASOR Books Vol 6, American School of Oriental Research,
Victor Mathews, editor. Boston, MA, 2000. http://www.bu.edu/asor/pubs
/books-monographs/macdonald.pdf) Accessed 2011. Aharoni (1979:202).

6   Springer, "Nature and Geology in Faynan," *Natural Science in Archaeology;*
reference to Schröder and Yalçin 1991. http://link.springer.com/chapter/10
.1007%2F978-3-540-72238-0_3, Accessed 2010.

7   Levy, Thomas E., et al. *Antiquity Article: Early Bronze Age Metallurgy: a
newly discovered copper manufactory in southern Jordan* (Statistical Data
Included); http://www.highbeam.com/doc/1G1-89075891.html. Accessed
2011.

8   Levy, Thomas E., et al. *Early Bronze Age Metallurgy: a newly discovered copper*; levlab.ucsd.edu/resources/ELRAP-Publications/Ant0760425.pdf. (Costin 1991). Accessed 2010.

9   MacDonald, Burton. *East of Jordan Territories and Sites of the Hebrew Scriptures,* ASOR Books Vol 6, American School of Oriental Research, Victor Mathews, editor. Boston, MA, 2000. http://www.bu.edu/asor/pubs /books-monographs/macdonald.pdf) Accessed 2011. Aharoni (1979:202).

10 Salopek, Paul. *About Feynan,* Feynan Ecolodge, Out of Eden Walk (National Geographic); http://ecohotels.me/en/feynan/about-archaeological _history.

11 Jacobson, Simon. *42 Journeys*; 2008, Meaningful Life Center www.meaningfullife.com – Rokeach, Targum Yonathan.

12 Jacobson, Simon. *42 Journeys*; 2008, Meaningful Life Center www.meaningfullife.com – Lekach Tov, Numbers 21:10.

JERUSALEM THORN – OBOTH: CAMP 37

1   Numbers 33:43.

2   Hillel ben David (Greg Killian). *The Journeys of the Sons of Israel*; http://www.betemunah.org/stages.html -Targum.

3   MacDonald, Burton. *East of Jordan Territories and Sites of the Hebrew Scriptures;* ASOR Books Vol 6, American School of Oriental Research, Victor Mathews, editor. Boston, MA 2000. http://www.bu.edu/asor/pubs /books-monographs/macdonald.pdf) Accessed 2011.

4   "Ir Ovot." Wikipedia. https://en.wikipedia.org/wiki/Ir_Ovot.

5   Hillel ben David (Greg Killian). *The Journeys of the Sons of Israel*; http://www.betemunah.org/stages.html.

6   Hillel ben David (Greg Killian). *The Journeys of the Sons of Israel*; http://www.betemunah.org/stages.html.

7   Jacobson, Simon. *42 Journeys;* 2008, Meaningful Life Center www.meaningfullife.com.

CHAPTER 8

RUINS OF COPULATION AND TERRIFYING WASTELANDS – IYAY HA'AVARIM: CAMP 38

1   Numbers 33:34.

2   Hillel ben David (Greg Killian). *The Journeys of the Sons of Israel*; http://www.betemunah.org/stages.html.

3   Jacobson, Simon, *42 Journeys*: 2008. Meaningful Life Center www.meaningfullife.com.

4   Numbers 21:11.

5   Numbers 21:12.

6   Rabbi Kaplan, Aryeh. *The Living Torah: A New Translation Based On Traditional Jewish Sources (The Five Books of Moses)*; New York /Jerusalem: Maznaim Publishing Corporation, June 1, 1981.

7   Rabbi Kaplan, Aryeh. *The Living Torah: A New Translation Based On Traditional Jewish Sources (The Five Books of Moses)*; New York /Jerusalem: Maznaim Publishing Corporation, June 1, 1981.

8   "Zoar," *Net Bible*. In Bible versions: http://classic.net.bible.org/dictionary .php?word=ZOAR.

9   MacDonald, Burton. *East of Jordan Territories and Sites of the Hebrew Scriptures;* ASOR Books Vol 6, American School of Oriental Research, Víctor Mathews, editor. Boston MA, 2000. http://www.bu.edu/asor/pubs /books-monographs/macdonald.pdf), Accessed 2011.

10   *Dead Sea, Jordan*. Atlas Tours; http://www.atlastours.net/jordan/deadsea .html, Accessed 2011.

11   *Dead Sea*, http://www.votedeadsea.com/why-vote-dead-sea.

12   Rast, Walter E., and R Thomas Schaub, R. Thomas, et al.; *Bâb edh-Dhrâ: excavations at the town site (1975-1981)*. Winona Lake, Ind.: Eisenbrauns, 2003.

13   Jacobson, Simon. *42 Journeys*; 2008, Meaningful Life Center www.meaningfullife.com.

14   Rabbi Kaplan, Aryeh. *The Living Torah: A New Translation Based On Traditional Jewish Sources (The Five Books of Moses);* New York/Jerusalem: Maznaim Publishing Corp, June 1, 1981.

15   Neubauer, Adolf. La Geographie du Talmud (Mémoire Couronne par l'Academie des Inscriptions et Belles-Lettres); Paris: Michel Levy Freres, 1868.

16   MacDonald, Burton. *East of Jordan Territories and Sites of the Hebrew Scriptures*; ASOR Books Vol 6, American School of Oriental Research, Victor Mathews, editor. Boston MA, 2000. http://www.bu.edu/asor/pubs /books-monographs/macdonald.pdf), Accessed 2011.

17   MacDonald, Burton. *East of Jordan Territories and Sites of the Hebrew Scriptures*; ASOR Books Vol 6, American School of Oriental Research, Victor Mathews, editor. Boston MA, 2000. http://www.bu.edu/asor/pubs /books-monographs/macdonald.pdf), Accessed 2011.

18   Deuteronomy 2:1-8.

19   Numbers 20:17-18 and 21:22.

20   Numbers 21:19-21.

21   Numbers 21:16.

22   "Desert Castles," All in Jordan: Darcizia Multimedia International Est. 2005. http://www.allinjordan.com/index.php?cGc9Q2loaWVzJmN1c3Rvb WVyPURlc2VydCtDYXNobGVz.

23   Al–Kheder, Sharaf, Al-Shawabkeh, Yahya, and Haala, Norbert. "Developing a documentation system for desert palaces in Jordan using 3D laser scanning and digital photogrammetry," *Journal of Archaeological Science* 36,

2009. http://www.ifp.uni-stuttgart.de/publications/2009/haala-jas-2009
.pdf. Accessed 2010.

24   MacDonald, Burton. *East of Jordan Territories and Sites of the Hebrew
Scriptures*; ASOR Books Vol 6, American School of Oriental Research,
Victor Mathews, editor. Boston MA, 2000. http://www.bu.edu/asor/pubs
/books-monographs/macdonald.pdf) Accessed 2009.

25   MacDonald, Burton. *East of Jordan Territories and Sites of the Hebrew
Scriptures*; ASOR Books Vol 6, American School of Oriental Research,
Victor Mathews, editor. Boston MA, 2000. http://www.bu.edu/asor/pubs
/books-monographs/macdonald.pdf.

26   Numbers 21:16

27   Hubner, Manu Marcus. *A Rota do Exodo*; Sao Paulo: Universidade de Sao
Paulo, 2009. https://sistemas.usp.br/tycho/CurriculoLattesMostrar
?codpub. Accessed 2012.

28   Numbers 21:23

29   "Khirbat al-Mudayna, Jordan." Find a Dig: Biblical Archaeological Society,
June 17 – July 31, 2010. http://digs.bib-arch.org/digs/khirbat-al-mudayna
.asp. Accessed 2010.

30   Bolen, Todd. *Discoveries at Khirbet al-Mudayna, possible Jahaz*; BiblePlaces
Blog; Thursday, October 07, 2010. http://blog.bibleplaces.com/2010/10
/discoveries-at-khirbet-al-mudayna.html. Accessed 2010.

31   MacDonald, Burton. *East of Jordan Territories and Sites of the Hebrew
Scriptures*; ASOR Books Vol 6, American School of Oriental Research,
Victor Mathews, editor. Boston MA, 2000. http://www.bu.edu/asor/pubs
/books-monographs/macdonald.pdf), Accessed 2011.

32   Numbers 21:19

33   MacDonald, Burton. *East of Jordan Territories and Sites of the Hebrew
Scriptures*; ASOR Books Vol 6, American School of Oriental Research,
Victor Mathews, editor. Boston MA, 2000. http://www.bu.edu/asor/pubs
/books-monographs/macdonald.pdf) Accessed 2011.

34   Numbers 21:21-22

35   Deuteronomy 3:1-11

36   Hillel ben David (Greg Killian). *The Journeys of the Sons of Israel*;
http://www.betemunah.org/stages.html- Avot 5:21.

CHAPTER 9

MOSQUES AND FLOWERS – DIBONGAD: CAMP 39

1   Numbers 33: 45

2   Hillel ben David (Greg Killian). *The Journeys of the Sons of Israel*;
http://www.betemunah.org/stages.html

3   Numbers 21:26-31

4   Isaiah 15:1-9

5   "The Moabite Stone." Palestine Exploration Fund Quarterly Statement; Biblical Studies, Office of the Fund. https://biblicalstudies.org.uk/pdf /pefqs/1869-71_169.pdf.

6   Jordan's Department of Antiquities and Divan Excavation and Development Project; Dhiban Excavation and Development Project. http://nes.berkeley.edu/Web_Porter/Dhiban/Welcome.html.

7   Dhiban, Jordan. Wikipedia; http://en.wikipedia.org/wiki/Dhiban,_Jordan.

8   The Dhiban Excavation and Development Project (DEDP); http://www.dhiban.org/ and http://nes.berkeley.edu/Web_Porter/Dhiban /Welcome.html, Accessed 2010.

9   Jacobson, Simon. *42 Journeys*; 2008, Meaningful Life Center www.meaningfullife.com.

10 Jacobson, Simon, *42 Journeys;* 2008, Meaningful Life Center www.meaningfullife.com.

11 Hillel ben David (Greg Killian). *The Journeys of the Sons of Israel;* http://www.betemunah.org/stages.html. Avot 5:21.

ALMONDS AND KINGS' BATTLES – ALMON DIVLATHAYMAH: CAMP 40

1   Numbers 33: 46-47.

2   Hillel ben David (Greg Killian). *The Journeys of the Sons of Israel*; http://www.betemunah.org/stages.html.

3   Hillel ben David (Greg Killian). *The Journeys of the Sons of Israel*; http://www.betemunah.org/stages.html.

4   Hubner, Manu Marcus. *A Rota do Exodo*; Sao Paulo: Universidade de Sao Paulo, 2009. https://sistemas.usp.br/tycho/CurriculoLattesMostrar ?codpub. Accessed 2012.

5   Deuteronomy 3:1.

6   Numbers 21:33.

7   Deuteronomy 2:33-35.

8   Numbers 21-30.

9   MacDonald, Burton. *East of Jordan Territories and Sites of the Hebrew Scriptures*; ASOR Books Vol 6, American School of Oriental Research, Victor Mathews, editor. Boston MA, 2000. http://www.bu.edu/asor/pubs /books-monographs/macdonald.pdf. Accessed 2011.

10 Jacobson, Simon. *42 Journeys*; 2008, Meaningful Life Center www.meaningfullife.com.

11 Jacobson, Simon. *42 Journeys*; 2008, Meaningful Life Center www.meaningfullife.com – Lekach Tov Numbers 21:19 and Targum Pseudo Yonathan for Numbers 33:46.

12 Jacobson, Simon. *42 Journeys;* 2008, Meaningful Life Center www.meaningfullife.com.

13 "Madaba," Wikipedia. http://en.wikipedia.org/wiki/Madaba.

14 Numbers 21:19

15 MacDonald, Burton. *East of Jordan Territories and Sites of the Hebrew Scriptures*; ASOR Books Vol 6, American School of Oriental Research, Victor Mathews, editor. Boston MA, 2000. http://www.bu.edu/asor/pubs /books-monographs/macdonald.pdf Accessed 2011.

MOSES' SANCTUARY – ABARIM: CAMP 41

1   Numbers 21:20.

2   Numbers 33:47.

3   Numbers 33;47-48.

4   MacDonald, Burton. *East of Jordan Territories and Sites of the Hebrew Scriptures*; ASOR Books Vol 6, American School of Oriental Research, Victor Mathews, editor. Boston MA, 2000. http://www.bu.edu/asor/pubs /books-monographs/macdonald.pdf. Accessed 2012.

5   "Abarim," Wikipedia. http://en.wikipedia.org/wiki/Abarim.

6   Numbers 27:12.

7   Deuteronomy 32:49

8   Eusebius of Caesarea. *The Onomasticon and the Exodus Route (Dictionary of Places)*; 325 A.D.

9   MacDonald, Burton. *East of Jordan Territories and Sites of the Hebrew Scriptures*; ASOR Books Vol 6, American School of Oriental Research, Victor Mathews, editor. Boston MA, 2000. http://www.bu.edu/asor/pubs /books-monographs/macdonald.pdf. Accessed 2012.

10 Deuteronomy 34:1.

11 Numbers 22:2-25:9, Talmud Sanhedrin 106a. http://www.come-and-hear .com/sanhedrin/sanhedrin_106.html.

12 MacDonald, Burton. *East of Jordan Territories and Sites of the Hebrew Scriptures*; ASOR Books Vol 6, American School of Oriental Research, Victor Mathews, editor. Boston MA, 2000. http://www.bu.edu/asor/pubs /books-monographs/macdonald.pdf Accessed 2012.

13 "The Memorial of Moses on Mount Nebo," Franciscan Cyberspot. http:// 198.62.75.1/www1/ofm/pope/10GPen/12/12GPsho1.html. Accessed 2011.

14 Eusebius of Caesarea. *The Onomasticon and the Exodus Route (Dictionary of Places)*; 325 A.D.

15 Jennings, James E. "Nebo," The New International Dictionary of Biblical Archaeology, ed. Edward M. Blaiklock and R. K. Harrison; Grand Rapids: The Zondervan Corporation, 1983.332 http://claudemariottini.com/2007 /08/29/mount-nebo. Accessed 2012.

16 Jennings, James E. "Nebo," The New International Dictionary of Biblical Archaeology, ed. Edward M. Blaiklock and R. K. Harrison; Grand Rapids: The Zondervan Corporation, 1983.332 http://claudemariottini.com/2007 /08/29/mount-nebo. Accessed 2012.

17 Numbers 27:12-13.

18 Deuteronomy 32:49-50.

19 Jacobson, Simon. *42 Journeys*; 2008, Meaningful Life Center www.meaningfullife.com Zohar 3:183b; Bachya on 20:28, Deuteronomy 32:49.

DELICIOUS FRUIT AND BLOODY BATTLES:
B'ARVOS MOAB – CAMP 42

1   Numbers 33:49.
2   Hillel ben David (Greg Killian). *The Journeys of the Sons of Israel*;
    http://www.betemunah.org/stages.html.
3   Hillel ben David (Greg Killian). *The Journeys of the Sons of Israel*;
    http://www.betemunah.org/stages.html Ramban Genesis 14:6.
4   Hillel ben David (Greg Killian). *The Journeys of the Sons of Israel*;
    http://www.betemunah.org/stages.html.
5   Deuteronomy 3:1-11.
6   MacDonald, Burton. *East of Jordan Territories and Sites of the Hebrew
    Scriptures*; ASOR Books Vol 6, American School of Oriental Research,
    Victor Mathews, editor. Boston MA, 2000. http://www.bu.edu/asor/pubs
    /books-monographs/macdonald.pdf. Accessed 2011.
7   Tall el-Hammam Excavation Project (TeHEP); Trinity Southwest
    University's College of Archaeology & Biblical History (Albuquerque,
    New Mexico, USA) and the Department of Antiquities of the Hashemite
    Kingdom of Jordan. http://www.tallelhammam.com/Tall_el_Hammam
    .html. Accessed 2012.
8   MacDonald, Burton. *East of Jordan Territories and Sites of the Hebrew
    Scriptures*; ASOR Books Vol 6, American School of Oriental Research,
    Victor Mathews, editor. Boston MA, 2000. http://www.bu.edu/asor/pubs
    /books-monographs/macdonald.pdf. Accessed 2010.
9   MacDonald, Burton. *East of Jordan Territories and Sites of the Hebrew
    Scriptures*; ASOR Books Vol 6, American School of Oriental Research,
    Victor Mathews, editor. Boston MA, 2000. http://www.bu.edu/asor/pubs
    /books-monographs/macdonald.pdf. Accessed 2010.
10 MacDonald, Burton. *East of Jordan Territories and Sites of the Hebrew
    Scriptures*; ASOR Books Vol 6, American School of Oriental Research,
    Victor Mathews, editor. Boston MA, 2000. http://www.bu.edu/asor/pubs
    /books-monographs/macdonald.pdf. Accessed 2010.
11 Hillel ben David (Greg Killian), The Journeys Of The Sons of Israel.
    http://www.betemunah.org/stages.html.
12 MacDonald, Burton. *East of Jordan Territories and Sites of the Hebrew
    Scriptures*; ASOR Books Vol 6, American School of Oriental Research,
    Victor Mathews, editor. Boston MA, 2000. http://www.bu.edu/asor/pubs
    /books-monographs/macdonald.pdf. Accessed 2010.
13 Joshua 2:1, 3:1.
14 Mullins, Eustace. "The Curse of Canaan," *Encyclopedia Judaica*, Vol 2, page
    62, 1987.
15 Warnke, Mike. *Schemes of Satan*; Tulsa, OK: Victory House, 1991. p. 29.
16 *Esau, Edomites, Phoenicians, Canaanites & Jews,* reference to Edwin O.
    James, *Sacrifice and Sacrament*, p. 94 (1962);
    http://www.biblebelievers.org.au/edomites.html Accessed 2011.

17 Mullins, Eustace. "The Curse of Canaan," *Encyclopedia Judaica*, Vol 2, page 62, 1987.

18 Numbers 33:50-55.

19 Exodus 23:24.

20 Deuteronomy 12:3.

21 Deuteronomy 7:2-4.

22 Exodus 23:23.

23 Jacobson, Simon. *42 Journeys*; 2008, Meaningful Life Center www.meaningfullife.com – Likkutei Levi Yitzchak Igros, p. 400.

24 Jacobson, Simon. *42 Journeys*; 2008, Meaningful Life Center www.meaningfullife.com.

25 Jacobson, Simon. *42 Journeys*, 2008, Meaningful Life Center www.meaningfullife.com.

26 Hillel ben David (Greg Killian). *The Journeys of the Sons of Israel*; http://www.betemunah.org/stages.html – Ramban Genesis 14:6, Sefat Emet.